Praise for *The Old New Thing*

"Raymond Chen is the original raconteur of Windows."

—Scott Hanselman, ComputerZen.com

"Raymond has been at Microsoft for many years and has seen many nuances of Windows that others could only ever hope to get a glimpse of. With this book, Raymond shares his knowledge, experience, and anecdotal stories, allowing all of us to get a better understanding of the operating system that affects millions of people every day. This book has something for everyone, is a casual read, and I highly recommend it!"

—Jeffrey Richter, Author/Consultant, Cofounder of Wintellect

"Very interesting read. Raymond tells the inside story of why Windows is the way it is."

—Eric Gunnerson, Program Manager, Microsoft Corporation

"Absolutely essential reading for understanding the history of Windows, its intricacies and quirks, and why they came about."

—Matt Pietrek, *MSDN Magazine*'s Under the Hood Columnist

"Raymond Chen has become something of a legend in the software industry, and in this book you'll discover why. From his high-level reminiscences on the design of the Windows Start button to his low-level discussions of GlobalAlloc that only your inner-geek could love, *The Old New Thing* is a captivating collection of anecdotes that will help you to truly appreciate the difficulty inherent in designing and writing quality software."

—Stephen Toub, Technical Editor, *MSDN Magazine*

The Old New Thing

THE OLD NEW THING

Practical Development
Throughout the Evolution of Windows

Raymond Chen

✦ Addison-Wesley

Upper Saddle River, NJ ✦ Boston ✦ Indianapolis ✦ San Francisco
New York ✦ Toronto ✦ Montreal ✦ London ✦ Munich ✦ Paris ✦ Madrid
Capetown ✦ Sydney ✦ Tokyo ✦ Singapore ✦ Mexico City

Many of the designations used by manufacturers and sellers to distinguish their products are claimed as trademarks. Where those designations appear in this book, and the publisher was aware of a trademark claim, the designations have been printed with initial capital letters or in all capitals.

The author and publisher have taken care in the preparation of this book, but make no expressed or implied warranty of any kind and assume no responsibility for errors or omissions. No liability is assumed for incidental or consequential damages in connection with or arising out of the use of the information or programs contained herein.

The publisher offers excellent discounts on this book when ordered in quantity for bulk purchases or special sales, which may include electronic versions and/or custom covers and content particular to your business, training goals, marketing focus, and branding interests. For more information, please contact:

U.S. Corporate and Government Sales
(800) 382-3419
corpsales@pearsontechgroup.com

For sales outside the United States please contact:

International Sales
international@pearsoned.com

 This Book Is Safari Enabled

The Safari® Enabled icon on the cover of your favorite technology book means the book is available through Safari Bookshelf. When you buy this book, you get free access to the online edition for 45 days.

Safari Bookshelf is an electronic reference library that lets you easily search thousands of technical books, find code samples, download chapters, and access technical information whenever and wherever you need it.

To gain 45-day Safari Enabled access to this book:

• Go to http://www.awprofessional.com/safarienabled
• Complete the brief registration form
• Enter the coupon code X2R8-XJGQ-LQQB-BNQE-RGW8

If you have difficulty registering on Safari Bookshelf or accessing the online edition, please e-mail customer-service@safaribooksonline.com.

Visit us on the Web: www.awprofessional.com

Library of Congress Cataloging-in-Publication Data

Chen, Raymond.
  The old new thing. Practical development throughout the evolution of Windows / Raymond Chen.
     p. cm.
  Includes index.
  ISBN 0-321-44030-7 (pbk. : alk. paper)
  1. Microsoft Windows (Computer file) 2. Operating systems (Computers) 3. Computer software—Development. I. Title.
  QA76.76.O63C45747 2007
  005.4'46—dc22   2006028949

ISBN 0-321-44030-7

Text printed in the United States on recycled paper at Courier in Stoughton, Massachusetts.
First printing, December 2006

FOR MY FAMILY

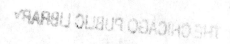

CONTENTS

CHAPTER ONE

Initial Forays into User Interface Design

CHAPTER TWO
Selected Reminiscences on Windows 95

CHAPTER THREE
The Secret Life of GetWindowText

CHAPTER FOUR
The Taskbar and Notification Area

CHAPTER FIVE
Puzzling Interface Issues

A History of the GlobalAlloc Function

Short Topics in Windows Programming

CHAPTER EIGHT

Window Management

CHAPTER NINE

Reminiscences on Hardware

CHAPTER TEN

The Inner Workings of the Dialog Manager

CHAPTER ELEVEN
General Software Issues

CHAPTER TWELVE
Digging into the Visual C++ Compiler

CHAPTER THIRTEEN
Backward Compatibility

CHAPTER FOURTEEN

Etymology and History

CHAPTER FIFTEEN

How Window Messages Are Delivered and Retrieved

CHAPTER SIXTEEN

International Programming

CHAPTER SEVENTEEN

Security

CHAPTER EIGHTEEN

Windows 2000 and Windows XP

CHAPTER NINETEEN
Win32 Design Issues

CHAPTER TWENTY
Taxes

CHAPTER TWENTY-ONE
Silliness

PREFACE

MUCH INK IS devoted to describing the "how" of using and developing software for Windows, but few authors go into the "why." What might appear at first to be quirks often turn out to have entirely logical explanations, reflecting the history, evolution, and philosophy of the Microsoft Windows operating system. This book attempts to provide knowledge not so much in the form of telling what needs to be done (although there is certainly plenty of that, too) but rather by helping to understand why things came to be that way. Thus informed of the history and philosophy of Windows, you can become a more effective Windows programmer.

The emphasis here, then, is on the rationale behind Windows. It is not a reference or even a tutorial, but rather a "practical history," taking a conversational rather than didactic approach in an attempt to give you an appreciation for the philosophy of Windows through a series of brief, largely independent essays. You can therefore skip freely to topics of momentary interest (or technical expertise). Essays have been grouped into general themes, and there is the occasional sequential pedagogical treatment when a topic is explored in depth; even in those cases, however, the topic is confined to a single self-contained chapter.

Writer and commentator David Sedaris is often asked whether his stories are true. He responds that they are "true enough." Like David Sedaris's stories, the material in this book is also "true enough." The focus is on the big picture, not on the minutiae; on making a single point without getting distracted by nitpicking detail. Key details are highlighted, but unimportant ones are set aside, and potentially interesting digressions may be neglected if they do not serve the topic at hand.

The primary audience is technology-savvy readers with an interest in Windows history. About half of the essays require no programming background. Most of the remaining topics assume a basic background in software design and development, although nothing particularly advanced. Topics specifically related to Windows programming assume reader familiarity with Win32 user interface programming and COM. The table on page xxv provides a breakdown of the chapters for nonprogrammers and for general programmers who do not have an interest in Win32 specifically. Of course, you are welcome to skim chapters not explicitly marked as of interest to you. Perhaps you will find something interesting in them after all.

What will you get out of this book? As noted previously, the primary goal is to convey the philosophy and rationale behind what might at first appear to be an irrational design. You will also understand that when something can't be done in Windows, it's often for a good reason; and you will gain an appreciation of the lengths to which Windows goes to preserve backward compatibility (and why it's important that it do so). And if nothing else, you will be able to tell amusing stories about Windows history at cocktail parties (that is, cocktail parties thrown by other geeks).

Much of the short-essay material here has already appeared in one form or another on the author's Web site, The Old New Thing (http://blogs.msdn.com/oldnewthing/), but is substantially supplemented by new material better suited to book form.

Visit the Web page for this book (www.awprofessional.com/title/0321440307) to download two bonus chapters, "Tales of Application Compatibility" and "How to Ensure That Your Program Does Not Run Under Windows 95." Think of them if you like as the book version of a movie's unique and insightful deleted scenes. The Web page also contains the code samples from the book as well as errata.

Breakdown of Chapters by Audience

Chapter	Title	General Audience	General Programmer	Win32 Programmer
Chapter 1	Initial Forays into User Interface Design	x	x	x
Chapter 2	Selected Reminiscences on Windows 95	x	x	x
Chapter 3	The Secret Life of GetWindowText			x
Chapter 4	The Taskbar and Notification Area	x	x	x
Chapter 5	Puzzling Interface Issues	x	x	x
Chapter 6	A History of the GlobalLock Function			x
Chapter 7	Short Topics in Windows Programming			x
Chapter 8	Window Management			x
Chapter 9	Reminiscences on Hardware	x	x	x
Chapter 10	The Inner Workings of the Dialog Manager			x
Chapter 11	General Software Issues		x	x
Chapter 12	Digging into the Visual C++ Compiler		x	x
Chapter 13	Backward Compatibility	x	x	x
Chapter 14	Etymology and History	x	x	x
Chapter 15	How Window Messages Are Delivered and Retrieved			x
Chapter 16	International Programming	First half	x	x
Chapter 17	Security		x	x
Chapter 18	Reminiscences on Windows 2000 and Windows XP	First half	First half	x
Chapter 19	Win32 Design Issues		Part	x
Chapter 20	Taxes		x	x
Chapter 21	Silliness	x	x	x
*	Tales of Application Compatibility	x	x	x
*	How to Ensure That Your Program Doesn't Run Under Windows 95		x	x

* These bonus chapters can be downloaded from www.awprofessional.com/title/0321440307.

ACKNOWLEDGMENTS

I WANT TO begin by thanking Joan Murray at Addison-Wesley for believing in a book as unusual as this one. Without her support, this project would never have come together. Others at Addison-Wesley have also been of great help, including Tyrrell Albaugh, Patty Boyd, Keith Cline, Curt Johnson, and Chris Zahn. Ben Ryan deserves credit for suggesting to me back in the late 1990s that I should write a book on Win32 (sorry it took so long), and I blame Brad Abrams for flat-out telling me to start a Web log in 2003.

Additional thanks to Betsy Aoki, Jeff Davis, Henry Gabryjelski, Jeffery Galinovsky, Michael Grier, Mike Gunderloy, Eric Gunnerson, Chris Guzak, Johnson M. Hart, Francis Hogle, Aleš Holecek, Michael Kaplan, KC Lemson, Shelley McKinley, Rico Mariani, Joseph Newcomer, Adrian Oney, Larry Osterman, Matt Pietrek, Jeffrey Richter, Mike Schmidt, Jan Shanahan, Joel Spolsky, Stephen Toub, and Ed Wax for their assistance in various capacities throughout this entire project (either intentional or unwitting).

Finally, I must acknowledge all the people who visit my Web site, which serves as the title as well as the inspiration for this book. They're the ones who convinced me to give this book thing another try.

ABOUT THE AUTHOR

RAYMOND CHEN IS a programmer in the Windows division at Microsoft. His Web site The Old New Thing deals with Windows history and Win32 programming. He also writes the Windows Confidential column for *TechNet Magazine*.

CHAPTER ONE

INITIAL FORAYS INTO USER
INTERFACE DESIGN

I F YOU ASK ten people for their thoughts on user interface design, you will get ten self-proclaimed expert opinions. Designing an interface for a single user grants you the luxury of just asking your customer what they want and doing it, but designing an interface for a large audience forces you to make tough decisions. Here are some stories on the subject of user interface design, starting with probably the most frequently asked question about the Windows 95 user interface.

Why do you have to click
the Start button to shut down?

BACK IN THE early days of what would eventually be named Windows 95, the taskbar didn't have a Start button. (Later, you'll learn that back in the early days of the project, the taskbar wasn't called the taskbar.)

Instead of the Start button, three buttons were displayed in the lower-left corner: the System button (icon: the Windows flag), the Find button (icon: an eyeball), and the Help button (icon: a question mark). Find and Help are self-explanatory. The System button gave you this menu:

Over time, the Find and Help buttons eventually joined the System button menu, and the System button menu itself gradually turned into the Windows 95 Start menu. Some menu options such as Arrange Windows (which led to options such as Cascade Windows and Tile Windows Horizontally) moved to other parts of the user interface; others such as Task List vanished completely.

One thing kept showing up during usability tests as a major hurdle: People turned on the computer and just sat there, unsure what to do next.

That's when someone got the idea of labeling the System menu Start. It says, "Psst. Click here." With this simple change, the usability results improved dramatically because, all of a sudden, people knew what to click when they wanted to do something.

So why is Shut down on the Start menu?

When we asked people to shut down their computers, they clicked the Start button. Because, after all, when you want to shut down, you have to start somewhere.

Why doesn't Windows have an "expert mode"?

WE OFTEN GET requests like this:

> There should be a slider bar somewhere, say on the Performance tab, that ranges from Novice to Advanced. At the highest level, all the advanced settings are turned on. At the Novice level, all the settings for beginners are turned on. In between, we can gradually enable stuff.

We've been trying to do something like this since even before Windows 95, and it doesn't work.

It doesn't work because those who might be whizzes at Excel will rate themselves as Advanced even though they can't tell a page file from a box of corn flakes. They're not stupid. They really are advanced users. Just not advanced at the skill we're asking them about.

And before you go mocking the beginners: Even so-called advanced users don't know everything. I know a lot about GUI programming, but I only know a little about disk partitioning, and I don't know squat about Active Directory. So am I an expert? When I need to format a hard drive, I don't want to face a dialog box filled with incomprehensible options. I just want to format the hard drive.

In the real world, people who are experts in one area are probably not experts in other areas. It's not something you can capture in a single number.

⌇

The default answer to every dialog box is Cancel

THE PROBLEM WITH displaying a dialog box is that people will take every opportunity to ignore it. One system administrator related a story in a *Network World* magazine online contest of a user who ignored a dozen virus security warnings and repeatedly tried to open an infected email attachment, complaining, "I keep trying to open it, but nothing happens." When the administrator asked why the user kept trying to open an attachment from a stranger, the answer was, "It might have been from a friend! They might have made up a new email address and didn't tell me!"[1] This story is a template for how users treat any unexpected dialog: They try to get rid of it.

We see this time and time again. If you are trying to accomplish task A, and in the process of doing it, an unexpected dialog box B appears, you aren't going to stop and read and consider B carefully. You're going to try to find the quickest path to getting rid of dialog B. For most people, this means minimizing it or clicking Cancel or just plain ignoring it.

---

1. "Why Some People Shouldn't Be Allowed Near Computers," *Network World*, August 23, 2003, http://napps.networkworld.com/compendium/archive/003362.html.

This manifests itself in many ways, but the basic idea is, "That dialog box is scary. I'm afraid to answer the question because I might answer it incorrectly and lose all my data. So I'll try to find a way to get rid of it as quickly as possible."

Here are some specific examples, taken from conversations I have had with real customers who called the Microsoft customer support line:

- "How do I make this error message go away? It appears every time I start the computer."

  "What does this error message say?"

  "It says, 'Updates are ready to install.' I've just been clicking the X to make it go away, but it's really annoying."

- "Every time I start my computer, I get this message that says that updates are ready to install. What does it mean?"

  "It means that Microsoft has found a problem that may allow a computer virus to get into your machine, and it's asking for your permission to fix the problem. You should click on it so the problem can be fixed."

  "Oh, that's what it is? I thought it was a virus, so I just kept clicking 'No.'"

- "When I start the computer I get this big dialog that talks about automatic updates. I've just been hitting Cancel. How do I make it stop popping up?"

  "Did you read what the dialog said?"

  "No. I just want it to go away."

- "Sometimes I get the message saying that my program has crashed and would I like to send an error report to Microsoft. Should I do it?"

  "Yes, we study these error reports so we can see how we can fix the problem that caused the crash."

  "Oh, I've just been hitting Cancel because that's what I always do when I see an error message."

  "Did you read the error message?"

"Why should I? It's just an error message. All it's going to say is 'Operation could not be performed because blah blah blah blah blah.'"

When most people buy a car, they don't expect to have to learn how an engine works and how to change spark plugs. They buy a car so that they can drive it to get from point A to point B. If the car makes a funny noise, they will ignore it as long as possible. Eventually, it may bother them to the point of taking it to a mechanic who will ask incredulously, "How long has it been doing this?" And the answer will be something like, "Oh, about a year."

The same goes for computers. People don't want to learn about gigabytes and dual-core processors and security zones. They just want to send email to their friends and surf the Web.

I myself have thrown out a recall notice because I thought it was junk mail. And computers are so filled with pop-up messages that any new pop-up message is treated as just another piece of junk mail to be thrown away.

Those who work at an information desk encounter this constantly. People ignore unexpected information. For example, even when a sign on a door says that "XYZ is closed today," you can bet that people will walk on in and ask, "Is XYZ open today?"

"No, it's closed today. Didn't you see the sign on the door?"

"Hmm, yeah, now that you mention it, there was a sign on the door, but I didn't read it."

Automobile manufacturers have learned to consolidate all their error messages into one message called "Check engine." Most people are conditioned to take the car in to a mechanic when the "Check engine" light goes on, and let the mechanic figure out what is wrong. Is it even possible to have a "Check engine" light for computers? Or would people just ignore that, too? How can a computer even tell whether a particular change in behavior is *normal* or *unintended?*

The best setting is the one you don't even sense, but it's there, and it works the way you expect

ONE SOLUTION THAT many people propose to the issue of "How should something be designed" is "Design it in every imaginable way, then let the end users pick the one they want with an option setting somewhere." This is a cop-out.

Computers need to be made simpler. This means fewer settings, not more. One way to reduce the number of settings is to make them implicit. You'll see more of this trend as researchers work on ways to make computers simpler, not more complicated.

Your toaster has a slider to set the darkness, which is remembered for your next piece of toast. There is no Settings dialog where you set the default darkness, but which you can override on a slice-by-slice basis.

Yes, this means that if you spent three weeks developing the perfect toaster slider position for Oroweat Honey Wheat Berry, and then you decide for a change of pace to have a slice of rye bread instead, you're going to have to move the slider and lose your old setting. People seem not to be particularly upset by this. The toaster works the way they expect.

Perhaps, you, the power-toaster-user, would want all toasters to let you save up to ten favorite darkness settings. But I suspect most people don't even sense that there are "missing options." If you started adding options to toasters, people would start wishing for the old days when toasters were simpler and easier to use.

"When I was a kid, you didn't have to log on to your toaster to establish your personal settings."

⤳

In order to demonstrate our superior intellect, we will now ask you a question you cannot answer

DURING THE DEVELOPMENT of Windows 95, a placeholder dialog was added with the title "In order to demonstrate our superior intellect, we will now ask you a question you cannot answer." The dialog itself asked a technical question that you need a brain the size of a planet to answer. (Okay, your brain didn't need to be quite that big.)

Of course, there was no intention of shipping Windows 95 with such a dialog. The dialog was there only until other infrastructure became available, permitting the system to answer the question automatically.

But when I saw that dialog, I was enlightened. As programmers, we often find ourselves unsure what to do next, and we say, "Well, to play it safe, I'll just ask users what they want to do. I'm sure they'll make the right decision."

Except that they don't. As we saw earlier, the default answer to every dialog box is Cancel. If you ask the user a technical question, odds are that they're just going to stare at it blankly for a while, then try to cancel out of it. The lesson they've learned is this: Computers are hard to use.

So don't ask questions the user can't answer. It doesn't get you anywhere, and it just frustrates the user.

⤳

Why doesn't Setup ask you if you want to keep newer versions of operating system files?

WINDOWS 95 SETUP would notice that a file it was installing was older than the file already on the machine and would ask you whether you wanted to keep the existing (newer) file or overwrite it with the older version.

Asking the user this question at all turned out to have been a bad idea. It's one of those dialogs that asks users a question they have no idea how to answer.

Suppose you're installing Windows 95 and you get the file version conflict dialog box. "The file Windows is attempting to install is older than the one already on the system. Do you want to keep the newer file?" What do you do?

Well, if you're like most people, you say, "Um, I guess I'll keep the newer one," so you click Yes.

And then a few seconds later, you get the same prompt for some other file. And you click Yes again.

And then a few seconds later, you get the same prompt for yet another file. Now you're getting nervous. Why is the system asking you all these questions? Is it second-guessing your previous answers? Often when this happens, it's because you're doing something bad and the computer is giving you one more chance to change your mind before something horrible happens. Like in the movies when you have to type Yes five times before you can launch the nuclear weapons.

Maybe this is one of those times.

Now you start clicking No. Besides, it's always safer to say "No," isn't it?

After a few more dialogs (clicking No this time), Setup finally completes. The system reboots, and … it blue-screens.

Why?

Because those five files were part of a matched set of files that together form your video driver. By saying "Yes" to some of them and "No" to others, you ended up with a mishmash of files that don't work together.

We learned our lesson. Setup doesn't ask this question any more. It always overwrites the files with the ones that come with the operating system. Sure, you may lose functionality, but at least you will be able to boot. Afterward, you can go to Windows Update and update that driver to the latest version.

Some have suggested that expanding the dialog with more explanatory text would solve the problem, but this misses the fact that people don't want to be bothered with these dialogs to begin with, as well as the fact that more information doesn't help anyway because the user doesn't have the background knowledge necessary to make an informed decision in the first place.

To a user, the dialog looks like this:

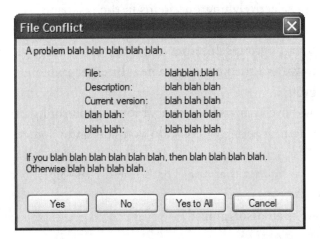

Making the dialog longer just increases the number of blahs. It's like trying to communicate with someone who doesn't speak your language by repeating yourself louder and more slowly. Users just want to surf the Web and send email to their grandchildren. Whatever you put in the dialog, they simply won't read it. Giving the dialog more buttons merely increases the paralysis factor.

Do you know the name of your printer driver? Or whether you should keep version 4.12.5.101 or downgrade it to 4.12.4.8? I sure don't.

Thinking through a feature

EVERYONE HAS A suggestion for a taskbar grouping feature. It's just a little bit of code; why not just do it?

Writing the code is the easy part.

Designing a feature is hard.

You have several audiences to consider. It's not just about the alpha geeks; you have to worry about the grandmothers, the office workers, the IT departments. They all have different needs. Sometimes a feature that pleases one group offends another.

So let's look at some of the issues surrounding the proposed feature of allowing users to selectively ungroup items in the taskbar.

One issue with selective grouping is deciding the scope of the feature. Suppose the user ungroups Internet Explorer, then closes all the Internet Explorer windows, and then opens two new Internet Explorer windows: Do the new ones group?

If so, you now have an invisible setting. How do you configure grouping for programs that aren't running? (How do you configure something that you can't see?)

Suppose you've figured that out. That's fine for the alpha geeks, but what about Grandma?

"The Internet is all disorganized."

"What do you mean?"

"My Internet windows are all disorganized."

"Can you explain a little more?"

"My taskbar used to be nice and organized, but now the Internet parts are disorganized and spread out all over the place. It used to be nice and neat. I don't know how it happened. I hate the Internet. It's always messing up my computer."

What is the user interface for selective ungrouping? Anything that is on a context menu will be executed accidentally by tens of thousands of people due to mouse twitching. Putting the regroup onto the context menu isn't necessarily good enough because those people don't even realize it was a context menu that did it. It was just a mouse twitch.

Mouse twitches cause all sorts of problems. Some people accidentally dock their taskbar vertically; others accidentally resize their taskbar to half the size of the screen. Do not underestimate the havoc that can be caused by mouse twitching.

Soon people will want to do arbitrary grouping. "I want to group this command prompt, that Notepad window, and this Calc window together."

What about selective ungrouping? "I have this group of ten windows, but I want to ungroup just two of them, leaving the other eight grouped together."

When you have selective/arbitrary grouping, how do you handle new windows? What group do they go into?

Remember: If you decide, "No, that's too much," thousands of people will be cursing you for not doing enough. Where do you draw the line? And also remember that each feature you add will cost you another feature somewhere else. Manpower isn't free.

But wait, the job has just begun. Next, you get to sit down and do the usability testing.

Soon you'll discover that everything you assumed to be true is completely wrong, and you have to go back to the drawing board. Eventually, you might conclude that you overdesigned the feature and you should go back to the simple on/off switch.

Wait, you're still not done. Now you have to bounce this feature off corporate IT managers. They will probably tear it to shreds, too. In particular, they're going to demand things such as remote administration and the capability to force the setting on or off across their entire company from a central location. (And woe unto you if you chose something more complicated than an on/off switch: Now you have to be able to deploy that complex setting across tens of thousands of computers, some of which may be connected to the corporate network via slow modems.)

Those are just some of the issues involved in designing a feature. Sometimes I think it's a miracle that features happen at all!

(Disclaimer: I'm not saying this is how the grouping feature actually came to be. I just used it as an illustration.)

Curiously, when I bring up this issue, the reaction of most people is not to consider the issue of trade-offs in feature design but rather to chip in with their vision of how the taskbar should work. "All I want is for the taskbar to do X. That other feature Y is useless." The value of X and Y changes from person to person; these people end up unwittingly proving my point rather than refuting it.

When do you disable an option, and when do you remove it?

WHEN YOU'RE DISPLAYING a menu item or a dialog option, and the option is not available, you can either disable it or you can remove it. What is the rule for deciding which one to do?

Experiments have shown that if something is shown but disabled, users expect that they will be able to get it enabled if they tinker around enough.

Therefore, leave a menu item shown but disabled if there is something the user can do to cause the operation to become available. For example, in a media playback program, the option to stop playback is disabled if the media file is not playing. When it starts playing, however, the option becomes available again.

On the other hand, if the option is not available for a reason the user has no control over, remove it. Otherwise the user will go nuts looking for the magic way to enable it. For example, if a printer is not capable of printing color, don't show any of the color management options, because there's nothing the user can do with your program to make that printer a color printer.

By analogy, consider a text adventure game. The player tries something clever, such as "Take the torch from the wall," and the computer replies, "You can't do that, yet." This is the adventure game equivalent to graying out a menu item. The user is now going to go nuts trying to figure out what's happening: "Hmm, maybe I need a chair, or the torch is too hot, or I'm carrying too much stuff, or I have to find another character and ask him to do it for me."

If it turns out that the torch is simply not removable, what you've done is send the user down fruitless paths to accomplish something that simply can't be done. For an adventure game, this frustration is part of the fun. But for a computer program, frustration is not something people tend to enjoy.

Note that this isn't a hard-and-fast rule; it's just a guideline. Other considerations might override this principle. For example, you may believe that a consistent menu structure is more desirable because it is less confusing. (A media playback program, for example, might decide to leave the video-related options visible but grayed when playing a music file.)

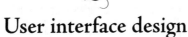

When do you put ...
after a button or menu?

SAVE AS... APPEARS on some menus. You'll also find plenty of Customize... buttons. What is the rule for dots?

Many people believe that the rule for dots is this: "If it's going to display a dialog, you need dots." This is a misapprehension.

The rules are spelled out in the Windows User Interface Design Specifications and Guidelines (what a mouthful) in the section titled "Ellipses."

You should read the guidelines for the full story, but here's the short version: Use an ellipsis if the command requires additional information before it can be performed. Sometimes the dialog box is the command itself, such as About or Properties. Even though they display a dialog, the dialog *is the result*, as opposed to commands such as Print, where the dialog is *collecting additional information prior to the result.*

User interface design
for vending machines

How HARD CAN it be to design the user interface of a vending machine? You accept money, you have some buttons, users push the buttons, and they get their product and their change.

At least in the United States, many vending machines arrange their product in rows and columns. To select a product, you press the letter of the row and the number of the column. Could it be any simpler?

It turns out that subtleties lurk even in something this simple.

If the vending machine contains ten items per row, and you number them 1 through 10, a person who wants to buy product C10 has to push the buttons C and 10. But in our modern keyboard-based world, there is no 10 key. Instead, people press 1 followed by 0.

What happens if you type C + 1 + 0? After you type the 1, product C1 drops. Then the user realizes that there is no 0 key. And he bought the wrong product.

This is not a purely theoretical problem. I have seen this happen myself. How would you fix this?

One solution is simply not to put so many items on a single row, considering that people have difficulty making decisions if given too many options. On the other hand, the vendor might not like that design; their goal might be to maximize the number of products.

Another solution is to change the labels so that the number of button presses needed always matches the number of characters in the label. In other words, no buttons with two characters on them (for example, a 10 button).

You could switch the rows and columns so that the products are labeled 1A through 1J across the top row and 9A through 9J across the bottom. This assumes you don't have more than nine rows, however. Some vending machines have many more selections on display, resulting in a very large number of rows.

If you have exactly ten items per row, you can call the tenth column 0. Notice, however that you also should remove rows I and O to avoid possible confusion with 1 and 0.

Some vending machines use numeric codes for all items rather than a letter and a digit. For example, if the cookies are product number 23, you punch 2 + 3. If you want the chewing gum (product code 71), you punch 7 + 1. What are some problems with having your products numbered from 1 to 99?

Here are a few problems. You may have come up with others:

- Products with codes 11, 22, 33, and so on may be selected accidentally. A faulty momentary switch might cause a single key-press to register as two, or a user may press the button twice by mistake or frustration.

- Product codes less than ten are ambiguous. Is a 3 a request for product number 3, or is the user just being slow at entering 32? Solving this by adding a leading zero will not work because people are in the habit of ignoring leading zeros.

- Product codes should not coincide with product prices. If there is a bag of cookies that costs 75 cents, users are likely to press 75 when they want the cookies, even though the product code for the cookies is 23.

User interface design for interior door locks

How HARD CAN it be to design the user interface of an interior door lock?

Locking or unlocking the door from the inside is typically done with a latch that you turn. Often, the latch handle is in the shape of a bar that turns.

Now, there are two possible ways you can set up your lock. One is that a horizontal bar represents the locked position, and a vertical bar represents the unlocked position. The other is to have a horizontal bar represent the unlocked position and a vertical bar represent the locked position.

For some reason, it seems that most lock designers went for the latter interpretation. A horizontal bar means unlocked.

This is wrong.

Think about what the bar represents. When the deadbolt is locked, a horizontal bar extends from the door into the door jamb. Clearly, the horizontal bar position should reflect the horizontal position of the deadbolt. It also resonates with the old-fashioned way of locking a door by placing a wooden or metal bar horizontally across the face. (Does no one say "bar the door" any more?)

Car doors even followed this convention, back when car door locks were little knobs that popped up and down. The up position represented the removal of the imaginary deadbolt from the door/jamb interface. Pushing the button down was conceptually the same as sliding the deadbolt into the locked position.

But now, many car door locks don't use knobs. Instead, they use rocker switches. (Forward means lock. Or is it backward? What is the intuition there?) The visual indicator of the door lock is a red dot. But what does it mean? Red clearly means *danger*, so is it more dangerous to have a locked door or an unlocked door? I can never remember; I always have to tug on the door handle.

(Horizontally mounted power window switches have the same problem. Does pushing the switch forward raise the window or lower it?)

⬱

The evolution of mascara in Windows UI

THE LOOK OF the Windows user interface has gone through fashion cycles.

In the beginning, there was Windows 1.0, which looked very flat because screen resolutions were rather low in those days, and color depth was practically nonexistent. If you had 16 colors, you were doing pretty well. You couldn't afford to spend very many pixels on fluff such as borders, and shadows were out of the question because of lack of color depth.

The *flat look* continued in Windows 2.0, but Windows 3.0 added a hint of 3D, with a touch of beveling in push buttons.

Other people decided that the 3D look was the hot new thing, and libraries sprang up to add 3D shadow and outlining effects to nearly everything. The library CTL3D.DLL started out as just an Excel thing, but it grew in popularity until it became the standard way to make your dialog boxes *even more 3D*.

Come Windows 95, and even more of the system had a 3D look. For example, beveling appeared along the inside edge of the panes in the Explorer window. Furthermore, 3D-ness was turned on by default for all programs that marked themselves as designed for Windows 95. For programs that wanted to run on older versions of Windows as well, a new dialog style DS_3DLOOK was added, so that they could indicate that they wanted 3D-ization if available.

And if the 3D provided by Windows 95 by default wasn't enough, you could use CTL3D32.DLL to make your controls *even more 3D than ever before*. By this point, things started getting really ugly. Buttons on dialog boxes had so many heavy black outlines that it started to look like a really bad mascara job.

Fortunately, like many fashions that get out of hand, people realized that too much 3D is not a good thing. User interfaces got flatter. Instead of using 3D effects and bold outlines to separate items, subtler cues were used. Divider lines became more subdued and sometimes disappeared entirely.

Microsoft Office and Microsoft Money were two programs that embraced the *less-is-more* approach. The beveling is gone, and there are no 3D effects. Buttons are flat and unobtrusive. The task pane separates itself from the content pane by a simple gray line and a change in background shade. Even the toolbar has gone flat. Office 2000 also went largely flat, although some simple 3D effects linger (in the grooves and in the scrollbars, for example).

Windows XP jumped on the *flat-is-good* bandwagon and even got rid of the separator line between the tasks pane and the contents pane. The division is merely implied by the change in color. "Separation through juxtaposition" has become the new mantra.

Office XP and Outlook 2003 continue the trend and flatten nearly everything aside from the scrollbar elements. Blocks of color are used to separate elements onscreen, sometimes with the help of simple outlines.

So now the pendulum of fashion has swung away from 3D back toward flatness. Who knows how long this school of visual expression will hold the upper hand? Will 3D return with a vengeance when people tire of the starkness of the flat look?

CHAPTER TWO

SELECTED REMINISCENCES ON WINDOWS 95

WINDOWS 95 WAS perhaps the most heavily anticipated software of its era. At the Windows 95 tenth anniversary party, I happened to run into one of the lead marketing people for Windows 95, and we got to reminiscing about people lining up for hours at software stores to buy their copy at the stroke of midnight. Having Jay Leno (an actual celebrity!) host the launch event turned operating systems from boring software that only geeks understood to something with mass appeal (that only geeks understood). And he wrapped up our brief chat by saying, "And we'll never see anything like it ever again." Although you, my dear reader, weren't able to join us for our little nostalgia trip, here are some stories you can use to pretend that you were.

Why isn't my time zone highlighted on the world map?

IN THE ORIGINAL release of Windows 95, you could change your time zone by clicking on the map, and the time zone you selected would highlight. Similarly, you could change your Region settings by clicking on the world map.

This was one of those little touches that made Windows 95 that much more fun to use.

But we had to remove those features, even though we based both of the maps on the borders officially recognized by the United Nations.

In early 1995, a border war broke out between Peru and Ecuador, and the Peruvian government complained to Microsoft that the border was incorrectly placed. Of course, if we complied and moved the border northward, we'd get an equally angry letter from the Ecuadorian government demanding that we move it back. So we removed the map feature of the Region settings altogether.

The time zone map met a similar fate. The Indian government threatened to ban all Microsoft software from the country because we assigned a disputed region to Pakistan in the time zone map.[1] (Any map that depicts an unfavorable border must bear a government stamp warning the end user that the borders are incorrect. You can't stamp software.) The drawing of regional boundaries in the time zone map was removed from the International version of Windows 95.

It isn't good enough to remove it only from the Indian version of Windows 95. Maintaining multiple code bases is an expensive proposition, and besides, no one can predict what country will get upset next.

Geopolitics is a sensitive subject.

⌒

Why didn't Windows 95 boot with more than 1GB of memory?

SHORT VERSION: Windows 95 will fail to boot if you have more than around 480MB of memory. (This was considered an insane amount of memory back then. Remember, Windows 95's target machine was a 4MB 386SX, and a powerful machine had 16MB. So according to Moore's law, that gave us seven years before we had to do something about it. One of my friends got 96MB of memory on his machine to test that we didn't tank under "insanely huge memory configurations," and we all drooled.)

---

1. Lance Lattig, "A Dispute Over India's Borders Had Microsoft Mapping a Retreat," *Wall Street Journal*, August 24, 1995.

Windows 98 bumped the limit to 1GB because there existed a vendor (who shall remain nameless) who was insane enough to want to sell machines with 1GB of memory and preinstall Windows 98 rather than the much more suitable Windows NT.

Now the long version.

One of the first things that happens in the Windows 95 boot process after you have transitioned into 32-bit mode is to initialize the 32-bit memory manager. But now you have a chicken-and-egg problem: The memory manager needs to allocate some memory to keep track of the memory it is managing (keeping track of which pages are paged in and which are paged out, that sort of thing). However, it can't allocate memory until the memory manager is initialized. Eek!

The solution is to initialize the memory manager twice.

The first time the memory manager is initialized, it gets all its memory from a fixed block of memory preallocated in the init-data segment. It sets up this fixed block as the memory manager heap. So now a heap is available to satisfy memory allocations.

Next, the memory manager starts looking for the real memory in the system, and when it finds some, it allocates memory (from the initial fixed block) to keep track of the real memory.

After the memory manager has found all the real memory in the system, it's time to initialize the memory manager a second time: It carves out a chunk of that real memory to use as the "real heap" and copies the information from the heap that it has been using so far (the fixed-sized heap) to the "real heap."

After everything has been copied and all the pointers fixed up, the global memory manager heap pointers are changed to point at the new ("real") heap, and the original heap is abandoned.

The memory consumed by the original heap is reclaimed when the init-data segment is discarded (which happens at the end of system initialization).

The total memory limitation occurs because the size of the fixed block in the init-data segment needs to be large enough to satisfy all the memory allocations performed during the memory scan. If you have too much memory, an allocation during the memory scan fails, and the system halts.

The size of the init-data segment was chosen to balance two factors. The larger you make it, the more memory you can have in the system before hitting an allocation failure during the memory scan. But you can't make it too large or machines with small amounts of memory won't even be able to load the operating system into memory because of all the space required by your new, bigger init-data segment.

The Windows NT series (which includes Windows 2000, Windows XP, and Windows Vista) has a completely different kernel-mode architecture and fortunately suffers from none of these problems.

〜

Why did Windows 95 have functions called BEAR, BUNNY, and PIGLET?

IF YOU DIG back into your Windows 95 files, you'll find that some internal system functions are given names such as BEAR35, BUNNY73, and PIGLET12. Surely there is a story behind these silly names, isn't there?

Of course there is.

Bear is the name of the Windows 3.1 mascot, a stuffed teddy bear seemingly obsessively carried around by Dave, one of the most senior programmers on the team. If he came into your office, he might bounce Bear on your monitor to get your attention. As a prank, we would sometimes steal Bear and take him on "vacation," in the same way people take garden gnomes on vacation and send back postcards.

If you play the Windows 3.1 Easter egg, one of the pictures you will see is a cartoon of Bear.

Bear took a lot of abuse. He once had the power cord to an arcade-style video game run through his head between his ears. Another developer tried to stick a firecracker up Bear's butt (presumably not while it had the power cord in its head).

By Windows 95, Bear was in pretty bad repair. (The children of one of the program managers once took pity on Bear and did a nice job of getting Bear back in cuddle-able condition.)

So Bear was retired from service and replaced with a pink bunny rabbit, named Bunny. We actually had two of them, a small one called 16-bit Bunny and a big one called 32-bit Bunny. Two bunnies means twice as many opportunities for theft, of course, and the two bunnies had their own escapades during the Windows 95 project. (When Dave got married, we helped 32-bit Bunny crash the party and sent back pictures of Bunny drunk on wine.)

Dave was primarily responsible for the user-interface side of things, so you'll see the BEAR and BUNNY functions in the components responsible for the user interface. On the kernel side, Mike had a Piglet plush toy (from Winnie the Pooh). When we needed to name an internal kernel function, we chose PIGLET. Piglet survived the Windows 95 project without a scratch.

What about BOZOSLIVEHERE and TABTHETEXTOUTFORWIMPS?

FOR THIS, YOU need a deeper history lesson.

Back in the old days of real-mode Windows, all callback functions had to be exported. The exporting was necessary because of the way real-mode Windows managed memory, the details of which are unimportant here. Consequently, the window procedures for all the standard window classes (edit controls, list boxes, check boxes, and so on) were exported from USER. And those were on top of the usual collection of internal functions that enabled USER, KERNEL, and GDI to coordinate their efforts.

Some people reverse-engineered all these internal functions and printed books about how they worked. As a result, a lot of programs actually used them; which was quite a surprise to us because they were internal functions. And then when we wanted to redesign these internal functions (for example, to add a parameter, or if we decided that we didn't need it any more and tried to delete it), we found that the programs stopped working.

So we had to put the functions back, with their old behavior. The new features we were contemplating had to be redesigned, redirected, or possibly even abandoned entirely. (If we wanted to delete a function, the work could continue; but the old function had to stay around with its old behavior. It was basically dead code from the operating system's point of view, hanging around just because some random program or other decided to cheat and bypass the documented way of doing things.) But to teach people a lesson, they often got given goofy names.

For example, BOZOSLIVEHERE was originally the window procedure for the edit control, with the rather nondescript name of EditWndProc. Then some people who wanted to use the edit control window procedure decided that GetWindowLong(GWL_WNDPROC) was too much typing, so they linked to EditWndProc directly. Then when a later version of Windows no longer required window procedures to be exported, we removed them all, only to find that programs stopped working. So we had to put them back, but they got goofy names as a way of scolding the programs that were doing these invalid things.

Things got even worse in Windows 95, when all our window procedures were converted to 32-bit versions. The problem is that the old window procedures were only 16 bit. So we couldn't even simply export the 32-bit window procedure under the name BOZOSLIVEHERE. We had to write a conversion function that took an illegal 16-bit function call and converted it to the corresponding illegal 32-bit function call.

This is just the tip of the iceberg with respect to application compatibility. I can tell dozens upon dozens of stories about bad things programs did and what we had to do to get them to work again (often in spite of themselves). Which is why I get particularly furious when people accuse Microsoft of maliciously breaking applications during operating system upgrades. If any application failed to run on Windows 95, I took it as a personal failure. I spent many sleepless nights fixing bugs in third-party programs just so they could keep running on Windows 95. (Games were the worst. Often the game vendor didn't even care that their program didn't run on Windows 95!)

What was in the Windows 95 Special Edition box?

AT THE WINDOWS 95 launch and at various other marketing events, guests were given a copy of Windows 95 Special Edition. What is so special about the box?

Answer: the box.

The contents of the box are exactly the same as a regular copy of Windows 95. The only thing special about it is the box itself.

Windows brings out the Rorschach test in everyone

IT SEEMS THAT no matter what you do, somebody will get offended.

Every Windows 95 box has an anti-piracy hologram on the side. The photographer chose his infant son as his model because the human face is hard to copy accurately. The baby sits next to a computer, and as you turn the hologram, his arm rises and points at the computer monitor, which bursts into a Windows 95 logo.

How cute. And everybody loves babies.

Until we got a complaint from a government (who shall remain nameless for obvious reasons) that was upset with Windows 95 because it depicted naked children.

"Naked children!?" we all thought to ourselves.

They were complaining about the hologram on the box. The baby wasn't wearing a shirt. Even though the baby was visible only from the waist up, the offended government assumed that he wasn't wearing pants either.

We had to produce a new hologram. In the new hologram, the baby is wearing a shirt and overalls. But because this was a rush job, we didn't have time to do the arm animation.

So if you still have your copy of Windows 95, go look at the hologram. If the baby in your hologram isn't wearing a shirt, you have a genuine collector's item. I have seen the "naked baby" hologram, but unfortunately my copy of Windows 95 has a clothed baby.

If you hunt around the Web, you can find lots of other people who claim to have found subliminal messages in Windows 95. My favorite is the one who claims to have found images in the clouds bitmap. Hey, they're clouds. They're nature's Rorschach test.

Windows XP had its own share of complaints. The original wallpaper for Windows XP was Red Moon Desert, until people claimed that Red Moon Desert looked like a pair of buttocks. People also thought that one of the generic people used in the User Accounts Control Panel looked like Hitler. And one government claimed the cartoon character in the original Switch Users dialog looked like an indecent body part. We had to change them all. But it makes me wonder about the mental state of our beta testers!

∾

The martial arts logon picture

ALONG THE LINES of Windows as Rorschach test, here's an example of someone attributing malicious behavior to randomness.

Among the logon pictures that come with Windows XP is a martial arts kick. I remember one bug we got that complained, "Windows XP is racist. It put a picture of a kung fu fighter next to my name, just because my name is Chinese. This is an insult!"

The initial user picture is chosen at random from among the pictures in the %ALLUSERSPROFILE%\Application Data\Microsoft\User Account Pictures\Default Pictures directory. It just so happened that the random number generator picked the martial arts kick out of the 21 available pictures.

I'm also frustrated by people who find quirks in spell checkers and attribute malicious intent to them. You know what I'm talking about. "Go to Word and type in ‹some name that's not in the dictionary› and tell it to check your spelling. Word will flag the word and recommend ‹some other word that is somehow opposite to the first word in meaning› instead. This is an insult!

Microsoft intentionally taught the spell checker to suggest ‹that word› when you type ‹this word›. This is clear proof of ‹some bad thing›."

🙡

Why a really large dictionary is not a good thing

SOMETIMES YOU'LL HEAR people brag about how many words are in their spell-checking dictionary. It turns out that having too many words in a spell checker's dictionary is worse than having too few.

Suppose you have a spell checker whose dictionary contains every word in the Oxford English Dictionary. Then you hand it this sentence:

```
Therf werre eyght bokes.
```

That sentence would pass with flying colors because all the words in the preceding sentence are valid English words, although most people would be hard-pressed to provide definitions.

The English language has so many words that if you included them all, common typographical errors would often match (by coincidence) a valid English word and therefore not be detected by the spell checker. Which would go against the whole point of a spell checker: to catch spelling errors.

So be glad that your spell checker doesn't have the largest dictionary possible. If it did, it would end up doing a worse job.

🙡

An insight into the Windows 95 startup sound

DOO, DUDUDUDINGGGGGG … ding … ding … ding.

In an interview with Joel Selvin at the *San Francisco Chronicle*, Brian Eno explains how he came to compose "The Microsoft Sound," the default system startup sound for Windows 95. He compared writing a 3.25-second music piece to "making a tiny little jewel," and when he returned to writing longer works, 3 minutes "seemed like oceans of time."[2]

The Windows 95 CD contained extra multimedia toss-ins. The ones I remember are a cartoon or two by Bill Plympton, a Weezer music video, and a music video of Edie Brickell singing "Good Times."

For some reason, everybody wanted to know the artist from the "Good Times" video. Nobody was interested in the artists who did any of the other stuff. (Okay, probably nobody asked about Weezer because, well, that's the group right there in the filename.)

Hint: Right-click and select Properties. That will tell you the artist.

Oh, and the question nobody asked but I'm going to answer it anyway: The composer of the Windows 95 Easter egg theme is Brian Orr. You can read his story of how it came to be on his Web site (www.brianorr.com/music/compositions/clients.asp).

It's a lot easier to write a column if you don't care about accuracy

THE GREAT THING about writing a rumors column is that you don't have to be right! Even if you're wrong, you can just say, "Well, Microsoft changed it before they shipped," and nobody can say you were wrong. It's a victimless crime! The only victim is Microsoft!

A classic example from early 1995 came from a technology rumor columnist who reported that Windows 95 would employ a hardware key, informally known in the industry as a *dongle*. A dongle is a device that plugs into the computer and that the software uses to confirm that the copy is legitimate. The report concluded with "it should be classified as a rumor. Microsoft could change its mind on the dongle security strategy tomorrow."

Note that last sentence. And the great thing is, if the story turns out untrue, you can even take credit for it! "Thanks to public uproar over my amazing scoop, Microsoft changed its mind and decided not to do this thing" (that it wasn't planning on doing anyway).

---

2. Joel Selvin, "Q and A with Brian Eno," *San Francisco Chronicle*, June 2, 1996, www.sfgate.com/cgi-bin/article.cgi?file=/chronicle/archive/1996/06/02/PK70006.DTL.

It's frustrating reading rampant bogus rumors about your product and not being able to do anything about it.

So remember, all you rumor-consumers: Just because you saw it in the newspaper doesn't mean that it's true.

⤳

Why does the System Properties page round the memory size?

DURING WINDOWS 95 beta testing, people ran the System Properties page and complained about "missing memory."

The Windows 95 System Properties page reports the amount of memory available to Windows as system memory, which is not necessarily the same as the amount of memory installed in your computer.

For example, you may have an old DOS device driver that allocates a large amount of memory for itself, which prevents Windows 95 from using it. Or you may have a dreaded Unified Memory Architecture (UMA) machine, where your so-called 8MB of memory is actually being divided between main system memory and video memory. So if you have an 8MB UMA machine and you're running at 800 × 600 pixels in 256 colors, you actually have only 7.5MB of memory; the other half megabyte got taken by the video card.

When we displayed the actual amount of memory available to Windows, we got lots of bug reports from people asking, "I paid for 8 megabytes of memory, where is it?"

That's why Windows 95 takes the actual amount of memory and rounds it up to the nearest multiple of 4MB and displays that.

⤳

Why does my hard drive light flash every few seconds?

BACK IN WINDOWS 95, people would notice that their hard drive light would blink every few seconds. What's that all about?

Actually, it wasn't the hard drive light after all.

Windows 95 was polling your CD-ROM drive to see whether you had inserted a new CD. Some computers wired up the "hard drive light" not to the hard drive but rather to the SCSI and/or IDE bus. So the light didn't indicate hard drive activity necessarily. It turned on for any bus activity.

Fortunately, motherboard manufacturers discovered their mistake, and nowadays you don't find any of them that mis-wire the hard drive access light.

Or do you? I keep my computer under my desk, so I never see the hard drive light anyway. I'm just surmising that in the past seven years, motherboard manufacturers have gotten their act together.

⬤

The hunt for a faster syscall trap

THE PERFORMANCE OF the syscall trap gets a lot of attention.

I was reminded of a meeting that took place between Intel and Microsoft more than 15 years ago. (Sadly, I was not myself at this meeting, so the story is second-hand.)

Because Microsoft is one of Intel's biggest customers, their representatives often visit Microsoft to show off what their latest processor can do, to lobby the kernel development team to support a new processor feature, and to solicit feedback on what sort of features would be most useful to add.

At this meeting, the Intel representatives asked, "So if you could ask for only one thing to be made faster, what would it be?"

Without hesitation, one of the lead kernel developers (who happens to be a bit of a jokester) replied, deadpan, "Speed up faulting on an invalid instruction."

The Intel half of the room burst out laughing. "Oh, you Microsoft engineers are so funny!" And so the meeting ended with a cute little joke.

After returning to their labs, the Intel engineers ran profiles against the Windows kernel and, lo and behold, they discovered that Windows spent a lot of its time dispatching invalid instruction exceptions. How absurd! Was the Microsoft engineer not kidding around after all?

No, he wasn't.

It so happens that on the 80386 chip of that era, the fastest way to get from 8086 emulation mode into kernel mode was to execute an invalid instruction! Consequently, Windows/386 used an invalid instruction as its syscall trap.

What's the moral of this story? I'm not sure. Perhaps it's that when you create something, you may find people using it in ways you had never considered.

⤳

One byte used to cost a dollar

BACK IN THE days when software was distributed on floppy disks (remember floppy disks?), the rule of thumb for Windows was "one byte costs a dollar."

In other words, considering the cost of materials, the additional manufacturing time, the contribution to product weight, the cost of replacing materials that became defective after they left the factory (for example, during shipping), after taking data compression into account, and so on, the incremental cost of adding another megabyte to the Windows product was around $1,000,000 (or about $1 per byte).

This was a cute rule of thumb to have because it let you put a (admittedly somewhat artificial) monetary value on code bloat. Was your feature even worth the disk space?

Of course, the advent of the CD as the primary distribution medium changed the mathematics, but there is still great concern over the size of the operating system. It is my understanding that the Windows Server 2003 CD is basically "full." It might not look full to you, but remember that your CD is probably the 32-bit English version. Additional space needs to be reserved for translations into other languages, and don't forget that the 64-bit edition of Windows needs to contain two operating systems, the native 64-bit one and the emulated 32-bit one. (It's not quite that bad, because some files can be shared, and many 32-bit components can be jettisoned.)

Each product-support call costs a sale

ANOTHER MONETARY RULE of thumb is that "each product-support call costs a sale."

What this means is that, if you look at all the Windows product-support calls—some of which are handled in minutes, others of which take days—the average cost of a product-support call is approximately the same as the revenue for one copy of Windows.

Sometimes you'll hear somebody say, "The odds of someone hitting this problem are one in a million." I read one estimate that there are 200 million Windows PCs in the world. Who knows how accurate that is, but it's enough to illustrate my point.

Suppose something happens once a day, and it has a one in a million chance of going wrong. With 200 million Windows PCs, that's 200 failures a day, or more than 70,000 failures a year. Congratulations, your *one-in-a-million* bug just cost the company 70,000 copies' worth of Windows revenue each year (not to mention, of course, 70,000 dissatisfied users).

Why isn't Tweak UI included on the Windows CD?

WE TRIED THAT. It was a disaster.

In the original version of Windows 98, a copy of Tweak UI was placed in an Extras folder on the CD. And it didn't take long for us to realize that this was a bad idea.

Because there was no explicit download step, where you could see the Web page and read all the warnings, people just ran the program and started fiddling with their settings. Some time later, their computer would start acting strange, and they would call the product-support lines to get help. The product-support folks would spend hours trying to figure out what happened, only to discover that the users had actually done it to themselves.

For example, they would go into Tweak UI's Control Panel page and hide some Control Panel icons. A few weeks later, they would get an error message that said something like, "Cannot connect to your printer. Please go to the Wireless Link Control Panel and check your settings." But when they went to the Control Panel, there was no Wireless Link icon.

The product-support people are smart, but they aren't psychic. There are hundreds of reasons why the Wireless Link icon might be missing from the Control Panel. It could be a corrupted file. It might be that the infrared port is not being detected by Plug and Play. Maybe the user has the wrong infrared driver. Or the infrared port is incompatible. The printer might be positioned at the wrong angle, or the air might be too dusty to establish a good infrared connection.

Tweak UI hides the Wireless Link icon by using Group Policy, which is a technique that is used by corporations to apply settings to all computers in their organization. But if a home user calls the product-support line, the product-support people won't even bother looking into Group Policy settings because home users don't use Group Policy. Group Policy is for corporations.

Only after exhausting the most likely reasons will the product-support technician be likely to say, "Hmm, I know this is a home computer and Group Policy shouldn't be set, but let's go check it anyway." Then they'll find that the policy has been set to hide the Wireless Link icon. "Oh, yeah, a few months ago, I used that Tweak UI program to hide some icons I wasn't using. Was that wrong?" The product-support person politely walks the user through reenabling the Wireless Link icon via Group Policy and concludes the service call.

Based on feedback from the product-support team, the Windows team realized that putting Tweak UI on the CD was a horrible mistake; and when Windows 98 was updated as Windows 98 SE, one of the files missing from the CD was Tweak UI.

∽

Turns out that you can't install
Windows via xcopy

A COLLEAGUE OF mine reminded me of a story from Windows 95. A major magazine reviewer excoriated a beta of Windows 95 because it blue-screened the moment he opened his Control Panel. We contacted the reviewer and asked to borrow the machine to investigate the problem.

It turns out that this particular magazine reviewer decided that running the Windows 95 Setup program was too much work. Instead, he copied the contents of the hard drive of an existing Windows 95 machine to his laptop. Never mind that the old machine was a desktop and the new machine was a laptop. Never mind that they had completely different hardware from different manufacturers with different preinstalled drivers and utilities.

It so happens that it was one of these preinstalled utilities that was causing the problem. It was a 16-bit Control Panel utility designed for controlling various bonus features of Brand X computers.

The authors of this Control Panel utility didn't want to show their icon unless they were running on an authentic Brand X computer. Therefore, when the Control Panel started up and looked for icons, their utility said, "Hang on a second, let me decide whether I should show an icon or not."

The utility allocated a selector manually and set its base and limit so that it could grovel around the BIOS memory and then freed the temporary selector. If it confirmed that the BIOS was a Brand X BIOS, the function returned success, and the icon was shown. If it decided that you didn't have a Brand X BIOS, it freed the selector and returned failure, thereby preventing the icon from appearing in the Control Panel.

Do you see the bug?

Because the reviewer's laptop computer was not Brand X, the Control Panel utility exercised its failure path, which contains a double-free bug, resulting in a corrupted free list. It so happens that selectors are used a lot in 16-bit Windows, and the corrupted free list didn't take long to manifest itself in a selector load failure, followed by more selector load failures trying to handle the first failure, and so on, until the recursive death spiral finally proved too much for Windows to handle and it just gave up.

Such was the world of 16-bit Windows, where programs were trusted not to screw up.

Buying an entire Egghead Software store

DURING THE DEVELOPMENT of Windows 95, application compatibility was a high priority. To make sure that coverage was as broad as possible, the development manager for Windows 95 took his pickup truck, drove down to the local Egghead Software store (back when Egghead still existed), and bought *one copy of every single PC program in the store.*

He then returned to Microsoft, unloaded all the software onto tables in the cafeteria, and invited every member of the Windows 95 team to come in and take responsibility for up to two programs. The ground rules were that you had to install and run the program, use it like a normal end user, and file a bug against everything that didn't work right, even the minor stuff. (Of course, you had to provide the program to the person investigating the bug upon request.) In exchange for taking responsibility for ensuring that Windows 95 was compatible with your adopted programs, you got to keep them after Windows 95 shipped. If you did a good job with your two, you could come back for more.

The cafeteria was filled with Windows 95 team members, browsing through the boxes upon boxes of software like bargain hunters at a flea market. And there were the inevitable "What'd you get?" comparisons afterward.

I picked up only one program, an English/German automatic translator. It ran fine but produced pretty bad translations (not that the quality of the translations was in any way the fault of Windows!).

The history of the Windows PowerToys

DURING THE DEVELOPMENT of Windows 95, as with the development of any project, the people working on the project wrote side programs to test the features they were adding or to prototype a feature. After Windows 95 shipped, some of those programs were collected into the first edition of the Windows 95 PowerToys.

As I recall, the first edition consisted of the following toys:

- **CabView.** This was a handy internal tool that also served as a test of the shell folder design.
- **CD AutoPlay, DeskMenu, FlexiCD, QuickRes.** These were side toys originally written by shell developers for their own personal use.
- **Command Prompt Here, Explore From Here.** These were proof-of-concept toys that tested the shell command extension design.
- **Round Clock.** This was a program to test regional windows.
- **Shortcut Target Menu.** This was a feature idea that didn't make the final cut.

I wasn't around when the decision was made to package these toys up and ship them, so I don't know what the rule was for deciding what was PowerToy-worthy and what wasn't. Nor do I know where the name PowerToy came from. (Probably somebody just made it up because it sounded neat.)

Upon the enormous success of the PowerToys, a second edition was developed. This time, people knew that they were writing a PowerToy, in contrast to the first edition of the PowerToys, which was merely cobbled together from stuff lying around. The second edition of the Windows 95 PowerToys added FindX, Send To X, the Telephony Locator Selector, XMouse, and Tweak UI.

Later, the kernel team released their own set of toys, known as the Windows 95 Kernel Toys. Here was the original introductory text:

```
The Windows 95 Kernel PowerToys
-------------------------------
The Windows 95 kernel team got kind of jealous of all the atten-
tion the shell team has been getting from its PowerToys, so they
decided to polish off their own personal toys and make their own
web page. Mind you, the kernel folks aren't experts at intuitive
user interfaces, so don't expect to see jumping icons and friend-
ly things to click on. (These are the people who do their taxes
in hexadecimal.)
```

In reality, it was I who wrote all the Kernel Toys, except for the Time Zone Editor, which came from the Windows NT Resource Kit. I also wrote the somewhat whimsical original blurb.

This was all back in the day when it was easy to put up something for download. No digital signatures, no virus checking, no paperwork. Just throw it up there and watch what happens. Today, things are very different. Putting something up for download is a complicated process with forms to fill out in triplicate and dark rooms with card readers. I wouldn't be surprised if an abandoned salt mine in Montana were somehow involved.

Nowadays, every team at Microsoft seems to have their own PowerToys, trading on the good name of the Windows shell team who invented the whole PowerToys idea. As far as I can tell, we don't get any royalties from other divisions calling *their* toys PowerToys.

What's frustrating is that because they are all called PowerToys, questions about them tend to go to the shell team, because we are the ones who invented PowerToys. We frequently have to reply, "Oh, no, you're having a problem with the XYZ PowerToys, not the classic Windows PowerToys. We're the folks who do the classic Windows PowerToys."

Some people claim that Tweak UI was written because Microsoft got tired of responding to customer complaints. I don't know where they got that from. Tweak UI was written because I felt like writing it.

People also claim that sometimes PowerToys vanish without warning. That's true. A few years ago, all the Windows XP PowerToys were taken down so that they could be given a security review. Some of them didn't survive and didn't come back. Other times, a PowerToy is pulled because a serious bug is found. Because PowerToys are spare-time projects, it can take a long time for a bug to get fixed, tested, and republished. For example, the HTML Slide Show Wizard was pulled after a (somewhat obscure) data-loss bug was found. Fixing the bug itself took just a few days, but testing and filling out all the associated paperwork took six months.

There's no moral to this story. Just a quick history lesson.

≈

How did Windows choose its final build numbers?

IT VARIES FROM project to project.

Windows NT used a strictly incrementing build number scheme. It was Windows 95 that first introduced the "cute" final build number. But there was a serious reason behind the cuteness.

Windows 95 started with build number one and typically incremented the build number each day. However, when a beta release approached, things got interesting. The source code was forked into two versions: one that continued to develop towards the final version, and one that developed towards the beta release. For illustrative purposes, suppose that the build number at the time of the fork was 123.

```
beta release code base    124 → 125 → 126
                         ↗
primary code base   122 → 123 → 200 → 201 → 202 → 203 → 204 → ⋯
```

After the fork, work proceeds in two source trees simultaneously. Most work continues in the primary code base, but important fixes are applied to the beta fork as well as to the primary fork. During this time, both the beta and primary build numbers increment daily.

Notice that at the point of the fork, the primary code base's build number artificially jumps. This jump ensures that no two builds have the same number, and ensures that any machine that installs the beta release can eventually upgrade to a build from the primary code base (by keeping the primary build number greater than any beta build number). The release management team typically chooses a generous gap to ensure that there is absolutely no chance that the two build numbers will ever collide.

Why such a generous gap? Because there's no benefit to conserving build numbers. They're just numbers.

Okay, but this doesn't explain why the final build number is so cute.

One of the big points of excitement surrounding the Windows 95 launch was that there would be many programs available for sale that were specifically designed for Windows 95. To coordinate this simultaneous release process, software vendors needed a way to detect whether they were running on a beta version of Windows 95 or the final version. Software vendors were told to check the build number, with the assurance that the final version would have a build number greater than or equal to 900. Less than 900 was a beta version.

That's why the final Windows 95 release was build number 950. (More precisely, it was build number 950.6. It took six release candidates before the product was declared to have passed all exit criteria.) The value 950 met the requirement of being greater than or equal to 900, and it lent an air of "cuteness" to the build number.

Windows 98 went through a similar procedure, settling upon the number 1998 for their release build number. Windows Me was released with a build number of 2222.

The first product from the Windows NT series to use a cute final build number was Windows XP, which chose the value 2600, a nod to a well-known hacker magazine.

🖎

Why doesn't the build number increment for service packs?

BECAUSE THERE'S A lot of software that uses strict equality checks for build numbers. Rather than risk having all these programs fail with "Unsupported operating system" when the user installs a service pack, it's safer just to hold the operating system build number constant and update the service pack version number instead.

"Why not use an application compatibility shim for those programs?"

Because the problem is so widespread that it would be unlikely that all such affected programs would be found in the limited testing cycle of a service pack. And even if they were, by some miracle, all found (highly unlikely because many of them are probably not commercial programs but rather internal programs used as a company's line of business applications), the application compatibility database would be crammed to overflowing with entries for all of these programs. This would in turn slow down overall application startup because there would be many more entries to search through to determine whether a program requires a compatibility shim.

⁓

CHAPTER THREE

THE SECRET LIFE OF GetWindowText

T HE GetWindowText function is more complicated than you think. The documentation tries to explain its complexity with small words, which is great if you don't understand long words, but it also means that the full story becomes obscured.

Here's an attempt to give the full story.

How windows manage their text

THERE ARE TWO ways window classes can manage their text. They can do it manually or they can let the system do it. The default is to let the system do it.

If a window class lets the system manage its text, the system will do the following:

- Default handling of the WM_NCCREATE message takes the lpWindowName parameter passed to CreateWindow/Ex and saves the string in a "special place."

- Default handling of the WM_GETTEXT message retrieves the string from that special place.

- Default handling of the WM_SETTEXT message copies the string to that special place.

On the other hand, if a window class manages its window text manually, the system does not do any special handling, and it is the window class's responsibility to respond to the WM_GETTEXT/WM_SETTEXT messages and return/save the strings explicitly.

Frame windows typically let the system manage their window text. Custom controls typically manage their window text manually.

Enter GetWindowText

THE GETWINDOWTEXT function has a problem: Window text needs to be readily available without hanging. FindWindow needs to get window text to find a window. Task-switching applications need to get window text so that they can display the window title in the switcher window. It should not be possible for a hung application to clog up other applications. This is particularly true of the task-switcher scenario.

This argues *against* sending WM_GETTEXT messages, because the target window of the WM_GETTEXT might be hung. Instead, GetWindowText should use the "special place" because that cannot be affected by hung applications.

On the other hand, GetWindowText is used to retrieve text from controls on a dialog, and those controls frequently employ custom text management. This argues *for* sending WM_GETTEXT messages, because that is the only way to retrieve custom-managed text.

GetWindowText strikes a compromise:

- If you are trying to get the window text from a window in your own process, GetWindowText will send the WM_GETTEXT message.
- If you are trying to get the window from a window in another process, GetWindowText will use the string from the special place and not send a message.

According to the first rule, if you are trying to get text from a window in your own process, and the window is hung, `GetWindowText` will also hang. But because the window belongs to your process, it's your own fault, and you deserve to lose. Sending the `WM_GETTEXT` message ensures that text from windows that do custom text management (typically, custom controls) are properly retrieved.

According to the second rule, if you are trying to get text from a window in another process, `GetWindowText` will not send a message; it just retrieves the string from the special place. Because the most common reason for getting text from a window in another process is to get the title of the frame, and because frame windows typically do not do custom window text manipulation, this usually gets the right string.

The documentation simplifies this as "`GetWindowText` cannot retrieve text from a window from another application."

What if I don't like these rules?

IF THE SECOND rule bothers you because you need to get text from a custom control in another process, you can send the `WM_GETTEXT` message manually. Because you are not using `GetWindowText`, you are not subject to its rules.

Note, however, that if the target window is hung, your application will also hang because `SendMessage` will not return until the target window responds.

Note also that because `WM_GETTEXT` is in the system message range (0 to `WM_USER-1`), you do not need to take any special action to get your buffer transferred into the target process and to get the result transferred back to the calling process (a procedure known as *marshalling*). In fact, any special steps you take to this end are in error. The window manager does the marshalling for you.

⤳

Can you give an example
where this makes a difference?

CONSIDER THIS CONTROL:

```
SampleWndProc(...)
{
    case WM_GETTEXT:
        lstrcpyn((LPTSTR)lParam, TEXT("Booga!"), (int)wParam);
        return lstrlen((LPTSTR)lParam);
    case WM_GETTEXTLENGTH: return 7; // lstrlen("Booga!") + null
    ...
}
```

And application A, which does this:

```
hwnd = CreateWindow("Sample", "Frappy", ...);
```

Now consider process B, which gets the handle to the window created by application A (by whatever means):

```
TCHAR szBuf[80];
GetWindowText(hwnd, szBuf, 80);
```

This will return szBuf = "Frappy" because it is getting the window text from the special place. However

```
SendMessage(hwnd, WM_GETTEXT, 80, (LPARAM)szBuf);
```

will return szBuf = "Booga!"

⤳

Why are the rules
for GetWindowText so weird?

SET THE WAYBACK machine to 1983. Your typical PC had an 8086 processor running at a whopping 4.7MHz, two 360K 5¼-inch floppy drives (or if you were really loaded, one floppy drive and a 10MB hard drive), and 256KB of memory

This was the world of Windows 1.0.

Windows 1.0 was a cooperatively multitasked system. No preemptive multitasking here. When your program got control, it had control for as long as it wanted it. Only when you called a function such as `PeekMessage` or `GetMessage` did you release control to other applications.

This was important because in the absence of a hardware memory manager, you really had to make sure that your memory didn't get ripped out from under you.

One important consequence of cooperative multitasking is that if your program is running, not only do you know that no other program is running, but you also know that *every window is responding to messages*. Why? Because if they are hung, they won't release control to you!

This means that it was *always* safe to send a message. You never had to worry about the possibility of sending a message to a hung window, because you knew that no windows were hung.

In this simpler world, `GetWindowText` was a straightforward function:

```
int WINAPI
GetWindowText(HWND hwnd, LPSTR pchBuf, int cch)
{
    // ah for the simpler days
    return SendMessage(hwnd, WM_GETTEXT, (WPARAM)cch, (LPARAM)pchBuf);
}
```

This worked for all windows, all the time. No special handling of windows in a different process.

It was the transition to Win32 and preemptive multitasking that forced the change in the rules, because for the first time, there was the possibility that (gasp) the window you were trying to communicate with was not responding to messages.

Now you have the backward-compatibility problem. As noted previously, many parts of the system and many programs rely on the capability to retrieve window text without hanging. So how do you make it possible to retrieve window text without hanging, while still enabling controls such as the edit control to do their own window text management?

The Win32 rules on `GetWindowText` are the result of this attempt to reconcile conflicting goals.

⁐

CHAPTER FOUR

The Taskbar and Notification Area

I F THE MOST noticeable element of the Windows 95 user interface is the Start menu, the second most noticeable element of the Windows 95 user interface is probably the taskbar. To achieve its simple and intuitive design took quite a bit of work and experimentation. After a brief discussion of taskbar nomenclature, we look at some of the decisions and rationales behind the taskbar design.

Why do some people call the taskbar the "tray"?

SHORT ANSWER: because they're wrong.

Okay, here's the long answer.

The official name for the thingy at the bottom of the screen is the *taskbar*. The taskbar contains a variety of elements, such as the Start button, a collection of taskbar buttons, the clock, and the taskbar notification area.

One of the most common errors is to refer to the taskbar notification area as the tray or the system tray. This has never been correct. If you find any documentation that refers to it as the tray, you've found a bug.

In early builds of Windows 95, the taskbar originally wasn't a taskbar; it was a folder window docked at the bottom of the screen that you could drag/drop things into/out of, sort of like the organizer tray in the top drawer of your desk. That's where the name tray came from. (Some might argue that this was taking the desktop metaphor a bit too far.)

Take a look at this artist's conception (that is, Raymond sat down with Paint and tried to reconstruct it from memory) of what the tray looked like at that time:

The tray could be docked to any edge of the screen or it could be undocked and treated like any other window.

Then we ditched the tray and replaced it with the taskbar. We went through a doc scrub to change all occurrences of *tray* to *taskbar*. If you go through the shell documentation, you should not find the word *tray* anywhere.

A little while later, we added notification icons to the taskbar.

I think the reason people started calling it the system tray is that Windows 95 contained a program called systray.exe that displayed some icons in the notification area: volume control, PCMCIA (as it was then called) status, battery meter. If you killed systray.exe, you lost those notification icons. So people thought, "Ah, systray must be the component that manages those icons, and I bet its name is 'system tray.'" Thus began the misconception that we have been trying to eradicate for more than ten years!

Even worse, other groups (not the shell) picked up on this misnomer and started referring to the tray in their own documentation and samples, some of which even erroneously claim that system tray is the official name of the notification area.

"But why do you care? That's what everybody calls it now, may as well go with the flow."

How would you like it if everybody started calling you by the wrong name?

Summary: It is never correct to refer to the notification area as the tray. It has always been called the notification area, and the icons that appear in the notification icon are called notification icons.

Now, you might argue, "Well, come on, everybody knows what I mean what I say 'system tray.'" That might be true for your social circle, but if you talk about the system tray to a member of the shell team, you'll probably get a confused look. That's because the taskbar internally retains the name *tray* as a remnant from the days when it was, well, a tray.

⬄

Why does the taskbar default to the bottom of the screen?

IT DIDN'T ALWAYS.

The original taskbar didn't look at all like what you see today. It defaulted to the top of the screen and looked something like this:

This is definitely not what it actually looked like. It has been so long I forgot precisely what it looked like (I didn't realize there was going to be a quiz ten years later), but this captures the basic flavor, at least for the purpose of this discussion.

The point is that the bar took the form not of buttons, but of tabs. Each tab corresponded to a running window, which melded into the tab. You switched windows by clicking the corresponding tab.

You can see vestiges of this style in the TCS_BUTTONS style in the tab control. When we switched to the button look for the taskbar, we still had a lot of switching code based on the tabs metaphor, and it was less work to add a button look to the tab control than it was to rewrite all the switching code.

The tabbed look was abandoned for various reasons, one of which was what many people have noticed on their own: If you put the taskbar at the top of the screen, lots of windows end up sliding under it, because they assume that the usable area of the screen begins at (0, 0). Other windows "creep" up the screen because they use `GetWindowPlacement` to save their window position (which returns workspace coordinates, where (0, 0) is the first usable pixel) but use `SetWindowPos` to restore it (which uses screen coordinates, where (0, 0) is the upper-left pixel of the primary monitor).

Too many apps kept sliding under the top-docked taskbar, so we had to abandon that idea and move it to the bottom.

It's somewhat disheartening to observe that now, ten years later, apps still mess up their coordinate systems and keep sliding under a top-docked or left-docked taskbar.

Why doesn't the clock in the taskbar display seconds?

EARLY BETA VERSIONS of the taskbar clock did display seconds, and it even blinked the colon like some clocks do. But we had to remove it.

Why?

Because that blinking colon and the constantly updating time were killing our benchmark numbers.

On machines with only 4MB of memory (which was the minimum memory requirement for Windows 95), saving even 4KB of memory had a perceptible impact on benchmarks. By blinking the clock every second, this prevented not only the code paths related to text rendering from ever being paged out, it also prevented the taskbar's window procedure from being paged out, plus the memory for stacks and data, plus all the context structures related to the Explorer process. Add up all the memory that was being forced to remain continuously present, and you had significantly more than 4KB.

So out it went, and our benchmark numbers improved. The fastest code is code that doesn't run.

Why doesn't the taskbar show an analog clock?

BELIEVE IT OR not, we actually did studies on the possibility of having an analog clock. Problem is, some disturbingly large percentage of people can't read an analog clock. (Is it 30%? 60%? I forget, but it is a lot.) And besides, it's hard to draw a readable analog clock in a 16×16-pixel space.

But the main reason for not having an analog clock is that it would have been yet more code to be written, tested, and documented. You have to draw the line somewhere or you'll be constantly adding features and never ship. Windows 95 was originally Windows 93, after all.

When I dock my taskbar vertically, why does the word "Start" disappear?

BECAUSE THE ALTERNATIVE is even worse.

If the taskbar is not wide enough to display the entire word *Start*, then the word *Start* is hidden. To get it back, resize the taskbar wider until the word *Start* reappears.

This behavior is intentional. From a design point of view, a partial word looks very broken.

Also, there is an apocryphal story of clipping text causing embarrassment during localization. The word *Start*, after being translated into some language, and then being clipped, turned into a rude word. (As an analogy, suppose the text on the Start button said "Start button," but it got clipped to "Start butt." Now you have to explain to people why they have to click on the Start butt.)

Why don't notification icons get a message when the user clicks the "X" button?

IF SUCH A notification were generated, ill-behaved programs would just react to a click on the balloon's X button with an annoying follow-up dialog like, "Are you sure you want to ignore my wonderful message?" So there was a conscious decision not to give them the chance.

In the Before Time, software was trusted not to be actively evil, not to second-guess a user's action, not to invade a user's private space.

Over the years, we've learned that this was a naive position to take. So now, when we decide that something is an end-user setting, we actively avoid giving programmatic access to it, so that programs won't be tempted to weasel themselves into it.

CHAPTER FIVE

PUZZLING INTERFACE ISSUES

HERE ARE SOME short answers to simple questions about the Windows user interface. Behind many of the simple questions lie lessons for software designers, because the situations that lead to these questions are often triggered by programming errors or by a suboptimal program design.

What are those little overlay icons?

WINDOWS XP SHIPS with a number of icon overlays:

- **A small arrow.** Everybody knows this one: It's the shortcut overlay.
- **A hand, palm up.** This is the "sharing" overlay. A folder with this overlay is the root of a file share.
- **A downward-pointing blue arrow.** This is the "to be written to CD" overlay.
- **A pair of blue swirling arrows.** This sometimes baffles people. This means that the item is available offline. (You have to enable offline folders to get this.)

- **A black clock.** This really baffles people. This means that the file
  has been archived to tape and will take a long time to access.

The black clock is particularly baffling because you sometimes see it even if your system is not equipped with Hierarchical Storage Management. When this happens, it's because some program (typically a setup program) didn't check error codes properly.

```
void CopyFileAttributes(LPCTSTR pszSrc, LPCTSTR pszDst)
{
    SetFileAttributes(pszDst, GetFileAttributes(pszSrc));
}
```

The preceding code fragment fails to check for an error code from GetFileAttributes. It so happens that GetFileAttributes fails by returning the value 0xFFFFFFFF. If you fail to check this error code, you end up setting every possible attribute on the destination, including FILE_ATTRIBUTE_OFFLINE, which is the attribute that indicates that a file has been archived to tape.

⟩

Why are these unwanted files/folders opening when I log on?

I GET CALLED on frequently to do troubleshooting, so I figure I'd share some entries from my private bag of tricks. (And there are some remarks for programmers hidden here, too.)

First problem: A folder like C:\Program Files\LitWare opens each time you log on.

Reason: Your system contains two sibling directories where one is a strict prefix of the second (for example, C:\Program Files\LitWare and C:\Program Files\LitWare Deluxe). If you run the Registry Editor, you will likely find under the Registry key

HKEY_LOCAL_MACHINE\Software\Microsoft\Windows\CurrentVersion\Run or

```
HKEY_CURRENT_USER\Software\Microsoft\Windows\CurrentVersion\Run
```

an entry that refers to a program in the longer directory, such as the following:

```
C:\Program Files\LitWare Deluxe\reminder.exe /silent
```

What's more, the reference such as the preceding one will not have quotation marks to protect the embedded spaces in the name.

What's going on is that LitWare Deluxe wants to run `C:\Program Files\ LitWare Deluxe\reminder.exe`, but because of the spaces, this first gets parsed as this:

```
app = C:\Program
command line=Files\LitWare Deluxe\reminder.exe /silent
```

This fails, so the system tries again with the following:

```
app = C:\Program Files\LitWare
command line=Deluxe\reminder.exe /silent
```

And this succeeds because you have a folder called `C:\Program Files\ LitWare`. Result: The `C:\Program Files\LitWare` folder opens.

To fix this, edit the string and add the quotation marks, resulting in this:

```
"C:\Program Files\LitWare Deluxe\reminder.exe" /silent
```

Note to programmers: This is why it's important to quote your filenames if they contain spaces.

Second problem: A `desktop.ini` file opens when you log on.

Reason: The System and Hidden attributes for the file `desktop.ini` in the directory

```
C:\Documents and Settings\All Users\Start Menu\Startup
```

or

```
C:\Documents and Settings\yourname\Start Menu\Startup
```

have been lost. Alternatively, you went to the advanced Folder Options and disabled the Hide protected operating system files (Recommended) option.

If a file is marked with both the System and Hidden attributes, Explorer will not enumerate it, thereby hiding it from the user. If you disable Hide protected operating system files, this rule is suppressed.

When you log on, one of the things that Explorer does is enumerate the contents of your Startup folders and run each file it finds. If the `desktop.ini` is not marked with both the System and Hidden attributes (or you disabled the rule that filters them out), it will be opened.

What is this file for?

This file is used to support the Windows XP Multilingual User Interface, which enables you to change the language you use to interact with Windows; for example, you could say, "I want everything to be in French," and Windows will translate all its menus, shortcuts, dialog boxes, and so on into French. Specifically, this file instructs Windows how to translate the word *Startup* into French, German, Spanish, and so forth.

Programmatically, you use the `SHSetLocalizedName` function to set the multilingual name for a file or folder.

To fix this, restore the Hidden and System attributes to the `desktop.ini` file and reenable Hide protected operating system files.

🐦

What do the text label colors mean for files?

BLUE MEANS COMPRESSED; green means encrypted.

Why the colors blue and green? Nothing profound; they just seemed like good colors to choose. It's unfortunate that blue conflicts with the color of hyperlinks, but the compressed file coloration was done long before Web browsers burst onto the scene.

This is an example of one of those "come on, it's a tiny, simple feature" requests. Yes, the code to do this isn't particularly complicated, but it adds another element of "I'm going to do something in a way that you will never be able to figure out unless somebody tells you."

We get a lot of these little requests. If we accepted them all, you'd have icons with so many decorations you'd never be able to figure out what all the colors and markers mean. And each of those decorations would have to have a specification and a test plan. Automated testing would have to be developed and run to make sure the feature didn't break. It would create another burden for the product-support teams. Its presence constrains future innovation because of backward-compatibility concerns. (Nobody likes it when a favorite feature is dropped from the next version of the operating system.)

So the next time you say to yourself, "Windows should change the appearance of *X* if simple condition *Y*," imagine what it would be like if we actually did even 20 of those simple things.

As another example, a gray item on the Start menu indicates a program that is available to run but has not yet been installed (or is only partially installed). Install-on-use is a feature of Windows Installer (MSI), which uses the term *advertised* to describe a program in this *available-but-not-installed* state. And I suspect you would never have figured this out on your own.

⮑

Why does my advanced options dialog say ON and OFF after every option?

Because Windows thinks a screen reader is running.

If a screen reader is running, the Advanced Options dialog will add ON and OFF to the end of each check box item so that the screen reader program can read the state to a blind user. This mechanism for expressing the state of the option is a throwback to the early days of ActiveAccessibility, where the capability to annotate tree view items had not yet been developed. The workaround for this missing functionality was to put the state of the option directly in its text.

What determines the order in which icons appear in the Alt+Tab list?

THE ICONS APPEAR in the same order as the windows appear on the screen, front to back (known programmatically as the *Z-order*). When you switch to a window, it comes to the top of the Z-order. If you minimize a window, it goes to the bottom of the Z-order. The Alt+Esc hotkey (gosh, does anybody still use Alt+Esc?) takes the current top window and sends it to the bottom of the Z-order (and the window next in line comes to the top). The Alt+Shift+Esc hotkey (I bet you didn't know that hotkey even existed) takes the bottom-most window and brings it to the top, but does not open the window if it is minimized.

The presence of an always-on-top window makes this a little more complicated. The basic rule is that an always-on-top window always appears on top of a not-always-on-top window. So if the preceding rules indicate that a not-always-on-top window comes to the top, it really just goes as high as it can without getting on top of any always-on-top windows.

You may have run across the term *fast task switching*. This was the term used to describe the precursor to the current Alt+Tab switching interface. The old way of switching via Alt+Tab (Windows 3.0 and earlier) was just like Alt+Esc, except that the window you switched to was automatically opened if it had been minimized. When the new Alt+Tab was added to Windows 3.1, we were concerned that people might prefer the old way, so there was a switch in the control panel to set it back to the slow way. (There was also a setting SPI_SETFASTTASKSWITCH that let you change it programmatically.) It turns out nobody complained, so the old slow way of task switching was removed entirely, and the setting now has no effect.

This does highlight the effort we take to try to allow people who don't like the new way of doing something to go back to the old way. It turns out that corporations with 10,000 employees don't like it when the user interface changes, because it forces them to spend millions of dollars retraining all their employees. If you open up the Group Policy Editor, you can see the zillions of deployment settings that IT administrators can use to disable a variety of new Windows user interface features.

〰

Why is the read-only property for folders so strange?

IT'S ACTUALLY A signal to Explorer to look harder. It doesn't mean that the directory is read-only.

If a folder has the Read-only or System flag set, Explorer looks for a desk-top.ini file, which describes the folder customizations. For performance reasons, Explorer does this only if the directory has the +R or +S flag. (This is enormously important on slow networks.)

Two Knowledge Base articles deal with this subject, and I defer to them for the gory details. Article Q326549 applies to Windows XP and Windows Server 2003, and article Q256614 applies to older versions of Windows, although the UseSystemForSystemFolders policy still applies.

Programmers should use the function PathMakeSystemFolder to mark a folder as requiring special attention from Explorer.

〰

What's with those blank taskbar buttons that go away when I click on them?

SOMETIMES YOU'LL FIND a blank taskbar button that goes away when you click on it. What's the deal with that?

Some basic rules apply as to which windows go into the taskbar (as spelled out in more detail in MSDN). In short

- If the WS_EX_APPWINDOW extended style is set, it shows (when visible).

- If the window is a top-level unowned window, it shows (when visible).

- Otherwise, it doesn't show.

(However, the ITaskbarList interface muddies this up a bit.)

When a taskbar-eligible window becomes visible, the taskbar creates a button for it. When a taskbar-eligible window becomes hidden, the taskbar removes the button.

The blank buttons appear when a window changes between taskbar-eligible and taskbar-ineligible *while it is visible*. Follow:

- Window is taskbar-eligible.
- Window becomes visible: Taskbar button created.
- Window goes taskbar-ineligible.
- Window becomes hidden: Because the window is not taskbar-eligible at this point, the taskbar ignores it.

Result: a taskbar button that hangs around with no window attached to it.

This is why the documentation also advises, "If you want to dynamically change a window's style to one that doesn't support visible taskbar buttons, you must hide the window first (by calling the ShowWindow function with SW_HIDE), change the window style, and then show the window."

Bonus question: Why doesn't the taskbar pay attention to *all* windows as they come and go?

Answer: because that would be expensive. The filtering out of windows that aren't taskbar-eligible happens inside the window manager, and it then notifies the taskbar (or anybody else who has installed a WH_SHELL hook) via one of the HSHELL_* notifications only if a taskbar-eligible window has changed state. That way, the taskbar code doesn't get paged in when there's nothing for it to do.

⮌

What is the difference between Minimize All and Show Desktop?

THE KEYBOARD SHORTCUT for "Minimize All" is ⊞+M and the keyboard shortcut for "Show Desktop" is ⊞+D. How are they different?

"Minimize All" is easier to describe. It minimizes all the windows that support the "Minimize" command. You can minimize a window by selecting Minimize from its System menu, or by clicking the ⬓ button in the title bar. Minimize All is effectively the same as going to each window that is open and clicking the Minimize button. If there is a window that doesn't have a Minimize button, it is left alone. To undo the Minimize All command, press ⊞+Shift+M.

Show Desktop takes Minimize All one step further. After minimizing all the windows that can be minimized, it then takes the desktop and "raises" it to the top of the window stack so that no other windows cover it. (Well, okay, topmost windows continue to cover it.) As a result, Show Desktop manages to get a few more windows out of your way than Minimize All.

Note, however, that when you return the desktop to its normal state (either by pressing ⊞+D again, selecting Show Open Windows, or just by switching to another window), all the un-minimizable windows come back because the desktop has "lowered" itself back to the bottom of the window stack.

You may have noticed that occasionally when you undo a Minimize All or Show Desktop, the windows are not stacked in precisely the order they were stacked when you issued the original command. Why is that?

Because the alternative is worse.

Guaranteeing that the window order is restored can result in Explorer hanging.

When the windows are restored when you undo a Show Desktop, Explorer goes through and asks each window that it had minimized to restore itself. If each window is quick to respond, the windows are restored, and the order is preserved.

However, if there is a window that is slow to respond (or even hung), it loses its chance, and Explorer moves on to the next window in the list. That way, a hung window doesn't cause Explorer to hang, too. But it does mean that the windows restore out of order.

What does boldface on a menu mean?

ON MANY CONTEXT menus, you will see an item in boldface. For example, if you right-click a text file, you will most likely see **Open** in boldface at the top of the menu. What does the boldface mean?

The boldface menu item is the default command for that menu. It represents the action that would have occurred if you had double-clicked the item instead of viewing its context menu.

In this example, the fact that **Open** is in boldface means that if you had double-clicked the text file instead of right-clicking it, you would have opened the document.

Programmatically, the default menu item is set via the `SetMenuDefaultItem` function and can be retrieved with the corresponding `GetMenuDefaultItem` function.

If you put a default menu item in a submenu, Windows invokes the default item in the submenu when you double-click the submenu's parent. If you put a default menu item in a top-level pop-up menu (that is, not on a submenu), it is your responsibility to invoke the default menu item when the user double-clicks the object that led to the menu. After all, the menu manager doesn't get involved when you handle a double-click event. It's all up to your program.

Where do those customized Web site icons come from?

MANY PEOPLE HAVE noticed the customized icon that appears in the Internet Explorer address bar … sometimes.

There's actually method to the madness.

Each Web site can put a customized icon called `favicon.ico` into the root of the site, or the page can use a custom LINK tag in the HTML to specify a nondefault location for that icon (handy if the page author does not have write permission into the root directory of the server).

For the `favicon.ico` to show up in the address bar, (1) the site needs to offer a customized icon, (2) you have to have added the site to your favorites, and (3) the site icon must still be in your Internet Explorer cache.

When this feature was introduced, Internet Explorer was careful not to go and hit every site you visit for a `favicon.ico` file; that would have put too much strain on the server. Only when you added the site to your Favorites did Internet Explorer go looking for the `favicon.ico` and stash it in the cache for future use.

Mind you, when the `favicon.ico` feature was first introduced, many Web server administrators blew a gasket, calling it pollution, exceedingly obnoxious, and even declaring the feature enough reason not to use Internet Explorer. And this from Internet Explorer probing for `favicon.ico` files *at all*. Imagine the apoplectic fits people would have had if Internet Explorer had probed for the file at every hit!

Paradoxically, one of them declared, "One can only hope Netscape among others does not repeat this mistake." Indeed, Netscape repeated this "mistake" and took it a step further, downloading the `favicon.ico` file upon first visit, even before you chose to add it to your Favorites.

Who's wasting bandwidth now?

Where did my task manager tabs and buttons go?

AH, WELCOME TO "tiny footprint mode."

This mode exists for the ultra-geeks who want to put a tiny little CPU meter in the corner of the screen. To switch between normal mode and tiny footprint mode, double-click in a blank gray area of the Task Manager window (not counting the menu or status bar).

This is an excellent example of one of those geek features that has created more problems than it solved. Sure, the geeks get their cute little CPU meter in the corner; but for each geek that does this, there are thousands of normal users who accidentally go into tiny mode and can't figure out how to get back.

⤜

Will dragging a file result in a move or a copy?

SOME PEOPLE ARE confused by the seemingly random behavior when you drag a file. Do you get a move or a copy?

And you're right to be confused because it's not obvious until you learn the secret. Mind you, this secret hasn't changed since 1989, but an old secret is still a secret just the same. (Worse: An old secret is a compatibility constraint.)

- If Ctrl+Shift are held down, the operation creates a shortcut.
- If Shift is held down, the operation is a move.
- If Ctrl is held down, the operation is a copy.
- If no modifiers are held down and the source and destination are on the same drive, the operation is a move.
- If no modifiers are held down and the source and destination are on different drives, the operation is a copy.

This is one of the few places where the fact that there are things called *drives* makes itself known to the end user in a significant way.

But why make the distinction between intra-drive and inter-drive moves? Consider various scenarios:

- **Dragging a file from a CD to your hard drive.** This is obviously a copy operation.
- **Dragging a file from your hard drive to a floppy.** This is also obviously a copy operation.
- **Dragging a file from one folder** on your hard drive to another. This time, you are rearranging documents on your machine, so it is obviously a move operation.

Any rules that you come up with need to do the "obvious" thing when faced with these three scenarios, but should nevertheless be simple enough that the results can be explained. (And, of course, the rule needs to make sense in the context of 1989 technology, because that's when the rule was invented.) The "Am I crossing a drive boundary?" test satisfies these criteria.

If you can't keep these rules in your head, you can always drag with the right mouse button. When you drop the files, you will get a context menu asking you what you would like to do. At this point, you can specify explicitly whether you want to move, copy, or create a shortcut.

⪧

Why does the Links folder keep re-creating itself?

THOSE OF YOU who dislike the Links folder have probably tried to delete it, only to discover that it keeps coming back. Why is that?

This is Internet Explorer trying to do some auto-repair. It noticed that the Links folder is missing, so it figures, "Gosh, it must be corrupted! I'd better fix the problem by creating a replacement."

People complain that computers can't perform self-repair, and then when the software tries to perform self-repair, they get mad. "But I wanted it to stay broken." You can't win.

The way to indicate "Yes, I know about the Links folder, but I don't want to use it" is to hide it: View its properties and check the Hidden box.

This is extraordinarily similar to a problem some people have with Device Manager. They don't want Windows to use a particular device, so they delete it. And then it gets redetected and added back.

Because when you delete the device, you're saying, "Forget everything you know about this device." Then when it gets redetected, Windows says, "Gosh, here's a device I've never seen before! The user must have bought it recently. Let me add it to the device tree so that the user can use it."

In other words, Windows behaves the way it does because the alternative is even worse: You buy a device, plug it in, and nothing happens.

If you have a device that you don't want Windows to use, go into the Device Manager and disable it rather than deleting it. This means, "Yes, I know about this device, but I don't want to use it."

Why are documents printed out of order when you multiselect and choose Print?

IF YOU SELECT five files, for example, and then right-click them and choose Print, they tend to print in a random order. Why?

The shell invokes the Print verb on each file in turn, and depending on how the program responsible for printing the document is registered, one of several things can happen:

- Most commonly, the program that prints the document registered a simple command line under the `shell\print\command` Registry key. In this case, the program is launched five times, each with a different file. All these print commands are now racing to the printer, and it's a question of which copy of the program submits its print job first that determines the order in which they come out of the printer. (You're probably going to see the shortest and simplest documents come out first because they take less time to render.) A program could, in principle, detect that another copy is already printing and coordinate the printing of all the documents so that the order is preserved, but in practice, extremely few programs go to this extra effort.

- Occasionally, the program that prints the document registered a DDE verb under the `shell\print\ddeexec` Registry key. In this case, one copy of the program is launched, and it is given each filename one at a time. What it does with those filenames is now up to the program. If the program supports background printing, it will probably shunt the printing of the document onto a background thread, and now you're roughly in the same fix as the previous scenario: five background threads each racing to see who can submit their print job first.

- Extremely rarely, the program that prints the document registered a drop handler under the `shell\print\DropTarget` key. In this case, the drop target is instantiated and is given the list of files. It is then up to the drop target to decide what to do with the documents.

These three ways of registering print actions are described in the MSDN documentation section titled "Verbs and File Associations." The common thread is that in all cases, it is up to the program that prints the document to decide what to do when multiple documents are being printed simultaneously; as a general rule, few programs go to the effort of trying to preserve the original print order.

Raymond spends the day doing product support

I GOT UP at five one morning to spend the day at Product Support Services answering phones: It was the day the Blaster worm launched its second wave. And by a startling coincidence, the person at the station next to me was Michael Howard, our Senior Security Program Manager and author of *Writing Secure Code* (Microsoft Press, 2003). Getting Michael Howard to help you secure your computer is like getting Lance Armstrong to help you change a flat tire on your bicycle.

As enlightening yet humbling experiences go, for a software designer, it's hard to top (1) watching a usability session, and (2) answering product-support calls. You get to observe users—customers, the people your job it is to make more productive—struggle with the software you helped create.

Usability sessions are particularly frustrating because you are hidden behind a one-way mirror, watching somebody struggle to accomplish something you designed to be the most obvious thing on the planet. It's a hard lesson to learn:

Not everybody is a geek like you. (Watching a usability session is a lot like being a member of the studio audience at *The Price Is Right* trying to help the contestant onstage guess the price of a new car.)

Product-support calls let you participate in the other end of the pipeline. The software is written, it's out there, and now you have to pay for all your mistakes and bad designs when people call in with their problems. It's software karma.

Blow the dust out of the connector

OKAY, I'M ABOUT to reveal one of the tricks of product support.

Sometimes you're on the phone with somebody and you suspect that the problem is something as simple as forgetting to plug it in, or that the cable was plugged into the wrong port. This is easy to do with those PS/2 connectors that fit both a keyboard and a mouse plug, or with network cables that can fit both into the upstream and downstream ports on a router.

Here's the trick: Don't ask, "Are you sure it's plugged in correctly?"

If you do this, they will get all insulted and say indignantly, "Of course it is! Do I look like an idiot?" without actually checking.

Instead, say, "Okay, sometimes the connection gets a little dusty and the connection gets weak. Could you unplug the connector, blow into it to get the dust out, and then plug it back in?"

They will then crawl under the desk, find that they forgot to plug it in (or plugged it into the wrong port), blow out the dust, plug it in, and reply, "Um, yeah, that fixed it, thanks."

If the problem was that it was plugged into the wrong port, the act of unplugging it and blowing into the connector *takes their eyes off the port.* Then when they go to plug it in, they will look carefully and get it right the second time because they're paying attention.

Customer saves face, you close a support case, everybody wins.

The face-saving aspect is also important when customers are in a situation where they cannot admit that they made a mistake. For example, their boss or client may be in the room with them. If you offer to shoulder the blame for the problem—perhaps by admitting, "You're right, that dialog box really is confusing, isn't it"—that may make them more willing to work with you toward the solution.

This technique has many variations. For example, instead of asking, "Are you sure it's turned on?" ask them to turn it off and back on. For symmetric cables, you can ask them to reverse the cable: This ensures that *both* ends are plugged in. The underlying trick is to have the user perform some nonthreatening action that tricks them into doing something they would normally resist doing.

⌒

How much is that gigabyte in the window?

In 2003, a lawsuit charging computer manufacturers of misleading consumers over hard drive capacity caused a momentary uproar. The manufacturers use the ISO definition, wherein a gigabyte is one billion bytes, even though most people consider a gigabyte to be 1,024 megabytes.

This is a tricky one. The computer industry is itself inconsistent as to whether the *kilo*, *mega*, and so on prefixes refer to powers of ten or powers of two. The only place powers of two have the upper hand is when describing storage capacity. Everything else is powers of ten: Your 1GHz processor is running at one billion cycles per second, not 1,073,741,824 cycles per second. Your 28.8K modem has a theoretical top speed of 28,800 bits per second, not 29,491. And your 19-inch monitor measures only 17.4 inches diagonally. (Okay, that last one was a joke, but it's another case where the quoted value isn't necessarily measured the way you expect.)

IEC standard designations do exist for power-of-two multipliers. A kibibyte (KiB) is 1,024 bytes, a mebibyte (MiB) is 1,024 KiB, and a gibibyte (GiB) is 1,024 MiB. Good luck finding anybody who actually uses these terms.

At least they don't report sizes in terms of unformatted capacity any more.

Why can't I remove the "For test/ evaluation purposes only" tag?

"Why can't I remove the 'For test/evaluation purposes only' tag? I know I'm running an evaluation edition; I don't need it rubbed in my face."

This prevents unscrupulous manufacturers from selling machines with the evaluation edition of the product rather than the retail version. Yes, this has happened before, many times. For example, one major manufacturer apparently couldn't wait for Windows 95 to be released, so they shipped thousands of machines with a late beta version of Windows 95 instead. This worked out really great. For six months. And then all their computers expired. They had a lot of cleaning up to do.

The "For test purposes only" tag prevents computer manufacturers from selling machines with uncertified drivers. (You learn more about driver-cheating later in the section titled "Defrauding the WHQL driver certification process" in Chapter 9, "Reminiscences on Hardware.") To install an uncertified driver without a warning prompt, you need to install the test root certificate. The presence of the test root certificate causes the "For test purposes only" tag to appear.

We have also had many cases of corporate customers (and technology reporters!) who have had machines expire because they forgot that they were running the evaluation edition. When the machines expire on them, they are stuck with thousands of machines that don't work. This tends to make them rather unhappy.

In summary, the tag is there for your own good. It's there to remind you that what you're running is *not the real thing*.

CHAPTER SIX

A HISTORY OF THE GLOBALALLOC FUNCTION

THE GLOBALALLOC FUNCTION was once the center of Windows memory allocation. Everything came from GlobalAlloc, be it code or data, private application data, or shared clipboard data. In this chapter, we follow the history of this function (as well as its close friend GlobalLock) from its salad days as the king of the heap to its current position of faded glory in Win32. And as you'll see, many of the strange requirements regarding the use of memory allocated on the *global heap* date back to the days when the global heap behaved very differently from how it does today.

The early years

ONCE UPON A time, there was Windows 1.0. This was truly the Before Time. 640K. Segments. Near and far pointers. No virtual memory. Cooperative multitasking.

Because there was no virtual memory, swapping had to be done with the cooperation of the application. When there was an attempt to allocate memory (either for code or data) and insufficient contiguous memory was available, the memory manager had to perform a process called *compaction* to make the desired amount of contiguous memory available.

Code segments could be discarded completely, because they could be reloaded from the original EXE. (No virtual memory—there is no such thing as *paged out*.) Discarding code requires extra work to make sure that the next time the code is called, it is refetched from memory. How this was done is not relevant here, although it was quite a complicated process in and of itself.

Memory containing code could be moved around, and references to the old address were patched up to refer to the new address. This was also a complicated process not relevant here.

Memory containing data could be moved around, but references to the old addresses were not patched up. It was the application's job to protect against its memory moving out from under it if it had a cached pointer to that memory.

Memory that was locked or fixed (or a third category, *wired*, which we'll see in Chapter 14, "Etymology and History") would never be moved.

When you allocated memory via the `GlobalAlloc` function, you first had to decide whether you wanted *movable* memory (memory that could be shuffled around by the memory manager) or *fixed* memory (memory that was immune from motion). Conceptually, a fixed memory block was like a movable block that was permanently locked.

Applications were strongly discouraged from allocating fixed memory because it gummed up the memory manager. Think of it as the memory equivalent of an immovable disk block faced by a defragmenter.

The return value of the `GlobalAlloc` function was a handle to a global memory block, or an `HGLOBAL`. This value was useless by itself. You had to call the `GlobalLock` function to convert this `HGLOBAL` into a pointer that you could use.

The `GlobalLock` function did a few things.

It forced the memory to be present if it had been discarded. Other memory blocks may have needed to be discarded or moved around to make room for the memory block being locked.

If the memory block was movable, it also incremented the *lock count* on the memory block, thus preventing the memory manager from moving the memory block during compaction. (Lock counts on fixed memory aren't necessary because they can't be moved anyway.)

Applications were encouraged to keep global memory blocks locked only as long as necessary to avoid fragmenting the heap. Pointers to unlocked movable memory were forbidden because even the slightest breath—like calling a function that happened to have been discarded—would cause a compaction and invalidate the pointer.

Okay, so how did this all interact with the GlobalReAlloc function?

It depends on how the memory was allocated and what its lock state was.

If the memory was allocated as movable and it wasn't locked, the memory manager was allowed to find a new home for the memory elsewhere in the system and update its bookkeeping so the next time somebody called the GlobalLock function, the caller got a pointer to the new location.

If the memory was allocated as movable but it was locked, or if the memory was allocated as fixed, the memory manager could only resize it in place. It couldn't move the memory either because (if movable and locked) there were still outstanding pointers to it, as evidenced by the nonzero lock count, or (if fixed) the fixed memory was allocated on the assumption that it would never move.

If the memory was allocated as movable and was locked, or if it was allocated as fixed, you can pass the GMEM_MOVEABLE flag to *override the "may only resize in place" behavior*, in which case the memory manager attempts to move the memory if necessary. Passing the GMEM_MOVEABLE flag means, "No, really, I know that according to the rules, you can't move the memory, but I want you to move it anyway. I promise to take the responsibility of updating all pointers to the old location to point to the new location."

(Raymond actually remembers using Windows 1.0. Fortunately, the therapy sessions have helped tremendously.)

Selectors

WITH THE ADVENT of the 80286, Windows could take advantage of that processor's *protected mode*. There was still no virtual memory, but you did have memory protection. Global handles turned into *descriptors*, more commonly known as *selectors*.

Architectural note: The 80286 did have support for both a local descriptor table and a global descriptor table, thereby making it possible to have each process run in something vaguely approximating a separate address space, but doing so would have broken compatibility with real-mode Windows, where all memory was global.

Addresses on the 80286 in protected mode consisted of a selector and an offset rather than a segment and an offset. This change might seem trivial, but it actually is important because a selector acts like a handle table *in hardware*.

When you created a selector, you specified a whole bunch of attributes, such as whether it was a code selector or a data selector, whether it was present or discarded, and where in memory it resided. (Still no virtual memory, so all memory is physical.)

The GlobalAlloc function now returned a selector. If you wanted to, you could just use it directly as the selector part of an address. When you loaded a selector, the CPU checked whether the selector was present, discarded, or invalid.

If present, everything was fine.

If discarded, a "not present" exception was raised. (Wow, we have exceptions now!) The memory manager trapped this exception and did whatever was necessary to make the selector present. This meant allocating the memory (possibly compacting and discarding to make room for it), and if it was a code selector, loading the code back off the disk and fixing it up.

If the selector was invalid, an Unrecoverable Application Error was raised, the infamous UAE.

Because memory accesses were now automatically routed through the descriptor table by the hardware, it meant that memory could be moved around with relative impunity. All existing pointers would remain valid because the selector remains the same; all that changes is the internal book-keeping in the descriptor table that specified which section of memory the descriptor referred to.

What's more, because global handles were really selectors, reallocating memory could be done without changing the numeric value of the selector.

All the memory manager had to do was copy the memory to its new location and update the descriptor table. As a result, the `GlobalReAlloc` function had only two return values: If the memory could not be reallocated, it returned NULL. If the memory was reallocated successfully, it returned the original handle back. (There was an exception to this rule for memory blocks larger than 64KB, but let's not go there.) In other words, the following code fragment actually worked:

```
HGLOBAL hglob = GlobalAlloc(GMEM_MOVEABLE, 100);
if (hglob) {
  void *p = MAKELP(hglob, 0);  // p points to the data!
  if (GlobalReAlloc(hglob, 200, GMEM_MOVEABLE)) {
   // p still points to the data, even if it moved!
   // hglob is still the correct handle to the data
  }
  GlobalFree(hglob);
}
```

For compatibility with real-mode Windows, the `GlobalAlloc` function continued to emulate all the rules on movable memory as before. It's just that the numeric value of the selector never really changed any more.

Transitioning to Win32

Now THAT YOU know how the 16-bit memory manager handled the global heap, it's time to see how this got transitioned to the new 32-bit world.

The `GlobalAlloc` function continued to emulate all its previous rules on movable memory, but the return value of `GlobalAlloc` was no longer a selector because Win32 used the processor in *flat mode*.

This means that the trick described earlier of not having to update any pointers after a `GlobalReAlloc` no longer worked.

The rules on movable memory were preserved. Memory blocks still had a lock count, even though it didn't really accomplish anything because Win32 never compacted memory. (Recall that the purpose of the lock count was to prevent memory from moving during a compaction.)

Movable memory and locking could have been eliminated completely if it weren't for the `GlobalFlags` function. This function returns several strange bits of information—now entirely irrelevant—the most troubling of which is the lock count. Consequently, the charade of locking must be maintained just in case there's some application that actually snoops at the lock count, or a program that expected the `GlobalReAlloc` function to fail on a locked block.

Aside from that, movable memory gets you nothing aside from overhead.

The `LocalAlloc` function also carries the movability overhead; but because local memory was never passed between DLLs in Win16, the local heap functions don't carry as much 16-bit compatibility overhead as the global heap functions. `LocalAlloc` is preferred over `GlobalAlloc` in Win32 for that reason. (Of course, many functions require a specific type of memory allocation, in which case you don't have any choice. The clipboard, for example, requires movable global handles. You'll learn more about the peculiar memory requirements of the clipboard when we discuss the `GMEM_SHARE` flag.)

≈

A peek at the implementation

ON ONE OF our internal discussion mailing lists, someone posted the following question:

> We have some code that was using `DragQueryFile` to extract file paths. The prototype for `DragQueryFile` appears as follows:

```
UINT DragQueryFile(HDROP hDrop, UINT iFile,
                   LPTSTR lpszFile, UINT cch);
```

> In the code we have, instead of passing an `HDROP` as the first parameter, we were passing in a pointer to a `DROPFILES` structure. This code was working fine for the last few months until some protocol changes we made in packet layouts over the weekend.
>
> I know that the bug is that we should be passing an `HDROP` handle instead of a pointer, but I am just curious as to why this worked so flawlessly until now. In other words, what determines the validity of a handle and how come a pointer can sometimes be used instead of a handle?

The `GlobalLock` function accepts `HGLOBAL`s that refer to either `GMEM_MOVEABLE` or `GMEM_FIXED` memory. The rule for Win32 is that for fixed memory, the `HGLOBAL` is itself a pointer to the memory, whereas for movable memory, the `HGLOBAL` is a handle that needs to be converted to a pointer.

The `GlobalAlloc` function works closely with the `GlobalLock` function so that the `GlobalLock` function can be fast. If the memory happens to be aligned just right and to pass some other tests, the `GlobalLock` function says, "Woo-hoo, this is a handle to a `GMEM_FIXED` block of memory, so I should just return the pointer back."

The packet layout changes probably altered the alignment, which in turn caused the `GlobalLock` function no longer to recognize (mistakenly) the invalid parameter as a `GMEM_FIXED` handle. It then went down other parts of the validation path and realized that the handle wasn't valid at all.

This is not, of course, granting permission to pass bogus pointers to the `GlobalLock` function; I'm just explaining why the problem kicked up all of a sudden even though it has always been there.

With that lead-in, what's the real story behind `GMEM_MOVEABLE` in Win32?

`GMEM_MOVEABLE` memory allocates a *handle*. This handle can be converted to memory via the `GlobalLock` function. You can call the `GlobalReAlloc` function on an unlocked `GMEM_MOVEABLE` block (or a locked `GMEM_MOVEABLE` block when you pass the `GMEM_MOVEABLE` flag to the `GlobalReAlloc` function, which means "move it even if it's locked") and the memory *will move*, but the handle will continue to refer to it. You have to relock the handle to get the new address it got moved to.

The `GMEM_MOVEABLE` flag is largely unnecessary; it provides additional functionality that most people have no use for. Most people don't mind when `GlobalRealloc` hands back a value that differs from the original. The `GMEM_MOVEABLE` flag is primarily for the case where you hand out a memory handle, and then you decide to reallocate it behind the handle's back. If you use `GMEM_MOVEABLE`, the handle remains valid even though the memory it refers to has moved.

This might sound like a neat feature, but in practice it's much more trouble than it's worth. If you decide to use movable memory, you have to lock it before accessing it, and unlock it when done. All this lock/unlock overhead becomes a real pain because you can't use pointers any more. You have to use handles and convert them to pointers right before you use them. (This also means no pointers into the middle of a movable object.)

Consequently, movable memory is useless in practice.

Note, however, that GMEM_MOVEABLE still lingers on in various places for compatibility reasons. For example, clipboard data must be allocated as movable. If you break this rule, some programs will crash because they made undocumented assumptions about how the heap manager internally manages handles to movable memory blocks instead of calling the GlobalLock function to convert the handle to a pointer.

A common error is forgetting to lock global handles before using them. If you forget and instead just cast a movable memory handle to a pointer, you will get strange results (and will likely corrupt the heap). Specifically, global handles passed via the hGlobal member of the STGMEDIUM structure, returned via the GetClipboardData function, as well as lesser-known places such as the hDevMode and hDevNames members of the PRINTDLG structure are all potentially movable. What's scary is that if you make this mistake, you might actually get away with it for a long time (if the memory you're looking at happens to be allocated as GMEM_FIXED), and then one day it crashes because all of a sudden somebody gave you memory that was allocated as GMEM_MOVEABLE.

Yes, I've seen this happen. It's not pretty.

⌇

CHAPTER SEVEN

SHORT TOPICS IN WINDOWS PROGRAMMING

I'M SORRY TO do this, but I'm going to have to introduce some code. I'll try to make it only as long as necessary, however. Nonprogrammers may want to skip this chapter and the next. I'll see you when we talk about hardware.

All of these topics were inspired by actual programming problems people were having. Some of the problems were solved with clever tricks; others were solved by clearing up a misconception.

Do not be distracted by the code, however. The code exists only to illustrate the principles being presented. To that end, the code presentation is unusually compact so as not to distract from the text. I don't want this to become one of those books with page after page of tiresome program listings. I know you don't read those listings; I don't either.

The scratch program

OCCASIONALLY, THERE IS need to illustrate a point with a full program. To avoid reproducing the boring parts of the program, let's agree on using the following template for our sample programs. This is a program skeleton I have kept around for years for when I need a quick-and-dirty program to test out an idea; it's called a *scratch* program because it is typically used one time and then thrown away. This program contains only one item of interest, but it's buried amid the boilerplate. (If you're in a hurry, skip ahead to the WM_PRINTCLIENT message handler.)

For expository purposes, I won't use a C++ class. I'll just keep all my variables global. In a real program, of course, the data would be attached to the window instead of being global variables. However, the additional work necessary to keep track of this so-called *instance data* would be distracting from the point of the program, so I will take the perhaps ill-advised approach of merely using global variables.

We will be using a handful of header files rather often, so I'll just make them part of the template:

```
#define STRICT
#include <windows.h>
#include <windowsx.h>
#include <ole2.h>
#include <commctrl.h>
#include <shlwapi.h>
```

The windowsx.h header file is a collection of handy macros that give more meaningful names to many Windows programming idioms. It was introduced in Windows 3.1 to facilitate the transition to 32-bit Windows. If your 16-bit program used these macros (especially the so-called message cracker macros), it was much easier to port to 32-bit Windows because the macros hid the details of message passing, particularly those details that changed between 16-bit and 32-bit Windows. Of course, the capability to compile your source code as a 16-bit Windows program is not very compelling nowadays, but the macros are nevertheless quite handy, and I use them liberally.

A few of our sample programs are really just wrappers around another control such as a list view control. The g_hwndChild variable holds the handle to that inner control, if any. Keeping it in a variable saves us the trouble of having to hunt for it each time we want to do something with our child window. Sometimes my test program has multiple child windows, in which case having all the child window handles available in variables is a significant convenience:

```
HINSTANCE g_hinst;              /* This application's HINSTANCE */
HWND g_hwndChild;               /* Optional child window */
```

If we are wrapping another control, we position it to fill our client area when we are resized:

```
void
OnSize(HWND hwnd, UINT state, int cx, int cy)
{
    if (g_hwndChild) {
        MoveWindow(g_hwndChild, 0, 0, cx, cy, TRUE);
    }
}
```

This skeleton of an OnCreate function is fleshed out with actual work when we get around to making this template program do something interesting:

```
BOOL
OnCreate(HWND hwnd, LPCREATESTRUCT lpcs)
{
    return TRUE;
}
```

Because this is our main window, closing it ends the program. Post a quit message to tell the message pump to exit:

```
void
OnDestroy(HWND hwnd)
{
    PostQuitMessage(0);
}
```

Here is another skeleton function that will be filled in as necessary. To make it agree with what most programmers expect to see in a paint function, I make the second parameter a PAINTSTRUCT:

```
void
PaintContent(HWND hwnd, PAINTSTRUCT *pps)
{
}
```

All painting gets funneled through the PaintContent function. The obvious first case where we want to paint content is when actually handling a WM_PAINT message:

```
void
OnPaint(HWND hwnd)
{
    PAINTSTRUCT ps;
    BeginPaint(hwnd, &ps);
    PaintContent(hwnd, &ps);
    EndPaint(hwnd, &ps);
}
```

The less-obvious second case where we want to paint content is when handling a WM_PRINTCLIENT message. In this case, we use a fake PAINTSTRUCT structure so that the PaintContent function is blissfully unaware that the rendering is being redirected. (Supporting the WM_PRINTCLIENT message also permits the window to be animated with the AnimateWindow function.) In addition to the obvious steps of setting the DC and paint rectangle, we also set the fErase member to FALSE because the WM_PRINT message handler will already have taken care of erasing the background for us. This last step is not necessary in principle because paint handlers don't erase the background (it was done by the BeginPaint function), but we'll set it for the sake of completeness:

```
void
OnPrintClient(HWND hwnd, HDC hdc)
{
    PAINTSTRUCT ps;
    ps.hdc = hdc;
    GetClientRect(hwnd, &ps.rcPaint);
    ps.fErase = FALSE;
    PaintContent(hwnd, &ps);
}
```

Our window procedure takes advantage of the message-cracker macros in the windowsx.h header file. The WM_PRINTCLIENT message, however, did not exist in Windows 3.1, so there is no corresponding HANDLE_WM_PRINTCLIENT macro we can use. We have to dispatch the WM_PRINTCLIENT message manually:

```
LRESULT CALLBACK
WndProc(HWND hwnd, UINT uiMsg, WPARAM wParam, LPARAM lParam)
{
    switch (uiMsg) {
    HANDLE_MSG(hwnd, WM_CREATE, OnCreate);
    HANDLE_MSG(hwnd, WM_SIZE, OnSize);
    HANDLE_MSG(hwnd, WM_DESTROY, OnDestroy);
    HANDLE_MSG(hwnd, WM_PAINT, OnPaint);
    case WM_PRINTCLIENT: OnPrintClient(hwnd, (HDC)wParam); return 0;
    }

    return DefWindowProc(hwnd, uiMsg, wParam, lParam);
}
```

Initialization consists of registering our window class and initializing the common controls library, just in case we need a common control in a sample program someday. (The history behind the InitCommonControlsEx function is taken up later in the section "If InitCommonControls doesn't do anything, why do you have to call it?")

```
BOOL
InitApp(void)
{
    WNDCLASS wc;

    wc.style = 0;
    wc.lpfnWndProc = WndProc;
    wc.cbClsExtra = 0;
    wc.cbWndExtra = 0;
    wc.hInstance = g_hinst;
    wc.hIcon = NULL;
    wc.hCursor = LoadCursor(NULL, IDC_ARROW);
    wc.hbrBackground = (HBRUSH)(COLOR_WINDOW + 1);
    wc.lpszMenuName = NULL;
    wc.lpszClassName = TEXT("Scratch");

    if (!RegisterClass(&wc)) return FALSE;

    InitCommonControls(); /* In case we use a common control */

    return TRUE;
}
```

The main program initializes the application as well as COM, because some of our sample programs may need to use COM, so we initialize it in the template so that we don't need to worry about it in the future:

```
int WINAPI WinMain(HINSTANCE hinst, HINSTANCE hinstPrev,
                   LPSTR lpCmdLine, int nShowCmd)
{
    MSG msg;
    HWND hwnd;

    g_hinst = hinst;

    if (!InitApp()) return 0;

    if (SUCCEEDED(CoInitialize(NULL))) {/* In case we use COM */

        hwnd = CreateWindow(
          TEXT("Scratch"),                 /* Class Name */
          TEXT("Scratch"),                 /* Title */
          WS_OVERLAPPEDWINDOW,             /* Style */
          CW_USEDEFAULT, CW_USEDEFAULT,    /* Position */
          CW_USEDEFAULT, CW_USEDEFAULT,    /* Size */
          NULL,                            /* Parent */
          NULL,                            /* No menu */
          hinst,                           /* Instance */
          0);                              /* No special parameters */
        ShowWindow(hwnd, nShowCmd);

        while (GetMessage(&msg, NULL, 0, 0)) {
          TranslateMessage(&msg);
          DispatchMessage(&msg);
        }

        CoUninitialize();
    }

    return 0;
}
```

Other than the trickiness with painting, there really isn't anything here that you shouldn't already know. The point of this program is to be a template for the other programs in this chapter.

Getting a custom right-click menu for the caption icon

WHEN YOU RIGHT-CLICK on the miniature icon in the upper-left corner of the caption of an Explorer window on Windows XP, the context menu that appears is not the standard system menu but rather the context menu for the folder itself.

It's a simple matter of detecting a context menu on the caption icon and displaying a custom context menu. Here are the simple changes to our scratch program to display a rather pointless one-item menu:

```
// Add to WndProc
   case WM_CONTEXTMENU:
        if (lParam != -1 &&
            SendMessage(hwnd, WM_NCHITTEST,
                        0, lParam) == HTSYSMENU) {
            HMENU hmenu = CreatePopupMenu();
            if (hmenu) {
                AppendMenu(hmenu, MF_STRING, 1,
                        TEXT("Custom menu"));
                TrackPopupMenu(hmenu, TPM_LEFTALIGN |
                            TPM_TOPALIGN |
                            TPM_RIGHTBUTTON,
                        GET_X_LPARAM(lParam),
                        GET_Y_LPARAM(lParam), 0, hwnd,
                        NULL);
                DestroyMenu(hmenu);
            }
            return 0;
        }
        break;
```

When we receive a WM_CONTEXTMENU message, we check that it did not come from the keyboard (lParam != -1) and that the mouse is on the caption icon (called HTSYSMENU because it displays the system menu by default). If so, we create a little pop-up menu and display it. Don't forget to return 0 instead of passing the message to DefWindowProc, because the default behavior is to display the system menu.

(Of course, in real life, you probably would use the LoadMenu function to get the menu so that you could just use the resource editor to create it, rather than creating it in code. I just created it in code to keep the sample short.)

Beware of the HANDLE_WM_CONTEXTMENU macro from windowsx.h. If you give it a closer look, you'll see that it uses the LOWORD and HIWORD macros to extract the coordinates rather than using the multiple-monitor-friendly GET_X_LPARAM and GET_Y_LPARAM macros we use here.

You might also notice that on a multiple-monitor system, the coordinates (−1, −1) are valid even though they are used here as a sentinel value. It means that if you manage to right-click at the pixels immediately above and to the left of the origin of the primary monitor, the system will mistake it for a keyboard-triggered context menu. This is sad but true, and the reason for this is historical.

The WM_CONTEXTMENU message was introduced in Windows 95, whereas support for multiple monitors didn't appear until Windows 98. As a result, the people who designed the WM_CONTEXTMENU message chose a sentinel value that made sense at the time, unaware that it would cause problems in the future. But what's done is done, and the somewhat-suboptimal sentinel value is retained for compatibility purposes.

⁕

What's the difference between CreateMenu and CreatePopupMenu?

THE CREATEMENU FUNCTION creates a horizontal menu bar, suitable for attaching to a top-level window. This is the sort of menu that says "File, Edit," and so on. The LoadMenu function loads menu bars, too.

The CreatePopupMenu function creates a vertical pop-up menu, suitable for use as a submenu of another menu (either a horizontal menu bar or another pop-up menu) or as the root of a context menu.

If you get the two confused, you can get strange menu behavior. Windows on rare occasions detects that you confused the two and converts as appropriate, but I wouldn't count on Windows successfully reading your mind. (Indeed, I was surprised when I ran across this behavior myself.)

There is no way to take a menu and ask it whether it is horizontal or vertical. You just have to know.

Note that menu resources are always menu bars. But what if you want to load a pop-up menu from a resource? Simple: Put the pop-up menu inside a placeholder horizontal menu bar:

```
1 MENU
BEGIN
    POPUP ""
    BEGIN
        MENUITEM "Custom Menu", 1
        MENUITEM "Another Menu", 2
        MENUITEM "Cancel", 3
    END
END
```

Here is a short function that illustrates how we can display this pop-up menu embedded inside a horizontal menu:

```
// Sample usage: UsePopupMenu(hwnd, g_hinst, MAKEINTRESOURCE(1));
void UsePopupMenu(HWND hwnd, HINSTANCE hinst, LPCTSTR pszMenu)
{
 HMENU hmenu = LoadMenu(hinst, pszMenu);
 if (hmenu) {
  HMENU hmenuPopup = GetSubMenu(hmenu, 0);
  TrackPopupMenu(hmenuPopup,
                 TPM_LEFTALIGN | TPM_TOPALIGN | TPM_RIGHTBUTTON,
                 GET_X_LPARAM(lParam),
                 GET_Y_LPARAM(lParam), 0, hwnd, NULL);
  DestroyMenu(hmenu);
 }
}
```

We load the horizontal menu, extract the submenu via GetSubMenu (which is a pop-up menu), and track the pop-up menu. When the pop-up menu is no longer needed, we destroy the horizontal menu.

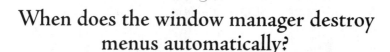

It can be cumbersome keeping track of both the horizontal menu and the pop-up menu. An alternative method is to detach the pop-up menu from the horizontal menu, destroy the horizontal menu, and return the pop-up:

```
HMENU LoadPopupMenu(HINSTANCE hinst, LPCTSTR pszMenu)
{
 HMENU hmenuPopup = NULL;
 HMENU hmenu = LoadMenu(hinst, pszMenu);
 if (hmenu) {
  hmenuPopup = GetSubMenu(hmenu, 0);
  RemoveMenu(hmenu, 0, MF_BYPOSITION);
  DestroyMenu(hmenu);
 }
 return hmenuPopup;
}

// sample usage
void Sample(HWND hwnd)
{
 HMENU hmenuPopup = LoadPopupMenu(g_hinst, MAKEINTRESOURCE(1));
 if (hmenuPopup) {
  TrackPopupMenu(hmenuPopup,
                 TPM_LEFTALIGN | TPM_TOPALIGN | TPM_RIGHTBUTTON,
                 GET_X_LPARAM(lParam),
                 GET_Y_LPARAM(lParam), 0, hwnd, NULL);
  DestroyMenu(hmenuPopup);
 }
```

The LoadPopupMenu thus functions as the pop-up version of LoadMenu.

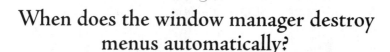

When does the window manager destroy menus automatically?

WHEN A WINDOW is destroyed, its menu is also destroyed. When a menu is destroyed, the entire menu tree is destroyed. (All its submenus are destroyed, all the submenu's submenus, and so forth). And when you destroy a menu, it had better not be the submenu of some other menu. That other menu would have an invalid menu as a submenu!

If you remove a submenu from its parent, you become responsible for destroying it, because it no longer gets destroyed automatically when the parent is destroyed.

It is legal (although highly unusual) for a menu to be a submenu of multiple parent menus. Doing this is not recommended, because if one of the parents is destroyed, it will destroy the submenu with it, leaving the other parent with an invalid submenu.

⌒

Painting only when your window is visible onscreen

SOMETIMES YOU WANT to perform an activity, such as updating a status window, only so long as the window is not covered by another window. After all, what's the point of going to the effort of updating something the user can't see anyway?

The easiest way to determine this is by not actually trying to determine it. For example, here's how the taskbar clock updates itself:

1. It computes how much time will elapse before the next minute ticks over.

2. It calls `SetTimer` with the amount of time it needs to wait.

3. When the timer fires, it does an `InvalidateRect` of itself and kills the timer.

4. The `WM_PAINT` handler draws the current time, then returns to step 1.

If the taskbar clock is not visible, because it got auto-hidden or because somebody covered it, Windows will not deliver a `WM_PAINT` message, so the taskbar clock will simply go idle and consume no CPU time at all. Here's how we can make our scratch program do the same thing.

Our scratch program will display the current time in its client area as well as in the title bar, so we can watch the taskbar to see the painting action (or lack thereof) when the window is covered or minimized. (This is just a scratch program, so let's not obsess over the right way of obtaining the time in string form.)

```
void
PaintContent(HWND hwnd, PAINTSTRUCT *pps)
{
    TCHAR szTime[100];
    if (GetTimeFormat(LOCALE_USER_DEFAULT, 0, NULL, NULL,
                      szTime, 100)) {
        SetWindowText(hwnd, szTime);
        TextOut(pps->hdc, 0, 0, szTime, lstrlen(szTime));
    }
}
```

Here is the timer callback that fires when we decide it's time to update. It merely kills the timer and invalidates the rectangle. The next time the window becomes uncovered, we get a WM_PAINT message. (And if the window is uncovered right now, we get one almost immediately.)

```
void CALLBACK
InvalidateAndKillTimer(HWND hwnd, UINT uMsg,
                       UINT_PTR idTimer, DWORD dwTime)
{
    KillTimer(hwnd, idTimer);
    InvalidateRect(hwnd, NULL, TRUE);
}
```

Finally, we add some code to our WM_PAINT handler to restart the timer each time we paint a nonempty rectangle before continuing with our normal processing with PaintContent:

```
void
OnPaint(HWND hwnd)
{
    PAINTSTRUCT ps;
    BeginPaint(hwnd, &ps);
    if (!IsRectEmpty(&ps.rcPaint)) {
        // compute time to next update - we update once a second
        SYSTEMTIME st;
        GetSystemTime(&st);
        DWORD dwTimeToNextTick = 1000 - st.wMilliseconds;
        SetTimer(hwnd, 1, dwTimeToNextTick,
                 InvalidateAndKillTimer);
    }
    PaintContent(hwnd, &ps);
    EndPaint(hwnd, &ps);
}
```

Run this program on Windows XP, and watch it update the time. When you minimize the window or cover it with another window, the time stops updating. If you take the window and drag it to the bottom of the screen so only the caption is visible, it also stops updating: The WM_PAINT message is used to paint the client area, and the client area is no longer onscreen.

This method also stops updating the clock when you switch to another user or lock the workstation, although you can't really tell because there's no taskbar you can consult to verify. But you can use your speakers: Stick a call to MessageBeep(-1); in the PaintContent() function, so you will get an annoying beep each time the time is repainted. When you switch to another user or lock the workstation, the beeping will stop.

Note the significance of putting this update logic in the OnPaint function rather than PaintContent. In particular, putting the repaint-detection logic in the PaintContent handler would result in WM_PRINTCLIENT messages interfering with our repaint timer. (Although our design is somewhat resilient to this type of mistake: Notice that if the timer is mistakenly restarted, it corrects itself after one tick.) Programs should not perform so-called business logic while painting; paint handlers should worry themselves only with drawing. But what we're doing here is not business logic; it's just some work to optimize how we draw, and doing that from a draw handler is perfectly legitimate.

This technique of invalidation can be extended to cover the case where only one section of the screen is interesting: Instead of invalidating the entire client area, invalidate only the area that you want to update, and restart the timer only if that rectangle is part of the update region. For example, suppose that our window is responsible for displaying multiple pieces of information as well as the current time. If we had used the technique previously described, we would be updating the clock if any part of our window was visible, even if the clock itself was covered. Here are the changes we need to make to run the clock only if the clock portion of the window is visible:

```
// We'll put our clock here
RECT g_rcClock = { 50, 50, 200, 100 };
```

When the timer fires, we invalidate only the clock rectangle rather than the entire client area. (As an optimization, I disabled background erasure for reasons you'll see later.)

```
void CALLBACK
InvalidateAndKillTimer(HWND hwnd, UINT uMsg,
                       UINT_PTR idTimer, DWORD dwTime) {
    KillTimer(hwnd, idTimer);
    InvalidateRect(hwnd, &g_rcClock, FALSE);
}
```

To make it more obvious where the clock rectangle is, we draw it in the highlight color and put the time inside it. By using the ETO_OPAQUE flag, we draw both the foreground and background simultaneously. Consequently, we don't need to have it erased for us:

```
void
PaintContent(HWND hwnd, PAINTSTRUCT *pps)
{
    TCHAR szTime[100];
    if (GetTimeFormat(LOCALE_USER_DEFAULT, 0, NULL, NULL, szTime,
                      100)) {
        SetWindowText(hwnd, szTime);
        COLORREF clrTextPrev = SetTextColor(pps->hdc,
                                  GetSysColor(COLOR_HIGHLIGHTTEXT));
        COLORREF clrBkPrev = SetBkColor(pps->hdc,
                                  GetSysColor(COLOR_HIGHLIGHT));
        ExtTextOut(pps->hdc, g_rcClock.left, g_rcClock.top,
                   ETO_CLIPPED | ETO_OPAQUE, &g_rcClock,
                   szTime, lstrlen(szTime), NULL);
        SetBkColor(pps->hdc, clrBkPrev);
        SetTextColor(pps->hdc, clrTextPrev);
    }
}
```

Finally, the code in the WM_PAINT handler needs to check the clock rectangle for visibility instead of using the entire client area:

```
Void
OnPaint(HWND hwnd)
{
    PAINTSTRUCT ps;
    BeginPaint(hwnd, &ps);
```

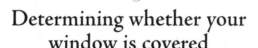

```
    if (RectVisible(ps.hdc, &g_rcClock)) {
        // compute time to next update - we update once a second
        SYSTEMTIME st;
        GetSystemTime(&st);
        DWORD dwTimeToNextTick = 1000 - st.wMilliseconds;
        SetTimer(hwnd, 1, dwTimeToNextTick, InvalidateAndKillTimer);
    }
    PaintContent(hwnd, &ps);
    EndPaint(hwnd, &ps);
}
```

Run this program and do various things to cover up or otherwise prevent the clock rectangle from painting. Observe that when you cover it up, the title stops updating.

This is one of those simple ideas, a small detail that nevertheless makes a big difference in the quality of your program. Notice, for example, that stopping the timer when there is nothing to do eliminates a source of polling, which has a significant impact on overall system performance.

As noted previously, this technique is usually enough for most applications, but there is an even more complicated (and more expensive) method, too, which we take up next.

Determining whether your window is covered

THE METHOD PREVIOUSLY described works great if you are using the window visibility state to control painting, because you're using the paint system itself to do the heavy lifting for you.

To obtain this information outside of the paint loop, you can use GetDC and GetClipBox. The HDC that comes out of GetDC is clipped to the visible region, and then you can use GetClipBox to extract information out of it.

Start with a new scratch program and add these lines:

```
void CALLBACK
PollTimer(HWND hwnd, UINT uMsg, UINT_PTR idTimer, DWORD dwTime)
```

```
{
    HDC hdc = GetDC(hwnd);
    if (hdc) {
        RECT rcClip, rcClient;
        LPCTSTR pszMsg;
        switch (GetClipBox(hdc, &rcClip)) {
        case NULLREGION:
            pszMsg = TEXT("completely covered");
            break;
        case SIMPLEREGION:
            GetClientRect(hwnd, &rcClient);
            if (EqualRect(&rcClient, &rcClip)) {
                pszMsg = TEXT("completely uncovered");
            } else {
                pszMsg = TEXT("partially covered");
            }
            break;
        case COMPLEXREGION:
            pszMsg = TEXT("partially covered");
            break;
        default:
            pszMsg = TEXT("Error");
            break;
        }
        // If we want to, we can also use RectVisible
        // or PtVisible - or go totally overboard by
        // using GetClipRgn
        ReleaseDC(hwnd, hdc);

        SetWindowText(hwnd, pszMsg);
    }
}

BOOL
OnCreate(HWND hwnd, LPCREATESTRUCT lpcs)
{
    SetTimer(hwnd, 1, 1000, PollTimer);
    return TRUE;
}
```

Once per second, the window title will update with the current visibility of the client rectangle. The GetClipBox function returns the bounding box of the DC's clip region as well as an integer describing what type of shape the clip region is, which is what we are primarily interested in. The null and complex region cases are straightforward, but the simple region is a bit tricky because a rectangular clip region could mean either that the window is complete uncovered (allowing the entire client region to show) or that the window is covered by a collection of other windows arranged so that the visible portion of the window just happens to be rectangular in shape. To distinguish these two cases, we need to compare the region's shape against the client rectangle. Fortunately, in the case of a simple clip region, the bounding box equals the region itself, so we can compare the result of GetClientRect against the clip region bounding box.

Note that we avoided using the GetClipRgn function. Most of the time, when you query information about a region's shape, the bounding box and shape type give you what you need. Only if you need to dig into the details of a complex clip region should you call functions such as GetRegionData.

As previously noted, polling is much more expensive than letting the paint system do the work for you, so do try to use the painting method first.

Note that the Windows Vista desktop composition feature changes the rules for painting significantly. If desktop composition is enabled, then all nonminimized windows behave as if they are completely uncovered because windows no longer draw directly to the screen but rather to offscreen buffers, which are then composed for final display. As a result, our sample programs act as if they are fully visible whenever they are restored, regardless of whether they are actually covered by other windows, because the composition engine maintains a copy of the entire window. The window contents are continuously available, for example, when the user views the window with the Flip3D feature or views the window thumbnail in the Alt+Tab window. In that sense, then, your window is always visible.

⟿

Using bitmap brushes for tiling effects

BITMAP BRUSHES USED to be these little 8 × 8 monochrome patterns that you could use for hatching and maybe little houndstooth patterns if you were really crazy. But you can do better.

The CreatePatternBrush function lets you pass in any old bitmap—even a huge one—and it will create a brush from it. The bitmap will automatically be tiled, so this is a quick way to get bitmap tiling. Let GDI do all the math for you! You can see this in some programs that have "watermark" effects such as the one Internet Explorer 3 used on its main toolbar.

This is particularly handy when you're stuck with a mechanism where you are forced to pass an HBRUSH but you really want to pass an HBITMAP (for example, when responding to one of the WM_CTLCOLOR messages). Convert the bitmap to a brush and return that brush instead.

For example, let's take our scratch program and give it a custom tiled background by using a pattern brush:

```
HBRUSH CreatePatternBrushFromFile(LPCTSTR pszFile)
{
    HBRUSH hbr = NULL;
    HBITMAP hbm = (HBITMAP)LoadImage(g_hinst, pszFile,
                    IMAGE_BITMAP, 0, 0, LR_LOADFROMFILE);
    if (hbm) {
        hbr = CreatePatternBrush(hbm);
        DeleteObject(hbm);
    }
    return hbr;
}

BOOL
InitApp(LPSTR lpCmdLine)
{
    BOOL fSuccess = FALSE;
    HBRUSH hbr = CreatePatternBrushFromFile(lpCmdLine);
    if (hbr) {
        WNDCLASS wc;

        wc.style = 0;
        wc.lpfnWndProc = WndProc;
        wc.cbClsExtra = 0;
        wc.cbWndExtra = 0;
        wc.hInstance = g_hinst;
        wc.hIcon = NULL;
        wc.hCursor = LoadCursor(NULL, IDC_ARROW);
        wc.hbrBackground = hbr;
        wc.lpszMenuName = NULL;
        wc.lpszClassName = TEXT("Scratch");
```

```
        fSuccess = RegisterClass(&wc);
        // Do not delete the brush - the class owns it now
    }
    return fSuccess;
}
```

With a corresponding adjustment to `WinMain` so that we know which file to use as the basis for our background brush:

```
if (!InitApp(lpCmdLine)) return 0;
```

Pass the path to a BMP file on the command line, and bingo, the window will tile its background with that bitmap. Notice that we did not have to change anything other than the class registration. No muss, no fuss, no bother.

Filling a shape with an image is another case where you wish you could use a bitmap rather than a brush, and therefore a case where bitmap brushes again save the day. Start with a new scratch program, copy the preceding `CreatePatternBrushFromFile` function, and make the following additional changes to draw a filled ellipse. The details of how the drawing is accomplished aren't important. All we're interested is the way the shape is filled:

```
HBRUSH g_hbr; // the pattern brush we created

void
PaintContent(HWND hwnd, PAINTSTRUCT *pps)
{
    BeginPath(pps->hdc);
    Ellipse(pps->hdc, 0, 0, 200, 100);
    EndPath(pps->hdc);
    HBRUSH hbrOld = SelectBrush(pps->hdc, g_hbr);
    FillPath(pps->hdc);
    SelectBrush(pps->hdc, hbrOld);
}
```

And add the following code to `WinMain` before the call to `CreateWindowEx`:

```
g_hbr = CreatePatternBrushFromFile(lpCmdLine);
if (!g_hbr) return 0;
```

This time, because we are managing the brush ourselves, we need to remember to destroy it, so add this to the end of the `WinMain` function before it returns:

```
DeleteObject(g_hbr);
```

This second program draws an ellipse filled with your bitmap. The FillPath function uses the currently selected brush, so we select our bitmap brush (rather than a boring solid brush) and draw with that. Result: a pattern-filled ellipse. Without a bitmap brush, you would have had to do a lot of work manually clipping the bitmap (and tiling it) to the ellipse.

What is the DC brush good for?

THE DC BRUSH you obtain by calling GetStockObject(DC_BRUSH) is a stock brush associated with the device context. Like the system color brushes you obtain by calling the GetSysColorBrush function, the color of the DC brush changes dynamically; but whereas the system color brushes change color based on the system colors, the color of the DC brush changes at your command.

The DC brush is handy when you need a solid color brush for a short time, because it always exists and doesn't need to be created or destroyed. Normally, you have to create a solid color brush, draw with it, and then destroy it. With the DC brush, you set its color and start drawing. But it works only for a short time, because the moment somebody else calls the SetDCBrushColor function on your DC, the DC brush color is overwritten. In practice, this means that the DC brush color is not trustworthy after you relinquish control to other code. (Note, however, that each DC has its own DC brush color, so you need only worry about somebody on another thread messing with your DC simultaneously, which doesn't happen under any of the painting models I am familiar with.)

The DC brush is quite useful when handling the various WM_CTLCOLOR messages. These messages require you to return a brush that will be used to draw the control background. If you need a solid-color brush, this usually means creating the solid-color brush and caching it for the lifetime of the window, and then destroying it when the window is destroyed. (Some people cache the brush in a static variable, which works great until somebody creates two copies of the dialog/window. Then you get a big mess.)

Let's use the DC brush to customize the colors of a static control. The program is not interesting as a program; it's just an illustration of one way you can use the DC brush.

Start, as always, with our scratch program and make the following changes:

```
BOOL
OnCreate(HWND hwnd, LPCREATESTRUCT lpcs)
{
  g_hwndChild = CreateWindow(TEXT("static"), NULL,
        WS_VISIBLE | WS_CHILD, 0, 0, 0, 0,
        hwnd, NULL, g_hinst, 0);
 if (!g_hwndChild) return FALSE;
 return TRUE;
}


HBRUSH OnCtlColor(HWND hwnd, HDC hdc, HWND hwndChild, int type)
{
  FORWARD_WM_CTLCOLORSTATIC(hwnd, hdc, hwndChild, DefWindowProc);
  SetDCBrushColor(hdc, RGB(255,0,0));
  return GetStockBrush(DC_BRUSH);
}
```

```
    HANDLE_MSG(hwnd, WM_CTLCOLORSTATIC, OnCtlColor);
```

Run this program and observe that we changed the background color of the static window to red.

The work happens inside the OnCtlColor function. When asked to customize the colors, we first forward the message to the DefWindowProc function so that the default foreground and background text colors are set (not relevant here because we draw no text, but a good thing to do on principle). Because we want to override the background brush color, we set the DC brush color to red and then return the DC brush as our desired background brush.

The static control then takes the brush we returned (the DC brush) and uses it to draw the background, which draws in red because that's the color we set it to.

Normally, when customizing the background brush, we have to create a brush, return it from the WM_CTLCOLORSTATIC message, and then destroy it when the parent window is destroyed. But by using the DC brush, we avoided having to do all that bookkeeping.

There is also a DC pen, GetStockObject(DC_PEN), that behaves in an entirely analogous manner.

⌇

Using ExtTextOut to draw solid rectangles

WHEN YOU NEED to draw a solid rectangle, the obvious choice is to call the Rectangle function. If you look at what the Rectangle function requires, however, you'll see that there's quite a bit of preparation necessary. You have to initialize the current pen to the null pen, select a solid-color brush, and then remember to increase the height and width of the rectangle by one to account for the decrement that the Rectangle function performs when given the null pen:

```
BOOL DrawSolidRect1(HDC hdc, LPCRECT prc, COLORREF clr)
{
 BOOL fDrawn = FALSE;
 HPEN hpenPrev =  SelectPen(hdc, GetStockPen(NULL_PEN));
 HBRUSH hbrSolid = CreateSolidBrush(clr);
 if (hbrSolid) {
  HBRUSH hbrPrev = SelectBrush(hdc, hbrSolid);
  fDrawn = Rectangle(hdc, prc->left, prc->top, prc->right + 1,
                     prc->bottom + 1);
  SelectBrush(hdc, hbrPrev);
  DeleteObject(hbrSolid);
 }
 SelectPen(hdc, hpenPrev);
 return fDrawn;
}
```

Slightly more convenient is the FillRect function, because you don't need to bother with the null pen:

```
BOOL DrawSolidRect2(HDC hdc, LPCRECT prc, COLORREF clr)
{
 BOOL fDrawn = FALSE;
 HBRUSH hbrSolid = CreateSolidBrush(clr);
 if (hbrSolid) {
  fDrawn = FillRect(hdc, prc, hbrSolid);
```

```
    DeleteObject(hbrSolid);
  }
  return fDrawn;
}
```

Note, however, that we still end up creating a GDI object and throwing it away shortly thereafter. We can avoid this if we allow ourselves to take advantage of the DC brush. (Doing so means that your program will not run on versions of Windows prior to Windows 2000.)

```
BOOL DrawSolidRect3(HDC hdc, LPCRECT prc, COLORREF clr)
{
  BOOL fDrawn = FALSE;
  COLORREF clrPrev = SetDCBrushColor(hdc, clr);
  if (clrPrev != CLR_INVALID) {
    fDrawn = FillRect(hdc, prc, GetStockBrush(DC_BRUSH));
    SetDCBrushColor(hdc, clrPrev);
  }
  return fDrawn;
}
```

At some point early in the days of Windows, developers who worry about such things experimented with all of these techniques and more (well, except for DrawSolidRect3, because the DC brush hadn't been invented yet) and found the fastest way to draw a solid rectangle: using the ExtTextOut function. The ETO_OPAQUE flag specifies that the contents of the rectangle parameter should be filled with the text background color, and it is this side effect that we will take advantage of:

```
BOOL DrawSolidRect4(HDC hdc, LPCRECT prc, COLORREF clr)
{
  BOOL fDrawn = FALSE;
  COLORREF clrPrev = SetBkColor(hdc, clr);
  if (clrPrev != CLR_INVALID) {
    fDrawn = ExtTextOut(hdc, 0, 0, ETO_OPAQUE, prc, NULL, 0, NULL);
    SetBkColor(hdc, clrPrev);
  }
  return fDrawn;
}
```

The DrawSolidRect4 function was the champion for many years, and its superiority faded into folklore. If you ask old-timers for the best way to draw solid rectangles, they'll tell you to use the ExtTextOut function. This created its own feedback loop: Driver vendors recognized that programs were using ExtTextOut to draw solid rectangles and consequently optimized for that scenario, thereby securing ExtTextOut's superiority into the next generation.

Even in Windows XP, after multiple changes in the video driver model, ExtTextOut still puts in a good showing compared to the other methods for drawing solid rectangles, coming in first place or tied for first place.

✑

Using StretchBlt to draw solid rectangles

IT IS A common need to fill a rectangle with a solid color taken from the upper-left pixel of an existing bitmap. For example, if you set the SS_CENTERIMAGE style on a static control, the image will be centered in the control's client area, using the color of the upper-left pixel of the bitmap as the background color. If you are providing a framework for laying out controls and bitmaps, you may find yourself having to do something similar. In these cases, the bitmap in question will already have been selected into a device context for rendering; while you're there, you can use a simple StretchBlt to fill the background.

Start with a fresh scratch program and make the following changes:

```
HBITMAP g_hbm;

void
PaintContent(HWND hwnd, PAINTSTRUCT *pps)
{
 HDC hdcMem = CreateCompatibleDC(pps->hdc);
 if (hdcMem) {
  HBITMAP hbmPrev = SelectBitmap(hdcMem, g_hbm);
  if (hbmPrev) {
    BITMAP bm;
    if (GetObject(g_hbm, sizeof(bm), &bm)) {
     RECT rcClient;
     GetClientRect(hwnd, &rcClient);
     int cxClient = rc.right - rc.left;
     int cyClient = rc.bottom - rc.top;
     StretchBlt(pps->hdc, rc.left, rc.top, cxClient, cyClient,
                hdcMem, 0, 0, 1, 1, SRCCOPY);
```

```
    BitBlt(pps->hdc, rc.left, rc.top, cxClient, cyClient,
            hdcMem, 0, 0, SRCCOPY);
    }
    SelectBitmap(hdcMem, hbmPrev);
  }
  DeleteDC(hdcMem);
  }
}
```

To `WinMain`, add before the call to `CreateWindowEx`:

```
    g_hbm = (HBITMAP)LoadImage(g_hinst, lpCmdLine,
                        IMAGE_BITMAP, 0, 0, LR_LOADFROMFILE);
    if (!g_hbm) return 0;
```

with a matching

```
DeleteObject(g_hbm);
```

at the end of `WinMain` before it returns.

When you run this program (with the name of a bitmap file on the command line, of course), the bitmap is drawn in the upper-left corner of the screen, and the one call to the `StretchBlt` function fills the unused portion of the client area with the upper-left pixel of the bitmap. Because we already had to set up the memory DC to draw the bitmap in the first place, a single call to `StretchBlt` is much more convenient than calling `GetPixel` to obtain the color and creating a solid brush to perform the fill.

Displaying a string
without those ugly boxes

YOU'VE ALL SEEN those ugly boxes. When you try to display a string and the font you have doesn't support all the characters in it, you get an ugly box for the characters that aren't available in the font.

Start with our scratch program and add this to the `PaintContent` function:

```
void
PaintContent(HWND hwnd, PAINTSTRUCT *pps)
```

```
{
    TextOutW(pps->hdc, 0, 0,
            L"ABC\x0410\x0411\x0412\x0E01\x0E02\x0E03", 9);
}
```

That string contains the first three characters from three alphabets: ABC from the Roman alphabet, АБВ from the Cyrillic alphabet, and กขฃ from the Thai alphabet.

If you run this program, you get a bunch of ugly boxes for the non-Roman characters because the SYSTEM font is very limited in its character set support.

But how to pick the right font? What if the string contains Korean or Japanese characters? There is no single font that contains every character defined by Unicode (or at least, none that is commonly available). What do you do?

This is where font linking comes in.

Font linking enables you to take a string and break it into pieces, where each piece can be displayed in an appropriate font.

The `IMLangFontLink2` interface provides the methods necessary to do this breaking. The `IMLangFontLink2::GetStrCodePages` method takes the string apart into chunks, such that all the characters in a chunk can be displayed by the same font, and the `IMLangFontLink::MapFont` method creates the font.

Okay, so let's write our font-link-enabled version of the `TextOut` function. We'll do this in stages, starting with the kernel of our solution. The *idea kernel* is my name for the "so this is what it all comes to" moment of programming. Most programming techniques are simple, but getting to that simple idea often entails many lines of tedious preparation that, although essential, also obscure the main point. Let's pretend that all the preparatory work has already been done: Somebody already set up the DC, created an `IMLangFontLink2` pointer in the `pfl` variable, and is keeping track of where the text needs to go. All that's left is this loop:

```
#include <mlang.h>

HRESULT TextOutFL(HDC hdc, int x, int y, LPCWSTR psz, int cch)
{
    ...
```

```
while (cch > 0) {
  DWORD dwActualCodePages;
  long cchActual;
  pfl->GetStrCodePages(psz, cch, 0, &dwActualCodePages,
                       &cchActual);
  HFONT hfLinked;
  pfl->MapFont(hdc, dwActualCodePages, 0, &hfLinked);
  HFONT hfOrig = SelectFont(hdc, hfLinked);
  TextOut(hdc, ?, ?, psz, cchActual);
  SelectFont(hdc, hfOrig);
  pfl->ReleaseFont(hfLinked);
  psz += cchActual;
  cch -= cchActual;
}
  ...
}
```

We walk through the string asking `IMLangFontLink2::GetStrCodePages` to give us the next chunk of characters and opaque information about what code pages those characters belong to. From that, we ask `IMLangFontLink2::MapFont` to create a matching font and then use `TextOut` to draw the characters in that font at the right place. Repeat until all the characters are done.

The rest is refinement and paperwork.

First of all, what is the right place? We want the next chunk to resume where the previous chunk left off. For that, we take advantage of the `TA_UPDATECP` text-alignment style, which says that GDI should draw the text at the current position and update the current position to the end of the drawn text (therefore, in position for the next chunk).

Therefore, part of the paperwork is to set the DC's current position and set the text mode to `TA_UPDATECP`:

```
SetTextAlign(hdc, GetTextAlign(hdc) | TA_UPDATECP);
MoveToEx(hdc, x, y, NULL);
```

Then we can just pass `0, 0` as the coordinates to `TextOut`, because the coordinates passed to `TextOut` are ignored if the text alignment mode is `TA_UPDATECP`; it always draws at the current position.

Of course, we can't just mess with the DC's settings like this. If the caller did not set `TA_UPDATECP`, the caller is not expecting us to be meddling with the current position. Therefore, we have to save the original position and restore it (and the original text alignment mode) afterward:

```
POINT ptOrig;
DWORD dwAlignOrig = GetTextAlign(hdc);
SetTextAlign(hdc, dwAlignOrig | TA_UPDATECP);
MoveToEx(hdc, x, y, &ptOrig);
while (cch > 0) {
  ...
  TextOut(hdc, 0, 0, psz, cchActual);
  ...
}
// if caller did not want CP updated, then restore it
// and restore the text alignment mode too
if (!(dwAlignOrig & TA_UPDATECP)) {
  SetTextAlign(hdc, dwAlignOrig);
  MoveToEx(hdc, ptOrig.x, ptOrig.y, NULL);
}
```

Next is a refinement: We should take advantage of the second parameter to `IMLangFontLink2::GetStrCodePages`, which specifies the code pages we would prefer to use if a choice is available. Clearly, we should prefer to use the code pages supported by the font we want to use, so that if the character can be displayed in that font directly, we shouldn't map an alternate font:

```
HFONT hfOrig = (HFONT)GetCurrentObject(hdc, OBJ_FONT);
DWORD dwFontCodePages = 0;
pfl->GetFontCodePages(hdc, hfOrig, &dwFontCodePages);
...
while (cch > 0) {
  pfl->GetStrCodePages(psz, cch, dwFontCodePages,
                       &dwActualCodePages, &cchActual);
  if (dwActualCodePages & dwFontCodePages) {
    // our font can handle it - draw directly using our font
    TextOut(hdc, 0, 0, psz, cchActual);
  } else {
    ... MapFont etc ...
  }
}
...
```

Of course, you probably wonder where this magical `pfl` comes from. It comes from the MultiLanguage Object in the MLang library:

```
IMLangFontLink2 *pfl;
CoCreateInstance(CLSID_CMultiLanguage, NULL,CLSCTX_ALL,
                IID_IMLangFontLink2,
                    (void**)&pfl);
...
pfl->Release();
```

And of course, all the errors we've been ignoring need to be taken care of. This does create a bit of a problem if we run into an error after we have already made it through a few chunks. What should we do?

I'm going to handle the error by drawing the string in the original font, ugly boxes and all. We can't erase the characters we already drew, and we can't just draw half of the string (for our caller won't know where to resume). So we just draw with the original font and hope for the best. At least it's no worse than it was before font linking.

Put all of these refinements together and you get this final function:

```
HRESULT TextOutFL(HDC hdc, int x, int y, LPCWSTR psz, int cch)
{
  HRESULT hr;
  IMLangFontLink2 *pfl;
  if (SUCCEEDED(hr = CoCreateInstance(CLSID_CMultiLanguage,
                   NULL, CLSCTX_ALL,IID_IMLangFontLink2,
                   (void**)&pfl))) {
    HFONT hfOrig = (HFONT)GetCurrentObject(hdc, OBJ_FONT);
    POINT ptOrig;
    DWORD dwAlignOrig = GetTextAlign(hdc);
    if (!(dwAlignOrig & TA_UPDATECP)) {
      SetTextAlign(hdc, dwAlignOrig | TA_UPDATECP);
    }
    MoveToEx(hdc, x, y, &ptOrig);
    DWORD dwFontCodePages = 0;
    hr = pfl->GetFontCodePages(hdc, hfOrig, &dwFontCodePages);
    if (SUCCEEDED(hr)) {
      while (cch > 0) {
        DWORD dwActualCodePages;
        long cchActual;
        hr = pfl->GetStrCodePages(psz, cch, dwFontCodePages,
                                &dwActualCodePages, &cchActual);
        if (FAILED(hr)) {
          break;
        }
```

```
      if (dwActualCodePages & dwFontCodePages) {
        TextOut(hdc, 0, 0, psz, cchActual);
      } else {
        HFONT hfLinked;
        if (FAILED(hr = pfl->MapFont(hdc, dwActualCodePages,
                                     0, &hfLinked))) {
          break;
        }
        SelectFont(hdc, hfLinked);
        TextOut(hdc, 0, 0, psz, cchActual);
        SelectFont(hdc, hfOrig);
        pfl->ReleaseFont(hfLinked);
      }
      psz += cchActual;
      cch -= cchActual;
    }
    if (FAILED(hr)) {
      // We started outputting characters so we must finish.
      // Do the rest without font linking since we have
      // no choice.
      TextOut(hdc, 0, 0, psz, cch);
      hr = S_FALSE;
    }
  }

  pfl->Release();

  if (!(dwAlignOrig & TA_UPDATECP)) {
    SetTextAlign(hdc, dwAlignOrig);
    MoveToEx(hdc, ptOrig.x, ptOrig.y, NULL);
  }
}

return hr;
}
```

Finally, we can wrap the entire operation inside a helper function that first tries with font linking, and then if that fails, just draws the text the old-fashioned way:

```
void TextOutTryFL(HDC hdc, int x, int y, LPCWSTR psz, int cch)
{
  if (FAILED(TextOutFL(hdc, x, y, psz, cch))) {
    TextOut(hdc, x, y, psz, cch);
  }
}
```

Okay, now that we have our font-linked `TextOut` with fallback, we can go ahead and adjust our `PaintContent` function to use it:

```
void
PaintContent(HWND hwnd, PAINTSTRUCT *pps)
{
    TextOutTryFL(pps->hdc, 0, 0,
              L"ABC\x0410\x0411\x0412\x0E01\x0E02\x0E03", 9);
}
```

Observe that the string is now displayed with no black boxes.

One refinement I did not do was to avoid creating the `IMlangFontLink2` pointer each time we want to draw text. In a real program, you would probably create the multilanguage object one time per drawing context (per window, perhaps) and reuse it to avoid going through the whole object creation code path each time you want to draw a string.

This technique of using the `IMlangFontLink2` interface to break a string up into pieces falls apart when you add right-to-left languages, however. (Try it and see what happens, and then see whether you can explain why.) The interface was introduced with Internet Explorer 4.0 to address a significant portion of the multilingual needs of the Web browser, but the solution is not perfect. With Internet Explorer 5.0 came Uniscribe, a more complete solution to the problem of rendering text. Rendering text with Uniscribe is comparatively anticlimactic given what we had to go through with the `IMlangFontLink2` interface:

```
#include <usp10.h>

HRESULT TextOutUniscribe(HDC hdc, int x, int y,LPCWSTR psz,
                         int cch)
{
 if (cch == 0) return S_OK;
 SCRIPT_STRING_ANALYSIS ssa;
 HRESULT hr = ScriptStringAnalyse(hdc, psz, cch, 0, -1,
                    SSA_FALLBACK | SSA_GLYPHS, MAXLONG,
                    NULL, NULL, NULL, NULL, NULL, &ssa);
 if (SUCCEEDED(hr)) {
  hr = ScriptStringOut(ssa, x, y, 0, NULL, 0, 0, FALSE);
  ScriptStringFree(&ssa);
 }
```

```
  return hr;
}
```

Rendering a single line of text is quite straightforward because the designers of Uniscribe streamlined the common case where all you want to do is display text. Most of the complexity of Uniscribe resides in the work you have to do if you intend to support editing of text. If you merely want to display it, things are simple. The single function ScriptStringAnalyse takes a string and produces a SCRIPT_STRING_ANALYSIS that describes the string in an internal format known only to Uniscribe. Passing the SSA_FALLBACK flag instructs Uniscribe to do font linking automatically, and the SSA_GLYPHS flag says that we want to see the characters themselves. Because we are an English program, the ambient text direction is left to right, and we are rendering the string all at once, so there is no context that needs to be carried over from one call to the next. Consequently, we don't need to pass any special SCRIPT_CONTROL or SCRIPT_STATE.

When ScriptStringAnalyse has performed its analysis, we ask ScriptStringOut to display the string, and then free the data structure that was used to perform the analysis. All that's left is to change our PaintContent function to use the TextOutUniscribe function rather than the TextOutFL function. Rendering mixed right-to-left and left-to-right text is an extremely difficult operation; fortunately, we can let the Uniscribe library do the work for us.

If Uniscribe does the right thing, why did I start by introducing IMLangFontLink2? First of all, IMLangFontLink2 predated Uniscribe, so I was presenting the technologies in chronological order. But more important, the purpose of the exploration of IMLangFontLink2 was to show how a simple *idea kernel* can be built up into a complete function.

⌒

Semaphores don't have owners

UNLIKE MUTEXES AND critical sections, semaphores don't have owners. They merely have counts. The ReleaseSemaphore function increases the count associated with a semaphore by the specified amount. (This increase might release waiting threads.) But the thread releasing the semaphore need not be the same one that claimed it originally. This differs from mutexes and critical sections, which require that the claiming thread also be the releasing one.

Some people use semaphores in a mutex-like manner: They create a semaphore with initial count 1 and use it like this:

```
WaitForSingleObject(hSemaphore, INFINITE);
... do stuff ..
ReleaseSemaphore(hSemaphore, 1, NULL);
```

If the thread exits (or crashes) before it manages to release the semaphore, the semaphore counter is not automatically restored. Compare mutexes, where the mutex is released if the owner thread terminates while holding it. For this pattern of usage, a mutex is therefore preferable.

A semaphore is useful if the conceptual ownership of a resource can cross threads:

```
WaitForSingleObject(hSemaphore, INFINITE);
... do some work ..
... continue on a background thread ...
HANDLE hThread = CreateThread(NULL, 0, KeepWorking, ...);
if (!hThread) {
    ... abandon work ...
    ReleaseSemaphore(hSemaphore, 1, NULL); // release resources
}

DWORD CALLBACK KeepWorking(void* lpParameter)
{
    ... finish working ...
    ReleaseSemaphore(hSemaphore, 1, NULL);
    return 0;
}
```

This trick doesn't work with a mutex or critical section because mutexes and critical sections have owners, and only the owner can release the mutex or critical section.

Note that if the KeepWorking function exits and forgets to release the semaphore, the counter is not automatically restored. The operating system doesn't know that the semaphore "belongs to" that work item.

Another common usage pattern for a semaphore is the opposite of the resource-protection pattern: It's the resource-generation pattern. In this model, the semaphore count normally is zero, but is incremented when there is work to be done:

```
... produce some work and add it to a work list ...
ReleaseSemaphore(hSemaphore, 1, NULL);

// There can be more than one worker thread.
// Each time a work item is signaled, one thread will
// be chosen to process it.
DWORD CALLBACK ProcessWork(void* lpParameter)
{
  for (;;) {
    // wait for work to show up
    WaitForSingleObject(hSemaphore, INFINITE);
    ... retrieve a work item from the work list ...
    ... perform the work ...
  }
  // NOTREACHED
}
```

Notice that in this case, there is not even a conceptual "owner" of the semaphore, unless you count the work item itself (sitting on a work list data structure somewhere) as the owner. If the ProcessWork thread exits, you do *not* want the semaphore to be released automatically; that would mess up the accounting. A semaphore is an appropriate object in this case.

⌇

An auto-reset event is just a stupid semaphore

WHEN YOU CREATE an event with the CreateEvent function, you get to specify whether you want an auto-reset event or a manual-reset event.

Manual-reset events are easy to understand: If the event is clear, a wait on the event is not satisfied. If the event is set, a wait on the event succeeds. Doesn't matter how many people are waiting for the event; they all behave the same way, and the state of the event is unaffected by how many people are waiting for it.

Auto-reset events are more confusing. Probably the easiest way to think about them is as if they were semaphores with a maximum token count of one. If the event is clear, a wait on the event is not satisfied. If the event is set, one waiter succeeds, and the event is reset; the other waiters keep waiting.

The gotcha with auto-reset events is the case where you set an event that is already set. Because an event has only two states (set and reset), setting an event that is already set has no effect. If you are using an event to control a resource producer/consumer model, the "setting an event that is already set" case will result in you appearing to "lose" a token. Consider the following intended pattern:

Producer	Consumer
	Wait
Produce work	
SetEvent	
	Wake up and reset event
	Do work
Produce work	
	Wait
SetEvent	
	Wake up and reset event
	Do work
...	...

But what if the timing doesn't quite come out? What if the consumer thread is a little slow to do the work (or the producer thread is a little fast in generating it):

Producer	Consumer
	Wait
Produce work	
SetEvent	
	Wake up and reset event

Producer	Consumer
Produce work	
SetEvent	
	Do work
Produce work	
SetEvent (has no effect)	
	Wait (satisfied immediately)
	and reset event
	Do work
	Wait

Notice that the producer produced three work items, but the consumer performed only two of them. The third SetEvent had no effect because the event was already set. (You have the same problem if you try to increase a semaphore's token count past its maximum.) If you want the number of wakes to match the number of sets, you need to use a semaphore with a maximum token count as high as the maximum number of outstanding work items you will support.

Moral of the story: Know your tools, know their limits, and use the right tool for the right job.

CHAPTER EIGHT

WINDOW MANAGEMENT

THIS CHAPTER FOCUSES on the window manager, starting with some basic design points and then introducing some code to illustrate the various types of modality and then investigating ways we can harness the design of Windows modal loops to accomplish some neat tricks. Nonprogrammers are welcome to skip to the next chapter when the subject matter here becomes a bit too technical.

⌒

Why do I get spurious WM_MOUSEMOVE messages?

TO UNDERSTAND THIS properly, it helps to know where WM_MOUSEMOVE messages come from.

When the hardware mouse reports an interrupt, indicating that the physical mouse has moved, Windows determines which thread should receive the mouse move message and sets a flag on that thread's input queue that says, "The mouse moved, in case anybody cares." (Other stuff happens, too, which we ignore here for now. In particular, if a mouse button event arrives, a lot of bookkeeping happens to preserve the virtual input state.)

When that thread calls a message retrieval function such as GetMessage, and the "The mouse moved" flag is set, Windows inspects the mouse position and does the work that is commonly considered to be part of mouse movement: determining the window that should receive the message, changing the cursor, and determining what type of message to generate (usually WM_MOUSEMOVE or perhaps WM_NCMOUSEMOVE).

If you understand this, you already see the answer to the question "Why does my program not receive all mouse messages if the mouse is moving too fast?"

If your program is slow to call GetMessage, multiple mouse interrupts may arrive before your program calls GetMessage to pick them up. Because all that happens when the mouse interrupt occurs is that a flag is set, if two interrupts happen in succession without a message retrieval function being called, the second interrupt merely sets a flag that is already set, which has no effect. The result is that the first interrupt acts as if it has been "lost" because nobody bothered to pick it up.

You should also see the answer to the question "How fast does Windows deliver mouse movement messages?"

The answer is, "As fast as you want." If you call GetMessage frequently, you get mouse messages frequently; if you call GetMessage rarely, you get mouse messages rarely.

Okay, so back to the original question, "Why do I get spurious WM_MOUSEMOVE messages?"

Notice that the delivery of a mouse message includes lots of work that is typically thought of as being part of mouse movement. Often, Windows wants to do that follow-on work even though the mouse hasn't actually moved. The most obvious example is when a window is shown, hidden, or moved. When that happens, the mouse cursor may be over a window different from the window it was over previously (or in the case of a move, it may be over a different part of the same window). Windows needs to recalculate the mouse cursor (for example, the old window may have wanted an arrow but the new window wants a pointy finger), so it *artificially sets the "The mouse moved, in case anybody* cares" *flag*. This causes all the follow-on work to happen, a side effect of which is the generation of a spurious WM_MOUSEMOVE message.

So if your program wants to detect whether the mouse has moved, you need to add a check in your WM_MOUSEMOVE that the mouse position is different from the position reported by the previous WM_MOUSEMOVE message.

Note that even though Windows generates spurious WM_MOUSEMOVE messages, it does so only in response to a relevant change to the window hierarchy. Some people have observed that their program receives a spurious WM_MOUSEMOVE message every two seconds even when the system is idle. This behavior is not normal. A constant stream of message traffic would quickly draw the attention of the performance team because it has the same effect as polling. If you are seeing a stream of spurious WM_MOUSEMOVE messages when the system is idle, you probably have a program that is continuously manipulating the window hierarchy or the mouse position. These programs typically do this to "enhance" the system in some way, such as translating the word under the cursor or animating a screen element to entertain you, but as a side effect keep fiddling with the mouse.

In addition to the problem of the spurious WM_MOUSEMOVE, there is also the problem of the missing WM_MOUSEMOVE. This typically happens when a program fails to update the cursor even though the content beneath it has changed, usually when the content changes as the result of scrolling. You can test this out yourself: Find a program where the cursor changes depending on where you are in a document. For example, a Web browser changes the cursor from an arrow to a hand if you are over a link; a word processor changes the cursor from an I-beam to an arrow when you move into the left margin. Position the mouse over the document and make a note of the cursor. Now use the keyboard or mouse wheel to scroll the document so that the cursor is now over a portion of the document where the cursor should be something different. Did your cursor change? If you try this out on a handful of different programs, you'll probably find that some correctly change the cursor after scrolling and others don't.

If you haven't figured it out by now, here's the reason for the problem of the missing WM_MOUSEMOVE: Because the mouse cursor is updated as the result of a WM_SETCURSOR message, operations that change what lies under the mouse (scrolling being the most common example) do not generate the WM_SETCURSOR message and consequently do not result in the cursor being updated to match the new contents. The solution to this problem is to put your cursor computation in a function that you call when you receive a WM_SETCURSOR message. After you make a change that requires the cursor to be recalculated, check whether the cursor is in your window, and if so, call that helper function.

The "missing WM_MOUSEMOVE" problem is quite common. It's admittedly a subtle problem, but when it happens, it can lead to end-user confusion because the cursor ends up being "wrong" until the user wiggles the mouse to "fix" it. To me, programs that exhibit this problem just feel unfinished.

Why is there no WM_MOUSEENTER message?

THERE IS A WM_MOUSELEAVE message. Why isn't there a WM_MOUSEENTER message? Because you can easily figure that out for yourself.

Here's what you do. When you receive a WM_MOUSELEAVE message, set a flag that says, "The mouse is outside the window." When you receive a WM_MOUSE-MOVE message and the flag is set, the mouse has entered the window. (And you should clear the flag while you're at it.)

Note that this provides another use for that spurious WM_MOUSEMOVE message: If the window appears at the mouse location, the spurious WM_MOUSE-MOVE message will cause your program's "mouse has entered" code to run, which is what you want.

The white flash

IF YOU HAD a program that didn't process messages for a while, but it needed to be painted for whatever reason (say, somebody uncovered it), Windows would eventually lose patience with you and paint your window white.

Or at least, that's what people would claim. Actually, Windows is painting your window with your class background brush. Because most people use COLOR_WINDOW and because COLOR_WINDOW is white in most color schemes, the end result is a flash of white.

Why paint the window white? Why not just leave it alone?

Well, that's what it used to do in Windows 3.1, but the result was that the previous contents of the screen would be shown where the window *would be*. Suppose you were looking at Explorer, and then you restored a program that stopped responding. Inside the program's main window would be … a picture of Explorer. And then people would try to double-click on what they thought was Explorer but was really a hung program.

In Windows XP, the behavior for a window that has stopped painting is different. Now, the system captures the pixels of the unresponsive window and just redraws those pixels if the window is unable to draw anything itself. Note, however, that if the system can't capture all of the pixels—say because the window was partially covered—then the parts that it couldn't get are filled in with the class brush.

Which is usually white.

What is the hollow brush for?

THE HOLLOW BRUSH is a brush that doesn't do anything. You can use it when you're forced to use a brush but you don't want to.

As one example, you can use it as your class brush. Then when your program stops responding and Windows decides to do the "white flash," it grabs the hollow brush and ends up not drawing anything. (At least, that's how it worked on Windows 2000. Things have changed in Windows XP, as described previously.)

Another place you can use the hollow brush is when handling the WM_CTL-COLOR* messages. Those messages require you to return a brush, which will be used to erase the background. If you don't want to erase the background, a hollow brush does the trick.

What's so special about the desktop window?

THE WINDOW RETURNED by the GetDesktopWindow function is very special, and I see people abusing it all over the place.

For example, many functions in the shell (such as IShellFolder::EnumObjects) accept a window handle parameter to be used in case a dialog box is needed.

What happens if you pass GetDesktopWindow()?

If a dialog box does indeed need to be displayed, you hang the system. Why?

- A modal dialog disables its owner.
- Every window is a descendant of the desktop.
- When a window is disabled, all its descendants are also disabled.

Put this together: If the owner of a modal dialog is the desktop, the desktop becomes disabled, which disables all of its descendants. In other words, it disables every window in the system. Even the one you're trying to display!

You also don't want to pass GetDesktopWindow() as your hwndParent. If you create a child window whose parent is GetDesktopWindow(), your window is now glued to the desktop window. If your window then calls something like MessageBox(), well, that's a modal dialog, and then the rules above kick in and the desktop gets disabled and the machine is toast.

The situation in real life is not quite as dire as I described it, however. The dialog manager detects that you've passed GetDesktopWindow() as the hwndParent and converts it to NULL. You'll see more details on this subject when we discuss the workings of the dialog manager.

So what window do you pass if you don't have a window?

If there is no UI being displayed on the thread yet, pass NULL. To the window manager, an owner equal to NULL means "Create this window without an owner." To the shell, a UI window of NULL typically means "Do not display UI," which is likely what you wanted anyway.

Be careful, however: If your thread does have a top-level unowned window, creating a second such window modally will create much havoc if the user switches to and interacts with the first window. (You'll see more of this when we discuss modality.) If you have a window, use it.

⮑

The correct order for disabling and enabling windows

IF YOU CHOOSE to display a modal window manually rather than using a function such as `DialogBoxParam` or `MessageBox`, you need to disable the owner and enable the modal child, and then reverse the procedure when the modal child is finished.

And if you do it wrong, focus will get all messed up.

If you are finished with a modal dialog, your temptation would be to clean up in the following order:

1. Destroy the modal dialog.

2. Reenable the owner.

But if you do that, you'll find that foreground activation doesn't go back to your owner. Instead, it goes to some random other window. Explicitly setting activation to the intended owner "fixes" the problem, but you still have all the flicker, and the Z-order of the interloper window gets all messed up.

What's going on?

When you destroy the modal dialog, you are destroying the window with foreground activation. The window manager now needs to find somebody else to give activation to. It tries to give it to the dialog's owner, but the owner is *still disabled*, so the window manager skips it and looks for some other window, somebody who is not disabled.

That's why you get the weird interloper window.

The correct order for destroying a modal dialog is

1. Reenable the owner.
2. Destroy the modal dialog.

This time, when the modal dialog is destroyed, the window manager looks to the owner and, hey, this time it's enabled, so it inherits activation.
No flicker. No interloper.

⫷

A subtlety in restoring the previous window position

A COMMON FEATURE for many applications is to record their screen location when they shut down and reopen at that location when relaunched. Even if you do the right thing and use the GetWindowPlacement and SetWindowPlacement functions mentioned in "Why does the taskbar default to the bottom of the screen?" (Chapter 4) to save and restore your window positions, you can still run into a problem if you restore the window position unconditionally.

If a user runs two copies of your program, the two windows end up in exactly the same place on the screen. Unless the user is paying close attention to the taskbar, it looks like running the second copy had no effect. Now things get interesting.

Depending on what the program does, the second copy may encounter a sharing violation, or it may merely open a second copy of the document for editing, or two copies of the song may start playing, resulting in a strange echo effect because the two copies are out of sync. Even more fun is if the user clicks the Stop button and the music keeps playing! Why? Because only the second copy of the playback was stopped. The first copy is still running.

I know one user who not infrequently gets as many as *four* copies of a multimedia title running, resulting in a horrific cacophony as they all play their opening music simultaneously, followed by mass confusion as the user tries to fix the problem, which usually consists of hammering the Stop button on the topmost copy. This stops the topmost instance, but the other three are still running!

If a second copy of the document is opened, the user may switch away from the editor, switch back to the *first* instance, and think that all the changes were lost. Or the user may fail to notice this and make a conflicting set of changes to the first instance. Then all sorts of fun things happen when the two copies of the same document are saved.

Moral of the story: If your program saves and restores its screen position, you may want to check whether a copy of the program is already running at that screen position. If so, move your second window somewhere else so that it doesn't occupy exactly the same coordinates, or just use the CW_USEDEFAULT values to ask the window manager to choose a position for you.)

UI-modality versus code-modality

FROM THE END-USERS' point of view, modality occurs when the users are locked into completing a task after it is begun, with the only escape being to cancel the entire operation. Opening a file is an example of a modal operation: When the Open command has been selected, users have no choice but to select a file for opening (or to cancel the operation). While attempting to open a document, the users cannot interact with the existing document, say, to scroll it around to look for some text that would give a clue as to what file to open next. This is typically manifested in the window manager and exhibited to the end user by disabling the document window for the duration of the task (for example, while the common File Open dialog is displayed).

From a programmer's point of view, modality can be viewed as a function that performs some operation that displays UI and doesn't return until that operation is complete. In other words, modality is a nested message loop that continues processing messages until some exit condition is reached. In our example above, the modality is inherent in the GetOpenFileName function, which does not return until the user selects a filename or cancels the dialog box.

Note that these two senses of modality do not necessarily agree. You can create something that is UI-modal—that is, does not let the user interact with the main window until some other action is complete—while internally coding it as a nonmodal function.

Let's code up an example of this behavior, to drive the point home.

As always, start with our scratch program from Chapter 7, "Short Topics in Windows Programming," and then make the following changes:

```
#include <commdlg.h>

HWND g_hwndFR;
TCHAR g_szFind[80];
FINDREPLACE g_fr = { sizeof(g_fr) };
UINT g_uMsgFindMsgString;

void CreateFindDialog(HWND hwnd)
{
  if (!g_hwndFR) {
    g_uMsgFindMsgString = RegisterWindowMessage(FINDMSGSTRING);
    if (g_uMsgFindMsgString) {
      g_fr.hwndOwner = hwnd;
      g_fr.hInstance = g_hinst;
      g_fr.lpstrFindWhat = g_szFind;
      g_fr.wFindWhatLen = 80;
      g_hwndFR = FindText(&g_fr);
    }
  }
}

void OnChar(HWND hwnd, TCHAR ch, int cRepeat)
{
  switch (ch) {
  case ' ': CreateFindDialog(hwnd); break;
  }
}

void OnFindReplace(HWND hwnd, FINDREPLACE *pfr)
{
  if (pfr->Flags & FR_DIALOGTERM) {
    DestroyWindow(g_hwndFR);
    g_hwndFR = NULL;
  }
}
```

```
// Add to WndProc
   HANDLE_MSG(hwnd, WM_CHAR, OnChar);

   default:
      if (uiMsg == g_uMsgFindMsgString && g_uMsgFindMsgString) {
         OnFindReplace(hwnd, (FINDREPLACE*)lParam);
      }
      break;

// Edit WinMain
   while (GetMessage(&msg, NULL, 0, 0)) {
         if (g_hwndFR && IsDialogMessage(g_hwndFR, &msg)) {
         } else {
            TranslateMessage(&msg);
            DispatchMessage(&msg);
         }
   }
```

This is an unexciting example of a modeless dialog; in our case, the Find dialog is displayed when you press the spacebar. Observe that you can click back to the main window while the Find dialog is up; that's because the Find dialog is modeless. As is typical for modeless dialogs, dispatching its messages is handled in the main message loop with a call to the `IsDialogMessage` function.

We can turn this into a UI-modal dialog very simply:

```
void CreateFindDialog(HWND hwnd)
{
  if (!g_hwndFR) {
    g_uMsgFindMsgString = RegisterWindowMessage(FINDMSGSTRING);
    if (g_uMsgFindMsgString) {
      g_fr.hwndOwner = hwnd;
      g_fr.hInstance = g_hinst;
      g_fr.lpstrFindWhat = g_szFind;
      g_fr.wFindWhatLen = 80;
      g_hwndFR = FindText(&g_fr);
      if (g_hwndFR) {
         EnableWindow(hwnd, FALSE);
      }
    }
  }
}
```

```
void OnFindReplace(HWND hwnd, FINDREPLACE *pfr)
{
  if (pfr->Flags & FR_DIALOGTERM) {
    EnableWindow(hwnd, TRUE);
    DestroyWindow(g_hwndFR);
    g_hwndFR = NULL;
  }
}
```

Notice that we carefully observed the rules for enabling and disabling windows.

When you run this modified program, everything seems the same except that the Find dialog is now modal. You can't interact with the main window until you close the Find dialog. The Find dialog is modal in the UI sense. However, the code is structured in the nonmodal manner. There is no dialog loop; the main window loop dispatches dialog messages as necessary.

You typically do not design your modal UI in this manner because it makes the code harder to structure. Observe, for example, that the code to manage the dialog box is scattered about, and the management of the dialog needs to be handled as a state machine because each phase returns back to the main message loop. The purpose of this demonstration is to show that UI modality need not be coupled to code modality.

It is also possible to have code modality without UI modality. In fact, this is far more common than the UI-modal-but-not-code-modal scenario.

You encounter modal loops without a visible change in UI state when you drag the scrollbar thumb, drag the window caption, display a pop-up menu, or initiate a drag/drop operation, among other places. Any time a nested message loop is constructed, you have code modality.

➤

The WM_QUIT message and modality

THE TRICK WITH modality is that when you call a modal function, the responsibility of message dispatch is handled by that function rather than by your main program. Consequently, if you have customized your main program's message pump, those customizations are lost when you lose control to a modal loop.

The other important thing about modality is that a WM_QUIT message always breaks the modal loop. Remember this in your own modal loops! If ever you call the PeekMessage function or the GetMessage function and get a WM_QUIT message, you must not only exit your modal loop, but you must also regenerate the WM_QUIT message (via the PostQuitMessage function) so that the next outer layer sees the WM_QUIT message and does its cleanup, too. If you fail to propagate the message, the next outer layer will not know that it needs to quit, and the program will seem to "get stuck" in its shutdown code, forcing the user to terminate the process the hard way.

Here's the basic idea of how your modal loops should repost the quit message to the next outer layer:

```
BOOL WaitForSomething(void)
{
  MSG msg;
  BOOL fResult = TRUE; // assume it worked
  while (!SomethingFinished()) {
    if (GetMessage(&msg, NULL, 0, 0)) {
      TranslateMessage(&msg);
      DispatchMessage(&msg);
    } else {
      // We received a WM_QUIT message; bail out!
      CancelSomething();
      // Re-post the message that we retrieved
      PostQuitMessage(msg.wParam);
      fResult = FALSE; // quit before something finished
      break;
    }
  }
  return fResult;
}
```

Suppose your program starts some operation and then calls Wait ForSomething(). While waiting for something to finish, some other part of your program decides that it's time to exit. (Perhaps the user clicked on a Quit button in another window.) That other part of the program will call Post QuitMessage(wParam) to indicate that the message loop should terminate.

The posted quit message will first be retrieved by the GetMessage in the WaitForSomething function. The GetMessage function returns FALSE if the retrieved message is a WM_QUIT message. In that case, the "else" branch of the conditional is taken, which cancels the "Something" operation in progress, and then posts the quit message back into the message queue for the next outer message loop to handle.

When WaitForSomething returns, control presumably will fall back out into the program's main message pump. The main message pump will then retrieve the WM_QUIT message and do its exit processing before finally exiting the program.

And if there were additional layers of modality between WaitForSomething and the program's main message pump, each of those layers would retrieve the WM_QUIT message, do their cleanup, and then repost the WM_QUIT message (again, via PostQuitMessage) before exiting the loop.

In this manner, the WM_QUIT message gets handed from modal loop to modal loop, until it reaches the outermost loop, which terminates the program. Reposting the WM_QUIT message ensures that the program really does quit.

"But wait," I hear you say. "Why do I have to do all this fancy WM_QUIT footwork? I could just have a private little global variable named something like g_fQuitting. When I want the program to quit, I just set this variable, and all of my modal loops check this variable and exit prematurely if it is set. Something like this:

```
// Warning: This code is wrong
BOOL MyWaitForSomething(void)
{
  MSG msg;
  while (!SomethingFinished()) {
    if (g_fQuitting) {
      CancelSomething();
      return FALSE;
    }
    if (GetMessage(&msg, NULL, 0, 0)) {
      TranslateMessage(&msg);
      DispatchMessage(&msg);
    }
  }
  return TRUE;
}
```

"And so I can solve the problem of the nested quit without needing to do all this `PostQuitMessage` nonsense."

And you'd be right, if you controlled every single modal loop in your program. But you don't. For example, when you call the `DialogBox` function, the dialog box code runs its own private modal loop to do the dialog box UI until you get around to calling the `EndDialog` function. And whenever the user clicks on any of your menus, Windows runs its own private modal loop to do the menu UI. Indeed, even the resizing of your application's window is handled by a Windows modal loop.

Windows, of course, has no knowledge of your little `g_fQuitting` variable, so it has no idea that you want to quit. It is the `WM_QUIT` message that serves this purpose of coordinating the intention to quit among separate parts of the system.

Notice that this convention regarding the `WM_QUIT` message cuts both ways. You can use this convention to cause modal loops to exit, but it also obliges you to respect this convention so that *other* components (including the window manager itself) can get your modal loops to exit.

⤳

The importance of setting the correct owner for modal UI

IF YOU DECIDE to display some modal UI, it is important that you set the correct owner for that UI. If you fail to heed this rule, you will find yourself chasing some very strange bugs.

Let's return to our scratch program and intentionally set the wrong owner window, so that you can see the consequences:

```
void OnChar(HWND hwnd, TCHAR ch, int cRepeat)
{
  switch (ch) {
  case ' ':
    // Wrong!
    MessageBox(NULL, TEXT("Message"), TEXT("Title"), MB_OK);
    if (!IsWindow(hwnd)) MessageBeep(-1);
    break;
  }
}
```

```
// Add to WndProc
   HANDLE_MSG(hwnd, WM_CHAR, OnChar);
```

Run this program, press the spacebar, and instead of dismissing the message box, click the X button in the corner of the main window. Notice that you get a beep before the program exits.

What happened?

The beep is coming from our call to the MessageBeep function, which in turn is telling us that our window handle is no longer valid. In a real program that kept its state in per-window instance variables (instead of in global variables like we do), you would more likely crash because all the instance variables would have gone away when the window was destroyed. In this case, the window was destroyed while inside a nested modal loop. As a result, when control returned to the caller, it is now a method running inside an object that has been destroyed. Any access to an instance variable is going to access memory that was already freed, resulting in memory corruption or an outright crash. The visual state has fallen out of sync with the stack state.

Here's an explanation in a call stack diagram:

```
WinMain
  DispatchMessage(hwnd, WM_CHAR)
   OnChar
    MessageBox(NULL)
     ... modal dialog loop ...
     DispatchMessage(hwnd, WM_CLOSE)
      DestroyWindow(hwnd)
       WndProc(WM_DESTROY)
        ... clean up the window ...
```

When you clean up the window, you typically destroy all the data structures associated with the window. Notice, however, that you are freeing data structures *that are still being used* by the OnChar handler deeper in the stack. Eventually, control unwinds back to the OnChar, which is now running with an invalid instance pointer. (If you believe in C++ objects, you would find that its this pointer has gone invalid.)

This was caused by failing to set the correct owner for the modal `MessageBox` call, allowing the user to interact with the frame window at a time when the frame window isn't expecting to have its state changed.

Even more problematic, the user can switch back to the frame window and press the spacebar again. The result: another message box. Repeat another time and you end up with a stack that looks like this:

```
WinMain
 DispatchMessage(hwnd, WM_CHAR)
  OnChar
   MessageBox(NULL)
    ... modal dialog loop ...
    DispatchMessage(hwnd, WM_CHAR)
     OnChar
      MessageBox(NULL)
       ... modal dialog loop ...
      DispatchMessage(hwnd, WM_CHAR)
       OnChar
        MessageBox(NULL)
         ... modal dialog loop ...
```

There are now four top-level windows, all active. If the user dismisses them in any order other than the reverse order in which they were created, you're going to have a problem on your hands. For example, if the user dismisses the second message box first, the part of the stack corresponding to that nesting level will end up returning to a destroyed window when the third message box is finally dismissed.

Here is the very simple fix:

```
// pass the correct owner window
MessageBox(hwnd, TEXT("Message"), TEXT("Title"), MB_OK);
```

Because `MessageBox` is modal, it disables the owner while the modal UI is being displayed, thereby preventing the user from destroying or changing the owner window's state when it is not expecting it.

This is why functions that can potentially display UI accept a window handle as one of its parameters. They need to know which window to use as the owner for any necessary dialogs or other modal operations. If you call such functions from a thread that is hosting UI, you must pass the handle to the window you want to use as the UI owner. If you pass NULL (or worse, GetDesktopWindow), you may find yourself in the same bad state that our buggy sample program demonstrated.

If you are displaying a modal dialog from another modal dialog, it is important to pass the correct window as the owner for the second dialog. Specifically, you need to pass the modal dialog initiating the subdialog and not the original frame window. Here's a stack diagram illustrating:

```
MainWindow
  DialogBox(hwndOwner = main window) [dialog 1]
    ... dialog manager ...
    DlgProc
      DialogBox(hwndOwner = dialog 1) [dialog 2]
```

If you mess up and pass the main window handle when creating the second modal dialog, you will find yourself back in a situation analogous to what we had last time: The user can dismiss the first dialog while the second dialog is up, leaving its stack frames orphaned.

Interacting with a program that has gone modal

So FAR, WE'VE been highlighting the importance of setting the right owner window for modal UI. It is also important, when manipulating a window, to respect its modality. For example, consider the program we ended up with last time, the one which calls the MessageBox function to display a modal dialog. If we want to get that program to exit and send a WM_CLOSE message to the main window instead of its modal pop-up, the main window would likely exit and leave the message box stranded, resulting in the same stack trace without support we saw when we neglected to set the correct owner for the MessageBox.

Respect the modality of a window. If it is disabled, don't try to get it to do things; it's disabled because it doesn't want to do anything right now. You can go hunting for its modal pop-up and talk to that pop-up. (Unless, of course, that pop-up is itself disabled; in which case, you get to keep on hunting.)

A timed MessageBox, the cheap version

As NOTED PREVIOUSLY, when you know the conventions surrounding the WM_QUIT message, you can put them to your advantage.

The more robust you want the TimedMessageBox function to be, the more work you need to do. Here's the cheap version, based on the sample in Knowledge Base article Q181934, but with some additional bug fixes:

```
static BOOL s_fTimedOut;
static HWND s_hwndMBOwnerEnable;

void CALLBACK
CheapMsgBoxTooLateProc(HWND hWnd, UINT uiMsg,
                       UINT_PTR idEvent, DWORD dwTime)
{
    s_fTimedOut = TRUE;
    if (s_hwndMBOwnerEnable)
     EnableWindow(s_hwndMBOwnerEnable, TRUE);
    PostQuitMessage(0); // value not important
}

// Warning! Not thread-safe! See discussion.
int CheapTimedMessageBox(HWND hwndOwner, LPCTSTR ptszText,
    LPCTSTR ptszCaption, UINT uType, DWORD dwTimeout)
{
    s_fTimedOut = FALSE;
    s_hwndMBOwnerEnable = NULL;
    if (hwndOwner && IsWindowEnabled(hwndOwner)) {
        s_hwndMBOwnerEnable = hwndOwner;
    }
    UINT idTimer = SetTimer(NULL, 0, dwTimeout,
                            CheapMsgBoxTooLateProc);
    int iResult = MessageBox(hwndOwner,
                             ptszText, ptszCaption, uType);
    if (idTimer) KillTimer(NULL, idTimer);
    if (s_fTimedOut) {               // We timed out
      MSG msg;
      // Eat the fake WM_QUIT message we generated
      PeekMessage(&msg, NULL, WM_QUIT, WM_QUIT, PM_REMOVE);
      iResult = -1;
    }
    return iResult;
}
```

This `CheapTimedMessageBox` function acts just like the `MessageBox` function, except that if the user doesn't respond within `dwTimeout` milliseconds, we return –1. The limitation is that only one timed message box can be active at a time. If your program is single threaded, this is not a serious limitation, but if your program is multithreaded, this will be a problem.

Do you see how it works?

The global static variable `s_fTimedOut` tells us whether we generated a fake `WM_QUIT` message as a result of a timeout. When the `MessageBox` function returns because we timed out, we use the `PeekMessage` function to remove the fake `WM_QUIT` message from the queue before returning.

Note that we remove the `WM_QUIT` message only if we are the ones who generated it. In this way, `WM_QUIT` messages generated by other parts of the program remain in the queue for processing by the main message loop.

Note further that when we decide that the timeout has occurred, we reenable the original owner window before we cause the message box to bail out of its message loop by posting a quit message. Those are the rules for the correct order for disabling and enabling windows.

Note also that we used a thread timer rather than a window timer. That's because we don't own the window being passed in and therefore don't know what timer IDs are safe to use. Any timer ID we pick might happen to collide with a timer ID being used by that window, resulting in erratic behavior.

Recall that when you pass `NULL` as the `hwnd` parameter to the `Set Timer` function and also pass zero as the `nIDEvent` parameter, the `SetTimer` function creates a brand new timer, assigns it a unique ID, and returns the ID. Most people, when they read that part of the specification for `SetTimer`, scratch their heads and ask themselves, "Why would anybody want to use this?"

Well, this is one scenario where this is exactly what you want.

Next comes the job of making the function a tad more robust. But before we do that, we'll need to cover two side topics.

≈

The scratch window

SOMETIMES YOU NEED a quick-and-dirty window and you don't want to go through all the hassle of registering a class for it. For example, you might need a window to listen for notifications, or you just need a window to own a message box.

To save yourself the trouble of registering a class for every single thing you might need a window for, you can get lazy and register a single "scratch window" class and simply subclass it on an as-needed basis:

```c
ATOM RegisterScratchWindowClass(void)
{
  WNDCLASS wc = {
        0,                              // style
        DefWindowProc,                  // lpfnWndProc
        0,                              // cbClsExtra
        0,                              // cbWndExtra
        g_hinst,                        // this file's HINSTANCE
        NULL,                           // hIcon
        LoadCursor(NULL, IDC_ARROW),    // hCursor
        (HBRUSH)(COLOR_BTNFACE+1),      // hbrBackground
        NULL,                           // lpszMenuName
        TEXT("ScratchWindow"),          // lpszClassName
  };

  return RegisterClass(&wc);
}

HWND
CreateScratchWindow(HWND hwndParent, WNDPROC wp)
{
  HWND hwnd;
  hwnd = CreateWindow(TEXT("ScratchWindow"), NULL,
                    hwndParent ? WS_CHILD : WS_OVERLAPPED,
                  0, 0, 0, 0, hwndParent, NULL, NULL, NULL);
  if (hwnd) {
    SubclassWindow(hwnd, wp);
  }
  return hwnd;
}
```

Now if you need a quick one-off window, you can just create a scratch window instead of creating a custom window class just to handle that specific task.

The bonus window bytes at GWLP_USERDATA

THE WINDOW MANAGER provides a pointer-sized chunk of storage you can access via the GWLP_USERDATA constant. You pass it to the GetWindowLongPtr and SetWindowLongPtr functions to read and write that value. Most of the time, all you need to attach to a window is a single pointer value anyway, so the free memory in GWLP_USERDATA is all you need.

Officially, these window bytes belong to the window class and not to the code that creates the window. However, this convention is not adhered to consistently. If you cannot be sure that your clients will keep their hands off the GWLP_USERDATA bytes, then it's probably safest to avoid those bytes.

A timed MessageBox, the better version

WE CAN NOW address a limitation of our first attempt at a timed MessageBox, namely that it could be used from only one thread at a time. Now we work to remove that limitation.

As you might recall, the reason why it could be used from only one thread at a time was that we kept the "Did the message box time out?" flag in a global. To fix it, we will move the flag to a per-instance location, namely a helper window.

Start with the scratch program, add the code for the scratch window class, and then add the following:

```
#define IDT_TOOLATE      1

typedef struct TOOLATEINFO {
  BOOL fTimedOut;
```

```
  HWND hwndReenable;
} TOOLATEINFO;

void CALLBACK
MsgBoxTooLateProc(HWND hwnd, UINT uiMsg,
                  UINT_PTR idEvent, DWORD dwTime)
{
  TOOLATEINFO *ptli = reinterpret_cast<TOOLATEINFO*>(
    GetWindowLongPtr(hwnd, GWLP_USERDATA));
  if (ptli) {
    ptli->fTimedOut = TRUE;
    if (ptli->hwndReenable) {
        EnableWindow(ptli->hwndReenable, TRUE);
    }
    PostQuitMessage(0);
  }
}

int TimedMessageBox(HWND hwndOwner, LPCTSTR ptszText,
    LPCTSTR ptszCaption, UINT uType, DWORD dwTimeout)
{
  TOOLATEINFO tli;
  tli.fTimedOut = FALSE;
  BOOL fWasEnabled = hwndOwner && IsWindowEnabled(hwndOwner);
  tli.hwndReenable = fWasEnabled ? hwndOwner : NULL;

  HWND hwndScratch = CreateScratchWindow(hwndOwner,
                                         DefWindowProc);
  if (hwndScratch) {
      SetWindowLongPtr(hwndScratch, GWLP_USERDATA,
                       reinterpret_cast<LONG_PTR>(&tli));
      SetTimer(hwndScratch, IDT_TOOLATE,
               dwTimeout, MsgBoxTooLateProc);
  }
  int iResult = MessageBox(hwndOwner, ptszText,
                           ptszCaption, uType);
  if (hwndScratch) {
    KillTimer(hwndScratch, IDT_TOOLATE);
    if (tli.fTimedOut) { // We timed out
      MSG msg;
      // Eat the fake WM_QUIT message we generated
      PeekMessage(&msg, NULL, WM_QUIT, WM_QUIT, PM_REMOVE);
      iResult = -1;
    }
    DestroyWindow(hwndScratch);
  }
```

```
    return iResult;
}

void OnChar(HWND hwnd, TCHAR ch, int cRepeat)
{
    switch (ch) {
    case ' ':
        TimedMessageBox(hwnd, TEXT("text"), TEXT("caption"),
                        MB_OK, 2000);
        break;
    }
}

// add to WndProc
    HANDLE_MSG(hwnd, WM_CHAR, OnChar);

// add to InitApp
    RegisterScratchWindowClass();
```

This is basically the same as the previous cheap version, just with slightly different bookkeeping.

The state of the timed message box is kept in the structure TOOLATEINFO. But how to pass this state to the timer callback? You can't pass any parameters to timer callbacks.

Aha, but timer callbacks do get a window handle. As we discovered above, however, we can't just hang the callback off the hwndOwner window because we don't know how to pick a timer ID that doesn't conflict with an existing one.

The solution: Hang it on a window of our own creation. That way, we get a whole new space of timer IDs to play in, separate from the timer IDs that belong to hwndOwner. The scratch window is a convenient window to use. We don't pass an interesting window procedure to CreateScratchWindow because there is no need; all we wanted was a window to own our timer.

A timed context menu

THIS IS SORT of in the same spirit as our preceding exercise in writing a timed message box, but this is much easier. Here, we use the handy-dandy WM_CANCELMODE message to get us out of menu mode:

```
void CALLBACK
MenuTooLateProc(HWND hwnd, UINT uiMsg,
    UINT_PTR idEvent, DWORD dwTime)
{
  SendMessage(hwnd, WM_CANCELMODE, 0, 0);
}

BOOL
TimedTrackPopupMenuEx(HMENU hMenu, UINT uFlags, int x, int y,
    HWND hwnd, LPTPMPARAMS pTpm, DWORD dwTimeout)
{
    UINT idTimer = SetTimer(NULL,0,
                                dwTimeout, MenuTooLateProc);
    BOOL fResult = TrackPopupMenuEx(hMenu, uFlags, x, y,
                                        hwnd, pTpm);
    if (idTimer) KillTimer(NULL, idTimer);
    return fResult;
}
```

Before displaying the menu, we set a timer. (And we use a thread timer because we don't own the `hwnd` window and therefore don't know what timer IDs are safe to use.) If the timer fires, we send ourselves a `WM_CANCELMODE` message to cancel menu mode. This causes the system to act as if the user had dismissed the menu without selecting anything, either by pressing the Escape key or clicking outside the menu. The call to the `TrackPopupMenuEx` function returns after the user has selected something (or the timeout has elapsed), at which point we clean up by destroying our timer before returning.

Why does my window receive messages after it has been destroyed?

WHAT LOOKS LIKE a window receiving a message after it was destroyed usually, upon closer inspection, isn't. For example, you might have a function that goes like this:

```
Victim(HWND hwnd)
{
  Something* p = GetSomethingAssociatedWithWindow(hwnd);
  p->BeforeSomethingElse();
```

```
DoSomethingElse(hwnd);
p->AfterSomethingElse(); // crash here!
}
```

When you investigate this in the debugger, you see a stack trace like this:

```
YourApp!Victim
YourApp!WndProc
user32!...
```

And when you ask the debugger for the condition of the window hwnd, it tells you that it isn't a valid window handle. How did your window procedure get a message for a window after it was destroyed?

Because the window still existed when the message was delivered.

What has usually happened is that somewhere during the processing of the DoSomething function, the window hwnd was destroyed. As part of its destruction, its associated Something data was also destroyed. After the DoSomething function returns, the Victim function tries to use the pointer p, which is no longer valid because the object was destroyed when the window was. The stack trace looks, on casual inspection, as if the window procedure was called for a window after it was destroyed. But a deeper study of the steps that led up to this condition usually reveals that the real problem is that the window was destroyed while it was busy processing a message.

⬲

CHAPTER NINE

REMINISCENCES ON HARDWARE

ONE OF THE roles of an operating system is to insulate applications from hardware to some degree or other. This is hard enough with properly functioning hardware, but bad hardware makes the problem even more difficult. Here are some hardware-related stories, some dealing with bad hardware, and others just with the complexity of dealing with hardware in the first place, even the type that works just fine.

Hardware backward compatibility

BACKWARD COMPATIBILITY APPLIES not only to software. It also applies to hardware. And when hardware goes bad, the software usually takes the blame.

The HLT instruction tells the CPU to stop ("halt") executing instructions until the next hardware interrupt. This is a big win on laptops because it reduces power consumption and thereby saves your lap from third-degree burns.

One of my colleagues had this implemented and working in Windows 95 but discovered to his dismay that many laptops (some from a major manufacturer) locked up unrecoverably if you issued a HLT instruction.

So we had to back it out.

Then the aftermarket HLT programs came out and people wrote, "Stupid Microsoft. Why did they leave this feature out of Windows?" I had to sit quietly while people accused Microsoft of being stupid and/or lazy and/or selfish.

But now the statute of limitations has expired, so at least I can say something (although I'm still not going to name that major manufacturer, nice try).

My favorite bad hardware, however, was a system which would crash if the video card was put in an expansion slot too far away from the power supply. Manufacturers will do anything to save a nickel.

And yet Windows 95 ran on almost all of this bad hardware. Why did we go to all this effort to accommodate bad hardware? Consider the following:

- You have a computer that works okay.
- You go to the store and buy Windows 95.
- You take it home and install it.
- Your computer crashes.

Whom do you blame? Hint: not your computer manufacturer.

☙

The ghost CD-ROM drives

MY FAVORITE BAD CD-ROM drive from Windows 95 was one where the manufacturer cut a corner to save probably twenty-five cents.

The specification for CD-ROM controllers indicates that each can host up to four CD-ROM drives. When you talk to the controller, you specify which drive you want to communicate with.

The manufacturer of a certain brand of CD-ROM controller decided that listening for the "Which drive?" was too much work, so they ignored the drive number in every I/O request and always returned the status of drive 1. When Windows 95 Plug and Play went off to detect your CD-ROM drives, it first asked the controller, "Is drive 1 installed?"

The controller responded, "Yes, it is."

Then Plug and Play asked, "Is drive 2 installed?"

Because the controller ignored the drive number in the request, it interpreted this as a request for the status of drive 1 and consequently responded, "Yes, it is."

Repeat for drives 3 and 4.

Result: Windows 95 detected four CD-ROM drives.

Apparently, this was a popular card because the question came up about once a week. (And the solution was to go into the Device Manager and disable three of the devices. Deleting them doesn't work, as mentioned in Chapter 5, "Puzzling Interface Issues," when we discussed why the Links folder keeps re-creating itself.)

The Microsoft corporate network: 1.7 times worse than hell

ONE OF THE tests performed by Windows Hardware Quality Labs (WHQL) was the network card packet stress test that had the nickname *Hell*. The purpose of the test was to flood a network card with an insane number of packets, to see how it handled extreme conditions. It uncovered packet-dropping bugs, timing problems, all sorts of great stuff. Network card vendors used it to determine what size internal hardware buffers should be to cover "all reasonable network traffic scenarios."

It so happened that at the time this test had currency (1996 era), the traffic on the Microsoft corporate network was approximately 1.7 times worse than the NCT packet stress test. A card could pass the Hell test with flying colors, yet drop 90% of its packets when installed on a computer at Microsoft because the card simply couldn't keep up with the traffic.

The open secret among network card vendors was, "If you want your card to work with Windows, submit one card to WHQL and send another to a developer on the Windows team."

Why was the Microsoft corporate network so horrible? Because there was more traffic going over the corporate network than in any other network that anyone had ever seen. Vendors would regularly show up at Microsoft to pitch their newest coolest hardware solutions. And we'd put them on the corporate network and watch the vendors' solutions collapse under the traffic. Few vendors had systems that could handle the load.

The Microsoft network administrators selected the NetBEUI protocol as the campus standard. This was really a "best of a bad lot" decision, because none of the existing network standards supported by Windows could handle a single network as large as Microsoft's. TCP/IP was not a good choice at this time, because neither the Domain Name Service (DNS) nor the Dynamic Host Configuration Protocol (DHCP) had been invented yet. Static host tables are absurd on a network with 50,000 computers.

NetBEUI had the major shortcoming of not being a routable protocol; as a result, name resolution had to be performed via broadcasts. Consequently, an unbelievable amount of broadcast traffic was going out on the network.

The shift from NetBEUI to TCP/IP began around 1996 and was made possible by the availability of DHCP and Windows Internet Name Services (WINS) to bring the tasks of IP address assignment and name resolution down to a manageable level. Although Microsoft long ago moved away from NetBEUI, an insane amount of traffic is still on our corporate network. The Microsoft corporate network is one of the most complicated corporate networks in the world, and it's a remarkable tribute to the IT department that it just works.

⁓

When vendors insult themselves

DURING WINDOWS 95, when we were building the Plug and Play infrastructure, we got an angry letter from a hardware vendor (who shall remain nameless) complaining that we intentionally misspelled the vendor company name in our configuration files in a manner that made the name similar to an insulting word.

Of course, this is a serious accusation, and we set to work to see what happened. It didn't take long to find the misspelling. The question now was why we spelled it wrong.

Further investigation revealed that the reason the company name was misspelled is that they misspelled their own name in their hardware devices' firmware. When Plug and Play asked the device for its manufacturer name, it replied with the misspelled name. So, of course, our INF file had to have an entry with the misspelled name so that we could identify the device when the user connected it. (The name displayed to the user did not contain the misspelling.)

We sent a polite letter to the company explaining the reason for the misspelling. As far as I am aware, they never brought up the subject again.

⌒

Defrauding the WHQL driver certification process

PEOPLE HAVE HAD all sorts of interesting experiences with drivers. Some people noticed a driver that blue-screened under normal conditions, but when you enabled the Driver Verifier (to try to catch the driver doing whatever bad thing it was doing), the problem went away. Others bemoan that certification by the Windows Hardware Quality Labs (WHQL) didn't seem to improve the quality of the drivers.

Video drivers will do anything to outdo their competition. Every so often, a company is caught cheating on benchmarks, for example. I remember one driver that ran the DirectX "3D Tunnel" demonstration program extremely fast, demonstrating how totally awesome their video card was. Except that if you renamed TUNNEL.EXE to FUNNEL.EXE, it ran slowly again.

Another one checked whether you were printing a specific string used by a popular benchmark program. If so, it only drew the string a quarter of the time and merely returned without doing anything the other three-quarters of the time. Bingo! Their benchmark numbers just quadrupled.

Anyway, similar shenanigans are not unheard of when submitting a driver to WHQL for certification. Some unscrupulous drivers detect that they are being run by WHQL and disable various features so that they pass certification. Of course, they also run dog slow in the WHQL lab, but that's okay, because

WHQL is interested in whether the driver contains any bugs, not whether the driver has the fastest triangle fill rate in the industry.

The most common cheat I've seen is drivers that check for a secret "Enable Dubious Optimizations" switch in the Registry or some other place external to the driver itself. They take the driver and put it in an installer which does not turn the switch on and submit it to WHQL. When WHQL runs the driver through all its tests, the driver is running in "safe but slow" mode and passes certification with flying colors.

The vendor then takes that driver (now with the WHQL stamp of approval) and puts it inside an installer that enables the secret "Enable Dubious Optimizations" switch. Now the driver sees the switch enabled and performs all sorts of dubious optimizations, none of which were tested by WHQL.

A twenty-foot-long computer

BACK IN THE days of Windows 95, when Plug and Play was in its infancy, one of the things the Plug and Play team did was push a newly introduced interface card standard to an absurd extreme.

They took a computer and put it at one end of a hallway. They then built a chain of bridge cards that ran down the hallway, and at the end of the chain, plugged in a video card.

And then they turned the whole thing on.

Amazingly, it actually worked. The machine booted and used a video card 20 feet away. (I'm guessing at the distance. It was a long time ago.) It took two people to operate this computer, one to move the mouse and type, and another to watch the monitor at the other end and report where the pointer was and what was happening on the screen.

And the latency was insane.

But it did work and served as a reassuring test of Plug and Play.

Other Plug and Play trivia: The phrase *Plug and Play* had already been trademarked at the time, and Microsoft had to obtain the rights to the phrase from the original owners.

⌇

The USB cart of death

DURING THE WINDOWS 2000 project, the USB team did something similar to what the Windows 95 Plug and Play team did with their 20-foot-long computer. To test Plug and Play and to test the Driver Verifier, they created the "USB Cart of Death."

They started with a two-level cart similar to what you'd see in a library. About ten eight-port hubs were wired together, and then every port was filled with some different type of USB device. A USB steering wheel adorned the back of the cart, and a USB radio provided the antenna. Two cameras were on the front. All power went to a USB UPS. The entire cart, completely mobile, came down to two cables (power and USB). The final USB cable was plugged into a USB PCMCIA card.

They plugged the card into a laptop, watched the operating system start up the 50 or so devices on it, and then (before or after it finished) unceremoniously yanked the PCMCIA card. If a blue screen occurred or the Driver Verifier detected a bug, the appropriate developer was asked to look at the machine. In the meantime, the cart was wheeled to the next laptop, in hopes of finding a different bug.

⌇

New device detected:
Boeing 747

BACK IN 1994, Boeing considered equipping each seat with a serial modem. Laptop users could hook up to the modem and dial out. (Dial-up was the primary means of connecting to the Internet back in those days.)

We chuckled at the thought of attaching the serial cable and getting a Plug and Play pop-up message: "New device detected: Boeing 747."

⤳

There's an awful lot of
overclocking out there

A BUNCH OF us were going through some Windows crashes that people sent in by clicking the Send Error Report button in the crash dialog. And there were huge numbers of them that made no sense whatsoever. For example, there would be code sequences like this:

```
mov ecx, dword ptr [someValue]
mov eax, dword ptr [otherValue]
cmp ecx, eax
jnz generateErrorReport
```

This code generates an error report if the ecx and eax registers are unequal. Yet when we looked at the error report, the ecx and eax registers were equal! There were other crashes of a similar nature, where the CPU simply lost its marbles and did something "impossible."

We had to mark these crashes as "possibly hardware failure." Because the crash reports are sent anonymously, we have no way of contacting the submitter to ask them follow-up questions. (The ones that my group was investigating were failures that were hit only once or twice, but were of the type deemed worthy of close investigation because the types of errors they uncovered—if valid—were serious.)

One of my colleagues had a large collection of failures where the program crashed at the instruction

```
xor eax, eax
```

How can you crash on an instruction that simply sets a register to zero? And yet there were hundreds of people crashing in precisely this way.

He went through all the published errata to see whether any of them would affect an xor eax, eax instruction. Nothing.

The next theory was some sort of hardware failure. Overheating, perhaps? Or overclocking?

Overclocking is analogous to setting a musician's metronome to a higher speed than the person was trained to play at. Sure, the music is faster, but it's more stressful on the musician, and the likelihood of an eventual mistake increases. A computer has a so-called clock chip whose purpose is to serve as the computer's metronome. Overclockers increase the speed of that clock chip to get the computer to "play music faster." There is an entire subculture devoted to overclocking.

My colleague sent email to some Intel people he knew to see whether they could think of anything else that could have caused this problem. They said that the only other thing they could think of was that perhaps somebody had mis-paired memory chips on the motherboard, but their description of what sorts of things go wrong when you mis-pair didn't match this scenario.

Because the failure rate for this particular error was comparatively high (certainly higher than the one or two I was getting for the failures I was looking at), he requested that the next ten people to encounter this error be given the opportunity to leave their email address and telephone number so that he could call them and ask follow-up questions. Some time later, he got word that ten people took him up on this offer, and he sent each of them email asking various questions about their hardware configurations, including whether they were overclocking.

Five people responded saying, "Oh, yes, I'm overclocking. Is that a problem?"

The other half said, "What's overclocking?" He called them and walked them through some configuration information and was able to conclude that they were indeed all overclocked. But these people were not overclocking on purpose. *The computer was already overclocked when they bought it.* These "stealth overclocked" computers came from small, independent "Bob's Computer Store"-type shops, not from one of the major computer manufacturers or retailers.

For both groups, he suggested that they stop overclocking or at least not overclock as aggressively. And in all cases, the people reported that their computer that used to crash regularly now runs smoothly.

Moral of the story: There's a lot of overclocking out there, and it makes Windows look bad.

I wonder whether it would be possible to detect overclocking from software and put up a warning in the crash dialog, "It appears that your computer is overclocked. This may cause random crashes. Try running the CPU at its rated speed to improve stability." But it takes only one false positive to get people saying, "Oh, there goes Microsoft blaming other people for its buggy software again."

CHAPTER TEN

The Inner Workings of the Dialog Manager

I think a lot of confusion about the dialog manager stems from not really understanding how it works. It's not that bad. After some warm-up discussion on dialog procedures, I go into the history of dialog templates, using that as a basis for understanding how dialog boxes are created, then move on to the dialog message loop, and wrap up with some topics regarding navigation.

On the dialog procedure

There really isn't much to a dialog procedure. For each message, you can choose to handle it or not, just like a window procedure. But unlike a window procedure, the way you express this decision is done by the return value.

Returning values from a dialog procedure

For some reason, the way values are returned from a dialog procedure confuses people, so I'm going to try to explain it a different way.

The trick with dialog box procedures is realizing that they actually need to return *two* pieces of information:

- Was the message handled?
- If so, what should the return value be?

Because two pieces of information have to be returned, but a C function can have only one return value, there needs to be some other way to return the second piece of information.

The return value of the dialog procedure is whether the message was handled. The second piece of information—what the return value should be—is stashed in the DWLP_MSGRESULT window long.

In other words, DefDlgProc goes something like this:

```
LRESULT CALLBACK DefDlgProc(
    HWND hdlg, UINT uMsg, WPARAM wParam, LPARAM lParam)
{
    DLGPROC dp = (DLGPROC)GetWindowLongPtr(hdlg, DWLP_DLGPROC);
    SetWindowLongPtr(hdlg, DWLP_MSGRESULT, 0);
    INT_PTR fResult = dp(hdlg, uMsg, wParam, lParam);
    if (fResult) return GetWindowLongPtr(hdlg, DWLP_MSGRESULT);
    else ... do default behavior ...
}
```

If you return anything other than 0, the value you set via SetWindowLongPtr(hdlg, DWLP_MSGRESULT, value) is used as the message result.

(Old-timers might wonder what happened to GetWindowLong and DWL_MSGRESULT. With the introduction of 64-bit Windows, functions like GetWindowLong gained "pointer-sized" counterparts like GetWindowLongPtr, which operate on integer values the same size as a native pointer. Because the return value from a window procedure is a 64-bit value on 64-bit Windows, the name of the window bytes that store the desired return value from a dialog procedure changed from DWL_MSGRESULT to DWLP_MSGRESULT, with the P indicating that the parameter should be used with SetWindowLongPtr rather than

SetWindowLong. If this is too much of a shock to your system, you can ignore the P's for now and make a mental note to learn about 64-bit programming later.)

For example, many WM_NOTIFY notifications allow you to override default behavior by returning TRUE. To prevent a list view label from being edited, you can return TRUE from the LVN_BEGINLABELEDIT notification. If you are doing this from a dialog procedure, however, you have to do this in two steps:

```
SetWindowLongPtr(hdlg, DWLP_MSGRESULT, TRUE);
return TRUE;
```

The second line sets the return value for the dialog procedure, which tells DefDlgProc that the message has been handled and default handling should be suppressed. The first line tells DefDlgProc what value to return back to the sender of the message (the listview control). If you forget either of these steps, the desired value will not reach the listview control.

Notice that DefDlgProc sets the DWLP_MSGRESULT to zero before sending the message. That way, if the dialog procedure neglects to set a message result explicitly, the result will be zero.

This also highlights the importance of calling SetWindowLongPtr *immediately* before returning from the dialog procedure and no sooner. If you do anything between setting the return value and returning TRUE, that may trigger a message to be sent to the dialog procedure, which would set the message result back to zero.

Caution: A small number of "special messages" do not follow this rule. The list is given in the documentation for DialogProc in MSDN. Why do these exceptions exist? Because when the dialog manager was first designed, it was determined that special treatment for these messages would make dialog box procedures easier to write, because you wouldn't have to go through the extra step of setting the DWLP_MSGRESULT. Fortunately, since those original days, nobody has added any new exceptions. The added mental complexity of remembering the exceptions outweighs the mental savings of not having to write SetWindowLongPtr.

A different type of dialog procedure

But what if you prefer the window procedure design for your dialog procedure, where you just call DefDlgProc to do default actions rather than returning TRUE/FALSE? (Some people prefer this model because it makes dialog procedures and window procedures more similar.)

Well, let's do that. In fact, we're going to do it twice in completely different ways. Each method consists of a simple kernel of an idea; the rest is just scaffolding to make that idea work.

The first way uses a recursive call from the dialog procedure back into DefDlgProc to make DefDlgProc perform the default behavior. This technique requires that you have a flag that lets you detect (and therefore break) the recursion. Because you typically have data attached to your dialog box anyway, it's not too hard to add another member to it.

The key idea is to detect that this recursive call is taking place and break the recursion. DefDlgProc calls your dialog procedure to see what you want to do. When you want to do the default action, just call DefDlgProc recursively. The inner DefDlgProc calls your dialog procedure to see whether you want to override the default action. Detect this recursive call and return FALSE ("do the default"). The recursive DefDlgProc then performs the default action and returns its result. Now you have the result of the default action, and you can modify it or augment it before returning that as the result for the dialog box procedure, back to the outer DefDlgProc, which returns that value back as the final message result.

Here's the flow diagram, for those who prefer pictures:

```
Message delivered
-> DefDlgProc
   -> your dialog procedure
      decide what to do
      want to do the default action
      -> DefDlgProc
         -> your dialog procedure
            detect recursion
         <- return FALSE
         DefDlgProc sees FALSE
         performs default behavior
```

```
   <- returns result of default behavior
   you do other stuff (perhaps modify
   default behavior after it occurred)
   set DWLP_MSGRESULT to desired result
<- return TRUE
retrieve DWLP_MSGRESULT
<- return it as message result
```

Given this sketch, you should be able to write it up yourself. Here's what I came up with. I call it a Wndproc-like dialog:

```
class WLDialogBox
{
public:
  virtual LRESULT WLDlgProc(HWND hdlg, UINT uMsg,
                            WPARAM wParam, LPARAM lParam)
  {
    return DefDlgProcEx(hdlg, uMsg, wParam, lParam,
                        &m_fRecursing);
  }

  INT_PTR DoModal(HINSTANCE hinst, LPCTSTR pszTemplate,
                  HWND hwndParent)
  {
    m_fRecursing = FALSE;
    return DialogBoxParam(hinst, pszTemplate, hwndParent,
                          s_DlgProc, (LPARAM)this);
  }

private:
  static INT_PTR CALLBACK s_DlgProc(HWND hdlg, UINT uMsg,
                                    WPARAM wParam, LPARAM lParam)
  {
    if (uMsg == WM_INITDIALOG) {
      SetWindowLongPtr(hdlg, DWLP_USER, lParam);
    }

    WLDialogBox *self =
            (WLDialogBox*)GetWindowLongPtr(hdlg, DWLP_USER);
    if (!self) {
      return FALSE;
    }

    CheckDefDlgRecursion(&self->m_fRecursing);

    return SetDlgMsgResult(hdlg, uMsg,
             self->WLDlgProc(hdlg, uMsg, wParam, lParam));
```

```
    }
private:
    BOOL m_fRecursing;
};
```

Let's walk through this class.

The WLDlgProc method is virtual because we expect derived classes to do custom actions in their dialog procedure that we invoke from our s_DlgProc. The default implementation in the base class uses the DefDlgProcEx macro from windowsx.h to do the dirty work. That's right; this technique has been published by Microsoft since 1992. If you look at DefDlgProcEx, it sets the recursion flag to TRUE and then calls DefDlgProc, which triggers the recursive call.

I could have had a separate WLDefDlgProc method that calls DefDlgProcEx and have WLDlgProc call WLDefDlgProc. (In fact, my first version did exactly that.) But I decided against this design because people would be tempted to call WLDefDlgProc from their WLDlgProc instead of forwarding to the WLDlgProc of their base class. Instead, the design is simply to forward unhandled messages to the base class's implementation of WLDlgProc.

The s_DlgProc method is the dialog procedure used for all instances of Wndproc-like dialogs. It initializes itself in the WM_INITDIALOG message so that future messages can identify which instance of the dialog is handling the message. After short-circuiting messages that arrive before the dialog box has initialized, it uses the CheckDefDlgRecursion macro, also from windowsx.h. This macro checks the recursion flag; if set, it resets the flag and just returns FALSE immediately. This is what stops the recursion. Otherwise, it calls the WLDlgProc method (which has probably been overriden in a derived class), and then sets the dialog procedure return value and returns.

The SetDlgMsgResult macro also comes from windowsx.h: It stores the return value into the DWLP_MSGRESULT and returns TRUE. Well, unless the message is one of the special exceptions, in which case it returns the value directly. Note to 64-bit developers: There is a bug in this macro as currently written. The expression (BOOL)(result) should be changed to

(INT_PTR)(result) so that the upper 32 bits of the return value are not truncated.

The last method is DoModal, which initializes the recursion flag and kicks off the dialog box.

Here's a sample program that illustrates the use of this class:

```
class SampleWLDlg : public WLDialogBox
{
  LRESULT WLDlgProc(HWND hdlg, UINT uMsg,
                    WPARAM wParam, LPARAM lParam)
  {
    switch (uMsg) {
    HANDLE_MSG(hdlg, WM_COMMAND, OnCommand);
    HANDLE_MSG(hdlg, WM_SETCURSOR, OnSetCursor);
    }
    return __super::WLDlgProc(hdlg, uMsg, wParam, lParam);
  };

  void OnCommand(HWND hdlg, int id,
                 HWND hwndCtl, UINT codeNotify)
  {
    switch (id) {
    case IDCANCEL:
      MessageBox(hdlg, TEXT("Bye"), TEXT("Title"), MB_OK);
      EndDialog(hdlg, 1);
      break;
    }
  }

  BOOL OnSetCursor(HWND hdlg, HWND hwndCursor,
                   UINT codeHitTest, UINT msg)
  {
    if (codeHitTest == HTCAPTION) {
      SetCursor(LoadCursor(NULL, IDC_SIZEALL));
      return TRUE;
    }
    return FORWARD_WM_SETCURSOR(hdlg, hwndCursor,
                  codeHitTest, msg, __super::WLDlgProc);
  }
};

int WINAPI WinMain(HINSTANCE hinst, HINSTANCE hinstPrev,
                   LPSTR lpCmdLine, int nShowCmd)
{
    SampleWLDlg dlg;
```

```
    dlg.DoModal(hinst, MAKEINTRESOURCE(1), NULL);
    return 0;
}
```

```
1 DIALOGEX DISCARDABLE  0, 0, 200,200
STYLE DS_SHELLFONT | WS_POPUP | WS_VISIBLE |
      WS_CAPTION | WS_SYSMENU
CAPTION "sample"
FONT 8, "MS Shell Dlg"
BEGIN
DEFPUSHBUTTON "&Bye",IDCANCEL,"Button",WS_TABSTOP,7,4,50,14
END
```

To illustrate a custom return value, I override the WM_SETCURSOR message to display a custom cursor when the mouse is over the caption area. It's not exciting, but it gets the point across.

Observe that in two places, we forwarded the message to our base class by calling __super::WLDlgProc. The __super keyword is a Visual C++ extension that resolves to the base class of your derived class. This is quite handy because it saves the reader the trouble of figuring out "So which level in the class hierarchy are we forwarding this call to?" If you wanted to forward a call to your grandparent class, you would use this:

__super::__super:: WLDlgProc.

If your compiler doesn't support __super, you can fake it by adding this line to the definition of SampleWLDlg

typedef WLDialogBox super;

and using super::WLDlgProc without the underscores. In fact, this is the technique I use because I was doing it before the Visual C++ folks added the __super keyword and now it's just habit.

As written, the m_fRecursing member is an instance member. Does it need to be? Can it be global? What is the weakest condition you can place on m_fRecursing?

The m_fRecursing flag does not need to be per instance. It only needs to be valid long enough that the recursive call that comes immediately afterward can be detected. However, a global variable would not work because two threads might be inside the recursive DefDlgProc call simultaneously. But a thread-local variable would work.

Another different type of dialog procedure

The other method of using a window-procedure-like dialog box is to change the rules of the game. Normally, the window procedure for a dialog box is the DefDlgProc function, which calls the dialog procedure and then takes action if the dialog procedure indicated that it desired the default action to take place.

The dialog procedure is subservient to DefDlgProc, providing advice when requested. The kernel of the idea for this technique is to "turn the tables." Make DefDlgProc be the one who gives advice and you be the one that asks for the advice when you want it.

We do this by making the window procedure be our own function which decides whether it wants the default action to happen. If so, it calls DefDlgProc to do it, after giving the dialog a dummy dialog procedure that always says "Just do the default."

Here's the flow diagram:

```
Message delivered
-> WLWndProc
    -> your WLDlgProc
       decide what to do
       want to do the default action
       -> DefDlgProc
           -> dummy dialog procedure
           <- always returns FALSE
           DefDlgProc does default action
       <- returns result of default behavior
       you do other stuff (perhaps modify
       default behavior after it occurred)
    <- returns result
<- returns result
```

To do this, we need to register a custom dialog class. You always wondered what that was for. Now you know.

```
BOOL
InitApp(void)
{
  WNDCLASS wc;

  wc.style = CS_DBLCLKS | CS_SAVEBITS | CS_BYTEALIGNWINDOW;
  wc.lpfnWndProc = WLWndProc;
  wc.cbClsExtra = 0;
  wc.cbWndExtra = DLGWINDOWEXTRA + sizeof(WLDLGPROC);
  wc.hInstance = g_hinst;
  wc.hIcon = NULL;
  wc.hCursor = LoadCursor(NULL, IDC_ARROW);
  wc.hbrBackground = NULL;
  wc.lpszMenuName = NULL;
  wc.lpszClassName = TEXT("WLDialog");

  if (!RegisterClass(&wc)) return FALSE;

  return TRUE;
}
```

This creates a new window class called WLDialog, which we will use as our custom dialog class. When you create a custom dialog class, you must set the cbWndExtra to DLGWINDOWEXTRA bytes, plus any additional bytes you want to use for yourself. We need to store an extra WLDLGPROC, so we add that in.

To use our custom dialog procedure, the dialog template must use the CLASS keyword to specify the custom dialog class:

```
1 DIALOGEX DISCARDABLE  0, 0, 200,200
STYLE DS_SHELLFONT | WS_POPUP | WS_VISIBLE |
      WS_CAPTION | WS_SYSMENU
CLASS "WLDialog"
CAPTION "sample"
FONT 8, "MS Shell Dlg"
BEGIN
    DEFPUSHBUTTON "&Bye", IDCANCEL, 7,4,50,14, WS_TABSTOP
END
```

This is exactly the same as a regular dialog box template, except that there is a CLASS entry that specifies that this dialog box should use our new class. Paralleling the `DialogBoxParam` function we have our own:

```
typedef LRESULT (CALLBACK* WLDLGPROC)(HWND, UINT, WPARAM, LPARAM);

struct WLDIALOGINFO {
  WLDLGPROC wldp;
  LPARAM lParam;
};

INT_PTR
WLDialogBoxParam(HINSTANCE hinst, LPCTSTR pszTemplate,
  HWND hwndParent, WLDLGPROC wldp, LPARAM lParam)
{
  WLDIALOGINFO wldi = { wldp, lParam };
  return DialogBoxParam(hinst, pszTemplate,
          hwndParent, WLDlgProc, (LPARAM)&wldi);
}
```

This packages up the WndProc-like dialog procedure and its reference data so that we can recover it in our window procedure:

```
LRESULT CALLBACK
WLWndProc(HWND hdlg, UINT uiMsg, WPARAM wParam, LPARAM lParam)
{
  if (uiMsg == WM_INITDIALOG) {
    WLDIALOGINFO *pwldi = (WLDIALOGINFO*)lParam;
    SetWindowLongPtr(hdlg, DLGWINDOWEXTRA,
                     (LONG_PTR)pwldi->wldp);
    lParam = pwldi->lParam;
  }
  WLDLGPROC wldp = (WLDLGPROC)GetWindowLongPtr(hdlg,
                                               DLGWINDOWEXTRA);
  if (wldp) {
    return wldp(hdlg, uiMsg, wParam, lParam);
  } else {
    return DefDlgProc(hdlg, uiMsg, wParam, lParam);
  }
}
```

This is the window procedure for the custom dialog. When the WM_INITDIALOG message comes in, we recover the original parameters to WLDialogBoxParam. The WLDLGPROC we save in the extra bytes we reserved, and the original LPARAM becomes the lParam that we pass to the WLDLGPROC. Then for each message that comes in, we pass the message and its parameters directly to the WLDLGPROC and return the value directly. No DWLP_MSGRESULT necessary.

The last piece of the puzzle is the dialog procedure we actually hand to the dialog manager:

```
INT_PTR CALLBACK
WLDlgProc(HWND hdlg, UINT uiMsg, WPARAM wParam, LPARAM lParam)
{
  return FALSE;
}
```

All it says is, "Do the default thing."

Okay, so let's write yet another version of our sample program, using this new architecture:

```
LRESULT CALLBACK SampleWLDialogProc(
HWND hdlg, UINT uiMsg, WPARAM wParam, LPARAM lParam)
{
  switch (uiMsg) {
  case WM_INITDIALOG:
    break;

  case WM_COMMAND:
    switch (GET_WM_COMMAND_ID(wParam, lParam)) {
    case IDCANCEL:
      MessageBox(hdlg, TEXT("Bye"), TEXT("Title"), MB_OK);
      EndDialog(hdlg, 1);
      break;
    }
    break;

  case WM_SETCURSOR:
    if (LOWORD(lParam) == HTCAPTION) {
      SetCursor(LoadCursor(NULL, IDC_SIZEALL));
      return TRUE;
    }
    break;
  }

  return DefDlgProc(hdlg, uiMsg, wParam, lParam);
}
```

```
int WINAPI WinMain(HINSTANCE hinst, HINSTANCE hinstPrev,
                   LPSTR lpCmdLine, int nShowCmd)
{
  InitApp();
  WLDialogBoxParam(hinst, MAKEINTRESOURCE(1),
                   NULL, SampleWLDialogProc, 0);
  return 0;
}
```

In this style of WndProc-like dialog, we just write our dialog procedure as if it were a window procedure, calling `DefDlgProc()` to perform default behavior. And to get this new behavior, we use `WLDialogBoxParam` rather than `DialogBoxParam`.

Now I've developed two quite different ways you can write WndProc-like dialog procedures. You might not like either one of them, so go ahead and write a third way if you prefer. But at least I hope you learned a little more about how `DefDlgProc` works.

🙑

The evolution of dialog templates

IN THE HISTORY of Windows, there have been four versions of dialog templates. And despite the changes, you'll see that they're basically all the same.

My secret goal in this chapter is to address questions people have had along the lines of "I'm trying to generate a dialog template in code, and it's not working. What am I doing wrong?"

As it turns out, you can get the resource compiler to tell you what you're doing wrong. Take the template that you're trying to generate, create an *.rc file for it and run it through the resource compiler. Attach the resource to a dummy program and dump the bytes! Compare the compiler-generated template against the one you generated. Look for the difference.

In other words: To see what you're doing wrong, take somebody who does it right and compare. Clearly there's a difference somewhere. It's just bytes.

Anyway, enough of the rant against laziness. The next several pages cover the evolution of the dialog template, with annotated byte dumps for people who are trying to figure out why their dialog template isn't working. We trace the evolution of dialog templates from the original 16-bit classic template to the two types of modern 32-bit templates, both of which you need to be familiar with if you intend to generate or parse dialog templates on your own. (The 16-bit templates, by comparison, are merely of historical interest.) The discussion does assume that you're familiar with how dialog templates are defined in the Resource Compiler and focuses on how those definitions turn into bytes in a template.

16-bit classic templates

First, there was the classic 16-bit dialog template as originally defined by Windows 1.0. It starts like this:

```
DWORD dwStyle;   // dialog style
BYTE  cItems;    // number of controls in this dialog
WORD  x;         // x-coordinate
WORD  y;         // y-coordinate
WORD  cx;        // width
WORD  cy;        // height
```

Notice that this is where the 255-controls-per-dialog limit comes from on 16-bit Windows, because the field that records the number of controls on the dialog is only a byte.

After this header comes a series of strings. All strings in the 16-bit dialog template permit a null-terminated ANSI string. For example, if you want to store the string "Hello", you write out the six bytes

```
48 65 6C 6C 6F 00   ; "Hello"
```

(As a special case of this: If you write out a single 00 byte, that represents a null string—handy when you don't actually want to store a string but the dialog format requires you to store one.)

Sometimes you are allowed to specify a 16-bit ordinal value rather than a string. In that case, you write out the byte `0xFF` followed by the ordinal. For example, if you want to specify the ordinal 42, you write out the three bytes

```
FF 2A 00            ; FF followed by WORD (little-endian)
```

Okay, back to the dialog template. After the header, there are three strings:

- The menu name, which can be a string or an ordinal. This is typically null, indicating that you don't want a menu. If non-null, the menu is loaded via `LoadMenu` using the specified string or resource from the instance handle passed to the dialog creation function via the `HINSTANCE` parameter.

- The class, which must be a string (no ordinals allowed). This is typically also null, indicating that you want the default dialog class. We saw how you can override the default dialog class if you would like a completely different window procedure for your dialog box. If non-null, the class will be also be looked up relative to the instance handle passed to the dialog creation function via the `HINSTANCE` parameter.

- The dialog title, which must be a string (no ordinals allowed).

If the `DS_SETFONT` style is set, what follows next is a `WORD` indicating the point size and a string specifying the font name. Otherwise, there is no font information.

That's the end of the header section. Next come a series of dialog item templates, one for each control. Each item template begins the same way:

```
WORD   x;        // x-coordinate (DLUs)
WORD   y;        // y-coordinate (DLUs)
WORD   cx;       // width (DLUs)
WORD   cy;       // height (DLUs)
WORD   wID;      // control ID
DWORD  dwStyle;  // window style
```

Recall that the dialog coordinates are recorded in dialog units (DLUs). Four x-DLUs and eight y-DLUs equal one "average" character.

After the fixed start of the item template comes the class name, either as a null-terminated ANSI string or (and this is particularly weird) as a single byte in the range 0x80 through 0xFF, which encodes one of the "standard" window classes:

0x80	"button"
0x81	"edit"
0x82	"static"
0x83	"listbox"
0x84	"scrollbar"
0x85	"combobox"

(Note that this encoding means that the first character of a window class name cannot be an extended character if you want to use it in a dialog template!)

After the class name comes the control text, either as a null-terminated string or as an ordinal. If you use an ordinal, the lpszName member of the CREATESTRUCT is a pointer to the three-byte ordinal sequence (0xFF followed by the ordinal); otherwise, it's a pointer to the string. The only control I know of that knows what to do with the ordinal is the static control if you put it into one of the image modes (SS_ICON or SS_BITMAP), in which case the ordinal is a resource identifier for the image that the static control displays.

After the control text comes up to 256 bytes of "extra data" in the form of a byte count, followed by the actual data. If there is no extra data, use a byte count of zero.

When the dialog manager creates a control, it passes a pointer to the extra data as the final LPVOID parameter to the CreateWindowEx function. (As far as I can tell, there is no way to tell the resource compiler to insert this extra data. It's one of those lurking features that nobody has taken advantage of yet.)

Okay, that's all great and theoretical. But sometimes you just need to see it in front of you to understand it. So let's take apart an actual 16-bit dialog resource. I took this one from COMMCTRL.DLL; it's the search/replace dialog:

```
0000   C0 00 C8 80 0B 24 00 2C-00 E6 00 5E 00 00 00 52   .....$.,...^...R
0010   65 70 6C 61 63 65 00 08-00 48 65 6C 76 00 04 00   eplace...Helv...
0020   09 00 30 00 08 00 FF FF-00 00 00 50 82 46 69 26   ..0........P.Fi&
```

```
0030  6E 64 20 57 68 61 74 3A-00 00 36 00 07 00 72 00   nd What:..6...r.
0040  0C 00 80 04 80 00 83 50-81 00 00 04 00 1A 00 30   .......P.......0
0050  00 08 00 FF FF 00 00 00-50 82 52 65 26 70 6C 61   ........P.Re&pla
0060  63 65 20 57 69 74 68 3A-00 00 36 00 18 00 72 00   ce With:..6...r.
0070  0C 00 81 04 80 00 83 50-81 00 00 05 00 2E 00 68   .......P......h
0080  00 0C 00 10 04 03 00 03-50 80 4D 61 74 63 68 20   ........P.Match
0090  26 57 68 6F 6C 65 20 57-6F 72 64 20 4F 6E 6C 79   &Whole Word Only
00A0  00 00 05 00 3E 00 3B 00-0C 00 11 04 03 00 01 50   ....>.;........P
00B0  80 4D 61 74 63 68 20 26-43 61 73 65 00 00 AE 00   .Match &Case....
00C0  04 00 32 00 0E 00 01 00-01 00 03 50 80 26 46 69   ..2........P.&Fi
00D0  6E 64 20 4E 65 78 74 00-00 AE 00 15 00 32 00 0E   nd Next......2..
00E0  00 00 04 00 00 03 50 80-26 52 65 70 6C 61 63 65   ......P.&Replace
00F0  00 00 AE 00 26 00 32 00-0E 00 01 04 00 00 03 50   ....&.2........P
0100  80 52 65 70 6C 61 63 65-20 26 41 6C 6C 00 00 AE   .Replace &All...
0110  00 37 00 32 00 0E 00 02-00 00 00 03 50 80 43 61   .7.2........P.Ca
0120  6E 63 65 6C 00 00 AE 00-4B 00 32 00 0E 00 0E 04   ncel....K.2.....
0130  00 00 03 50 80 26 48 65-6C 70 00 00                ...P.&Help..
```

Let's start with the header:

```
0000  C0 00 C8 80   // dwStyle
0004  0B            // cItems
0005  24 00 2C 00   // x, y
0009  E6 00 5E 00   // cx, cy
```

In other words, the header says this:

dwStyle	= 0x80C800C0	= WS_POPUP | WS_CAPTION | WS_SYSMENU |
		DS_SETFONT | DS_MODALFRAME
cItems	= 0x0B	= 11
x	= 0x0024	= 36
y	= 0x002C	= 44
cx	= 0x00E6	= 230
cy	= 0x005E	= 94

After the header come the menu name, class name, and dialog title:

```
000D  00                        // no menu
000E  00                        // default dialog class
000F  52 65 70 6C 61 63 65 00   // "Replace"
```

Now, because the DS_SETFONT bit is set in the style, the next section describes the font to be used by the dialog:

```
0017  08 00            // wSize = 8
0019  48 65 6C 76 00   // "Helv"
```

Aha, this dialog box uses 8pt Helv. Next come the 11 dialog item templates:

```
001E   04 00 09 00      // x, y
0022   30 00 08 00      // cx, cy
0026   FF FF            // wID
0028   00 00 00 50      // dwStyle
```

So this dialog item template says this:

x	= 0x0004	= 4	
y	= 0x0009	= 9	
cx	= 0x0030	= 48	
cy	= 0x0008	= 8	
wID	= 0xFFFF	= -1	
dwStyle	= 0x50000000	= WS_CHILD | WS_VISIBLE | SS_LEFT	

How did I know that the style value 0x0000 should be interpreted as SS_LEFT and not, say, BS_PUSHBUTTON? Because the window class tells me that what I have is a static control and therefore that the low word should be treated as a combination of SS_* values:

```
002C   82               // "static"
```

After the class name comes the control text:

```
002D   46 69 26 6E 64 20 57 68 61 74 3A 00 // "Fi&nd What:"
```

And finally (for this dialog item template), we specify that we have no extra data:

```
0039   00               // no extra data
```

Now we repeat the preceding exercise for the other ten controls. I'll just summarize here:

```
// Second control
003A   36 00 07 00      // x, y
003E   72 00 0C 00      // cx, cy
0042   80 04            // wID
0044   80 00 83 50      // dwStyle
0048   81               // "edit"
0049   00               // ""
004A   00               // no extra data
```

```
// Third control
004B    04 00 1A 00      // x, y
004F    30 00 08 00      // cx, cy
0053    FF FF            // wID
0055    00 00 00 50      // dwStyle
0059    82               // "static"
005A    52 65 26 70 6C 61 63 65 20 57 69 74 68 3A 00
                         // "Re&place With:"
0069    00               // no extra data

// Fourth control
006A    36 00 18 00      // x, y
006E    72 00 0C 00      // cx, cy
0072    81 04            // wID
0074    80 00 83 50      // dwStyle
0078    81               // "edit"
0079    00               // ""
007A    00               // no extra data

// Fifth control
007B    05 00 2E 00      // x, y
007F    68 00 0C 00      // cx, cy
0083    10 04            // wID
0085    03 00 03 50      // dwStyle
0089    80               // "button"
008A    4D 61 74 63 68 20 26 57 68 6F 6C 65 20 57
        6F 72 64 20 4F 6E 6C 79 00
                         // "Match &Whole Word Only"
00A1    00               // no extra data

// Sixth control
00A2    05 00 3E 00      // x, y
00A6    3B 00 0C 00      // cx, cy
00AA    11 04            // wID
00AC    03 00 01 50      // dwStyle
00B0    80               // "button"
00B1    4D 61 74 63 68 20 26 43 61 73 65 00
                         // "Match &Case"
00BD    00               // no extra data

// Seventh control
00BE    AE 00 04 00      // x, y
00C2    32 00 0E 00      // cx, cy
00C6    01 00            // wID
00C8    01 00 03 50      // dwStyle
00CC    80               // "button"
```

```
00CD    26 46 69 6E 64 20 4E 65 78 74 00
                        // "&Find Next"
00D8    00              // no extra data

// Eighth control
00D9    AE 00 15 00     // x, y
00DD    32 00 0E 00     // cx, cy
00E1    00 04           // wID
00E3    00 00 03 50     // dwStyle
00E7    80              // "button"
00E8    26 52 65 70 6C 61 63 65 00
                        // "&Replace"
00F1    00              // no extra data

// Ninth control
00F2    AE 00 26 00     // x, y
00F6    32 00 0E 00     // cx, cy
00FA    01 04           // wID
00FC    00 00 03 50     // dwStyle
0100    80              // "button"
0101    52 65 70 6C 61 63 65 20 26 41 6C 6C 00
                        // "Replace &All"
010E    00              // no extra data

// Tenth control
010F    AE 00 37 00     // x, y
0113    32 00 0E 00     // cx, cy
0117    02 00           // wID
0119    00 00 03 50     // dwStyle
011D    80              // "button"
011E    43 61 6E 63 65 6C 00
                        // "Cancel"
0125    00              // no extra data

// Eleventh control
0126    AE 00 4B 00     // x, y
012A    32 00 0E 00     // cx, cy
012E    0E 04           // wID
0130    00 00 03 50     // dwStyle
0134    80              // "button"
0135    26 48 65 6C 70 00
                        // "&Help"
013B    00              // no extra data
```

And that's the dialog template. We can now reconstruct the resource compiler source code from this template:

```
DIALOG 36, 44, 230, 94
STYLE WS_POPUP | WS_CAPTION | WS_SYSMENU |
     DS_MODALFRAME | NOT WS_VISIBLE
CAPTION "Replace"
FONT 8, "Helv"
BEGIN
    CONTROL "Fi&nd What:", -1, "static", SS_LEFT,
            4, 9, 48, 8

    CONTROL "", 0x0480, "edit",
            WS_BORDER | WS_GROUP | WS_TABSTOP | ES_AUTOHSCROLL,
            54, 7, 114, 12

    CONTROL "Re&place With:", -1, "static", SS_LEFT,
            4, 26, 48, 8

    CONTROL "", 0x0481, "edit",
            WS_BORDER | WS_GROUP | WS_TABSTOP | ES_AUTOHSCROLL,
            54, 24, 114, 12

    CONTROL "Match &Whole Word Only", 0x0410, "button",
            WS_GROUP | WS_TABSTOP | BS_AUTOCHECKBOX,
            5, 46, 104, 12

    CONTROL "Match &Case", 0x0411, "button",
            WS_TABSTOP | BS_AUTOCHECKBOX,
            5, 62, 59, 12

    CONTROL "&Find Next", IDOK, "button",
            WS_GROUP | WS_TABSTOP | BS_DEFPUSHBUTTON,
            174, 4, 50, 14

    CONTROL "&Replace", 0x0400, "button",
            WS_GROUP | WS_TABSTOP | BS_PUSHBUTTON,
            174, 21, 50, 14

    CONTROL "Replace &All", 0x0401, "button",
            WS_GROUP | WS_TABSTOP | BS_PUSHBUTTON,
            174, 38, 50, 14

    CONTROL "Cancel", IDCANCEL, "button",
            WS_GROUP | WS_TABSTOP | BS_PUSHBUTTON,
            174, 55, 50, 14

    CONTROL "Cancel", 0x040E, "button",
            WS_GROUP | WS_TABSTOP | BS_PUSHBUTTON,
            174, 75, 50, 14
END
```

Notice that we didn't explicitly say DS_SETFONT in the dialog's STYLE directive because that is implied by the FONT directive. And because WS_VISIBLE is on by default, we didn't have to say it; instead, we had to explicitly refute it in the places it wasn't wanted.

Now if you take a look in the Windows header files, you'll find dlgs.h and findtext.dlg which pretty much match up with the preceding template, giving names to the magic values like 0x0400 and positioning the controls in the same place as earlier. You'll find some minor differences, however, because the Windows header files are for the 32-bit Find/Replace dialog and the one here is the 16-bit Find/Replace dialog, but you'll see that it still matches up pretty well.

32-bit classic templates

We take the next step in the evolution of dialog templates and look at the 32-bit classic dialog template.

There really isn't much going on. Some 8-bit fields got expanded to 16-bit fields, some 16-bit fields got expanded to 32-bit fields, extended styles were added, and all strings got changed from ANSI to Unicode.

The template starts like this:

```
DWORD dwStyle;    // dialog style
DWORD dwExStyle;  // extended dialog style
WORD  cItems;     // number of controls in this dialog
WORD  x;          // x-coordinate
WORD  y;          // y-coordinate
WORD  cx;         // width
WORD  cy;         // height
```

This is basically the same as the 16-bit dialog template, except that there's a new dwExStyle field, and the cItems went from a BYTE to a WORD. Consequently, the maximum number of controls per 32-bit dialog is 65535. That should be enough for a while.

After this header come a series of strings, just like in 16-bit dialog templates. But this time, the strings are Unicode. For example, if you want to store the string "Hello", you write out the 12 bytes:

```
48 00 65 00 6C 00 6C 00 6F 00 00 00 ; "Hello"
```

As with the 16-bit case, in the 32-bit dialog template, you can often specify an ordinal rather than a string. Here, it's done by writing the bytes `FF 00` followed by the 16-bit ordinal (in little-endian format). For example, if you want to specify the ordinal 42, you write out the four bytes:

```
FF 00 2A 00        ; 00FF followed by WORD (little-endian)
```

The three strings are the same as last time:

- The menu name, which can be a string or an ordinal
- The class, which must be a string (no ordinals allowed)
- The dialog title, which must be a string (no ordinals allowed)

If the `DS_SETFONT` style is set, what follows next is a `WORD` indicating the point size and a string specifying the font name. Otherwise, there is no font information (same as in the 16-bit dialog template).

So far, everything has been `WORD`-aligned.

After the header comes a series of dialog item templates. Each item template begins on a `DWORD` boundary, inserting padding if required to achieve this. The padding is necessary to ensure that processors that are sensitive to alignment can access the memory without raising an exception:

```
DWORD dwStyle;     // window style
DWORD dwExStyle;   // window extended style
WORD  x;           // x-coordinate (DLUs)
WORD  y;           // y-coordinate (DLUs)
WORD  cx;          // width (DLUs)
WORD  cy;          // height (DLUs)
WORD  wID;         // control ID
```

As before, the dialog coordinates are recorded in dialog units (DLUs).

Next comes the class name, either as a null-terminated Unicode string, as an integer atom (which is of not much use in practice), or as an ordinal. A class name is encoded as a null-terminated Unicode string. An integer atom is encoded as the word `0x00FF` followed by the word integer atom. An ordinal is encoded as `0xFFFF` followed by a word specifying the ordinal code of one of the six "standard" window classes, which are the same as for 16-bit dialog templates:

0x0080	"button"
0x0081	"edit"
0x0082	"static"
0x0083	"listbox"
0x0084	"scrollbar"
0x0085	"combobox"

After the class name comes the control text, either as a null-terminated string or as an ordinal, following the same rules as for the 16-bit template. Extra weirdness: To specify an ordinal here, use FFFF rather than 00FF as the ordinal marker. I don't know why.

After the control text come up to 65535 bytes of "extra data" in the form of a 16-bit count, followed by the actual data. If there is no extra data, use a count of zero.

And that's all there is. As with last time, I'll present an annotated dialog template:

```
0000   C4 20 C8 80 00 00 00 00-0B 00 24 00 2C 00 E6 00   . ........$.,...
0010   5E 00 00 00 00 00 52 00-65 00 70 00 6C 00 61 00   ^.....R.e.p.l.a.
0020   63 00 65 00 00 00 08 00-4D 00 53 00 20 00 53 00   c.e.....M.S. .S.
0030   68 00 65 00 6C 00 6C 00-20 00 44 00 6C 00 67 00   h.e.l.l. .D.l.g.
0040   00 00 00 00 00 00 02 50-00 00 00 00 04 00 09 00   .......P........
0050   30 00 08 00 FF FF FF FF-82 00 46 00 69 00 26 00   0.........F.i.&.
0060   6E 00 64 00 20 00 77 00-68 00 61 00 74 00 3A 00   n.d. .w.h.a.t.:.
0070   00 00 00 00 80 00 83 50-00 00 00 00 36 00 07 00   .......P....6...
0080   72 00 0C 00 80 04 FF FF-81 00 00 00 00 00 00 00   r...............
0090   00 00 02 50 00 00 00 00-04 00 1A 00 30 00 08 00   ...P........0...
00A0   FF FF FF FF 82 00 52 00-65 00 26 00 70 00 6C 00   ......R.e.&.p.l.
00B0   61 00 63 00 65 00 20 00-77 00 69 00 74 00 68 00   a.c.e. .w.i.t.h.
00C0   3A 00 00 00 00 00 00 00-80 00 83 50 00 00 00 00   :..........P....
00D0   36 00 18 00 72 00 0C 00-81 04 FF FF 81 00 00 00   6...r...........
00E0   00 00 00 00 03 00 03 50-00 00 00 00 05 00 2E 00   .......P........
00F0   68 00 0C 00 10 04 FF FF-80 00 4D 00 61 00 74 00   h.........M.a.t.
0100   63 00 68 00 20 00 26 00-77 00 68 00 6F 00 6C 00   c.h. .&.w.h.o.l.
0110   65 00 20 00 77 00 6F 00-72 00 64 00 20 00 6F 00   e. .w.o.r.d. .o.
0120   6E 00 6C 00 79 00 00 00-00 00 00 00 03 00 01 50   n.l.y..........P
0130   00 00 00 00 05 00 3E 00-3B 00 0C 00 11 04 FF FF   ......>.;.......
0140   80 00 4D 00 61 00 74 00-63 00 68 00 20 00 26 00   ..M.a.t.c.h. .&.
0150   63 00 61 00 73 00 65 00-00 00 00 00 01 00 03 50   c.a.s.e........P
```

```
0160  00 00 00 00 AE 00 04 00-32 00 0E 00 01 00 FF FF  ........2.......
0170  80 00 26 00 46 00 69 00-6E 00 64 00 20 00 4E 00  ..&.F.i.n.d. .N.
0180  65 00 78 00 74 00 00 00-00 00 00 00 00 00 01 50  e.x.t..........P
0190  00 00 00 00 AE 00 15 00-32 00 0E 00 00 04 FF FF  ........2.......
01A0  80 00 26 00 52 00 65 00-70 00 6C 00 61 00 63 00  ..&.R.e.p.l.a.c.
01B0  65 00 00 00 00 00 00 00-00 00 01 50 00 00 00 00  e..........P....
01C0  AE 00 26 00 32 00 0E 00-01 04 FF FF 80 00 52 00  ..&.2.........R.
01D0  65 00 70 00 6C 00 61 00-63 00 65 00 20 00 26 00  e.p.l.a.c.e. .&.
01E0  41 00 6C 00 6C 00 00 00-00 00 00 00 00 00 01 50  A.l.l..........P
01F0  00 00 00 00 AE 00 37 00-32 00 0E 00 02 00 FF FF  ......7.2.......
0200  80 00 43 00 61 00 6E 00-63 00 65 00 6C 00 00 00  ..C.a.n.c.e.l...
0210  00 00 00 00 00 00 01 50-00 00 00 00 AE 00 4B 00  .......P......K.
0220  32 00 0E 00 0E 04 FF FF-80 00 26 00 48 00 65 00  2.........&.H.e.
0230  6C 00 70 00 00 00 00 00  l.p.....
```

As before, we start with the header:

```
0000  C4 20 C8 80   // dwStyle
0004  00 00 00 00   // dwExStyle
0008  0B 00         // cItems
000A  24 00 2C 00   // x, y
000E  E6 00 5E 00   // cx, cy
```

In other words, the header says this:

```
dwStyle    = 0x80C820C4  = WS_POPUP | WS_CAPTION | WS_SYSMENU |
                           DS_CONTEXTHELP | DS_SETFONT |
                           DS_MODALFRAME |
                           DS_3DLOOK

dwExStyle = 0x00000000
cItems    = 0x000B      = 11
x         = 0x0024      = 36
y         = 0x002C      = 44
cx        = 0x00E6      = 230
cy        = 0x005E      = 94
```

After the header come the menu name, class name, and dialog title:

```
0012  00 00                         // no menu
0014  00 00                         // default dialog class
0016  52 00 65 00 70 00 6C 00 61 00 63 00
      65 00 00 00                   // "Replace"
```

Again, because the DS_SETFONT bit is set in the style, the next section describes the font to be used by the dialog:

```
0026    08 00                    // wSize = 8
0028    4D 00 53 00 20 00 53 00 68 00 65 00 6C 00
        6C 00 20 00 44 00 6C 00 67 00 00 00
                                 // "MS Shell Dlg"
```

This dialog box uses 8pt MS Shell Dlg as its dialog font.

Next come the 11 dialog item templates. Now remember that each template must be DWORD-aligned, so we need some padding here to get up to a four-byte boundary:

```
0042 00 00              // Padding for alignment
```

Now that we are once again DWORD-aligned, we can read the first dialog item template:

```
0044    00 00 02 50              // dwStyle
0048    00 00 00 00              // dwExStyle
004C    04 00 09 00              // x, y
0050    30 00 08 00              // cx, cy
0054    FF FF                    // wID
0056    FF FF 82 00              // "static"
005A    46 00 69 00 26 00
0060    6E 00 64 00 20 00 77 00-68 00 61 00 74 00 3A 00
0070    00 00                    // "Fi&nd what:"
0072    00 00                    // no extra data
```

Notice here that the "static" class was encoded as an ordinal. The template for this item is therefore as follows:

dwStyle	= 0x50020000	= WS_CHILD | WS_VISIBLE |
		WS_GROUP | SS_LEFT
dwExStyle	= 0x00000000	
x	= 0x0004	= 4
y	= 0x0009	= 9
cx	= 0x0030	= 48
cy	= 0x0008	= 8
wID	= 0xFFFF	= -1
szClass	= ordinal 0x0082	= "static"
szText		= "Fi&nd what:"

The other controls are similarly unexciting:

```
// Second control
0074    80 00 83 50    // dwStyle
0078    00 00 00 00    // dwExStyle
007C    36 00 07 00    // x, y
0080    72 00 0C 00    // cx, cy
0084    80 04          // wID
0086    FF FF 81 00    // "edit"
008A    00 00          // ""
008C    00 00          // no extra data
008E    00 00          // padding to achieve DWORD alignment

// Third control
0090    00 00 02 50    // dwStyle
0094    00 00 00 00    // dwExStyle
0098    04 00 1A 00    // x, y
009C    30 00 08 00    // cx, cy
00A0    FF FF          // wID
00A2    FF FF 82 00    // "static"
00A6    52 00 65 00 26 00 70 00 6C 00
00B0    61 00 63 00 65 00 20 00 77 00 69 00 74 00 68 00
00C0    3A 00 00 00    // "Re&place with:"
00C4    00 00          // no extra data
00C6    00 00          // padding to achieve DWORD alignment

// Fourth control
00C8    80 00 83 50    // dwStyle
00CC    00 00 00 00    // dwExStyle
00D0    36 00 18 00    // x, y
00D4    72 00 0C 00    // cx, cy
00D8    81 04          // wID
00DA    FF FF 81 00    // "edit"
00DE    00 00          // ""
00E0    00 00          // no extra data
00E2    00 00          // padding to achieve DWORD alignment

// Fifth control
00E4    03 00 03 50    // dwStyle
00E8    00 00 00 00    // dwExStyle
00EC    05 00 2E 00    // x, y
00F0    68 00 0C 00    // cx, cy
00F4    10 04          // wID
00F6    FF FF 80 00    // "button"
00FA    4D 00 61 00 74 00
0100    63 00 68 00 20 00 26 00 77 00 68 00 6F 00 6C 00
```

```
0110   65 00 20 00 77 00 6F 00 72 00 64 00 20 00 6F 00
0120   6E 00 6C 00 79 00 00 00
                         // "Match &whole word only"
0128   00 00            // no extra data
012A   00 00            // padding to achieve DWORD alignment

// Sixth control
012C   03 00 01 50      // dwStyle
0130   00 00 00 00      // dwExStyle
0134   05 00 3E 00      // x, y
0138   3B 00 0C 00      // cx, cy
013C   11 04            // wID
013E   FF FF 80 00      // "button"
0142   4D 00 61 00 74 00 63 00 68 00 20 00 26 00
0150   63 00 61 00 73 00 65 00 00 00
                         // "Match &case"
015A   00 00            // no extra data

// Seventh control
015C   01 00 03 50      // dwStyle
0160   00 00 00 00      // dwExStyle
0164   AE 00 04 00      // x, y
0168   32 00 0E 00      // cx, cy
016C   01 00            // wID
016E   FF FF 80 00      // "button"
0172   26 00 46 00 69 00 6E 00 64 00 20 00 4E 00
0180   65 00 78 00 74 00 00 00
                         // "&Find Next"
0188   00 00            // no extra data
018A   00 00            // padding to achieve DWORD alignment

// Eighth control
018C   00 00 01 50      // dwStyle
0190   00 00 00 00      // dwExStyle
0194   AE 00 15 00      // x, y
0198   32 00 0E 00      // cx, cy
019C   00 04            // wID
019E   FF FF 80 00      // "button"
01A2   26 00 52 00 65 00-70 00 6C 00 61 00 63 00
01B0   65 00 00 00      // "&Replace"
01B4   00 00            // no extra data
01B6   00 00            // padding to achieve DWORD alignment

// Ninth control
01B8   00 00 01 50      // dwStyle
01BC   00 00 00 00      // dwExStyle
```

```
01C0    AE 00 26 00       // x, y
01C4    32 00 0E 00       // cx, cy
01C8    01 04             // wID
01CA    FF FF 80 00       // "button"
01CE    52 00
01D0    65 00 70 00 6C 00 61 00 63 00 65 00 20 00 26 00
01E0    41 00 6C 00 6C 00 00 00
                          // "Replace &All"
01E8    00 00             // no extra data
01EA    00 00             // padding to achieve DWORD alignment

// Tenth control
01EC    00 00 01 50       // dwStyle
01F0    00 00 00 00       // dwExStyle
01F4    AE 00 37 00       // x, y
01F8    32 00 0E 00       // cx, cy
01FC    02 00             // wID
01FE    FF FF 80 00       // "button"
0202    43 00 61 00 6E 00 63 00 65 00 6C 00 00 00
                          // "Cancel"
0210    00 00             // no extra data
0212    00 00             // padding to achieve DWORD alignment

// Eleventh control
0214    00 00 01 50       // dwStyle
0218    00 00 00 00       // dwExStyle
021C    AE 00 4B 00       // x, y
0220    32 00 0E 00       // cx, cy
0224    0E 04             // wID
0226    FF FF 80 00       // "button"
022A    26 00 48 00 65 00 6C 00 70 00 00 00
                          // "&Help"
0236    00 00             // no extra data
```

Whew. Tedious and entirely unexciting. Here's the original resource compiler source code that we reverse-engineered:

```
DIALOG 36, 44, 230, 94
STYLE WS_POPUP | WS_CAPTION | WS_SYSMENU |
      DS_MODALFRAME | DS_3DLOOK | NOT WS_VISIBLE
CAPTION "Replace"
FONT 8, "MS Shell Dlg"
BEGIN
      CONTROL "Fi&nd What:", -1, "static", WS_GROUP | SS_LEFT,
              4, 9, 48, 8
```

```
CONTROL "", 0x0480, "edit",
        WS_BORDER | WS_GROUP | WS_TABSTOP | ES_AUTOHSCROLL,
        54, 7, 114, 12

CONTROL "Re&place with:", -1, "static", WS_GROUP | SS_LEFT,
        4, 26, 48, 8

CONTROL "", 0x0481, "edit",
        WS_BORDER | WS_GROUP | WS_TABSTOP | ES_AUTOHSCROLL,
        54, 24, 114, 12

CONTROL "Match &whole word only", 0x0410, "button",
        WS_GROUP | WS_TABSTOP | BS_AUTOCHECKBOX,
        5, 46, 104, 12

CONTROL "Match &case", 0x0411, "button",
        WS_TABSTOP | BS_AUTOCHECKBOX,
        5, 62, 59, 12

CONTROL "&Find Next", IDOK, "button",
        WS_GROUP | WS_TABSTOP | BS_DEFPUSHBUTTON,
        174, 4, 50, 14

CONTROL "&Replace", 0x0400, "button",
        WS_TABSTOP | BS_PUSHBUTTON,
        174, 21, 50, 14

CONTROL "Replace &All", 0x0401, "button",
        WS_TABSTOP | BS_PUSHBUTTON,
        174, 38, 50, 14

CONTROL "Cancel", IDCANCEL, "button",
        WS_TABSTOP | BS_PUSHBUTTON,
        174, 55, 50, 14

CONTROL "Cancel", 0x040E, "button",
        WS_TABSTOP | BS_PUSHBUTTON,
        174, 75, 50, 14
END
```

As before, we didn't explicitly say DS_SETFONT in the dialog's STYLE directive because that is implied by the FONT directive, and we took advantage of the fact that WS_VISIBLE is on by default.

And you probably recognize this dialog. It's the Replace dialog from findtext.dlg. (Although it's not literally the same because the findtext.dlg template uses some shorthand directives such as DEFPUSHBUTTON instead of manually writing out the details of the button control as a CONTROL.)

16-bit extended templates

The next step in the evolution of dialog templates is the extended dialog, or DIALOGEX. First, let's look at the 16-bit version.

The 16-bit extended dialog template is purely historical. The only operating systems to support it were Windows 95 and its successors. It is interesting only as a missing link in the evolution toward the 32-bit extended dialog template.

The basic rules are the same as for the nonextended template. The extended dialog template starts off with a different header:

```
WORD   wDlgVer;      // version number - always 1
WORD   wSignature;   // always 0xFFFF
DWORD  dwHelpID;     // help ID
DWORD  dwExStyle;    // window extended style
DWORD  dwStyle;      // dialog style
BYTE   cItems;       // number of controls in this dialog
WORD   x;            // x-coordinate
WORD   y;            // y-coordinate
WORD   cx;           // width
WORD   cy;           // height
```

The first two fields specify a version number (so far, only version 1 extended dialogs have been defined), and a signature value 0xFFFF that allows this template to be distinguished from a nonextended dialog template.

Next come two new fields. The help identifier is an arbitrary 32-bit value that you can retrieve from the dialog later with the GetWindowContextHelpId function. The extended dialog style you've seen before.

As before, after the header come the strings. First comes the menu, then the class, and then dialog title, all encoded the same way as with the nonextended template.

If the DS_SETFONT style is set, a custom font exists in the template. The format of the font information is slightly different for extended templates.

In classic templates, all you get is a WORD of point size and a font name. But in the extended template, the font information is a little richer:

```
WORD  wPoint;           // point size
WORD  wWeight;          // font weight
BYTE  bItalic;          // 1 if italic, 0 if not
BYTE  bCharSet;         // character set (see CreateFont)
CHAR  szFontName[];     // variable-length
```

New fields are the weight, character set, and whether the font is italic.

After the header come the dialog item templates, each of which looks like this:

```
DWORD  dwHelpID;         // help identifier
DWORD  dwExStyle;        // window extended style
DWORD  dwStyle;          // window style
WORD   x;                // x-coordinate (DLUs)
WORD   y;                // y-coordinate (DLUs)
WORD   cx;               // width (DLUs)
WORD   cy;               // height (DLUs)
DWORD  wID;              // control ID
CHAR   szClassName[];    // variable-length (possibly ordinal)
CHAR   szText[];         // variable-length (possibly ordinal)
WORD   cbExtra;          // amount of extra data
BYTE   rgbExtra[cbExtra]; // extra data follows (usually none)
```

This takes the classic item template and adds the following:

- New dwHelpID and dwExStyle fields
- dwStyle field moved
- Control ID expanded to DWORD
- cbExtra expanded to WORD

Expanding the control ID to a 32-bit value doesn't accomplish much in 16-bit Windows, but it's there nonetheless.

And that's all.

Now the obligatory annotated hex dump:

```
0000   01 00 FF FF 00 00 00 00-00 00 00 00 C4 00 C8 80   ...............^...
0010   0B 24 00 2C 00 E6 00 5E-00 00 00 52 65 70 6C 61   .$.,...^...Repla
0020   63 65 00 08 00 90 01 00-00 4D 53 20 53 68 65 6C   ce.......MS Shel
0030   20 44 6C 67 00 00 00 00-00 00 00 00 00 00 00 02   Dlg.............
0040   50 04 00 09 00 30 00 08-00 FF FF FF FF 82 46 69   P....0........Fi
```

```
0050   26 6E 64 20 77 68 61 74-3A 00 00 00 00 00 00 00    &nd what:.......
0060   00 00 00 00 80 00 83 50-36 00 07 00 72 00 0C 00    .......P6...r...
0070   80 04 00 00 81 00 00 00-00 00 00 00 00 00 00 00    ................
0080   00 00 02 50 04 00 1A 00-30 00 08 00 FF FF FF FF    ...P....0.......
0090   82 52 65 26 70 6C 61 63-65 20 77 69 74 68 3A 00    .Re&place with:.
00A0   00 00 00 00 00 00 00 00-00 00 80 00 83 50 36 00    .............P6.
00B0   18 00 72 00 0C 00 81 04-00 00 81 00 00 00 00 00    ..r.............
00C0   00 00 00 00 00 00 03 00-03 50 05 00 2E 00 68 00    .........P...h.
00D0   0C 00 10 04 00 00 80 4D-61 74 63 68 20 26 77 68    .......Match &wh
00E0   6F 6C 65 20 77 6F 72 64-20 6F 6E 6C 79 00 00 00    ole word only...
00F0   00 00 00 00 00 00 00 00-03 00 01 50 05 00 3E 00    ...........P..>.
0100   3B 00 0C 00 11 04 00 00-80 4D 61 74 63 68 20 26    ;.......Match &
0110   63 61 73 65 00 00 00 00-00 00 00 00 00 00 00 01    case...........
0120   00 03 50 AE 00 04 00 32-00 0E 00 01 00 00 00 80    ..P....2........
0130   26 46 69 6E 64 20 4E 65-78 74 00 00 00 00 00 00    &Find Next......
0140   00 00 00 00 00 00 00 00-03-50 AE 00 15 00 32 00 0E    .......P....2..
0150   00 00 04 00 00 80 26 52-65 70 6C 61 63 65 00 00    ......&Replace..
0160   00 00 00 00 00 00 00 00-00 00 00 03 50 AE 00 26    ...........P..&
0170   00 32 00 0E 00 01 04 00-00 80 52 65 70 6C 61 63    .2........Replac
0180   65 20 26 41 6C 6C 00 00-00 00 00 00 00 00 00 00    e &All..........
0190   00 00 00 03 50 AE 00 37-00 32 00 0E 00 02 00 00    ....P..7.2......
01A0   00 80 43 61 6E 63 65 6C-00 00 00 00 00 00 00 00    ..Cancel........
01B0   00 00 00 00 00 03 50 AE-00 4B 00 32 00 0E 00 0E    ......P..K.2....
01C0   04 00 00 80 26 48 65 6C-70 00 00 00                ....&Help...
```

Again, we start with the header:

```
0000   01 00                  // wVersion
0002   FF FF                  // wSignature
0004   00 00 00 00            // dwHelpID
0008   00 00 00 00            // dwExStyle
000C   C4 00 C8 80            // dwStyle
0010   0B                     // cItems
0011   24 00 2C 00            // x, y
0015   E6 00 5E 00            // cx, cy
```

The header breaks down as follows:

```
wVersion      = 0x0001       = 1
wSignature    = 0xFFFF
dwHelpID      = 0x00000000   = 0
dwExStyle     = 0x00000000   = 0
dwStyle       = 0x80C800C4   = WS_POPUP | WS_CAPTION | WS_SYSMENU |
                               DS_SETFONT | DS_MODALFRAME | DS_3DLOOK
cItems        = 0x0B         = 11
```

```
x              = 0x0024    = 36
y              = 0x002C    = 44
cx             = 0x00E6    = 230
cy             = 0x005E    = 94
```

Next come the menu name, class name, and dialog title:

```
0019  00                       // no menu
001A  00                       // default dialog class
001B  52 65 70 6C 61 63 65 00  // "Replace"
```

Same as the 16-bit classic template.

The presence of DS_SETFONT means that there's font information ahead. This looks slightly different:

```
0023  08 00                    // wSize = 8
0025  90 01                    // wWeight = 0x02BC = 700 = FW_NORMAL
0027  00                       // Italic
0028  00                       // Character set = 0x00 = ANSI_CHARSET
0029  4D 53 20 53 68 65 6C 20 44 6C 67 00
                               // "MS Shell Dlg"
```

Now follow the extended dialog item templates. This should all be old hat by now, so I won't go into detail:

```
// First control
0035  00 00 00 00    // dwHelpID
0039  00 00 00 00    // dwExStyle
003D  00 00 02 50    // dwStyle
0041  04 00 09 00    // x, y
0045  30 00 08 00    // cx, cy
0049  FF FF FF FF    // dwID
004D  82             // szClass = ordinal 0x82 = "static"
004E  46 69 26 6E 64 20 77 68 61 74 3A 00
                     // "Fi&nd what:"
005A  00 00          // no extra data

// Second control
005C  00 00 00 00    // dwHelpID
0060  00 00 00 00    // dwExStyle
0064  80 00 83 50    // dwStyle
0068  36 00 07 00    // x, y
006C  72 00 0C 00    // cx, cy
0070  80 04 00 00    // dwID
```

```
0074    81                  // "edit"
0075    00                  // ""
0076    00 00               // no extra data

// Third control
0078    00 00 00 00         // dwHelpID
007C    00 00 00 00         // dwExStyle
0080    00 00 02 50         // dwStyle
0084    04 00 1A 00         // x, y
0088    30 00 08 00         // cx, cy
008C    FF FF FF FF         // dwID
0090    82                  // "static"
0091    52 65 26 70 6C 61 63 65 20 77 69 74 68 3A 00
                            // "Re&place with:"
00A0    00 00               // no extra data

// Fourth control
00A2    00 00 00 00         // dwHelpID
00A6    00 00 00 00         // dwExStyle
00AA    80 00 83 50         // dwStyle
00AE    36 00 18 00         // x, y
00B2    72 00 0C 00         // cx, cy
00B6    81 04 00 00         // dwID
00BA    81                  // "edit"
00BB    00                  // ""
00BC    00 00               // no extra data

// Fifth control
00BE    00 00 00 00         // dwHelpID
00C2    00 00 00 00         // dwExStyle
00C6    03 00 03 50         // dwStyle
00CA    05 00 2E 00         // x, y
00CE    68 00 0C 00         // cx, cy
00D2    10 04 00 00         // dwID
00D6    80                  // "button"
00D7    4D 61 74 63 68 20 26 77 68 6F 6C 65 20 77
        6F 72 64 20 6F 6E 6C 79 00
                            // "Match &whole word only"
00EE    00 00               // no extra data

// Sixth control
00F0    00 00 00 00         // dwHelpID
00F4    00 00 00 00         // dwExStyle
00F8    03 00 01 50         // dwStyle
00FC    05 00 3E 00         // x, y
0100    3B 00 0C 00         // cx, cy
```

```
0104   11 04 00 00        // dwID
0108   80                 // "button"
0109   4D 61 74 63 68 20 26 63 61 73 65 00
                          // "Match &case"
0115   00 00              // no extra data

// Seventh control
0117   00 00 00 00        // dwHelpID
011B   00 00 00 00        // dwExStyle
011F   01 00 03 50        // dwStyle
0123   AE 00 04 00        // x, y
0127   32 00 0E 00        // cx, cy
012B   01 00 00 00        // dwID
012F   80                 // "button"
0130   26 46 69 6E 64 20 4E 65 78 74 00
                          // "&Find Next"
013B   00 00              // no extra data

// Eighth control
013D   00 00 00 00        // dwHelpID
0141   00 00 00 00        // dwExStyle
0145   00 00 03 50        // dwStyle
0149   AE 00 15 00        // x, y
014D   32 00 0E 00        // cx, cy
0151   00 04 00 00        // dwID
0155   80                 // "button"
0156   26 52 65 70 6C 61 63 65 00
                          // "&Replace"
015F   00 00              // no extra data

// Ninth control
0161   00 00 00 00        // dwHelpID
0165   00 00 00 00        // dwExStyle
0169   00 00 03 50        // dwStyle
016D   AE 00 26 00        // x, y
0171   32 00 0E 00        // cx, cy
0175   01 04 00 00        // dwID
0179   80                 // "button"
017A   52 65 70 6C 61 63 65 20 26 41 6C 6C 00
                          // "Replace &All"
0187   00 00              // no extra data

// Tenth control
0189   00 00 00 00        // dwHelpID
018D   00 00 00 00        // dwExStyle
0191   00 00 03 50        // dwStyle
```

```
0195   AE 00 37 00      // x, y
0199   32 00 0E 00      // cx, cy
019D   02 00 00 00      // dwID
01A1   80               // "button"
01A2   43 61 6E 63 65 6C 00
                        // "Cancel"
01A9   00 00            // no extra data

// Eleventh control
01AB   00 00 00 00      // dwHelpID
01AF   00 00 00 00      // dwExStyle
01B3   00 00 03 50      // dwStyle
01B7   AE 00 4B 00      // x, y
01BB   32 00 0E 00      // cx, cy
01BF   0E 04 00 00      // dwID
01C3   80               // "button"
01C4   26 48 65 6C 70 00
                        // "&Help"
01CA   00 00            // no extra data
```

The original dialog template is the one you've seen twice already, with only one change: The DIALOG keyword has been changed to DIALOGEX.

```
DIALOGEX 36, 44, 230, 94
. . .
```

32-bit extended templates

At last we reach the modern era with the 32-bit extended dialog template, known in resource files as DIALOGEX. I will celebrate this with a gratuitous commutative diagram:

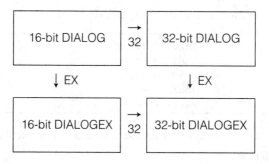

(So-called commutative diagrams are used in several branches of higher mathematics to represent the relationships among functions. Informally speaking, a commutative diagram says that if you pick a starting point and an ending point, then no matter which set of arrows you use to get from one to the other, you always get the same result.)

Okay, so let's get going. The 32-bit extended dialog template is the 32-bit version of the 16-bit extended dialog template, so you won't see any real surprises if you've been following along.

Again, we start with a header, this time the 32-bit extended header:

```
WORD   wDlgVer;        // version number - always 1
WORD   wSignature;     // always 0xFFFF
DWORD  dwHelpID;       // help ID
DWORD  dwExStyle;      // window extended style
DWORD  dwStyle;        // dialog style
WORD   cItems;         // number of controls in this dialog
WORD   x;              // x-coordinate
WORD   y;              // y-coordinate
WORD   cx;             // width
WORD   cy;             // height
```

The first two fields serve exactly the same purpose as the 16-bit extended template: They identify this header as an extended dialog template.

As before, the next two fields are new. The help identifier is attached to the dialog via the SetWindowContextHelpId function, and the extended dialog style shouldn't be a surprise.

You know the drill: Next come the three strings for the menu, class, and dialog title. Because this is the 32-bit template, the strings are Unicode.

As with the 16-bit extended template, the optional custom font consists of a little more information than the nonextended template:

```
WORD wPoint;           // point size
WORD wWeight;          // font weight
BYTE bItalic;          // 1 if italic, 0 if not
BYTE bCharSet;         // character set
WCHAR szFontName[];    // variable-length
```

As before, the point, weight, italic, and character set are all passed to the CreateFont function.

After the header come the dialog item templates, each of which must be aligned on a DWORD boundary:

```
DWORD  dwHelpID;        // help identifier
DWORD  dwExStyle;       // window extended style
DWORD  dwStyle;         // window style
WORD   x;               // x-coordinate (DLUs)
WORD   y;               // y-coordinate (DLUs)
WORD   cx;              // width (DLUs)
WORD   cy;              // height (DLUs)
DWORD  dwID;            // control ID
WCHAR  szClassName[];   // variable-length (possibly ordinal)
WCHAR  szText[];        // variable-length (possibly ordinal)
WORD   cbExtra;         // amount of extra data
BYTE   rgbExtra[cbExtra]; // extra data follows (usually none)
```

The changes here are as follows:

+ New dwHelpID and dwExStyle fields.

+ The dwStyle field has moved.

+ The control ID has grown to a 32-bit value.

Not that expanding the control ID to a 32-bit value helps any, because WM_COMMAND and similar messages still use a 16-bit value to pass the control ID. So in practice, you can't use a value greater than 16 bits. (Well, you can always ignore the control ID field and retrieve the full 32-bit control ID via the GetDlgCtrlID function, assuming you have the window handle of the control available.)

And that's all there is to it.

Here's the customary annotated hex dump:

```
0000   01 00 FF FF 00 00 00 00-00 00 00 00 C4 00 C8 80   ..............^.
0010   0B 00 24 00 2C 00 E6 00-5E 00 00 00 00 00 52 00   ..$.,...^.....R.
0020   65 00 70 00 6C 00 61 00-63 00 65 00 00 00 08 00   e.p.l.a.c.e.....
0030   00 00 00 01 4D 00 53 00-20 00 53 00 68 00 65 00   ....M.S. .S.h.e.
0040   6C 00 6C 00 20 00 44 00-6C 00 67 00 00 00 00 00   l.l. .D.l.g.....
0050   00 00 00 00 00 00 00 00-00 00 02 50 04 00 09 00   ...........P....
0060   30 00 08 00 FF FF FF FF-FF FF 82 00 46 00 69 00   0...........F.i.
0070   26 00 6E 00 64 00 20 00-57 00 68 00 61 00 74 00   &.n.d. .W.h.a.t.
0080   3A 00 00 00 00 00 00 00-00 00 00 00 00 00 00 00   :...............
0090   80 00 83 50 36 00 07 00-72 00 0C 00 80 04 00 00   ...P6...r.......
00A0   FF FF 81 00 00 00 00 00-00 00 00 00 00 00 00 00   ................
00B0   00 00 02 50 04 00 1A 00-30 00 08 00 FF FF FF FF   ...P....0.......
```

```
00C0   FF FF 82 00 52 00 65 00-26 00 70 00 6C 00 61 00    ....R.e.&.p.l.a.
00D0   63 00 65 00 20 00 77 00-69 00 74 00 68 00 3A 00    c.e. .w.i.t.h.:.
00E0   00 00 00 00 00 00 00 00-00 00 00 00 80 00 83 50    ...............P
00F0   36 00 18 00 72 00 0C 00-81 04 00 00 FF FF 81 00    6...r...........
0100   00 00 00 00 00 00 00 00-00 00 00 00 03 00 03 50    ...............P
0110   05 00 2E 00 68 00 0C 00-10 04 00 00 FF FF 80 00    ....h...........
0120   4D 00 61 00 74 00 63 00-68 00 20 00 26 00 77 00    M.a.t.c.h. .&.w.
0130   68 00 6F 00 6C 00 65 00-20 00 77 00 6F 00 72 00    h.o.l.e. .w.o.r.
0140   64 00 20 00 6F 00 6E 00-6C 00 79 00 00 00 00 00    d. .o.n.l.y.....
0150   00 00 00 00 00 00 00 00-00 03 00 01 50 05 00 3E 00    ..........P..>.
0160   3B 00 0C 00 11 04 00 00-FF FF 80 00 4D 00 61 00    ;...........M.a.
0170   74 00 63 00 68 00 20 00-26 00 63 00 61 00 73 00    t.c.h. .&.c.a.s.
0180   65 00 00 00 00 00 00 00-00 00 00 00 00 00 00 00    e...............
0190   01 00 03 50 AE 00 04 00-32 00 0E 00 01 00 00 00    ...P....2.......
01A0   FF FF 80 00 26 00 46 00-69 00 6E 00 64 00 20 00    ....&.F.i.n.d. .
01B0   4E 00 65 00 78 00 74 00-00 00 00 00 00 00 00 00    N.e.x.t.........
01C0   00 00 00 00 00 00 01 50-AE 00 15 00 32 00 0E 00    .......P....2...
01D0   00 04 00 00 FF FF 80 00-26 00 52 00 65 00 70 00    ........&.R.e.p.
01E0   6C 00 61 00 63 00 65 00-00 00 00 00 00 00 00 00    l.a.c.e.........
01F0   00 00 00 00 00 00 01 50-AE 00 26 00 32 00 0E 00    .......P..&.2...
0200   01 04 00 00 FF FF 80 00-52 00 65 00 70 00 6C 00    ........R.e.p.l.
0210   61 00 63 00 65 00 20 00-26 00 41 00 6C 00 6C 00    a.c.e. .&.A.l.l.
0220   00 00 00 00 00 00 00 00-00 00 00 00 00 00 01 50    ...............P
0230   AE 00 37 00 32 00 0E 00-02 00 00 00 FF FF 80 00    ..7.2...........
0240   43 00 61 00 6E 00 63 00-65 00 6C 00 00 00 00 00    C.a.n.c.e.l.....
0250   00 00 00 00 00 00 00 00-00 00 01 50 AE 00 4B 00    ..........P..K.
0260   32 00 0E 00 0E 04 00 00-FF FF 80 00 26 00 48 00    2...........&.H.
0270   65 00 6C 00 70 00 00 00-00 00                      e.l.p.....
```

As always, the header comes first:

```
0000   01 00                   // wVersion
0002   FF FF                   // wSignature
0004   00 00 00 00             // dwHelpID
0008   00 00 00 00             // dwExStyle
000C   C4 00 C8 80             // dwStyle
0010   0B 00                   // cItems
0012   24 00 2C 00             // x, y
0016   E6 00 5E 00             // cx, cy
```

Nothing surprising here; you've seen it before:

```
wVersion    = 0x0001      = 1
wSignature  = 0xFFFF
dwHelpID    = 0x00000000  = 0
dwExStyle   = 0x00000000  = 0
dwStyle     = 0x80C800C4  = WS_POPUP | WS_CAPTION | WS_SYSMENU |
```

```
                                   DS_SETFONT | DS_MODALFRAME | DS_3DLOOK
     cItems    = 0x000B    = 11
     x         = 0x0024    = 36
     y         = 0x002C    = 44
     cx        = 0x00E6    = 230
     cy        = 0x005E    = 94
```

After the header come the menu name, class name, and dialog title:

```
001A  00 00               // no menu
001C  00 00               // default dialog class
001E  52 00 65 00 70 00 6C 00 61 00 63 00
      65 00 00 00    // "Replace"
```

And because DS_SETFONT is set in the dialog style, font information comes next. Notice that the additional font characteristics are included in the extended template:

```
002E  08 00               // wSize = 8
0030  00 00               // wWeight = 0x0000 = FW_DONTCARE
0032  00                  // Italic
0033  01                  // Character set = 0x01 = DEFAULT_CHARSET
0034  4D 00 53 00 20 00 53 00 68 00 65 00 6C 00
      6C 00 20 00 44 00 6C 00 67 00 00 00
                          // "MS Shell Dlg"
```

You've seen this all before. Here come the extended dialog item templates. Remember, these must be DWORD-aligned:

```
004E  00 00               // padding to achieve DWORD alignment

// First control
0050  00 00 00 00         // dwHelpID
0054  00 00 00 00         // dwExStyle
0058  00 00 02 50         // dwStyle
005C  04 00 09 00         // x, y
0060  30 00 08 00         // cx, cy
0064  FF FF FF FF         // wID
0068  FF FF 82 00         // szClass = ordinal 0x0082 = "static"
006C  46 00 69 00
0070  26 00 6E 00 64 00 20 00 77 00 68 00 61 00 74 00
0080  3A 00 00 00         // "Fi&nd what:"
0084  00 00               // no extra data
```

```
0086    00 00                    // padding to achieve DWORD alignment

// Second control
0088    00 00 00 00             // dwHelpID
008C    00 00 00 00             // dwExStyle
0090    80 00 83 50             // dwStyle
0094    36 00 07 00             // x, y
0098    72 00 0C 00             // cx, cy
009C    80 04 00 00             // wID
00A0    FF FF 81 00             // "edit"
00A4    00 00                    // ""
00A6    00 00                    // no extra data

// Third control
00A8    00 00 00 00             // dwHelpID
00AC    00 00 00 00             // dwExStyle
00B0    00 00 02 50             // dwStyle
00B4    04 00 1A 00             // x, y
00B8    30 00 08 00             // cx, cy
00BC    FF FF FF FF             // wID
00C0    FF FF 82 00             // "static"
00C4    52 00 65 00 26 00 70 00 6C 00 61 00
00D0    63 00 65 00 20 00 77 00 69 00 74 00 68 00 3A 00
00E0    00 00                    // "Re&place with:"
00E2    00 00                    // no extra data

// Fourth control
00E4    00 00 00 00             // dwHelpID
00E8    00 00 00 00             // dwExStyle
00EC    80 00 83 50             // dwStyle
00F0    36 00 18 00             // x, y
00F4    72 00 0C 00             // cx, cy
00F8    81 04 00 00             // wID
00FC    FF FF 81 00             // "edit"
0100    00 00                    // ""
0102    00 00                    // no extra data

// Fifth control
0104    00 00 00 00             // dwHelpID
0108    00 00 00 00             // dwExStyle
010C    03 00 03 50             // dwStyle
0110    05 00 2E 00             // x, y
0114    68 00 0C 00             // cx, cy
0118    10 04 00 00             // wID
011C    FF FF 80 00             // "button"
```

```
0120    4D 00 61 00 74 00 63 00 68 00 20 00 26 00 77 00
0130    68 00 6F 00 6C 00 65 00 20 00 77 00 6F 00 72 00
0140    64 00 20 00 6F 00 6E 00 6C 00 79 00 00 00
                          // "Match &whole word only"
014E    00 00             // no extra data


// Sixth control
0150    00 00 00 00       // dwHelpID
0154    00 00 00 00       // dwExStyle
0158    03 00 01 50       // dwStyle
015C    05 00 3E 00       // x, y
0160    3B 00 0C 00       // cx, cy
0164    11 04 00 00       // wID
0168    FF FF 80 00       // "button"
016C    4D 00 61 00
0170    74 00 63 00 68 00 20 00 26 00 63 00 61 00 73 00
0180    65 00 00 00       // "Match &case"
0184    00 00             // no extra data
0186    00 00             // padding to achieve DWORD alignment


// Seventh control
0188    00 00 00 00       // dwHelpID
018C    00 00 00 00       // dwExStyle
0190    01 00 03 50       // dwStyle
0194    AE 00 04 00       // x, y
0198    32 00 0E 00       // cx, cy
019C    01 00 00 00       // wID
01A0    FF FF 80 00       // "button"
01A4    26 00 46 00 69 00 6E 00 64 00 20 00
01B0    4E 00 65 00 78 00 74 00 00 00
                          // "&Find Next"
01BA    00 00             // no extra data


// Eighth control
01BC    00 00 00 00       // dwHelpID
01C0    00 00 00 00       // dwExStyle
01C4    00 00 03 50       // dwStyle
01C8    AE 00 15 00       // x, y
01CC    32 00 0E 00       // cx, cy
01D0    00 04 00 00       // wID
01D4    FF FF 80 00       // "button"
01D8    26 00 52 00 65 00 70 00
                          // "&Replace"
01E0    6C 00 61 00 63 00 65 00 00 00
01EA    00 00             // no extra data
```

```
// Ninth control
01EC   00 00 00 00     // dwHelpID
01F0   00 00 00 00     // dwExStyle
01F4   00 00 03 50     // dwStyle
01F8   AE 00 26 00     // x, y
01FC   32 00 0E 00     // cx, cy
0200   01 04 00 00     // wID
0204   FF FF 80 00     // "button"
0208   52 00 65 00 70 00 6C 00
0210   61 00 63 00 65 00 20 00 26 00 41 00 6C 00 6C 00
0220   00 00           // "Replace &All"
0222   00 00           // no extra data

// Tenth control
0224   00 00 00 00     // dwHelpID
0228   00 00 00 00     // dwExStyle
022C   00 00 01 50     // dwStyle
0230   AE 00 37 00     // x, y
0234   32 00 0E 00     // cx, cy
0238   02 00 00 00     // wID
023C   FF FF 80 00     // "button"
0240   43 00 61 00 6E 00 63 00 65 00 6C 00 00 00
                       // "Cancel"
024E   00 00           // no extra data

// Eleventh control
0250   00 00 00 00     // dwHelpID
0254   00 00 00 00     // dwExStyle
0258   00 00 03 50     // dwStyle
025C   AE 00 4B 00     // x, y
0260   32 00 0E 00     // cx, cy
0264   0E 04 00 00     // wID
0268   FF FF 80 00     // "button"
026C   26 00 48 00
0270   65 00 6C 00 70 00 00 00
                       // "&Help"
0278   00 00           // no extra data
```

The original dialog template is, of course, the one you're probably sick of by now. The only change is that the DIALOG keyword has been changed to DIALOGEX:

```
DIALOGEX 36, 44, 230, 94
...
```

Summary

For those who want to compare the four forms of dialog templates, the highlights appear in tabular form on page 196. The table doesn't contain any new information, but it might give you a little glimpse into how things evolved to see the small changes highlighted against each other.

〜

Why dialog templates, anyway?

USING TEMPLATES IS hardly the only way dialogs could have been designed. A popular competing mechanism is to generate dialogs entirely in code, having each dialog explicitly create and position its child windows. This is the model used by some programming models such as Windows Forms. Win32 settled on the dialog template for a variety of reasons.

For one, memory was at a premium in the early days of Windows. A table-based approach is much more compact, requiring only one copy of the code that parses the template and generates the controls. Using a dialog procedure model means that the common behavior of dialog boxes need be written only once rather than repeated in each code-based dialog, especially because most dialog boxes have a fairly simple set of actions that can be covered in most part by the dialog manager itself.

Another reason for using resources is that it enables the use of interactive tools to design dialogs. These tools can read the dialog template and preview the results on the screen, allowing the designer to modify the layout of a dialog quickly.

Another important reason for using resources is to allow for localization. Isolating the portions of the program that require translation allows translation to be performed without having to recompile the program. Translators can use that same interactive tool to move controls around to accommodate changes in string lengths resulting from translation.

| | 16-Bit Classic | 32-Bit Classic |
	16-Bit Extended	32-Bit Extended
Header	Style	Extended style, style
	8-bit item count	16-bit item count
	Coordinates	Coordinates
	Help ID, extended style, style	Help ID, extended style, style
	8-bit item count	16-bit item count
	Coordinates	Coordinates
Menu	ASCIIZ or ordinal	UNICODEZ or ordinal
	ASCIIZ or ordinal	UNICODEZ or ordinal
Class	ASCIIZ or ordinal	UNICODEZ or ordinal
	ASCIIZ or ordinal	UNICODEZ or ordinal
Caption	ASCIIZ	UNICODEZ
	ASCIIZ	UNICODEZ
Font (if DS_SHELLFONT)	Size	Size
	ASCIIZ font name	UNICODEZ font name
	Size, weight, italic, charset	Size, weight, italic, charset
	ASCIIZ font name	UNICODEZ font name
Item template alignment	BYTE	DWORD
	BYTE	DWORD
Item templates	Size, position	Size, position
	16-bit ID	16-bit ID
	Style	Extended style, style
	Class, ASCIIZ text/ordinal	Class, UNICODEZ text/ordinal
	8-bit extra data	16-bit extra data
	Size, position	Size, position
	32-bit ID	32-bit ID
	Help ID, extended style, style	Help ID, extended style, style
	Class, ASCIIZ text/ordinal	Class, UNICODEZ text/ordinal
	16-bit extra data	16-bit extra data

⇌

How dialogs are created

NOW THAT YOU'VE seen how templates are constructed, we can move on to the next step in a dialog's life, namely its creation. This section relies heavily on previous topics covered in Chapter 8, "Window Management." It also assumes that you are already familiar with dialog templates and dialog styles.

Dialog creation warm-ups

All the CreateDialogXxx functions are just front ends to the real work that happens in the CreateDialogIndirectParam function. Some of them are already visible in the macros: CreateDialog is just a wrapper around CreateDialogParam, with a parameter of zero. Similarly, CreateDialog Indirect is just a wrapper around CreateDialogIndirectParam with a zero parameter.

Here's a slightly less-trivial wrapper:

```
HWND WINAPI CreateDialogParam(HINSTANCE hinst,
    LPCTSTR pszTemplate, HWND hwndParent,
    DLGPROC lpDlgProc, LPARAM dwInitParam)
{
  HWND hdlg = NULL;
  HRSRC hrsrc = FindResource(hinst, pszTemplate,
                        RT_DIALOG);
  if (hrsrc) {
    HGLOBAL hglob = LoadResource(hinst, hrsrc);
    if (hglob) {
      LPVOID pTemplate = LockResource(hglob);
      if (pTemplate) {
        hdlg = CreateDialogIndirectParam(hinst,
                pTemplate, hwndParent, lpDlgProc,
                dwInitParam);
      }
      FreeResource(hglob);
    }
  }
  return hdlg;
}
```

All the `CreateDialogParam` function does is use the `hinst` and `pszTemplate` parameters to locate the `lpTemplate`, and then use that template in `CreateDialogIndirectParam`.

Creating the frame window

The dialog template describes what the dialog box should look like, so the dialog manager walks the template and follows the instructions therein. It's pretty straightforward; there isn't much room for decision making. You just do what the template says.

For simplicity, I'm going to assume that the dialog template is an extended dialog template. This is a superset of the classic `DLGTEMPLATE`, so there is no loss of generality.

Furthermore, I will skip over some of the esoterica (such as the `WM_ENTERIDLE` message) because that would just be distracting from the main point. I am also going to ignore error checking for the same reason.

Finally, I assume you already understand the structure of the various dialog templates and ignore the parsing issues.

The first order of business is to study the dialog styles and translate the `DS_*` styles into `WS_*` and `WS_EX_*` styles.

Dialog Style	Window Style	Extended Window Style
DS_MODALFRAME		Add WS_EX_DLGMODALFRAME Add WS_EX_WINDOWEDGE
DS_CONTEXTHELP		Add WS_EX_CONTEXTHELP
DS_CONTROL	Remove WS_CAPTION Remove WS_SYSMENU	Add WS_EX_CONTROLPARENT

The `DS_CONTROL` style removes the `WS_CAPTION` and `WS_SYSMENU` styles to make it easier for people to convert an existing dialog into a `DS_CONTROL` sub-dialog by simply adding a single style flag. Note, however, that it does not add the `WS_CHILD` style, so you need to remember to specify that yourself.

If the template includes a menu, the menu is loaded from the instance handle passed as part of the creation parameters:

```
hmenu = LoadMenu(hinst, <resource identifier in template>);
```

This is a common theme in dialog creation: The instance handle you pass to the dialog creation function is used for all resource-related activities during dialog creation.

The algorithm for getting the dialog font goes like this:

```
if (DS_SETFONT) {
   use font specified in template
} else if (DS_FIXEDSYS) {
   use GetStockFont(SYSTEM_FIXED_FONT);
} else {
   use GetStockFont(SYSTEM_FONT);
}
```

Notice that DS_SETFONT takes priority over DS_FIXEDSYS. The historical reason for this will be taken up in Chapter 18, when we ask, "Why does DS_SHELLFONT = DS_FIXEDSYS | DS_SETFONT?"

When the dialog manager has the font, it is measured so that its dimensions can be used to convert dialog units (DLUs) to pixels, because everything in dialog box layout is done in DLUs. In explicit terms:

```
// 4 xdlu = 1 average character width
// 8 ydlu = 1 average character height
#define XDLU2Pix(xdlu) MulDiv(xdlu, AveCharWidth, 4)
#define YDLU2Pix(ydlu) MulDiv(ydlu, AveCharHeight, 8)
```

The dialog box size comes from the template:

```
cxDlg = XDLU2Pix(DialogTemplate.cx);
cyDlg = YDLU2Pix(DialogTemplate.cy);
```

The dialog size in the template is the size of the *client area*, so we need to add in the nonclient area, too:

```
RECT rcAdjust = { 0, 0, cxDlg, cyDlg };
AdjustWindowRectEx(&rcAdjust, dwStyle, hmenu != NULL, dwExStyle);
int cxDlg = rcAdjust.right - rcAdjust.left;
int cyDlg = rcAdjust.bottom - rcAdjust.top;
```

How do I know that it's the client area instead of the full window including nonclient area? Because if it were the full window rectangle, it would be impossible to design a dialog! The template designer doesn't know what nonclient metrics the end-user's system will be set to and therefore cannot take it into account at design time.

This is a special case of a more general rule: If you're not sure whether something is true, ask yourself, "What would the world be like if it were true?" If you find a logical consequence that is obviously wrong, you have just proven (by contradiction) that the thing you're considering is indeed not true. Many engineering decisions are really not decisions at all; of all the ways of doing something, only one of them is reasonable.

If the DS_ABSALIGN style is set, the coordinates given in the dialog template are treated as screen coordinates; otherwise, the coordinates given in the dialog template are relative to the dialog's parent:

```
POINT pt = { XDLU2Pix(DialogTemplate.x),
             YDLU2Pix(DialogTemplate.y) };
ClientToScreen(hwndParent, &pt);
```

But what if the caller passed hwndParent = NULL? In that case, the dialog position is relative to the upper-left corner of the primary monitor. But a well-written program is advised to avoid this functionality, which is retained for backward compatibility.

On a multiple-monitor system, it puts the dialog box on the primary monitor, even if your program is running on a secondary monitor.

The user may have docked the taskbar at the top or left edge of the screen, which will cover your dialog.

Even on a single-monitor system, your program might be running in the lower-right corner of the screen. Putting your dialog at the upper-left corner doesn't create a meaningful connection between the two.

If two copies of your program are running, their dialog boxes will cover each other precisely. You saw the dangers of this earlier ("A subtlety in restoring previous window position").

Moral of the story: Always pass a `hwndParent` window so that the dialog appears in a meaningful location relative to the rest of your program. (And as you saw earlier, don't just grab `GetDesktopWindow()` either!)

Okay, we are now all ready to create the dialog: We have its class, its font, its menu, its size, and position.

Oh wait, we have to deal with a subtlety of dialog box creation, namely that the dialog box is created initially hidden. (For an explanation, see the section "Why are dialog boxes initially created hidden?" in Chapter 14, "Etymology and History.")

```
BOOL fWasVisible = dwStyle & WS_VISIBLE;
dwStyle &= ~WS_VISIBLE;
```

The dialog class and title come from the template. Pretty much everyone just uses the default dialog class, although I explained earlier in this chapter how you might use a custom dialog class.

Okay, now we have the information necessary to create the window:

```
HWND hdlg = CreateWindowEx(dwExStyle, pszClass,
    pszCaption, dwStyle & 0xFFFF0000, pt.x, pt.y,
    cxDlg, cyDlg, hwndParent, hmenu, hinst, NULL);
```

Notice that we filter out all the low style bits (per class) because we already translated the DS_* styles into "real" styles.

This is why your dialog procedure doesn't get the window creation messages like `WM_CREATE`. At the time the frame is created, the dialog procedure hasn't yet entered the picture. Only after the frame is created can the dialog manager attach the dialog procedure:

```
// Set the dialog procedure
SetWindowLongPtr(hdlg, DWLP_DLGPROC, (LPARAM)lpDlgProc);
```

The dialog manager does some more fiddling at this point, based on the dialog template styles. The template may have asked for a window context help ID. And if the template did not specify window styles that permit resizing, maximizing, or minimizing, the associated menu items are removed from the dialog box's system menu.

And it sets the font:

```
SetWindowFont(hdlg, hf, FALSE);
```

This is why the first message your dialog procedure receives happens to be WM_SETFONT: It is the first message sent after the DWLP_DLGPROC has been set. Of course, this behavior can change in the future; you shouldn't rely on message ordering.

Now that the dialog frame is open for business, we can create the controls.

Creating the controls

This is actually a lot less work than creating the frame, believe it or not.

For each control in the template, the corresponding child window is created. The control's sizes and position are specified in the template in DLUs, so of course they need to be converted to pixels:

```
int x  = XDLU2Pix(ItemTemplate.x);
int y  = YDLU2Pix(ItemTemplate.y);
int cx = XDLU2Pix(ItemTemplate.cx);
int cy = YDLU2Pix(ItemTemplate.cy);
```

Note that the width and height of the control are converted directly from DLUs, rather than converting the control's rectangle as the following code fragment does:

```
// This is not how the dialog manager computes
// the control dimensions
int cxNotUsed = XDLU2Pix(ItemTemplate.x + ItemTemplate.cx) - x;
int cyNotUsed = YDLU2Pix(ItemTemplate.y + ItemTemplate.cy) - y;
```

The difference between cx and cxNotUsed is not normally visible, but it can manifest itself in discrepancies of up to two pixels if the rounding inherent in the DLU-to-pixel conversion happens to land just the wrong way. Let this be another warning to designers not to become attached to pixel-precise control positioning in dialogs. In addition to the DLU-to-pixel rounding we see here, you can also see this discrepancy when fonts change size and shape when the system's DPI (dots per inch) setting changes.

The class name and caption also come from the template. There are also the optional extra bytes pExtra that nobody uses but that nevertheless remain in the template definition, as you saw earlier in this chapter. When that information has been collected, we're ready to go:

```
HWND hwndChild = CreateWindowEx(
            ItemTemplate.dwExStyle | WS_EX_NOPARENTNOTIFY,
            pszClass, pwzCaption, ItemTemplate.dwStyle,
            x, y, cx, cy, hdlg, ItemTemplate.dwId,
            hinst, pExtra);
```

Notice that the WS_EX_NOPARENTNOTIFY style is forced on for dialog controls. There's no real point in notifying the parent window of the child window's comings and goings, because the parent is the dialog box, which is already quite aware of the child controls by other means.

This next part often trips people up. "When I try to create my dialog, it fails, and I don't know why." It's probably because one of the controls on the dialog could not be created, usually because you forgot to register the window class for that control. (For example, you forgot to call the InitCommon ControlsEx function or you forgot to LoadLibrary the appropriate version of the RichEdit control.)

```
if (!hwndChild) {
    DestroyWindow(hdlg);
    return NULL;
}
```

The DS_NOFAILCREATE style suppresses the failure check above.
But if the control did get created, it needs to be initialized:

```
SetWindowContextHelpId(hwndChild, ItemTemplate.dwHelpID);
SetWindowFont(hwndChild, hf, FALSE);
```

Repeat once for each item template, and you now have a dialog box with all its child controls. Tell the dialog procedure that it can initialize its child windows, show the (now-ready) dialog box if we had deferred the WS_VISIBLE bit when constructing the frame, and return the dialog box to our caller, ready for action:

```
    // The default focus is the first item that is a valid tab-stop
    HWND hwndDefaultFocus = GetNextDlgTabItem(hdlg, NULL, FALSE);
    if (SendMessage(hdlg, WM_INITDIALOG,
                    hwndDefaultFocus, lParam)) {
        SetDialogFocus(hwndDefaultFocus);
    }

    if (fWasVisible) ShowWindow(hdlg);
    return hdlg;
}
```

You will see the SetDialogFocus function in more detail later in this chapter; it sets the focus in a dialog-friendly manner.

So there you have it: You have now seen how dialog box sausages are made.

(Actually, reality is much sausagier, because I skipped over all the application compatibility hacks! For example, there's a program out there that relies on the subtle placement and absence of the WS_BORDER style to decide whether a control is a combo box or a list box. I guess the GetClassName function was too much work?)

~

The modal dialog loop

THE NEXT STEP in a dialog box's life is the modal loop that pumps and dispatches messages to the dialog. We start with a discussion of the basic dialog, then use that as a springboard for more advanced versions of the loop.

The basic dialog loop

The dialog loop is actually quite simple. At its core, it's a simple loop:

```
while (<dialog still active> &&
       GetMessage(&msg, NULL, 0, 0, 0)) {
  if (!IsDialogMessage(hdlg, &msg)) {
    TranslateMessage(&msg);
```

```
    DispatchMessage(&msg);
  }
}
```

If you want something fancier in your dialog loop, you can take the preceding loop and tinker with it.

But let's start from the beginning. The work happens in `DialogBox IndirectParam`. (We already saw how to convert all the `DialogBoxXxx` functions into `DialogBoxIndirectParam`.)

```
INT_PTR WINAPI DialogBoxIndirectParam(
    HINSTANCE hinst,
    LPCDLGTEMPLATE lpTemplate, HWND hwndParent,
    DLGPROC lpDlgProc, LPARAM lParam)
{
  /*
   * App hack!  Some people pass GetDesktopWindow()
   * as the owner instead of NULL.  Fix them so the
   * desktop doesn't get disabled!
   */
  if (hwndParent == GetDesktopWindow())
    hwndParent = NULL;
```

That's right, we start with an application compatibility hack. We discussed earlier the special position of the desktop window. ("What's so special about the desktop window?") So many people make the mistake of passing the desktop window instead of NULL that we had to put this application hack into the core operating system. It would be pointless to make a shim for it because that would mean that thousands of applications would need to be shimmed.

Because only top-level windows can be owners, we have to take the putative `hwndParent` (which might be a child window) and walk up the window hierarchy until we find a top-level window:

```
  if (hwndParent)
    hwndParent = GetAncestor(hwndParent, GA_ROOT);
```

(If you paid close attention, you might have noticed that there is still a way to sneak through the two layers of `hwndParent` parameter "repair" and end up with a dialog box whose owner is the desktop window, namely by creating a window as a child of the desktop and using it as the `hwndParent` for a dialog box. So don't do that.)

With that second application compatibility hack out of the way, we create the dialog:

```
HWND hdlg = CreateDialogIndirectParam(hinst,
                lpTemplate, hwndParent, lpDlgProc,
                lParam);
```

Note that as before, I am going to ignore error checking and various dialog box esoterica because it would just be distracting from the main point of this discussion.

As you saw earlier in our discussion of modality, modal windows disable their parent, so do it here:

```
BOOL fWasEnabled = EnableWindow(hwndParent, FALSE);
```

We then fall into the dialog modal loop:

```
MSG msg;
while (<dialog still active> &&
        GetMessage(&msg, NULL, 0, 0)) {
  if (!IsDialogMessage(hdlg, &msg)) {
   TranslateMessage(&msg);
   DispatchMessage(&msg);
  }
}
```

We observe the convention on quit messages by reposting any quit message we may have received so the next outer modal loop can see it:

```
if (msg.message == WM_QUIT) {
  PostQuitMessage((int)msg.wParam);
}
```

(Astute readers might have noticed an uninitialized variable bug: If `EndDialog` was called during `WM_INITDIALOG` handling, `msg.message` is never set. I decided to ignore this fringe case for expository purposes.)

Now that the dialog is complete, we clean up. As you saw earlier ("The correct order for disabling and enabling windows"), it is important to enable the owner before destroying the owned dialog:

```
if (fWasEnabled)
 EnableWindow(hwndParent, TRUE);
DestroyWindow(hdlg);
```

And that's all. Return the result:

```
 return <value passed to EndDialog>;
}
```

Congratulations, you are now an expert on the dialog loop. Now we'll put this new expertise to good use after a brief digression.

Why is the dialog loop structured this way, anyway?

The dialog loop is structured the way it is because of the way input messages are routed. The window manager delivers mouse input messages to the window that contains the coordinates of the cursor and it delivers keyboard input messages to the window with keyboard focus. This works out well under normal circumstances; but if we follow this model for dialogs, we quickly run into a problem: Because keyboard input is delivered to the window with keyboard focus, the dialog manager wouldn't get a chance to see them and implement dialog keyboard navigation. To see the messages before they continue on their way to the window with keyboard focus, the dialog loop needs to sneak a peek at the message before translating and dispatching it. The function that does this peeking is called `IsDialogMessage`. We take up the inner workings of `IsDialogMessage` after we finish exploring the details of the dialog modal loop.

Converting a nonmodal dialog box to a modal one

Let's convert a modeless dialog box into a modal one. Start with the scratch program and make the following additions:

```
INT_PTR CALLBACK DlgProc(
    HWND hdlg, UINT uMsg, WPARAM wParam, LPARAM lParam)
{
```

```
switch (uMsg) {
case WM_INITDIALOG:
 SetWindowLongPtr(hdlg, DWLP_USER, lParam);
 return TRUE;
case WM_COMMAND:
 switch (GET_WM_COMMAND_ID(wParam, lParam)) {
 case IDOK:
  EndDialog(hdlg, IDOK);
  break;
 case IDCANCEL:
  EndDialog(hdlg, IDCANCEL);
  break;
 }
}
 return FALSE;
}

int DoModal(HWND hwnd)
{
 return DialogBox(g_hinst, MAKEINTRESOURCE(1), hwnd, DlgProc);
}

void OnChar(HWND hwnd, TCHAR ch, int cRepeat)
{
 switch (ch) {
 case ' ': DoModal(hwnd); break;
 }
}

// Add to WndProc
    HANDLE_MSG(hwnd, WM_CHAR, OnChar);

// Resource file
1 DIALOGEX DISCARDABLE  32, 32, 200, 40
STYLE DS_MODALFRAME | DS_SHELLFONT | WS_POPUP |
      WS_VISIBLE | WS_CAPTION | WS_SYSMENU
CAPTION "Sample"
FONT 8, "MS Shell Dlg"
BEGIN
 DEFPUSHBUTTON "OK",IDOK,20,20,50,14
 PUSHBUTTON "Cancel",IDCANCEL,74,20,50,14
END
```

Not a very exciting program, I grant you that. It just displays a dialog box and returns a value that depends on which button you pressed. The DoModal function uses the DialogBox function to do the real work.

Now let's convert the DoModal function so that it implements the modal loop directly. Why? Just to see how it's done, because the best way to learn how something is done is by doing it. In real life, of course, there would normally be no reason to undertake this exercise; the dialog box manager does a fine job. But when you understand how the modal loop is managed, you will be on more solid ground when you need to add something a little out of the ordinary to your own dialog procedures. (In an extreme case, you might need to write code like this after all; for example, you might be developing your own modal dialog-box-like component such as a property sheet.)

First, we need to figure out where we're going to keep track of the flag we called <dialog still active> last time. We'll keep it in a structure that we hang off the dialog box's DWLP_USER window bytes. (I sort of planned ahead for this by having the DlgProc function stash the lParam into the DWLP_USER extra bytes when the dialog is initialized.)

```
// fEnded tells us if the dialog has been ended.
// When ended, iResult contains the result code.

typedef struct DIALOGSTATE {
 BOOL fEnded;
 int iResult;
} DIALOGSTATE;

void EndManualModalDialog(HWND hdlg, int iResult)
{
 DIALOGSTATE *pds = reinterpret_cast<DIALOGSTATE*>
     (GetWindowLongPtr(hdlg, DWLP_USER));
 if (pds) {
  pds->iResult = iResult;
  pds->fEnded = TRUE;
 }
}
```

The EndManualModalDialog takes the place of the EndDialog function: Instead of updating the dialog manager's internal "is the dialog finished?" flag, we update ours.

All we have to do to convert our DlgProc from one using the dialog manager's modal loop to our custom modal loop, therefore, is to change the calls to EndDialog to call our function instead:

```
INT_PTR CALLBACK DlgProc(
    HWND hdlg, UINT uMsg, WPARAM wParam, LPARAM lParam)
{
 switch (uMsg) {
 case WM_INITDIALOG:
  SetWindowLongPtr(hdlg, DWLP_USER, lParam);
  return TRUE;
 case WM_COMMAND:
  switch (GET_WM_COMMAND_ID(wParam, lParam)) {
  case IDOK:
   EndManualModeDialog(hdlg, IDOK);
   break;
  case IDCANCEL:
   EndManualModeDialog(hdlg, IDCANCEL);
   break;
  }
 }
 return FALSE;
}
```

All that's left is to write the custom dialog message loop:

```
int DoModal(HWND hwnd)
{
 DIALOGSTATE ds = { 0 };
 HWND hdlg = CreateDialogParam(g_hinst, MAKEINTRESOURCE(1),
           hwnd, DlgProc, reinterpret_cast<LPARAM>(&ds));
 if (!hdlg) {
  return -1;
 }

 EnableWindow(hwnd, FALSE);
 MSG msg;
 msg.message = WM_NULL; // anything that isn't WM_QUIT
 while (!ds.fEnded && GetMessage(&msg, NULL, 0, 0)) {
  if (!IsDialogMessage(hdlg, &msg)) {
   TranslateMessage(&msg);
   DispatchMessage(&msg);
  }
 }
 if (msg.message == WM_QUIT) {
```

```
    PostQuitMessage((int)msg.wParam);
  }
  EnableWindow(hwnd, TRUE);
  DestroyWindow(hdlg);
  return ds.iResult;
}
```

Most of this should make sense given what you've learned earlier.

We start by creating the dialog modelessly, passing a pointer to our dialog state as the creation parameter, which as we noted earlier, our dialog procedure squirrels away in the DWLP_USER window bytes for EndManualModalDialog to use.

Next we disable the owner window; this is done after creating the modeless dialog, observing the rules for enabling and disabling windows. We then fall into our message loop, which looks exactly like what we said it should look like. All we did was substitute !ds.fEnded for the pseudocode <dialog still active>. After the modal loop is done, we continue with the standard bookkeeping: reposting any quit message, reenabling the owner before destroying the dialog, and then returning the result.

As you can see, the basics of modal dialogs are really not that exciting. But now that you have this basic framework, you can start tinkering with it.

First, however, we're going to patch up a bug in the preceding code. It's rather subtle. See whether you can spot it. Hint: Look closely at the interaction between EndManualModalDialog and the modal message loop.

Subtleties in message loops

The subtlety is that EndManualModalDialog sets some flags but does nothing to force the message loop to notice that the flag was actually set. Recall that the GetMessage function does not return until a posted message arrives in the queue. If incoming sent messages arrive, they are delivered to the corresponding window procedure, but the GetMessage function doesn't return. It just keeps delivering incoming sent messages until a posted message finally arrives.

The bug, therefore, is that when you call EndManualModalDialog, it sets the flag that tells the modal message loop to stop running, but doesn't do anything to ensure that the modal message loop will wake up to notice. Nothing happens until a posted message arrives, which causes `GetMessage` to return. The posted message is dispatched and the `while` loop restarted, at which point the code finally notices that the `fEnded` flag is set and breaks out of the modal message loop.

There are a few ways of fixing this problem. The quick solution is to post a meaningless message:

```
void EndManualModalDialog(HWND hdlg, int iResult)
{
 DIALOGSTATE *pds = reinterpret_cast<DIALOGSTATE*>
     (GetWindowLongPtr(hdlg, DWLP_USER));
 if (pds) {
  pds->iResult = iResult;
  pds->fEnded = TRUE;
  PostMessage(hdlg, WM_NULL, 0, 0);
 }
}
```

This forces the `GetMessage` to return, because we made sure there is at least one posted message in the queue waiting to be processed. We chose the `WM_NULL` message because it doesn't do anything. We aren't interested in what the message does, just the fact that there is a message at all.

More subtleties in message loops

We solved the problem with the `EndManualDialog` function by posting a harmless message. Now let's solve the problem in an entirely different way, because it illustrates other subtleties of message loops.

The idea here is to make sure the modal message loop regains control, even if all that happened were incoming sent messages, so that it can detect that the `fEnded` flag is set and break out of the modal loop.

Instead of changing the `EndManualModalDialog` function, we will change the modal message loop:

```
int DoModal(HWND hwnd)
{
 DIALOGSTATE ds = { 0 };
```

```
HWND hdlg = CreateDialogParam(g_hinst, MAKEINTRESOURCE(1),
           hwnd, DlgProc, reinterpret_cast<LPARAM>(&ds));
if (!hdlg) {
 return -1;
}

EnableWindow(hwnd, FALSE);
MSG msg;
msg.message = WM_NULL; // anything that isn't WM_QUIT
while (!ds.fEnded) {
 if (PeekMessage(&msg, NULL, 0, 0, PM_REMOVE)) {
  if (msg.message == WM_QUIT) {
   break;
  } else
  if (!IsDialogMessage(hdlg, &msg)) {
   TranslateMessage(&msg);
   DispatchMessage(&msg);
  }
 } else if (!ds.fEnded) {
  WaitMessage();
 }
}
if (msg.message == WM_QUIT) {
 PostQuitMessage((int)msg.wParam);
}
EnableWindow(hwnd, TRUE);
DestroyWindow(hdlg);
return ds.iResult;
}
```

We changed the call to GetMessage into a call to the PeekMessage function, asking to remove the peeked message if any. Like GetMessage, this delivers any incoming sent messages, and then checks whether there are any posted messages in the queue. The difference is that whereas GetMessage keeps waiting if there are no posted messages, PeekMessage returns and tells you that there were no posted messages.

That's the control we want. If PeekMessage says that it couldn't find a posted message, we check our fEnded flag once again, in case an incoming sent message set the fEnded flag. If not, we call the WaitMessage function to wait until there is something to do (either an incoming sent message or a posted message).

Note that because we shifted from GetMessage to PeekMessage, we also have to check for the WM_QUIT message in a different way. Whereas the GetMessage function returns FALSE when the WM_QUIT message is received, the PeekMessage function does not call out that message in any special way. As a result, we need to check for it explicitly.

If the whole point was to regain control after sent messages are delivered, why isn't there a test of the fEnded flag immediately after DispatchMessage returns? Actually, the test is there. Control goes back to the top of the while loop, where the fEnded flag is tested.

Custom navigation in dialog boxes

Some dialog boxes contain custom navigation that goes beyond what the IsDialogMessage function provides. For example, property sheets use Ctrl+Tab and Ctrl+Shift+Tab to change pages within the property sheet. Remember the core of the dialog loop:

```
while (<dialog still active> &&
        GetMessage(&msg, NULL, 0, 0, 0)) {
 if (!IsDialogMessage(hdlg, &msg)) {
  TranslateMessage(&msg);
  DispatchMessage(&msg);
 }
}
```

(Or the modified version we created in the previous section.)

To add custom navigation, just stick it in before calling IsDialogMessage:

```
while (<dialog still active> &&
        GetMessage(&msg, NULL, 0, 0, 0)) {
 if (msg.message == WM_KEYDOWN &&
    msg.wParam == VK_TAB &&
    GetKeyState(VK_CONTROL) < 0) {
 ... do custom navigation ...
 } else if (!IsDialogMessage(hdlg, &msg)) {
  TranslateMessage(&msg);
  DispatchMessage(&msg);
 }
}
```

After retrieving a message, we check whether it was Ctrl+Tab before dispatching it or indeed even before letting `IsDialogMessage` see it. If so, treat it as a navigation key.

Note that if you intend to have modeless dialogs controlled by this message loop, your test needs to be a little more focused, because you don't want to pick off keyboard navigation keys destined for the modeless dialog:

```
while (<dialog still active> &&
       GetMessage(&msg, NULL, 0, 0, 0)) {
  if ((hdlg == msg.hwnd || IsChild(hdlg, msg.hwnd)) &&
     msg.message == WM_KEYDOWN &&
     msg.wParam == VK_TAB &&
     GetKeyState(VK_CONTROL) < 0) {
  ... do custom navigation ...
  } else if (!IsDialogMessage(hdlg, &msg)) {
  TranslateMessage(&msg);
  DispatchMessage(&msg);
  }
}
```

Next, you'll see another way of accomplishing this same task.

Custom accelerators in dialog boxes

The method for adding custom navigation can also be used to add custom accelerators to your dialog box. (In a sense, this is a generalization of custom navigation, because you can make your navigation keys be accelerators.)

So, let's use accelerators to navigate instead of picking off the keys manually. Our accelerator table might look like this:

```
IDA_PROPSHEET ACCELERATORS
BEGIN
     VK_TAB        , IDC_NEXTPAGE        , VIRTKEY, CONTROL
     VK_TAB        , IDC_PREVPAGE        , VIRTKEY, CONTROL, SHIFT
END
```

Here you can see my comma-placement convention for tables. I like to put commas at the far end of the field instead of jamming it up against the last word in the column. Doing this makes cut/paste a lot easier, because you can cut a column and paste it somewhere else without having to go back and twiddle all the commas.

Assuming you've loaded this accelerator table into the variable `hacc`, you can use that table in your custom dialog loop:

```
while (<dialog still active> &&
       GetMessage(&msg, NULL, 0, 0, 0)) {
  if (!TranslateAccelerator(hdlg, hacc, &msg) &&
      !IsDialogMessage(hdlg, &msg)) {
    TranslateMessage(&msg);
    DispatchMessage(&msg);
  }
}
```

The `TranslateAccelerator` function checks whether the message matches any entries in the accelerator table. If so, it posts a WM_COMMAND message to the window passed as its first parameter. In our case, we pass the dialog box handle. Not shown above is the WM_COMMAND handler in the dialog box that responds to IDC_NEXTPAGE and IDC_PREVPAGE by performing a navigation.

As before, if you think there might be modeless dialogs owned by this message loop, you will have to do filtering so that you don't pick off somebody else's navigation keys:

```
while (<dialog still active> &&
       GetMessage(&msg, NULL, 0, 0, 0)) {
  if (!((hdlg == msg.hwnd || IsChild(hdlg, msg.hwnd)) &&
        !TranslateAccelerator(hdlg, hacc, &msg)) &&
      !IsDialogMessage(hdlg, &msg)) {
    TranslateMessage(&msg);
    DispatchMessage(&msg);
  }
}
```

Nested dialogs and DS_CONTROL

AN IMPORTANT ENHANCEMENT to the dialog manager that first appeared in Windows 95 is support for nested dialogs via the DS_CONTROL style.

You're probably accustomed to seeing nested dialogs without even realizing it. Property sheets, for example, are a highly visible example: Each page on a property sheet is its own dialog, all of which are nested inside the property sheet frame. You also see nested dialogs when an application customizes the common file dialogs. For example, when you perform a Save As with Notepad, the encoding options at the bottom are a nested dialog.

Starter kit

Let's create a nested dialog so that we can see one in action, starting with the following program:

```
#include <windows.h>
#include <windowsx.h>

HINSTANCE g_hinst;

INT_PTR CALLBACK
OuterDlgProc(HWND hdlg, UINT wm, WPARAM wParam, LPARAM lParam)
{
 switch (wm) {
 case WM_INITDIALOG:
  return TRUE;
 case WM_COMMAND:
  switch (GET_WM_COMMAND_ID(wParam, lParam)) {
  case IDOK:
   EndDialog(hdlg, IDOK);
   break;
  case IDCANCEL:
   EndDialog(hdlg, IDCANCEL);
   break;
  }
 }
 return FALSE;
}

int PASCAL
WinMain(HINSTANCE hinst, HINSTANCE, LPSTR, int nShowCmd)
{
 g_hinst = hinst;
 INT_PTR iRc = DialogBox(g_hinst, MAKEINTRESOURCE(1),
                         NULL, OuterDlgProc);
 return 0;
}
```

Coupled with the following resource file:

```
1 DIALOG 0, 0, 212, 188
STYLE DS_SHELLFONT | WS_POPUP | WS_VISIBLE |
      WS_CAPTION | WS_SYSMENU
CAPTION "Sample"
FONT 8, "MS Shell Dlg"
BEGIN
    CONTROL         "",100,"static",SS_GRAYRECT,0,0,212,160
    DEFPUSHBUTTON   "OK",IDOK,98,167,50,14
    PUSHBUTTON      "Cancel",IDCANCEL,155,167,50,14
END
```

If you run this program, all you get is a rather bland dialog box with OK and Cancel buttons, and a large gray box filling the body. Let's fill the gray box with a nested dialog. Make the following changes to our program:

```
// New function
INT_PTR CALLBACK
InnerDlgProc(HWND hdlg, UINT wm, WPARAM wParam, LPARAM lParam)
{
 switch (wm) {
 case WM_INITDIALOG:
  return TRUE;
 }
 return FALSE;
}

// New function
void GetWindowRectRelative(HWND hwnd, LPRECT prc)
{
 GetWindowRect(hwnd, prc);
 MapWindowRect(NULL, GetAncestor(hwnd, GA_PARENT), prc);
}

// New function
void OnInitDialog(HWND hdlg)
{
 HWND hdlgInner = CreateDialog(g_hinst, MAKEINTRESOURCE(2),
                               hdlg, InnerDlgProc);
 if (hdlgInner) {
  RECT rc;
  GetWindowRectRelative(GetDlgItem(hdlg, 100), &rc);
  SetWindowPos(hdlgInner, HWND_TOP, rc.left, rc.top,
               rc.right - rc.left, rc.bottom - rc.top,
```

```
                    SWP_NOACTIVATE);
  } else {
   EndDialog(hdlg, IDCANCEL);
  }
}

// Add to OuterDlgProc
case WM_INITDIALOG:
  OnInitDialog(hdlg);
  return TRUE;
```

In the dialog procedure for our outer window, we respond to the WM_INITDIALOG message by creating the inner dialog box and positioning it in the outer dialog, using the gray box as a guide. The helper function Get WindowRectRelative is like GetWindowRect, except that it returns the window rectangle in parent-relative coordinates, which is the coordinate system of choice when performing child window positioning computations. The dialog procedure for the inner dialog box doesn't do anything, because this is just a demonstration:

```
1 DIALOG 0, 0, 212, 188
STYLE DS_SHELLFONT | WS_POPUP | WS_VISIBLE |
      WS_CAPTION | WS_SYSMENU
CAPTION "Sample"
FONT 8, "MS Shell Dlg"
BEGIN
    CONTROL             "",100,"static",
                        SS_GRAYRECT | NOT WS_VISIBLE,0,0,212,160
    DEFPUSHBUTTON       "OK",IDOK,98,167,50,14
    PUSHBUTTON          "Cancel",IDCANCEL,155,167,50,14
END

2 DIALOG 0, 0, 212, 160
STYLE DS_SHELLFONT | DS_CONTROL | WS_CHILD | WS_VISIBLE
CAPTION "Inner"
FONT 8, "MS Shell Dlg"
BEGIN
    GROUPBOX            "&Options",-1,7,7,198,153
    AUTOCHECKBOX        "&Autosave",100,14,24,184,10
    AUTOCHECKBOX        "&Resize images to fit window",
                        101,14,36,184,10
END
```

Because the gray box is merely a positioning guide, we remove the WS_ VISIBLE style so that it doesn't appear on the screen. The second dialog, the inner dialog, looks like a normal dialog, except that the styles are different: We add the DS_CONTROL style to indicate that this is a nested dialog. We also need to set the WS_CHILD style because it will be the child of the outer dialog. For the same reason, we remove the WS_POPUP, WS_CAPTION, and WS_SYSMENU styles. These steps are important to get the nested dialog to play friendly with its new parent.

Even with this limited example, many aspects of nested dialogs are apparent. First is the subservience of the nested dialog. The outer dialog takes responsibility for the combined dialog, running the message loop, managing the default button, and preserving the focus window across changes in activation. The inner dialog is reduced to merely managing its own controls.

Much more obvious is the unified tab order. The controls on the nested dialog are treated as if they belonged to the outer dialog, allowing the user to tab through all the controls seamlessly. The way this works is quite simple: When the dialog manager enumerates windows, it recurses into windows with the WS_EX_CONTROLPARENT extended style. Without the style, the dialog manager treats the window as a control; with the style, the dialog manager treats the window as a container. If a window is treated as a container, it loses the ability to receive focus directly; instead, its children become eligible for receiving focus.

Another way to visualize the effect of the WS_EX_CONTROLPARENT extended style is to treat it as a window that "promotes" its children.

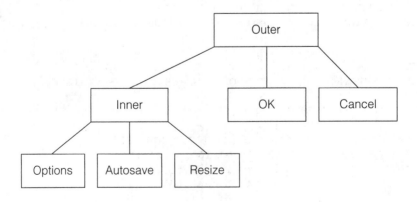

Without the WS_EX_CONTROLPARENT extended style, the outer dialog sees three children, namely "Inner", "OK", and "Cancel". When the WS_EX_ CONTROLPARENT extended style is added to "Inner", the children of the inner dialog are treated as if they were children of the outer dialog.

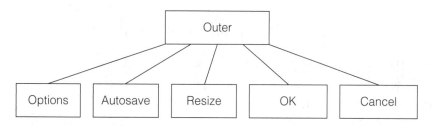

Either way you look at it, the effect is the same: The resulting tab order is the combination of the tab orders of the outer and inner dialogs.

It is important to be mindful of the unification of the tab order to avoid sending the dialog manager into an infinite loop. When you ask the GetNext DlgTabItem function to look for the previous item, it takes the control you pass as a starting point and walks through the controls on the dialog until it comes back to that starting point, at which point it returns the one it saw before that one. If you forget to mark your dialog as DS_CONTROL, and focus started out in the subdialog, the control enumeration will not recurse into the subdialog, and consequently the starting point will never be found. The dialog manager will just keep looping, hunting for that starting-point control and never finding it.

(This problem exists even without DS_CONTROL. If you start out on a disabled or invisible control, the walk through the controls will again never find the starting point, because disabled and invisible controls are skipped over when tabbing through a dialog.)

One aspect of nested dialogs we've conveniently glossed over is the communication between the outer and inner dialogs. There is no predefined protocol for the two dialogs to use; you get to invent whatever mechanism you feel works best for you. Typically, you pass information from the outer dialog to the inner dialog by passing it as the final parameter to the CreateDialog Param function. This at least lets the inner dialog know why it is being created.

Communication between the two dialogs after that point is up to you. The shell property sheet, for example, uses WM_NOTIFY messages to communicate from the outer to the inner dialog, and PSM_* messages to communicate from the inner back to the outer.

Resizing based on the inner dialog

Our previous example required a fixed size for the inner dialog; but in the case where the inner dialog is an extensibility point, you may choose to adapt to the size of the inner dialog rather than enforcing a size upon it. Implementing this is comparatively straightforward; it's just a variation on the general case of the resizable dialog. Replace the OnInitDialog function with this version:

```
void OnInitDialog(HWND hdlg)
{
 HWND hdlgInner = CreateDialog(g_hinst,
                    MAKEINTRESOURCE(2), hdlg, InnerDlgProc);
 if (hdlgInner) {
  RECT rcInner;
  GetWindowRectRelative(hdlgInner, &rcInner);
  RECT rcDst;
  GetWindowRectRelative(GetDlgItem(hdlg, 100), &rcDst);
  SetWindowPos(hdlgInner, HWND_TOP, rcDst.left, rcDst.top, 0, 0,
             SWP_NOSIZE | SWP_NOACTIVATE);

  int cxInner = rcInner.right - rcInner.left;
  int cyInner = rcInner.bottom - rcInner.top;
  int cxDst = rcDst.right - rcDst.left;
  int cyDst = rcDst.bottom - rcDst.top;
  int dx = cxInner - cxDst;
  int dy = cyInner - cyDst;
  SlideWindow(GetDlgItem(hdlg, IDOK), dx, dy);
  SlideWindow(GetDlgItem(hdlg, IDCANCEL), dx, dy);
  GrowWindow(hdlg, dx, dy);
 } else {
  EndDialog(hdlg, IDCANCEL);
 }
}
```

After creating the inner dialog, we measure it and position it. This time, instead of forcing the inner dialog to our desired size, we leave it at its original size and adapt the dialog to fit. We take advantage of the following helper functions:

```
void SlideWindow(HWND hwnd, int dx, int dy)
{
 RECT rc;
 GetWindowRectRelative(hwnd, &rc);
 SetWindowPos(hwnd, NULL, rc.left + dx, rc.top + dy, 0, 0,
          SWP_NOSIZE | SWP_NOZORDER | SWP_NOACTIVATE);
}

void GrowWindow(HWND hwnd, int dx, int dy)
{
 RECT rc;
 GetWindowRectRelative(hwnd, &rc);
 int cx = rc.right - rc.left;
 int cy = rc.bottom - rc.top;
 SetWindowPos(hwnd, NULL, 0, 0, cx + dx, cy + dy,
          SWP_NOMOVE | SWP_NOZORDER | SWP_NOACTIVATE);
}
```

These two simple functions move or resize a window given pixels deltas and should not be very much of a surprise.

To illustrate this dynamically resizable container dialog, we'll make some adjustments to the dimensions of the inner dialog:

```
2 DIALOG 0, 0, 148, 62
STYLE DS_SHELLFONT | DS_CONTROL | WS_CHILD | WS_VISIBLE
CAPTION "Inner"
FONT 8, "MS Shell Dlg"
BEGIN
    GROUPBOX        "&Options",-1,7,7,134,55
    AUTOCHECKBOX    "&Autosave",100,14,24,120,10
    AUTOCHECKBOX    "&Resize images to fit
                    window",101,14,36,120,10
END
```

I've reduced the overall size of the dialog box and tightened the controls. When you run the program with this dialog box, you'll see that it fits inside the outer dialog box, and the outer dialog box adjusts its size accordingly.

This technique can be extended to scenarios like tabbed property sheets, where multiple inner dialogs are displayed one at a time based on a user selection, but I'll stop here because I've given you the building blocks you need to build it; all that's left for you is to put them together: You now know how to create, measure, and position inner dialogs. Earlier I discussed how you can implement custom navigation in dialogs (so that, for example, you can use Ctrl+Tab to change pages in a property sheet), and I emphasized that when you have nested dialogs, it is the outermost dialog that controls the show. All that's left for you to do is to hide and show the appropriate inner dialog based on the user's selection.

Why do we need a dialog loop, anyway?

WHY IS THERE a dialog loop in the first place?

The first reason is modality. When you call the `MessageBox` function, you expect the function to wait for the user to respond to the dialog before returning. To wait, the thread needs some sort of message pump so that the user interface can respond to the user's actions.

But why do we need the `IsDialogMessage` function? Can't `DefDlgProc` do all the work?

The reason for the `IsDialogMessage` function is that input messages are directed to the target window. If keyboard focus is on a button control, say, and the user presses the Tab key, the `WM_KEYDOWN` message is created with the button control as the destination window. If no special action were taken, the `DispatchMessage` would deliver the message directly to the window procedure of the button control. The dialog window itself never sees the message, and consequently `DefDlgProc` doesn't get a chance to do anything about it.

For the dialog manager to get a chance to see the message, it needs to intercept the message at some point between the `GetMessage` and the button control's window procedure. How could this have been designed?

One possible solution would be for the dialog manager to subclass all the controls on the dialog. This approach requires that applications that add controls to the dialog dynamically go through a special procedure for creating those controls so that the dialog manager can subclass the new control.

Another possible solution would be to give the `DispatchMessage` itself special knowledge of dialog boxes. Not only would this violate the layering between the lower-level window manager and the higher-level dialog manager, it would tie the window manager to one specific dialog manager. If this had happened, many of the extensions to the dialog manager we've been experimenting with would have been impossible.

Therefore, given the design of the window manager, the simplest solution is add an explicit call to the dialog manager in the message loop so that it can intercept input messages destined for controls on the dialog and use them for dialog navigation and related purposes.

The people who developed the Windows Presentation Foundation had the advantage of more than a dozen years of experience with the Windows dialog manager and were able to come up with an elegant event-routing model that generalizes the Win32 method to situations such as control containment. Whereas Win32 requires an explicit call to the dialog manager, the Windows Presentation Foundation uses "event tunneling" by means of preview events. These tunneled events travel through the equivalent of the dialog box frame, at which point they can be handled in the manner of `IsDialogMessage`.

≈

Why do dialog editors start assigning control IDs with 100?

WHEN YOU USE a dialog editor and insert new controls, they typically are assigned control IDs starting at around 100. Why?

Because the small numbers are already taken:

```
/*
 * Dialog Box Command IDs
 */
#define IDOK          1
#define IDCANCEL      2
#define IDABORT       3
```

```
#define  IDRETRY            4
#define  IDIGNORE           5
#define  IDYES              6
#define  IDNO               7
#define  IDCLOSE            8
#define  IDHELP             9
#define  IDTRYAGAIN        10
#define  IDCONTINUE        11
```

The dialog manager knows about these special values and assumes that if your dialog box has a control whose ID matches one of these special values, it also behaves in a certain way.

The dialog manager assumes that a control whose ID is IDOK is an OK button. The default action when the user presses Enter is to push the default button; if no default button can be found, the OK button is pushed. Similarly, a control whose ID is IDCANCEL is assumed to be a Cancel button. If the user presses Esc or clicks the X button in the corner, the default behavior is to treat it as if the Cancel button had been pushed.

If your dialog box has OK and Cancel buttons, make sure to give them the IDOK and IDCANCEL control IDs so that they act like proper OK and Cancel buttons. Conversely, any control with those IDs had better be proper OK and Cancel buttons.

⁓

What happens inside DefDlgProc?

THE DEFAULT DIALOG box window procedure handles some bookkeeping, but it's really IsDialogMessage that does most of the heavy lifting, because it is in dialog navigation that most of the complexity of the dialog manager resides.

The most important job of the DefDlgProc function is to restore focus to the control on the dialog that most recently had focus when the dialog regains activation. This allows you to switch away from a dialog box then return to it, and the dialog box focus goes back to the control that had it when you switched away, as if nothing had happened.

As noted previously, the default dialog box window procedure treats the WM_CLOSE message as a click on the Cancel button. And the default dialog box window procedure also handles the WM_NEXTDLGCTL message, as we show in the next sections.

How to set focus in a dialog box

Setting focus in a dialog box is more than just calling the SetFocus function.

The MSDN documentation for the DM_SETDEFID message notes that messing directly with the default ID carelessly can lead to odd cases like a dialog box with two default buttons. Fortunately, you rarely need to change the default ID for a dialog.

A bigger problem is using SetFocus to shove focus around a dialog. If you do this, you are going directly to the window manager, bypassing the dialog manager. This means that you can create "impossible" situations such as having focus on a pushbutton without that button being the default!

To avoid this problem, don't use SetFocus to change focus on a dialog. Instead, use the WM_NEXTDLGCTL message:

```
void SetDialogFocus(HWND hdlg, HWND hwndControl)
{
  SendMessage(hdlg, WM_NEXTDLGCTL, (WPARAM)hwndControl, TRUE);
}
```

As the remarks for the WM_NEXTDLGCTL message observe, the DefDlgProc function handles the WM_NEXTDLGCTL message by updating all the internal dialog manager bookkeeping, deciding which button should be the default, all that good stuff.

Now you can update dialog boxes like the professionals, avoiding oddities such as having no default button, or worse, multiple default buttons!

Why doesn't the SetFocus function manage default IDs for me?

The Windows dialog manager is built on top of the window manager. The SetFocus function belongs to the window manager; consequently, it has no knowledge of whether the window receiving focus is part of a dialog box. You can't just check the window class of the parent to see whether it is a dialog box, because, as noted earlier, an application can register a custom dialog class. As you also saw earlier, applications can use the IsDialogMessage function to support keyboard navigation in windows that aren't dialog boxes at all. The window manager can't just send a DM_GETDEFID message to the focus window's parent, because DM_GETDEFID has a numeric value equal to WM_USER, which is in the class-defined message range. If the parent window isn't a dialog box, the result of sending it the WM_USER message is entirely unpredictable.

If you need to set focus in a dialog box, you need to talk to the dialog manager. This means using the WM_NEXTDLGCTL message and allowing the DefDlgProc function to handle the focus change.

➤

Never leave focus on a disabled control

ONE OF THE big no-no's in dialog box management is disabling the control that has focus without first moving focus somewhere else. When you do this, the keyboard becomes dead to the dialog box, because disabled windows do not receive input. For users who don't have a mouse (say, because they have physical limitations that confine them to the keyboard), this kills your dialog box.

I've seen this happen even in Microsoft software. It's very frustrating.

Before you disable a control, check whether it has focus. If so, move focus somewhere else before you disable it so that the user isn't left stranded.

If you don't know which control focus should go to, you can always let the dialog manager decide. The WM_NEXTDLGCTL message again comes to the rescue:

```
void DialogDisableWindow(HWND hdlg, HWND hwndControl)
{
  if (hwndControl == GetFocus()) {
    SendMessage(hdlg, WM_NEXTDLGCTL, 0, FALSE);
  }
  EnableWindow(hwndControl, FALSE);
}
```

And of course, you should never disable the last control on a dialog. That would leave the user completely stranded with no hope of escape!

Why does the window manager even let you disable the focus window, anyway? Suppose it tried to stop you. That adds another complication to the window manager. It also means that a call to `DestroyWindow` could fail even though the parameter is a valid window; this could lead to strange bugs, possibly even a security hole, because a program would end up leaving a window enabled when it intended for it to be disabled. After all, the program might be in a transition state where it disables the focus window momentarily, intending to move focus to an enabled window before returning to the message loop. In reality, the window manager is fine with a disabled focus window, just like it's fine with no focus window at all! From a user interface perspective, these conditions should be merely transitory; before you resume interacting with the user, you need to fix up your focus.

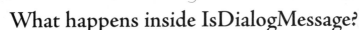

What happens inside IsDialogMessage?

As NOTED PREVIOUSLY, the job of the `IsDialogMessage` is to process input ahead of the destination window to implement keyboard navigation and other behaviors. The bulk of `IsDialogMessage` deals with keyboard accelerators, and the functionality is actually relatively straightforward. But before we dig into the details of `IsDialogMessage`, you need to understand a few other topics.

Using the Tab key to navigate in nondialogs

The `IsDialogMessage` function works even if you aren't a dialog. As long as your child windows have the `WS_TABSTOP` and/or `WS_GROUP` styles, they can be navigated as if they were part of a dialog box. One caveat is that `IsDialogMessage` sends `DM_GETDEFID` and `DM_SETDEFID` messages to your window, which are message numbers `WM_USER` and `WM_USER+1`, so you should avoid using those messages in your window procedure for some other purpose.

These changes to our scratch program illustrate how you can use the Tab key to navigate within a nondialog:

```
HWND g_hwndLastFocus;

void OnSetFocus(HWND hwnd, HWND hwndOldFocus)
{
    if (g_hwndLastFocus) {
        SetFocus(g_hwndLastFocus);
    }
}

void OnActivate(HWND hwnd, UINT state,
                HWND hwndActDeact, BOOL fMinimized)
{
    if (state == WA_INACTIVE) {
        g_hwndLastFocus = GetFocus();
    }
}

// Just display a messagebox so you can see something
void OnCommand(HWND hwnd, int id, HWND hwndCtl, UINT codeNotify)
{
    switch (id) {
    case 100:
        MessageBox(hwnd, TEXT("Button 1 pushed"),
                   TEXT("Title"), MB_OK);
        break;
    case 101:
        MessageBox(hwnd, TEXT("Button 2 pushed"),
                   TEXT("Title"), MB_OK);
        break;
    case IDCANCEL:
        MessageBox(hwnd, TEXT("Cancel pushed"),
                   TEXT("Title"), MB_OK);
        break;
    }
}

BOOL
OnCreate(HWND hwnd, LPCREATESTRUCT lpcs)
{
    HWND hwndChild =
        CreateWindow(
        TEXT("button"),                    /* Class Name */
        TEXT("Button &1"),                 /* Title */
```

```
            WS_CHILD | WS_VISIBLE | WS_TABSTOP |
            BS_DEFPUSHBUTTON | BS_TEXT,        /* Style */
            0, 0, 100, 100,                    /* Position and size */
            hwnd,                              /* Parent */
            (HMENU)100,                        /* Child ID */
            g_hinst,                           /* Instance */
            0);                                /* Special parameters */
    if (!hwndChild) return FALSE;
    g_hwndLastFocus = hwndChild;

    hwndChild =
        CreateWindow(
        TEXT("button"),                        /* Class Name */
        TEXT("Button &2"),                     /* Title */
        WS_CHILD | WS_VISIBLE | WS_TABSTOP |
        BS_PUSHBUTTON | BS_TEXT,               /* Style */
        100, 0, 100, 100,                      /* Position and size */
        hwnd,                                  /* Parent */
        (HMENU)101,                            /* Child ID */
        g_hinst,                               /* Instance */
        0);                                    /* Special parameters */
    if (!hwndChild) return FALSE;

    hwndChild =
        CreateWindow(
        TEXT("button"),                        /* Class Name */
        TEXT("Cancel"),                        /* Title */
        WS_CHILD | WS_VISIBLE | WS_TABSTOP |
        BS_PUSHBUTTON | BS_TEXT,               /* Style */
        200, 0, 100, 100,                      /* Position and size */
        hwnd,                                  /* Parent */
        (HMENU)IDCANCEL,                       /* Child ID */
        g_hinst,                               /* Instance */
        0);                                    /* Special parameters */
    if (!hwndChild) return FALSE;

    return TRUE;
}


// Add to WndProc

    HANDLE_MSG(hwnd, WM_COMMAND, OnCommand);
    HANDLE_MSG(hwnd, WM_ACTIVATE, OnActivate);
    HANDLE_MSG(hwnd, WM_SETFOCUS, OnSetFocus);
```

```
      // Add blank case statements for these
      // to ensure we don't use them by mistake.
      case DM_GETDEFID: break;
      case DM_SETDEFID: break;

// Change message loop
   MSG msg;
   while (GetMessage(&msg, NULL, 0, 0)) {
       if (IsDialogMessage(hwnd, &msg)) {
           /* Already handled by dialog manager */
       } else {
           TranslateMessage(&msg);
           DispatchMessage(&msg);
       }
   }
```

One subtlety is the additional handling of the WM_ACTIVATE and WM_SET-FOCUS messages to preserve the focus when the user switches away from the window and back. Notice also that we picked Button 1 as our initial default button by setting it with the BS_DEFPUSHBUTTON style.

Observe that all the standard dialog accelerators now work. The Tab key navigates, the Alt+1 and Alt+2 keys act as accelerators for the two buttons, the Enter key presses the default button, and the Esc key pushes the Cancel button because its control ID is IDCANCEL.

What is the "default ID" for a dialog box?

We glossed over those two messages DM_GETDEFID and DM_SETDEFID when we showed how to use the IsDialogMessage function to provide support for tabbing in nondialogs. But what is the "default ID"?

Recall that the default behavior when the user presses the Enter key in a dialog box is for the default button to be pushed. The default button is drawn with a distinctive look, typically a heavy outline or a different color. Programmatically, the default button identifies itself by having the BS_DEFPUSHBUTTON window style and by responding DLGC_DEFPUSHBUTTON to the WM_GETDLGCODE message. Note that default button status should not be confused with focus. For example, the Run dialog from the Start menu contains an edit control and three buttons. When it first appears, the OK button is the default button, but it does not have focus. Focus is instead on the edit control where you can type the command you want to run.

The rules for managing the default button are rather simple: If focus is on a pushbutton, that pushbutton is the default button. If focus is on some other control, the dialog manager sends the dialog the DM_GETDEFID message to determine which button it should make the default button. The default implementation of the DM_GETDEFID message returns the ID of the button that was the default button when the dialog box was first created, but you can change that ID by sending the dialog the DM_SETDEFID message.

(Astute observers might have noticed that the value returned by the DM_GETDEFID message packs the control ID in the low word and puts a signature in the high word. Consequently, control IDs are limited in practice to 16-bit values. Another scenario where the expansion of dialog control IDs to 32-bit values doesn't actually accomplish much.)

How to use the WM_GETDLGCODE message

The dialog manager uses the WM_GETDLGCODE message to learn about the controls on a dialog box. A control that wants to influence the behavior of the dialog manager should handle the WM_GETDLGCODE message by returning a bitmask of the DLGC_* values. These values break down into two groups:

- **The "want" group.** This group consists of the DLGC_WANTARROWS, DLGC_WANTTAB, DLGC_WANTALLKEYS (also known as DLGC_WANTMESSAGE), and DLGC_WANTCHARS flags. These values indicate which type of messages you want the dialog manager to pass through to the control. For example, if you return DLGC_WANT-ARROWS | DLGC_WANTTAB, the dialog manager lets arrows and tabs go through to your control instead of using them for dialog box navigation. The window that would normally have received the message is the one that gets to decide whether it wants it.

- **The "type" group.** This group consists of the DLGC_HASSETSEL (edit control), DLGC_DEFPUSHBUTTON, DLGC_UNDEFPUSHBUTTON,

DLGC_RADIOBUTTON, DLGC_BUTTON and DLGC_STATIC flags. You should return at most one of these flags (except for DLGC_BUTTON, which can be combined with the other button flags). They indicate what type of control the window is.

The dialog manager relies on the control reporting its own type rather than looking at the class name because looking only at the class name would cause the dialog manager to fail to recognize superclassed windows. Many user interface frameworks register their own enhanced versions of the standard window controls, and the dialog manager needs to know to treat an enhanced edit control as an edit control rather than as an unknown control. Because the superclass window procedure forwards to the original window procedure, the original window procedure's WM_GETDLGCODE handler will be available to report the "true" control type.

You rarely need to manipulate the dialog codes in the "type" group, but here they are for completeness.

The DLGC_SETSEL flag indicates that the window is an edit control and should have its contents selected when the user changes focus to the window. If you have an edit control on your dialog and you don't want this auto-select behavior, you can subclass the edit control and strip out the DLGC_SETSEL flag from the value returned by the original window procedure's WM_GETDLCCODE handler. (This is the only one of the "type" group of dialog codes that you will likely have need to tinker with.)

The DLGC_DEFPUSHBUTTON and DLGC_UNDEFPUSHBUTTON flags allow the dialog manager to determine which controls are pushbuttons and of them, which is the current default. The dialog manager needs to know this so that it can change the button from BS_PUSHBUTTON to BS_DEFPUSHBUTTON when it becomes the default button and to change it back when it ceases to be the default button.

The DLGC_RADIOBUTTON dialog code is used by button controls with the BS_AUTORADIOBUTTON style so that it can identify other radio buttons in its group and automatically uncheck all the other radio buttons when one of them is checked.

The DLGC_BUTTON dialog code tells the dialog manager that the window is a button control. The dialog manager knows that buttons should be clicked when the user types the corresponding accelerator (assuming there is only one window with that mnemonic). If you return any of the other DLGC_xxxBUTTON flags, then you also need to return DLGC_BUTTON.

The DLGC_STATIC dialog code is important because it tells the dialog manager that it should check for the SS_NOPREFIX style before scanning the control text for keyboard mnemonics.

One oft-neglected aspect of the WM_GETDLGCODE message is that if the window is being asked to produce its dialog code because the dialog manager wants to know whether it should process the message itself or let the control handle it, the lParam parameter to the message points to the MSG structure for the message being processed. Otherwise, the lParam is zero. If you want the dialog manager to pass a particular message to your window and it isn't covered by one of the existing "want" codes such as DLGC_WANTARROWS, you can look at the message yourself and return DLGC_WANTMESSAGE if the message is one that you want your window to process.

Consequently, many of the "want" codes are merely conveniences. For example, DLGC_WANTTAB is theoretically redundant, because you could simulate it by inspecting the message to see whether it is a WM_KEYDOWN or WM_CHAR with VK_TAB in the wParam and returning DLGC_WANTMESSAGE if so. Redundant they may be, but it's much easier just to say DLGC_WANTTAB instead of writing the code to see whether the message is a Tab keypress.

Okay, now what happens inside IsDialogMessage?

Now that we understand the WM_GETDLGCODE message, we can dig into how IsDialogMessage performs keyboard navigation.

When a character is typed, either with or without the Alt key pressed, the IsDialogMessage function tries to interpret it as a keyboard accelerator. The control's dialog code can override this behavior: If the DLGC_WANTMESSAGE (or DLGC_WANTCHARS in the case of a character typed without the Alt key) flag is set in the dialog code, the IsDialogMessage function will not interpret the key as an accelerator and instead will allow it to be delivered to the control normally. If you want your control to react to certain keys but not others, you can look at the message structure passed in the lParam parameter to decide whether your control wants to take the key. For example, check boxes return DLGC_WANTCHARS if the key is a space because they use the space bar to toggle the check mark.

If the control permits the IsDialogMessage to process the key as an accelerator, the IsDialogMessage function first looks for a matching accelerator inside the group that contains the control with focus, and then searches the entire dialog. The details of the searching algorithm are not worth repeating here because most discussions of the dialog manager cover the effect of the WS_GROUP and WS_TABSTOP styles, as well as the effect of hiding or disabling a control. The new wrinkle is the impact of the dialog code, for it is the dialog code that controls how the accelerator is determined. In addition to the other rules that govern which controls are searched, if the control's dialog code has the DLGC_WANTCHARS flag set, or if it has the DLGC_STATIC flag set and the control's window style includes the SS_NOPREFIX style, the control is skipped over in the search for a matching accelerator. The dialog manager also checks for the DLGC_DEFPUSHBUTTON and DLGC_UNDEFPUSHBUTTON codes because pushbuttons do not take focus when their accelerator is pressed; they merely fire the BN_CLICKED notification.

The processing for other keys is similarly straightforward, complicated only by constantly checking the dialog codes of the controls to see what type of special behaviors are required. Pressing an arrow key checks for DLGC_WANTARROWS (or the wildcard DLGC_WANTMESSAGE) before using the arrow key to navigate within a control group; and if the user navigated to a DLGC_RADIOBUTTON control that is an auto-radio button, the radio button is given a chance to uncheck its group siblings. Pressing the Tab key checks for DLGC_WANTTAB (or the wildcard DLGC_WANTMESSAGE) before using the Tab key to navigate among tab stops. Finally, pressing the Enter and Esc keys invokes the default button or the IDCANCEL button, respectively, again after checking with DLGC_WANTMESSAGE.

Why is the X button disabled on my message box?

SOME PEOPLE HAVE noticed that if you display a message box such as the following;

```
MessageBox(NULL, TEXT("Are you ready?"), TEXT("Message"),
        MB_YESNO);
```

the X button in the corner of the window is disabled. The reason for this is simultaneously obvious and subtle.

It's subtle in that it falls out of the default behavior of dialog boxes. Recall that the X button corresponds to WM_SYSCOMMAND/SC_CLOSE, which turns into WM_CLOSE, which cancels the dialog box by pressing the IDCANCEL button. But a Yes/No dialog doesn't have an IDCANCEL button; the buttons are IDYES and IDNO. No cancel button means nothing for the close button to do.

The answer is obvious by just looking at the question. Suppose the X button actually did something. What should it do? Does X mean Yes, or does it mean No? Certainly if it chose something at all, it should choose the safer option, but whether Yes or No is the safer answer depends on the question! Because there is no way to cancel out of a Yes/No question, there is no meaning that can be applied to the X button.

Note, however, that if you add Cancel to the list of responses, the X button becomes enabled and corresponds to the Cancel button.

The corollary to this little logic lesson is that if you are designing your own dialog box, and the only interactive control is a button (which I hope you have called OK or Close), you should give it the control ID IDCANCEL so that users can use the X button or press the Esc key to dismiss the dialog. More generally, you can use this trick any time you want the X button or Esc key to push a particular button on the dialog: Give that button the ID IDCANCEL.

CHAPTER ELEVEN

GENERAL SOFTWARE ISSUES

A LTHOUGH THESE TOPICS may take Windows as their starting point, they are nonetheless applicable to software development in general. We start with the insanity of time zone, then explore some simple software engineering principles, and end with topics related to performance.

Why daylight saving time is nonintuitive

A COMMON COMPLAINT is that all the Win32 time zone conversion functions such as `FileTimeToLocalFileTime` apply the *current* daylight saving time (DST) bias rather than the bias that was in effect at the time in question. (Outside North America, daylight saving time is typically called *summer time*.)

For example, suppose you have a `FILETIME` structure that represents 1 January 2000 12:00AM. If you are in Redmond, Washington, during the summer time, this converts to 31 December 1999 5:00PM, seven hours difference, even though the time difference between Redmond and coordinated universal time (UTC) was eight hours at that time. (When people in London were celebrating the New Year, it was 4 p.m. in Redmond, not 5 p.m.)

The reason is that the time got converted from 1 January 2000 12:00AM UTC to 31 December 1999 5:00PM *PDT*. So, technically, the conversion is correct. Of course, nobody was using Pacific daylight time (PDT) on December 31, 1999, in Redmond; everybody was on Pacific standard time (PST).

Why don't the time zone conversion functions use the time zone appropriate for the time of year?

One reason is that it means that `FileTimeToLocalFileTime` and `LocalFileTimeToFileTime` would no longer be inverses of each other. If you had a local time during the "limbo hour" during the cutover from standard time to daylight time, it would have *no corresponding UTC time* because there was no such thing as 2:30 a.m. local time. (The clock jumped from 2 a.m. to 3 a.m.) Similarly, a local time of 2:30 a.m. during the cutover from daylight time back to standard time would have *two* corresponding UTC times.

Another reason is that the laws regarding DST are in constant flux. For example, during 1974 and 1975, DST in the United States began in mid-winter because of the energy crisis. Of course, this information isn't encoded anywhere in the `TIME_ZONE_INFORMATION` structure. Similarly, during World War II, the United States went on DST all year round. And between 1945 and 1966, the DST rules varied from region to region.

DST rules are in flux even today. The DST cutover dates in Israel had been decided on a year-by-year basis by the Knesset before stabilizing in 2005. In the United States, new rules take effect in 2007. The dates in Brazil are determined every year by presidential decree. As a result, there is no deterministic formula for the day, and therefore no way to know it ahead of time.

The .NET Framework takes a different approach: They apply the time zone that was in effect at the time in question, on the assumption that the same DST transition rules applied then as they do now. Compare the last-modified time of a file as reported by `FileInfo.LastWriteTime` with what you see in the property sheet for a file that was last written to on the other side of the DST transition. For example, suppose the file was last modified on October 17, during DST but DST is not currently in effect. Explorer's file properties reports Thursday, October 17, 2003, 8:45:38 AM, but the .NET Framework's `FileInfo` reports Thursday, October 17, 2003, 9:45 AM.

To reiterate, Win32 does not attempt to guess which time zone rules were in effect at that other time. Win32 says, "Thursday, October 17, 2002, 8:45:38 AM PST." Note: Pacific *standard* time. Even though October 17 was during Pacific *daylight* time, Win32 displays the time as standard time because that's what time it is now.

.NET says, "Well, if the rules in effect now were also in effect on October 17, 2003, then that would be daylight time," so it displays "Thursday, October 17, 2003, 9:45 AM PDT"—*daylight* time.

So .NET gives a value which is more intuitively correct, but is also potentially incorrect, and which is not invertible. Win32 gives a value that is intuitively incorrect, but is strictly correct.

Why do timestamps change when I copy files to a floppy?

FLOPPY DISKS USE the FAT file system, as do DOS-based and Windows 95-based operating systems. On the other hand, Windows NT-based systems tend to use the NTFS file system. (Although you can format a hard drive as FAT on Windows NT-based systems, it is not the default option.)

The NTFS and FAT file systems store times and dates differently. Most notable, NTFS records file timestamps in UTC, whereas FAT records them in local time. Furthermore, FAT records last-write time only to two-second accuracy. Consequently, if you copy a file from NTFS to FAT, the last-write time can change by as much as two seconds.

Why is FAT so much lamer than NTFS? Because FAT was invented in 1977, back before people were worried about such piddling things like time zones, much less Unicode. And it was still a major improvement over CP/M, which didn't have timestamps at all. (Heck, CP/M didn't even keep track of how many bytes in size your file was!)

It is also valuable to read and understand the consequences of FAT storing file times in local time, compared to NTFS storing file times in UTC. In addition to the DST problems discussed earlier, you also will notice that the timestamp will appear to change if you take a floppy across time zones. Create a file at, say, 9 a.m. Pacific time, on a floppy disk. Now move the floppy disk to mountain time. The file was created at 10 a.m. mountain time, but if you look at the disk it will still say 9 a.m., which corresponds to 8 a.m. Pacific time. The file traveled backward in time one hour. (In other words, the timestamp *failed to change when it should have*.)

Don't trust the return address

SOMETIMES PEOPLE ASK, "I know that I can use the `_ReturnAddress()` intrinsic to get my function's return address, but how do I figure out what module that return address belongs to? I'm going to use this to make a security decision."

Beware.

Even if you call the `GetModuleHandleEx` function and pass the `GET_MOD`-`ULE_HANDLE_EX_FLAG_FROM_ADDRESS` flag, that doesn't mean that that is actually the DLL that called you.

A common trick is to search through a "trusted" DLL for some code bytes that coincidentally match ones you (the attacker) want to execute. This can be something as simple as a `retd` instruction, which is quite abundant. The attacker then builds a stack frame that looks like this, for, say, a function that takes two parameters:

```
trusted_return_address
hacked parameter 1
hacked parameter 2
hacker_code_addr
```

After building this stack frame, the attacker then jumps to the start of the function being attacked.

The function being attacked looks at the return address and sees `trusted_return_address`, which resides in a trusted DLL. It then foolishly trusts the caller and allows some unsafe operation to occur, using hacked parameters 1 and 2. The function being attacked then does a `ret 8` to return and clean the parameters. This transfers control to the `trusted_return_address`, which performs a simple `ret`, which now gives control to the `hacker_code_addr`, and the hacker can use the result to continue his nefarious work

This is why you should be concerned if somebody says, "This code verifies that its caller is trusted." How do they know who the caller really is?

Note that these remarks are in the context of unmanaged code, where malicious code can do things such as manipulate the call stack. Managed code (in the absence of unsafe operations) does not have the capability to manipulate arbitrary memory and consequently operates under a different set of rules.

Writing a sort comparison function

THE RULES FOR sort comparison functions have some interesting consequences.

When you are writing a sort comparison function (say, to be passed to `ListView_SortItems` or `qsort`), your comparison function needs to follow these rules:

- **Reflexivity.** `Compare(a, a) = 0`.
- **Anti-Symmetry.** `Compare(a, b)` has the opposite sign of `Compare(b, a)`, where 0 is considered to be its own opposite.
- **Transitivity.** If `Compare(a, b)` ≤ 0 and `Compare(b, c)` ≤ 0, then `Compare(a, c)` ≤ 0,

Here are some logical consequences of these rules (all easily proved). The first two are obvious, but the third might be a surprise:

- **Transitivity of equality.** If `Compare(a, b)` $= 0$ and `Compare(b, c)` $= 0$, then `Compare(a, c)` $= 0$.

- **Transitivity of inequality.** If `Compare(a, b) < 0` and `Compare(b, c) < 0`, then `Compare(a, c) < 0`.

- **Substitution.** If `Compare(a, b) = 0`, then `Compare(a, c)` has the same sign as `Compare(b, c)`.

Of the original three rules, the first two are hard to get wrong, but the third rule is often hard to get right if you try to be clever in your comparison function.

For one thing, these rules require that you implement a total order. If you merely have a partial order, you must extend your partial order to a total order *in a consistent manner.*

I've seen people get into trouble when they try to implement their comparison function on a set of tasks, where some tasks have other tasks as prerequisites. The comparison function implemented the following algorithm:

- If a is a prerequisite of b (possibly through a chain of intermediate tasks), then `a < b`.

- If b is a prerequisite of a (again, possibly through a chain of intermediate tasks), then `a > b`.

- Otherwise, `a = b`. "Neither task is a prerequisite of the other, so I don't care what order they are in."

Sounds great. Then you can sort with this comparison function and you get the tasks listed in some order such that all tasks come after their prerequisites.

Except that it doesn't work. Trying to sort with this comparison function results in all the tasks being jumbled together with apparently no regard for which tasks are prerequisites of which. What went wrong?

Consider this dependency diagram:

$$a \rightarrow b$$
$$c$$

Task a is a prerequisite for b, and task c is unrelated to both of them. If you used the above comparison function, it would declare that a = c and b = c (because c is unrelated to a or b), which in turn implies by transitivity that a = b, which contradicts a < b, because a is a prerequisite for b. If your comparison function is inconsistent, you will get garbled results.

Moral of the story: When you write a comparison function, you really have to know which items are less than which other items. Don't just declare two items "equal" because you don't know which order they should be in.

You can read a contract from the other side

AN INTERFACE IS a contract, but remember that a contract applies to both parties. Most of the time, when you read an interface, you look at it from the point of view of the client side of the contract, but often it helps to read it from the server side.

For example, let's look at the interface for control panel applications, documented in MSDN under the topic "Control Panel Items."

Most of the time, when you're reading this documentation, you are wearing your "I am writing a Control Panel application" hat. So, for example, the documentation says this:

> *When the controlling application first loads the Control Panel application, it retrieves the address of the* CPlApplet *function and subsequently uses the address to call the function and pass it messages.*

With your "I am writing a Control Panel application" hat, this means, "Gosh, I had better have a function called CPlApplet and export it so I can receive messages."

But if you are instead wearing your "I am hosting a Control Panel application" hat, this means, "Gosh, I had better call GetProcAddress() to get the address of the application's CPlApplet function so that I can send it messages."

Similarly, under the "Message Processing" section, it lists the messages that are sent from the controlling application to the Control Panel application. If you are wearing your "I am writing a Control Panel application" hat, this means, "Gosh, I had better be ready to receive these messages in this order."

But if you are wearing your "I am hosting a Control Panel application" hat, this means, "Gosh, I had better send these messages in the order listed."

And finally, when it says, "The controlling application releases the Control Panel application by calling the FreeLibrary function," your "I am writing a Control Panel application" hat says, "I had better be prepared to be unloaded," whereas your "I am hosting a Control Panel application" hat says, "This is where I unload the library."

So let's try it. As always, start with our scratch program and change the WinMain:

```c
#include <cpl.h>

int WINAPI WinMain(HINSTANCE hinst, HINSTANCE hinstPrev,
                   LPSTR lpCmdLine, int nShowCmd)
{
  HWND hwnd;

  g_hinst = hinst;

  if (!InitApp()) return 0;

  if (SUCCEEDED(CoInitialize(NULL))) {/* In case we use COM */

    hwnd = CreateWindow(
        "Scratch",                          /* Class Name */
        "Scratch",                          /* Title */
        WS_OVERLAPPEDWINDOW,                 /* Style */
        CW_USEDEFAULT, CW_USEDEFAULT,        /* Position */
        CW_USEDEFAULT, CW_USEDEFAULT,        /* Size */
        NULL,                                /* Parent */
        NULL,                                /* No menu */
        hinst,                               /* Instance */
        0);                                  /* No parameters */
      if (hwnd) {
        TCHAR szPath[MAX_PATH];
        LPTSTR pszLast;
        DWORD cch = SearchPath(NULL, TEXT("access.cpl"),
                    NULL, MAX_PATH, szPath, &pszLast);
        if (cch > 0 && cch < MAX_PATH) {
          RunControlPanel(hwnd, szPath);
        }
      }
    }
    CoUninitialize();
```

```
    }

    return 0;
}
```

Instead of showing the window and entering the message loop, we start acting like a Control Panel host. Our victim today is access.cpl, the accessibility Control Panel. After locating the program on the path, we ask RunControlPanel to do the heavy lifting:

```
void RunControlPanel(HWND hwnd, LPCTSTR pszPath)
{
    // — We'll talk about these lines later
    // Maybe this control panel application has a custom manifest
    ACTCTX act = { 0 };
    act.cbSize = sizeof(act);
    act.dwFlags = 0;
    act.lpSource = pszPath;
    act.lpResourceName = MAKEINTRESOURCE(123);
    HANDLE hctx = CreateActCtx(&act);
    ULONG_PTR ulCookie;
    if (hctx == INVALID_HANDLE_VALUE ||
        ActivateActCtx(hctx, &ulCookie)) {

        HINSTANCE hinstCPL = LoadLibrary(pszPath);
        if (hinstCPL) {
            APPLET_PROC pfnCPlApplet = (APPLET_PROC)
                GetProcAddress(hinstCPL, "CPlApplet");
            if (pfnCPlApplet) {
                if (pfnCPlApplet(hwnd, CPL_INIT, 0, 0)) {
                    int cApplets = pfnCPlApplet(hwnd, CPL_GETCOUNT, 0, 0);
                    // We're going to run application zero
                    // (In real life we might show a list of them
                    // and let the user pick one)
                    if (cApplets > 0) {
                        CPLINFO cpli;
                        pfnCPlApplet(hwnd, CPL_INQUIRE, 0, (LPARAM)&cpli);
                        pfnCPlApplet(hwnd, CPL_DBLCLK, 0, cpli.lData);
                        pfnCPlApplet(hwnd, CPL_STOP, 0, cpli.lData);
                    }
                }
                pfnCPlApplet(hwnd, CPL_EXIT, 0, 0);
            }

            FreeLibrary(hinstCPL);
```

```
    }

// ---- We'll talk about these lines later
if (hctx != INVALID_HANDLE_VALUE) {
    DeactivateActCtx(0, ulCookie);
    ReleaseActCtx(hctx);
}
    }
}
```

Ignore the highlighted lines for now; we discuss them later.

All we're doing is following the specification but reading it from the host side. So we load the library, locate its entry point, and call it with CPL_INIT, then CPL_GETCOUNT. If there are any Control Panel applications inside this library file, we inquire after the first one, double-click it (this is where all the interesting stuff happens), and then stop it. After all that excitement, we clean up according to the rules set out for the host (namely, by sending a CPL_EXIT message.)

So that's all. Well, except for the highlighted parts. What's that about?

Those lines are to support Control Panel applications that have a custom manifest. This is something new with Windows XP and is documented in MSDN under the topic "Using Windows XP Visual Styles."

If you go down to the "Using ComCtl32 Version 6 in Control Panel or a DLL That Is Run by RunDll32.exe" section, you'll see that the application provides its manifest to the Control Panel host by attaching it as resource number 123. That's what the shaded code does: It loads and activates the manifest, then invites the Control Panel application to do its thing (with its manifest active), and then cleans up. If there is no manifest, CreateActCtx returns INVALID_HANDLE_VALUE. We do not treat that as an error, because many programs don't yet provide a manifest.

These details regarding manifests and activation aren't important to the discussion; I included them only for completeness. The point of this exercise is showing how to read documentation from the point of view of the host rather than the client.

The battle between pragmatism and purity

As DISCUSSED IN "Why are these unwanted files/folder opening when I log on?" (Chapter 5), the CreateProcess function will try multiple times to split the command line into a program and arguments in an attempt to correct command lines that were mistakenly left unquoted. Why does the CreateProcess function do autocorrection at all?

Programs that weren't designed to handle long filenames would make mistakes like taking the path to the executable and writing it into the registry, unaware that the path might contain a space that needs quoting. (Spaces, although technically legal, were vanishingly rare in short filenames.) The CreateProcess function had to decide whether to "autocorrect" these invalid paths or to let those programs simply stop working.

This is the battle between pragmatism and purity.

Purity says, "Let them suffer for their mistake. We're not going to sully our beautiful architecture to accommodate such stupidity." Of course, such an attitude comes with a cost: People aren't going to use your "pure" system if it can't run the programs that they require.

Put another way, it doesn't matter how great your 1.0 version is if you don't survive long enough to make a 2.0.

Your choice is between "being pure and unpopular" or "being pragmatic and popular." Look at all the wonderful technologies that died for lack of popularity despite technical superiority. Sony Betamax, Mattel Intellivision. (And, in the United States: the metric system.)

Electric cars are another example. As great as electric cars are, they never reached any significant market success. Only after conceding to popularity and "sullying" their "purity" by adding a gasoline hybrid engine did they finally gain acceptance.

I see this happening over and over again. A product team that, hypothetically, makes automated diagramming software, says, "I can't believe we're losing to Z. Sure, Z's diagrams may be fast and snazzy, but ours gets ‹subtle detail› right, and when you go to ‹extreme case› their diagrams come out a little distorted, and they're faster only because they don't try to prevent X and Y from overlapping each other in ‹scenario Q›. We're doing all those things; that's why we're slower, but that's also why we're better. Those people over at Z just don't get it."

Guess what. People are voting with their wallets, and right now their wallets are saying that Z is better in spite of all those "horrible flaws." Whatever part of *it* they don't get, it's certainly not the "make lots of people so happy that they send you money" part.

~

Optimization is often counterintuitive

Anybody who's done intensive optimization knows that optimization is often counterintuitive. Things you think would be faster often aren't.

Consider, for example, the exercise of obtaining the current instruction pointer. There's the naive solution:

```
// Inlining this function would produce the wrong _ReturnAddress,
// so let's disable it.
__declspec(noinline)
void *GetCurrentAddress()
{
    return _ReturnAddress();
}

...
void *currentInstruction = GetCurrentAddress();
```

If you look at the disassembly, you'll get something like this:

```
GetCurrentAddress:
    mov eax, [esp]
    ret

...
    call GetCurrentAddress
    mov [currentInstruction], eax
```

"Pah," you say to yourself, "look at how inefficient that is. I can reduce that to two instructions. Watch:

```
void *currentInstruction;
__asm {
call L1
L1: pop currentInstruction
}
```

"That's half the instruction count of your bloated version."

But if you sit down and race the two code sequences, you'll find that the function-call version is faster by a factor of two! How can that be?

The reason is the "hidden variables" inside the processor. All modern processors contain much more state than you can see from the instruction sequence. You can read about TLBs, L1 and L2 caches, all sorts of stuff that you can't see in the instruction stream. The hidden variable that is important here is the return address predictor.

Modern x86 processors maintain an internal stack that is updated by each CALL and RET instruction. When a CALL is executed, the return address is pushed both onto the real stack (the one that the ESP register points to) as well as to the internal return address predictor stack; a RET instruction pops the top address of the return address predictor stack as well as the real stack.

The return address predictor stack is used when the processor decodes a RET instruction. It looks at the top of the return address predictor stack and says, "I bet that RET instruction is going to return to that address." It then speculatively executes the instructions at that address. Because programs rarely fiddle with return addresses on the stack, these predictions tend to be highly accurate.

That's why the "optimization" turns out to be slower. Let's say that at the point of the CALL L1 instruction, the return address predictor stack looks like this:

Return address predictor stack: caller1 → caller2 → caller3 → ...

Actual stack: caller1 → caller2 → caller3 → ...

Here, caller1 is the function's caller, caller1 is the function's caller's caller, and so on. So far, the return address predictor stack is right on target. (I've drawn the actual stack below the return address predictor stack so you can see that they match.)

Now you execute the CALL instruction. The return address predictor stack and the actual stack now look like this:

Return address predictor stack: L1 → caller1 → caller2 → caller3 → ...

Actual stack: L1 → caller1 → caller2 → caller3 → ...

But instead of executing a RET instruction, you pop off the return address. This removes it from the actual stack, but doesn't remove it from the return address predictor stack.

Return address predictor stack: L1   → caller1 → caller2 → caller3 → ...

Actual stack: caller1 → caller2 → caller3 → caller4 → ...

I think you can see where this is going.

Eventually your function returns. The processor decodes your RET instruction and looks at the return address predictor stack and says, "My predictor stack says that this RET is going to return to L1. I will begin speculatively executing there."

But oh no, the value on the top of the real stack isn't L1 at all. It's caller1. The processor's return address predictor predicted incorrectly, and it ended up wasting its time studying the wrong code!

The effects of this bad guess don't end there. After the RET instruction, the return address predictor stack looks like this:

Return address predictor stack: caller1 → caller2 → caller3 → ...

Actual stack: caller2 → caller3 → caller4 → ...

Eventually your caller returns. Again, the processor consults its return address predictor stack and speculatively executes at caller1. But that's not where you're returning to. You're really returning to caller2.

And so on. By mismatching the CALL and RET instructions, you managed to cause every single return address prediction on the stack to be wrong. Notice in the diagram that, in the absence of somebody playing games with the return address predictor stack of the type that created the problem initially, not a single prediction on the return address predictor stack will be correct. None of the predicted return addresses matches up with the actual return address.

Your peephole optimization has proven to be shortsighted.

Some processors expose this predictor more explicitly. The Alpha AXP, for example, has several types of control flow instructions, all of which have the same logical effect, but which hint to the processor how it should maintain its internal predictor stack. For example, the BR instruction says, "Jump to this address, but do not push the old address onto the predictor stack." On the other hand, the JSR instruction says, "Jump to this address, and push the old address onto the predictor stack." There is also a RET instruction that says, "Jump to this address, and pop an address from the predictor stack." (There's a fourth type that isn't used much.)

Moral of the story: Just because something looks better doesn't mean that it necessarily is better.

🙠

On a server, paging = death

I HAD OCCASION to meet somebody from another division who told me this little story: They had a server that went into thrashing death every 10 hours, like clockwork, and had to be rebooted. To mask the problem, the server was converted to a cluster, so what really happened was that the machines in the cluster took turns being rebooted. The clients never noticed anything, but the server administrators were really frustrated. ("Hey Clancy, looks like number two needs to be rebooted. She's sucking mud.")

The reason for the server's death? Paging.

There was a four-bytes-per-request memory leak in one of the programs running on the server. Eventually, all the leakage filled available memory and the server was forced to page. Paging means slower response, but of course the requests for service kept coming in at the normal rate. So the longer it took to turn a request around, the more requests piled up, and then it took even longer to turn around the new requests, so even more piled up, and so on. The problem snowballed until the machine just plain keeled over.

After much searching, the leak was identified and plugged. Now the servers chug along without a hitch. (Furthermore, because the reason for the cluster was to cover for the constant crashes, I suspect they reduced the size of the cluster and saved a lot of money.)

Don't save anything you can recalculate

NOWADAYS, A MAJOR barrier to performance for many classes of programs is paging. We just saw that paging can kill a server. Let's look at another example of how performance became tied to paging.

The principle is "Don't save anything you can recalculate." This of course, seems counterintuitive: Shouldn't you save the answer so you don't have to recalculate it?

The answer is, "It depends."

If recalculating the answer isn't very expensive and has good data locality, you might be better off recalculating it than saving it, especially if saving it reduces locality. For example, if the result is stored in a separate object, you now have to touch a second object—risking a page fault—to get the saved answer.

The window manager uses this principle, using the WM_PAINT message to generate the pixels on the screen instead of saving them. (An important consideration in the early days of Windows when there was precious little memory to go around.) Later, we will see how Windows 95 applied this principle so that rebasing a DLL didn't thrash your machine. I'm told that the Access team used this principle to reap significant performance gains. Instead of caching results, they just threw them away and recalculated them the next time they were needed.

Whether this technique works for you is hard to predict. If your program is processor bound, caching computations is probably a good idea. But if your program is memory bound, you may be better off getting rid of the cache, because the cache is just creating more memory pressure.

Performance gains at the cost of other components

IN THE OPERATING systems group, we have to take a holistic view of performance. The goal is to get the entire system running faster, balancing applications against each other for the greater good.

Applications, on the other hand, tend to have a selfish view of performance: "I will do everything possible to make myself run faster. The impact on the rest of the system is not my concern."

Some applications will put themselves into the Startup group so that they will load faster. This isn't really making the system run any faster; it's just shifting the accounting. By shoving some of the application startup cost into operating system startup, the amount of time between the user double-clicking the application icon and the application being ready to run has been reduced. But the total amount of time hasn't changed.

For example, consider the following time diagram. The asterisk (*) marks the point at which the user turns on the computer, the plus sign (+) marks the point at which Explorer is ready and the user double-clicks the application icon, and the exclamation point (!) marks the point at which the application is ready.

| * | OS Startup | + | Application Startup | ! |

The application developers then say, "Gosh, that 'Application Startup' section is awfully big. What can we do to make it smaller? I know, let's break our application startup into two pieces ...

"... and put part of it in the Startup group.

| ∗ | OS Startup | Application Startup 1 | + | Application Startup 2 | ! |

"Wow, look, the distance between the plus sign and the exclamation point (which represents how long it takes for our application to get ready after the user double-clicks the icon) is much shorter now!"

The team then puts this new shorter value in their performance status report, everybody gets raises all around, and maybe they go for a nice dinner to celebrate.

Of course, if you look at the big picture, from the asterisk all the way to the exclamation point, nothing has changed. It still takes the same amount of time for the application to be ready from a cold start. All this "performance" improvement did was rob Peter to pay Paul. The time spent doing "Application Startup 1" is now charged against the operating system and not against the application. You shuffled numbers around, but the end user gained nothing.

In fact, the user *lost* ground. For the preceding diagrams assume that the user wants to run your application at all! If users didn't want to run your application but instead just wanted to check their email, they are paying for "Application Startup 1" even though they will reap none of the benefits.

Another example of applications having a selfish view of performance came from a company developing an icon overlay handler. The shell treats overlay computation as a low-priority item, because it is more important to get icons on the screen so that users can start doing whatever it is they wanted to be doing. The decorations can come later. This company wanted to know whether they could somehow improve their performance and get their overlay onto the screen *even before the icon shows up*, demonstrating a phenomenally selfish interpretation of "performance."

Performance is about getting the user finished with their task sooner. If that task does not involve running your program, your "performance improvement" is really a performance impediment. I'm sure your program is very nice, but it would also be rather presumptuous to expect all users who install your program to think that it should take priority over everything else they do.

Performances consequences of polling

POLLING KILLS.

A program should not poll as a matter of course. Doing so can have serious consequences on system performance. It's like checking your watch every minute to see whether it's 3 o'clock yet instead of just setting an alarm.

First of all, polling means that a small amount of CPU time gets eaten up at each poll even though there is nothing to do. Even if you tune your polling loop so that its CPU usage is only, say, a measly one-tenth of 1%, when this program is placed on a Terminal Server with 800 simultaneous connections, your 0.1% CPU usage has magnified into 80% CPU usage.

Next, the fact that a small snippet of code runs at regular intervals means that it (and all the code that leads up to it) cannot be pruned from the system's working set. They remain present just to say, "Nope, nothing to do." If your polling code touches any instance data (and it almost certainly will), that's a minimum of one page's worth of memory per instance. On an x86-class machine, that is 4KB times the number of copies of the program running. On that 800-user Terminal Server machine, you've just chewed up 3MB of memory, all of which is being kept hot just in case some rare event occurs.

Finally, polling has deleterious effects even for people who aren't running humongous Terminal Server machines with hundreds of users. A single laptop will suffer from polling, because it prevents the CPU from going to more power-efficient sleep states, resulting in a hotter laptop and shorter battery life. Instead of polling, use a notification-based mechanism. That way, your code runs only when there is actually something to do.

Of course, Windows itself is hardly blame-free in this respect. But the performance team remains on the lookout for rogue polling in Windows and works with the people responsible for the offending component to fix the problem.

The poor man's way of identifying memory leaks

MANY DIFFERENT TOOLS are available for identifying resource leaks, but one method requires no tools or special compiler switches or support libraries: Just let the leak continue until the source becomes blatantly obvious.

Nightly automated stress testing is a regular part of any project. Some teams use a custom screen saver to initiate the stress test, others use a custom program, still others require manual launching of the stress test; but by whatever means, after you've gone home for the day, your computer connects to a central server and receives a set of tests that it runs all night.

One of the things that these overnight tests often turn up is a memory leak of one sort or another, identified by the stress team because your program's resource usage has gone abnormally high. But how do you debug these failures? These machines aren't running a special instrumented build with your leak detection tool, so you can't use that.

Instead, you use the "target-rich environment" principle.

Suppose you're leaking memory. After 15 hours of continuous heavy usage, your program starts getting out-of-memory failures. You're obviously leaking something, but what?

Think about it: If you are leaking something, there are going to be a lot of them. Whereas things you aren't leaking will be few in number. Therefore, if you grab something at random, it will most likely be a leaked object! In mathematical terms, suppose your program's normal memory usage is 15MB, but for some reason you've used up 1693MB of dynamically allocated memory. Because only 15MB of that is normal memory usage, the other 1678MB must be the leaked data. If you dump a random address from the heap, you have a greater-than-99% chance of dumping a leaked object.

So grab a dozen or so addresses at random and dump them. Odds are you'll see the same data pattern over and over again. That's your leak. If it's a C++ object with virtual methods, dumping the vtable will quickly identify what type of object it is. If it's a simple chunk of data, you can usually identify what it is by looking for string buffers or pointers to other data.

Your mileage may vary, but I've found it to be an enormously successful technique. Think of it as applied psychic powers.

A cache with a bad policy is another name for a memory leak

A COMMON PERFORMANCE trick is to reduce time spent in the heap by caching the last item freed (or maybe the last few) so that a subsequent allocation can just reuse the item instead of having to go make a new one. But you need to be careful how you do this or you can end up making things worse rather than better. Here's an example motivated by an actual problem the Windows performance team researched.

Consider a cache of variable-sized buffers. I will use only a one-entry cache for simplicity. In real life, the cache would be more complicated: People tend to have a deeper cache of 4 to 10 entries, and you would have to ensure that only one thread used the cache at a time; typically this is done by associating the cache with something that has thread affinity. Furthermore, you probably would keep the size of the cached buffer in a member variable instead of calling LocalSize all the time. I've left out all these complications to keep the presentation simple:

```
class BufferCache {
public:
  BufferCache() : m_pCache(NULL) { }
  ~BufferCache() { LocalFree(m_pCache); }

  void *GetBuffer(SIZE_T cb);
  void ReturnBuffer(void *p);

private:
  void *m_pCache;
};
```

If a request for a memory buffer arrives and it can be satisfied from the cache, the cached buffer is returned. Otherwise, a brand new buffer is allocated:

```
void *BufferCache::GetBuffer(SIZE_T cb)
{
 // Satisfy from cache if possible
 if (m_pCache && LocalSize(m_pCache) <= cb) {
  void *p = m_pCache;
  m_pCache = NULL;
  return p;
 }
 return LocalAlloc(LMEM_FIXED, cb);
}
```

When a buffer is returned to the cache, this particular implementation compares it against the item already in the cache and keeps the bigger one, on the theory that it is more likely to satisfy a GetBuffer in the future. (In the general case of a multiple-entry cache, we would free the smallest entry.)

```
// Flawed design - see discussion
void BufferCache::ReturnBuffer(void *p)
{
 SIZE_T cb = LocalSize(p);
 if (cb > LocalSize(m_pCache)) {
  // Returned buffer is bigger than the cache:
  // Keep the returned buffer
  LocalFree(m_pCache);
  m_pCache = p;
 } else {
  // Returned buffer is smaller than the cache:
  // Keep the cache
  LocalFree(p);
 }
}
```

This algorithm seems entirely reasonable at first, reasonable enough that I've seen it in production code more than once. Why is this a flawed design?

The distribution of buffer sizes in most programs is rarely uniform. The most common distribution is that small buffers are popular, with larger and larger buffers being required less and less often. Let's write a sample program that allocates and frees memory according to this pattern. To make the bad behavior easier to spot in a short run, I'm going to use a somewhat flat distribution and say that half of the buffers are small, with larger buffers becoming less popular according to exponential decay. In practice, the decay curve is usually much, much steeper:

```
#include <vector>
#include <iostream>

// Since this is just a quick test, we're going to be sloppy
using namespace std; //   sloppy
int __cdecl main(int argc, char **argv)
{
 BufferCache b;

 // seeding the random number generator is not important here
 // in fact, the distribution isn't important either
 vector<void *> v; // keeps track of allocated memory
 for (;;) {
  // randomly allocate and free
  if (v.size() == 0 || (rand() & 1)) { // allocate
   SIZE_T cb = 100;
   while (cb < 1024 * 1024 && (rand() & 1)) {
    cb *= 2; // exponential decay distribution up to 1MB
   }
   void* p = b.GetBuffer(cb);
   if (p) {
    cout << " A" << LocalSize(p) << "/" << cb;
    v.push_back(p); // append to vector
   }
  } else { // free
   int victim = rand() % v.size(); // choose one at random
   cout << " F" << LocalSize(v[victim]);
   b.ReturnBuffer(v[victim]); // free it
   v[victim] = v.back(); // remove it from the vector
   v.pop_back();
  }
 }
}
```

This short program randomly allocates and frees memory from the buffer cache, printing (rather cryptically) the size of the blocks allocated and freed. When memory is allocated, it prints "Ax/y" where x is the size of the block actually allocated and y is the size requested. When freeing memory, it prints

"Fz" where z is the size of the block allocated. Run this program, let it do its thing for maybe 10, 15 seconds, then pause the output and study it. I'll wait. If you're too lazy to actually compile and run the program (or perhaps you're unable to because you're reading this on the bus away from a computer), I've included some sample output for you to study. For example, the first few entries of this output say, "We freed a block of size 102400, then we allocated 102400 bytes to fulfill a request for 400 bytes, and then we freed 800 bytes."

```
F102400 A102400/400 F800 F200 A800/100 A200/200 A400/400
A400/400 A200/200 F1600 A1600/100 F100 F800 F25600 A25600/200
F12800 A12800/200 F200 F400 A400/100 F200 A200/100 A200/200
A100/100 F200 F3200 A3200/400 A200/200 F51200 F800 F25600
F1600 F1600 A51200/100 F100 A100/100 F3200 F200 F409600 F100
A409600/400 A100/100 F200 F3200 A3200/800 A400/400 F800 F3200
F200 F12800 A12800/200 A100/100 F200 F25600 F400 F6400
A25600/100 F100 F200 F400 F200 F800 F400 A800/800 A100/100
```

Okay, maybe you don't see it. Let's make the effect even more obvious by printing some statistics periodically. Of course, to generate the statistics, we need to keep track of them, so we'll have to remember how big the requested buffer was (which we'll do in the buffer itself):

```
int __cdecl main(int argc, char **argv)
{
 BufferCache b;

 // seeding the random number generator is not important here
 // in fact, the distribution isn't important either

 vector<void *> v; // keeps track of allocated memory
 SIZE_T cbAlloc = 0, cbNeeded = 0; // memory statistics
 for (int count = 0; ; count++) {
  // randomly allocate and free
  if (v.size() == 0 || (rand() & 1)) { // allocate
   SIZE_T cb = 100;
   while (cb < 1024 * 1024 && !(rand() % 4)) {
    cb *= 2; // exponential decay distribution up to 1MB
   }
   void* p = b.GetBuffer(cb);
   if (p) {
    *(SIZE_T*)p = cb;         // remember requested size
    cbAlloc += LocalSize(p); // update total memory allocated
```

```
    cbNeeded += cb;                // update total memory requested
    v.push_back(p);                // append to vector
  }
} else { // free
  int victim = rand() % v.size(); // choose one at random
  cbAlloc -= LocalSize(v[victim]); // total memory allocated
  cbNeeded -= *(SIZE_T*)v[victim]; // total memory requested
  b.ReturnBuffer(v[victim]); // free it
  v[victim] = v.back();
  v.pop_back();
}
if (count % 100 == 0) {
  cout << count << ": " << v.size() << " buffers, "
       << cbNeeded << "/" << cbAlloc << "="
       << cbNeeded * 100.0 / cbAlloc << "% used" << endl;
}
  }
}
```

This new version keeps track of how many bytes were allocated in addition to how many were actually needed, and prints a summary of those statistics every hundred allocations. Here is some sample output:

```
0: 1 buffers, 400/400=100% used
100: 7 buffers, 4300/106600=4.03377% used
200: 5 buffers, 1800/103800=1.7341% used
300: 19 buffers, 9800/115800=8.46287% used
400: 13 buffers, 5100/114000=4.47368% used
500: 7 buffers, 2500/28100=8.8968% used
...
37200: 65 buffers, 129000/2097100=6.15135% used
37300: 55 buffers, 18100/2031400=0.891011% used
37400: 35 buffers, 10400/2015800=0.515924% used
37500: 43 buffers, 10700/1869100=0.572468% used
37600: 49 buffers, 17200/1874000=0.917823% used
37700: 75 buffers, 26000/1889900=1.37573% used
37800: 89 buffers, 30300/1903100=1.59214% used
37900: 91 buffers, 29600/1911900=1.5482% used
```

By this point, the problem should be obvious: We're wasting insane quantities of memory. For example, after step 37900, we've allocated 1.8MB of memory when we needed only 30KB, for a waste of over 98%.

How did we go horribly wrong?

Recall that most of the time, the buffer being allocated is a small buffer, and most of the time, a small buffer is freed. But it's the rare case of a large buffer that messes up everything. The first time a large buffer is requested, it can't come from the cache, because the cache has only small buffers, so it must be allocated. And when it is returned, it is kept, because the cache keeps the largest buffer.

The next allocation comes in, and it's probably one of the common-case small buffers, and it is given the cached buffer—which is big. You're wasting a big buffer on something that needs only 100 bytes. Some time later, another rare big buffer request comes in, and because that other big buffer got wasted on a small allocation, you have to allocate a new big buffer. You allocated two big buffers even though you need only one. Because big buffers are rare, it is unlikely that a big buffer will be given to a caller that actually needs a big buffer; it is much more likely to be given to a caller that needs a small buffer.

Bad effect 1: Big buffers get wasted on small callers.

Notice that after a big buffer enters the system, it is hard to get rid of, because a returned big buffer will be compared against what is likely to be a small buffer, and the small buffer will lose.

Bad effect 2: Big buffers rarely go away.

The only way a big buffer can get freed is if the buffer in the cache is itself already a big buffer. If instead of a one-entry cache like we have here, you keep, say, 10 buffers in your buffer cache, then in order to free a big buffer, you have to have 11 consecutive `ReturnBuffer` calls, all of which pass a big buffer.

Bad effect 3: The more efficient you try to make your cache, the more wasteful it gets!

What's more, when that eleventh call to `ReturnBuffer` is made with a big buffer, it is only the smallest of the big buffers that gets freed. The biggest buffers stay.

Bad effect 4: When a big buffer does go away, it's only because you are keeping an even bigger buffer!

Corollary: The biggest buffer never gets freed.

What started out as an "obvious" decision in choosing which buffer to keep has turned into a performance disaster. By favoring big buffers, you allowed them to "poison" the cache, and the longer you let the system run, the more allocations end up being big "poisoned" buffers. It doesn't matter how rare those big blocks are; you will eventually end up in this state. It's just a matter of time.

When the performance team tries to explain this problem to people, many of them get the mistaken impression that the problem is merely that there is wasted space in the cache. But look at our example: Our cache has only one entry and we are still wasting over 90% of the memory. That's because the waste is not in the memory being held by the cache, but rather is in the memory that the cache hands out. (It's sort of like that scene in *It's a Wonderful Life* where George Bailey is explaining where all the money is. It's not in the bank; it's in all the places that got money *from* the bank.)

My recommendations: First, instrument your cache and understand what your program's memory allocation patterns are. Use that information to pick a size cutoff point beyond which you simply will not use the cache at all. This ensures that big buffers never get into the cache in the first place. Now, although you've taken the big buffers out of the picture, you will still have the problem that all the buffers in the cache will gradually grow up to your cutoff size. (That is, you still have the same problem, just in miniature.) Therefore, if the cache is full, you should just free the most recently returned buffer regardless of its size. And finally, reinstrument your cache to ensure that you're not suffering from yet some other pathological behavior that I haven't taken into account.

Here's a new `ReturnBuffer` implementation that takes the above advice into account. Instrumentation shows that most allocations are in the 100–200 byte range, so let's cap our cache at 200 bytes:

```
void BufferCache::ReturnBuffer(void *p)
{
 if (m_pCache == NULL && LocalSize(p) <= 200) {
  m_pCache = p;
 } else {
  LocalFree(p);
 }
}
```

With this one seemingly minor change, our efficiency stays above 90% and often gets close to 100%:

```
0: 1 buffers, 400/400=100% used
100: 7 buffers, 4300/4400=97.7273% used
200: 5 buffers, 1800/1800=100% used
300: 19 buffers, 9800/9800=100% used
400: 13 buffers, 5100/5100=100% used
500: 7 buffers, 2500/2600=96.1538% used
...
37200: 65 buffers, 129000/130100=99.1545% used
37300: 55 buffers, 18100/18700=96.7914% used
37400: 35 buffers, 10400/11000=94.5455% used
37500: 43 buffers, 10700/11000=97.2727% used
37600: 49 buffers, 17200/18000=95.5556% used
37700: 75 buffers, 26000/26800=97.0149% used
37800: 89 buffers, 30300/31900=94.9843% used
37900: 91 buffers, 29600/30600=96.732% used
```

Our performance guru Rico Mariani likes to point out that "caching implies policy." As he explained to me, "Cache policy is everything, so you must be dead certain that your policy is working as you intended. A cache with a bad policy is another name for a memory leak."

❧

CHAPTER TWELVE

DIGGING INTO THE VISUAL C++ COMPILER

FOR A LITTLE while, I'm going to abandon compiler agnosticism and dig into some details of Microsoft's Visual C++ compiler. Actually, the opening discussion on destructors applies to C++ in general, and the layout of a COM object is part of the Win32 application binary interface, so it is applicable to all compilers and languages that support COM, not just Microsoft's Visual C++ compiler. But as we dig deeper, we get into details that are more and more compiler specific.

Do you know when your destructors run?

DESTRUCTORS ARE A magical part of C++. They are not invoked explicitly under normal circumstances; instead, the compiler inserts calls to the destructor at appropriate points in program execution. And if you don't know when those points are, you can find yourself trying to figure out at a very nasty bug.

The classic example of mysterious destructor execution is in the destruction of global variables. Consider the following:

```
#include <stdafx.h> // Let's use ATL
CComPtr<IUnknown> g_pUnk;
```

```
int __cdecl main(int argc, char **argv)
{
 if (SUCCEEDED(CoInitialize(NULL)) {
  g_pUnk.CoCreateInstance(CLSID_IXMLDOMDocument);
  ...
  CoUninitialize();
 }
}
```

When you run this program, you'll discover that it crashes in the destructor for the g_pUnk variable. The reason is that the destructors for global variables run after the main program exits, in particular after COM has already been torn down by the main program. Part of COM teardown includes freeing all the dynamic link libraries (DLLs) that it had loaded because it "knows" that you aren't using them any more by virtue of the fact that you are shutting down COM entirely.

And then when you try to release one of those pointers that was squirreled away into a global variable, you crash trying to talk to a DLL that is no longer there.

But this problem is not exclusive to global objects. You need to take care even with local objects. Consider the following:

```
void Sample()
{
 if (SUCCEEDED(CoInitialize(NULL))) {
  CComPtr<IXMLDOMDocument> p;
  if (SUCCEEDED(p.CoCreateInstance(CLSID_IXMLDOMDocument))) {
   ...
  }
  CoUninitialize();
 }
}
```

Easy as pie. And there's a bug here. When does the destructor for that smart-pointer run? It runs when the object goes out of scope, which is at the closing brace of the outer if statement, *after* the CoUninitialize call. Your function shuts down COM and then tries to access a pointer to a COM object, resulting in the same type of crash you saw in the preceding example.

To fix this problem, you have to release all your COM pointers before the `CoUninitialize`. One way would be to insert a `p.Release()` at the end of the inner `if`. (But of course, if you're going to do that, why bother using a smart pointer?) An alternate fix is to introduce a seemingly unnecessary scope:

```
void Sample()
{
  if (SUCCEEDED(CoInitialize(NULL))) {
    {
      CComPtr<IXMLDOMDocument> p;
      if (SUCCEEDED(p.CoCreateInstance(CLSID_IXMLDOMDocument))) {
        ...
      }
    } // ensure p is destructed before the CoUninit
    CoUninitialize();
  }
}
```

Make sure you leave that comment there or the next person to come across this code is going to "clean it up" by removing the "redundant" braces.

Some might consider that solution too subtle. Here's another solution: Put the `CoUninitialize` inside a destructor of its own!

```
class CCoInitialize {
public:
  CCoInitialize() : m_hr(CoInitialize(NULL)) { }
  ~CCoInitialize() { if (SUCCEEDED(m_hr)) CoUninitialize(); }
  operator HRESULT() const { return m_hr; }
  HRESULT m_hr;
};

void Sample()
{
  CCoInitialize init;
  if (SUCCEEDED(init)) {
    CComPtr<IXMLDOMDocument> p;
    if (SUCCEEDED(p.CoCreateInstance(CLSID_IXMLDOMDocument))) {
      ...
    }
  }
} // CoUninitialize happens here
```

This technique works even if you put the smart pointer at the same scope, as long as you put it after the CCoInitialize object:

```
void Sample()
{
 CCoInitialize init;
 CComPtr<IXMLDOMDocument> p; // must declare after CCoInitialize
 if (SUCCEEDED(init) &&
     SUCCEEDED(p.CoCreateInstance(CLSID_IXMLDOMDocument))) {
   ...
 }
}
```

This works because objects with automatic storage duration are destructed in reverse order of declaration, so the object p will be destructed first, then the object init. Mind you, this is basically subtle no matter now you slice it. Nobody said programming was easy.

Up until now, we've seen destructors that run at the wrong time. Now, we're going to see destructors that don't run at all!

Assume there's an ObjectLock class that takes a lock in its constructor and releases it in its destructor:

```
DWORD ThreadProc(LPVOID p)
{
 ... do stuff ...
 ObjectLock lock(p);
 ... do stuff ...
 return 0;
}
```

Pretty standard stuff. The first batch of stuff is done without the lock, and the second batch is done inside the lock. When the function returns, the lock is automatically released. But suppose somebody adds a little code to this function like this:

```
DWORD ThreadProc(LPVOID p)
{
 ... do stuff ...
 ObjectLock lock(p);
 ...
 if (p->cancelled) ExitThread(1);
```

```
    . . .
    return 0;
}
```

The code change was just to add an early exit if the object was cancelled. But when does that `ObjectLock` destructor run?

It runs at the `return` statement, because that's when the lock goes out of scope. In particular, it is *not* run before you call `ExitThread`. Result: You left an object locked permanently.

Some might argue that calling `ExitThread` is poor programming practice, that threads must always be exited by falling through to the end of the thread procedure. But there is still a case in which you must exit a thread via one of the thread exit functions, and that is if you are a worker thread whose lifetime is not explicitly managed but whose code resides in a DLL. In that case, the standard approach is to use the `LoadLibrary` function to increment the load count for the DLL when the worker thread is started and to use the `FreeLibraryAndExitThread` function when the worker thread ends. (You can also use the `GetModuleHandleEx` function to increment the load count.) In that case, the thread procedure will look something like this:

```
DWORD ThreadProc(LPVOID p)
{
    ... do stuff ...
    ObjectLock lock(p);
    ...
    FreeLibraryAndExitThread(g_hinst, 0);
    // not reached
}
```

where g_hinst is a global variable that holds the DLL's instance handle. In this case, you suffer from the same problem described previously: The `ObjectLock` destructor runs at the function close brace, but the `FreeLibraryAndExitThread` function exits the thread never to return.

The destructor never runs. Again, a nested scope is needed to force the destructor to run earlier than normal:

```
DWORD ThreadProc(LPVOID p)
{
  {
  ... do stuff ...
  ObjectLock lock(p);
  ...
  } // ObjectLock destructor runs here
  FreeLibraryAndExitThread(g_hinst, 0);
  // not reached
}
```

The layout of a COM object

THE WIN32 COM calling convention specifies the layout of the virtual method table (vtable) of an object. If a language/compiler wants to support COM, it must lay out its object in the specified manner so other components can use it.

It is no coincidence that the Win32 COM object layout matches closely the C++ object layout. Even though COM was originally developed when C was the predominant programming language, the designers saw fit to "play friendly" with the up-and-coming new language C++.

The layout of a COM object is made explicit in the header files for the various interfaces. For example, here's IPersist from objidl.h, after cleaning up some macros:

```
typedef struct IPersistVtbl
{
    HRESULT ( STDMETHODCALLTYPE *QueryInterface )(
        IPersist * This,
        /* [in] */ REFIID riid,
        /* [iid_is][out] */ void **ppvObject);

    ULONG ( STDMETHODCALLTYPE *AddRef )(
        IPersist * This);

    ULONG ( STDMETHODCALLTYPE *Release )(
        IPersist * This);
```

```
HRESULT ( STDMETHODCALLTYPE *GetClassID )(
    IPersist * This,
    /* [out] */ CLSID *pClassID);

} IPersistVtbl;

struct IPersist
{
    const struct IPersistVtbl *lpVtbl;
};
```

This corresponds to the following memory layout:

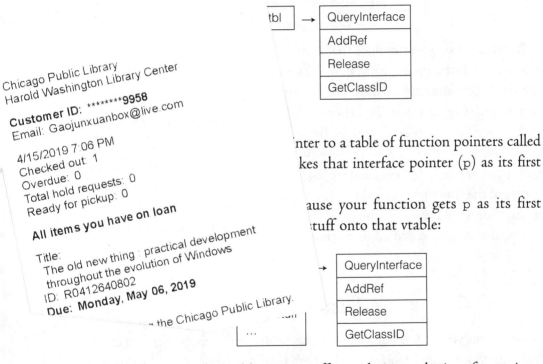

nter to a table of function pointers called
kes that interface pointer (p) as its first

ause your function gets p as its first
tuff onto that vtable:

The functions in the vtable can use offsets relative to the interface pointer to access its other stuff.

If an object implements multiple interfaces but they are all descendants of each other, a single vtable can be used for all of them. For example, the object above is already set to be used either as an IUnknown or as an IPersist, because the methods of the IUnknown interface are a subset of those of the IPersist interface, with the extra IPersist method coming at the end of the table.

On the other hand, if an object implements multiple interfaces that are not descendants of each other, you get multiple inheritance, in which case the object is typically laid out in memory like this:

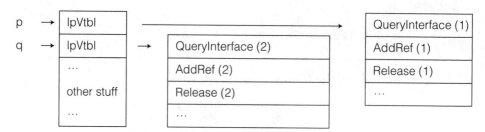

If you are using an interface that comes from the first vtable, the interface pointer is p. But if you're using an interface that comes from the second vtable, the interface pointer is q. Each of the methods in the first vtable can use offsets relative to p to access the "other stuff," whereas the methods in the second vtable can use offsets relative to q. Because the IUnknown interface is multiply-derived, however, there are now two copies of the IUnknown methods: QueryInterface, AddRef, and Release. The compiler could generate two copies of the function, one using p as its point of reference and the other using q, but that would result in multiple copies of the same function. Instead, the compiler uses a so-called adjustor thunk.

⇝

Adjustor thunks

IF YOU FIND yourself debugging in disassembly, you'll sometimes find strange little functions called *adjustor thunks*. Let's take another look at the object we laid out last time, giving it a bit more concreteness:

```
class CSample : public IPersist, public IServiceProvider
{
public:
  // *** IUnknown ***
```

```
STDMETHODIMP QueryInterface(REFIID riid, void** ppv);
STDMETHODIMP_(ULONG) AddRef();
STDMETHODIMP_(ULONG) Release();
// *** IPersist ***
STDMETHODIMP GetClassID(CLSID* pClassID);
// *** IQueryService ***
STDMETHODIMP QueryService(REFGUID guidService,
                 REFIID riid, void** ppv);
private:
  LONG m_cRef;
  ...
};
```

In the diagram, p is the pointer returned when the IPersist interface is needed, and q is the pointer for the IQueryService interface.

Now, there is only one QueryInterface method, but there are two entries, one for each vtable. Remember that each function in a vtable receives the corresponding interface pointer as its this parameter. That's just fine for QueryInterface (1); its interface pointer is the same as the object's interface pointer. But that's bad news for QueryInterface (2), because its interface pointer is q, not p.

This is where the adjustor thunks come in.

The entry for QueryInterface (2) is a stub function that changes q to p, and then lets QueryInterface (1) do the rest of the work. This stub function is the adjustor thunk:

```
[thunk]:CSample::QueryInterface'adjustor{4}':
  sub    DWORD PTR [esp+4], 4 ; this -= sizeof(lpVtbl)
  jmp    CSample::QueryInterface
```

The adjustor thunk takes the this pointer and subtracts the size of the vtable pointer, converting q into p, and then it jumps to the QueryInterface (1) function to do the real work.

Whenever you have multiple inheritance and a virtual function is implemented on multiple base classes, you will get an adjustor thunk for the second and subsequent base class methods in order to convert the this pointer into a common format.

Pointers to member functions
are very strange animals

WELL, OKAY, IF you only use single inheritance, pointers to member functions are just a pointer to the start of the function, because all the base classes share the same this pointer:

```
class Simple { int s; void SimpleMethod(); };
class Simple2 : public Simple
  { int s2; void Simple2Method(); };
class Simple3 : public Simple2
  { int s3; Simple3Method(); };
```

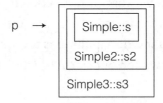

Because they all use the same this pointer (p), a pointer to a member function of Base can be used as if it were a pointer to a member function of Derived2 without any adjustment necessary.

The size of a pointer-to-member-function of a class that uses only single inheritance is just the size of a pointer.

But if you have multiple base classes, things get interesting:

```
class Base1 { int b1; void Base1Method(); };
class Base2 { int b2; void Base2Method(); };
class Derived : public Base1, Base2
  { int d; void DerivedMethod(); };
```

There are now two possible `this` pointers. The first (p) is used by both Derived and Base1, but the second (q) is used by Base2.

A pointer to a member function of Base1 can be used as a pointer to a member function of Derived because the two classes use the same `this` pointer. But a pointer to a member function of Base2 cannot be used as-is as a pointer to a member function of Derived because the `this` pointer needs to be adjusted.

There are many ways of solving this. Here's how the Visual Studio compiler decides to handle it: A pointer to a member function of a multiply-inherited class is really a structure.

| Address of function (pointer) |
| Adjustor (integer) |

The size of a pointer-to-member-function of a class that uses multiple inheritance is the size of a pointer plus the size of a `size_t`.

Compare this to the case of a class that uses only single inheritance.

The size of a pointer-to-member-function can change depending on the class!

To call through a pointer to a member function, the `this` pointer is adjusted by the adjustor, and then the function provided is called. A call through a function pointer might be compiled like this:

```
void (Derived::*pfn)();
Derived d;

(d.*pfn)();

    lea   ecx, d         ; ecx = "this"
    add   ecx, pfn[4]    ; add adjustor
    call  pfn[0]         ; call
```

When would an adjustor be nonzero? Consider the case above. The function `Derived::Base2Method()` is really `Base2::Base2Method()` and therefore expects to receive q as its this pointer. To convert a p to a q, the adjustor must have the value sizeof(Base1), so that when the first line of Base2::Base2Method() executes, it receives the expected q as its this pointer.

"But why not just use a thunk instead of manually adding the adjustor?" In other words, why not just use a simple pointer to a thunk that goes like this:

```
Derived::Base2Method thunk:
    add ecx, sizeof(Base1)    ; convert p to q
    jmp Base2::Base2Method    ; continue
```

And use that thunk as the function pointer?

The reason: function pointer casts. Consider the following code:

```
void (Base2::*pfnBase2)();
void (Derived::*pfnDerived)();

pfnDerived = pfnBase2;

    mov   ecx, pfnBase2                  ; ecx = address
    mov   pfnDerived[0], ecx

    mov   pfnDerived[4], sizeof(Base1)   ; adjustor!
```

We start with a pointer to a member function of Base2, which is a class that uses only single inheritance, so it consists of just a pointer to the code. To assign it to a pointer to a member function of Derived, which uses multiple inheritance, we can reuse the function address, but we now need an adjustor so that the pointer p can properly be converted to a q.

Notice that the code doesn't know which function pfnBase2 points to, so it can't just replace it with the matching thunk. It would have to generate a thunk at runtime and somehow use its psychic powers to decide when the memory can safely be freed. (This is C++. No garbage collector here.)

Notice also that when pfnBase2 got cast to a pointer to a member function of Derived, its size changed, because it went from a pointer to a function in a class that uses only single inheritance to a pointer to a function in a class that uses multiple inheritance.

Casting a function pointer can
change its size!

Consider the class:

```
class Base3 { int b3; void Base3Method(); };
class Derived2 : public Base3, public Derived { };
```

How would the following code be compiled?

```
void (Derived::*pfnDerived)();
void (Derived2::*pfnDerived2();

pfnDerived2 = pfnDerived;
```

Answer: The generated code for this sequence is likely to look something like this:

```
mov   ecx, pfnDerived[0]      ; ecx = address
mov   pfnDerived2[0], ecx

mov   ecx, pfnDerived2[4]     ; ecx = adjustor
add   ecx, sizeof(Base3)      ; adjust the adjustor!
mov   pfnDerived2[4], ecx
```

Let's use one of our fancy pictures:

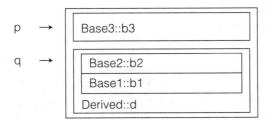

Just for fun, I swapped the order of `Base1` and `Base2`. There is no requirement in the standard about the order in which storage is allocated for base classes, so the compiler is completely within its rights to put `Base2` first, if it thinks that would be more efficient.

A pointer to member function for class `Derived` expects the `this` pointer to be at q. When we have a p, we need to add `sizeof(Base3)` to it to convert it to q, on top of whatever other adjustment the original function pointer wanted. That's why we add sizeof(Base3) to the existing adjustor to make a new combined adjustor.

⁓

What is __purecall?

BOTH C++ AND C# have the concept of virtual functions. These are functions that always invoke the most heavily derived implementation, even if called from a pointer to the base class. However, the two languages differ on the semantics of virtual functions during object construction and destruction.

C# objects exist as their final type before construction begins, whereas C++ objects change type during the construction process. Here's an example of a C++ class:

```
class Base {
public:
  Base() { f(); }
  virtual void f() { cout << 1; }
  void g() { f(); }
};

class Derived : public Base {
public:
  Derived() { f(); }
  virtual void f() { cout << 2; }
};
```

When a Derived object is constructed, the object starts as a Base, and then the Base::Base constructor is executed. Because the object is still a Base, the call to f() invokes Base::f and not Derived::f. After the Base::Base constructor completes, the object then becomes a Derived, and the Derived::Derived constructor is run. This time, the call to f() invokes Derived::f.

In other words, constructing a Derived object prints 12.

Similar remarks apply to the destructor. The object is destructed in pieces, and a call to a virtual function invokes the function corresponding to the stage of destruction currently in progress.

This is why some coding guidelines recommend against calling virtual functions from a constructor or destructor. Depending on what stage of construction/destruction is taking place, the same call to f() can have different effects. For example, the preceding function Base::g() will call Base::f if called from the Base::Base constructor or destructor, but will call Derived::f if called after the object has been constructed and before it is destructed.

On the other hand, if this sample were written (with suitable syntactic changes) in C#, the output would be 22 because a C# object is created as its final type. Both calls to f() invoke Derived::f, because the object is always a Derived. *This means a method can be invoked on a C# object before its constructor has run (and after its destructor has run).*

Sometimes your C++ program may crash with the error R6025 - pure virtual function call. This message comes from a function called __purecall. What does it mean?

C++ and C# both have the concept of a *pure virtual function* (which C# calls *abstract*). This is a method which is declared by the base class, but which derived classes must override. Typically, the base class provides no implementation whatsoever. In C++, the syntax for this is = 0:

```
class Base {
public:
  Base() { f(); }
  virtual void f() = 0;
};
```

If you attempt to create a Derived object, the base class will attempt to call Base::f, which is not implemented in the base class. When this happens, the "pure virtual function call" error is raised and the program is terminated.

Of course, the mistake is rarely as obvious as this. Typically, the call to the pure virtual function occurs deep inside the call stack of the constructor.

This raises the side issue of the novtable optimization. As noted previously, the identity of the object changes during construction. This change of identity is performed by swapping the vtables around during construction. If you have a base class that is never instantiated directly but always via a derived class, and *if you have followed the rules against calling virtual methods during construction or destruction,* you can use the `novtable` optimization to get rid of the vtable swapping during construction of the base class.

If you use this optimization, then *calling virtual methods during the base class's constructor or destructor will result in undefined behavior.* It's a nice optimization, but it's your own responsibility to make sure you conform to its requirements.

Why does C# not do type morphing during construction? One reason is that it would result in the possibility, given two objects A and B, that `typeof(A) == typeof(B)` yet `sizeof(A) != sizeof(B)`. This would happen if A were a fully constructed object and B were a partially constructed object on its way to becoming a derived object.

Why is this so bad? Because the garbage collector is really keen on knowing the size of each object so that it can know how much memory to free. It does this by checking the object's type. If an object's type did not completely determine its size, this would result in the garbage collector having to do extra work to figure out exactly how big the object is, which means extra code in the constructor and destructor, as well as space in the object, to keep track of which stage of construction/destruction is currently in progress. And all this for something most coding guidelines recommend against anyway.

❧

CHAPTER THIRTEEN

BACKWARD COMPATIBILITY

DEPENDING ON WHOM you ask, backward compatibility is either Windows's greatest strength or its greatest weakness. The purpose of this chapter is to illustrate some of the efforts that go into maintaining backward compatibility and highlight the obstacles that often stand in the way. More of these types of stories can be found in the bonus chapter, "Tales of Application Compatibility," available at www.awprofessional.com/title/0321440307.

Sometimes an app just wants to crash

I THINK IT was Internet Explorer 5.0 when we discovered that a third-party browser extension had a serious bug, the details of which aren't important. The point was that this bug was so vicious, it crashed Internet Explorer pretty frequently. Not good. To protect the users from this horrible fate, we marked the object as "bad" so that Internet Explorer wouldn't load it.

And then we got an angry letter from the company that wrote this browser extension. They demanded that we remove the marking from their object and let Internet Explorer crash in flames every time the user wanted to surf the Web. Why? Because they also wanted us to hook up Windows Error

Reporting to detect this crash and put up a dialog that says, "A fix for the problem you experienced is available. Click here for more information," and the "more information" was a redirect to the company's Web site, where you could upgrade to version x.y of Program ABC for a special price of only $nnn! (Actually I forget whether the upgrade was free or not, but the story is funnier if you had to pay for it.)

In other words, they were crashing on purpose in order to drive upgrades.

Astute readers may have noticed an additional irony: If the plug-in crashed Internet Explorer, how could the users view the company's Web page so that they could purchase and download the latest version?

⌐

When programs grovel into undocumented structures

THREE EXAMPLES OFF the top of my head of the consequences of groveling into and relying on undocumented structures:

+ Defragmenting things that can't be defragmented

  In Windows 2000, there are several categories of data structures in the NTFS file system that cannot be defragmented: directories, exclusively opened files, the master file table (MFT), the pagefile, and so forth. That didn't stop a certain software company from doing it anyway in their defragmenting software. They went into kernel mode, reverse-engineered NTFS's data structures, and modified them on-the-fly. Yee-haw cowboy! And then when the NTFS folks added support for defragmenting the MFT to Windows XP, these programs went in, modified NTFS's data structures (which changed in the meanwhile), and corrupted your disk.

  Of course, there was no mention of this illicit behavior in the documentation. So when the background defragmenter corrupted their disks, Microsoft got the blame.

- Parsing the Explorer view data structures

  A certain software company decided that they wanted to alter the behavior of the Explorer window from a shell extension. Because there is no way to do this (a shell extension is not supposed to mess with the view; the view belongs to the user), they decided to do it themselves anyway.

  From the shell extension, they used an undocumented window message to get a pointer to one of the internal Explorer structures. Then they walked the structure until they found something they recognized. Then they knew, "The thing immediately after the thing that I recognize is the thing that I want."

  Well, the thing that they recognized and the thing that they wanted happened to be base classes of a multiply-derived class. If you have a class with multiple base classes, there is no guarantee from the compiler which order the base classes will appear in memory. It so happened that they appeared in the order X,Y,Z in all the versions of Windows this software company tested against.

  Except Windows 2000.

  In Windows 2000, the compiler decided that the order should be X,Z,Y. So now they groveled in, saw the X, and said, "Aha, the next thing must be a Y," but instead they got a Z. And then they crashed your system some time later.

  I had to create a "fake X,Y" so that when the program went looking for X (so it could grab Y), it found the fake one first.

  This took the good part of a week to figure out.

- Reaching up the stack

  A certain software company decided that it was too hard to take the coordinates of the NM_DBLCLK notification and hit-test it against the tree view to see what was double-clicked. So instead, they took the address of the NMHDR structure passed to the notification, *added 60 to it*, and dereferenced a DWORD at that address. If it was zero, they did one thing, and if it was nonzero, they did some other thing.

It so happens that the NMHDR is allocated on the stack, so this program is reaching up into the stack and grabbing the value of some local variable (which happens to be two frames up the stack!) and using it to control their logic.

For Windows 2000, we upgraded the compiler to a version that did a better job of reordering and reusing local variables, and now the program couldn't find the local variable it wanted and stopped working.

I got tagged to investigate and fix this. I had to create a special NMHDR structure that "looked like" the stack the program wanted to see and pass that special "fake stack."

I think this one took me two days to figure out.

I hope you understand why I tend to go ballistic when people recommend relying on undocumented behavior. These weren't hobbyists in their garage seeing what they could do. These were major companies writing commercial software.

When you upgrade to the next version of Windows and you experience (1) disk corruption, (2) sporadic Explorer crashes, or (3) sporadic loss of functionality in your favorite program, do you blame the program or do you blame Windows?

If you say, "I blame the program," the first problem is of course figuring out which program. In cases (1) and (2), the offending program isn't obvious.

⮑

Why not just block the applications that rely on undocumented behavior?

BECAUSE EVERY APPLICATION that gets blocked is another reason for people not to upgrade to the next version of Windows. If you run the Registry Editor and look at HKEY_LOCAL_MACHINE\SOFTWARE\Microsoft\WindowsNT\ CurrentVersion\Compatibility, you'll see a list of programs that would have stopped working when you upgraded from Windows 3.0 to Windows 3.1. Actually, this list is only partial. Many times, the compatibility fix is made inside the core component for all programs rather than targeting a specific program, as this list does.

> **NOTE:** On Windows XP, the application compatibility database is stored in your `C:\WINDOWS\AppPatch` directory, in a binary format to permit rapid scanning. To inspect its contents, you can run the Compatibility Administrator tool, which is part of the Application Compatibility Toolkit.

Would you have bought Windows XP if you knew that all these programs were incompatible?

It takes only one incompatible program to sour an upgrade.

Suppose you're the IT manager of some company. Your company uses Program X for its word processor and you find that Program X is incompatible with Windows XP for whatever reason. Would you upgrade?

Of course not! Your business would grind to a halt.

"Why not call Company X and ask them for an upgrade?"

Sure, you could do that, and the answer might be, "Oh, you're using Version 1.0 of Program X. You need to upgrade to Version 2.0 for $150 per copy." Congratulations, the cost of upgrading to Windows XP just tripled.

And that's if you're lucky and Company X is still in business.

I recall a survey taken a few years ago by our Setup/Upgrade team of corporations using Windows. Pretty much every single one has at least one "deal-breaker" program, a program which Windows absolutely must support or they won't upgrade. In a high percentage of the cases, the program in question was developed by their in-house programming staff, written in Visual Basic (sometimes even 16-bit Visual Basic), and the person who wrote it doesn't work there any more. In some cases, they don't even *have* the source code any more.

And it's not just corporate customers. This affects consumers, too.

For Windows 95, my application compatibility work focused on games. Games are the most important factor behind consumer technology. The video card that comes with a typical computer has gotten better over time because games demand it. (Outlook certainly doesn't care that your card can do 20 bajillion triangles a second.) And if your game doesn't run on the newest version of Windows, you aren't going to upgrade.

Anyway, game vendors are very much like those major corporations. I made phone call after phone call to the game vendors trying to help them get their game to run under Windows 95. To a one, they didn't care. A game has a shelf life of a few months, and then it's gone. Why would they bother to issue a patch for their program to run under Windows 95? They already got their money. They're not going to make any more off that game; its three months are over. The vendors would slipstream patches and lose track of how many versions of their program were out there and how many of them had a particular problem. Sometimes they wouldn't even have the source code any more.

They simply didn't care that their program didn't run on Windows 95. (My favorite was the one that tried to walk me through creating a DOS boot disk.)

Oh, and that Application Compatibility Toolkit I mentioned earlier. It's a great tool for developers, too. One of the components is the Application Verifier: If you run your program under the verifier, it will monitor hundreds of operating system calls and break into the debugger when you do something wrong (such as close a handle twice or allocate memory with `GlobalAlloc` but free it with `LocalAlloc`).

The new application compatibility architecture in Windows XP carries with it one major benefit (from an OS development perspective): See all those DLL files in your `C:\WINDOWS\AppPatch` directory? That's where many of the compatibility changes live now. The compatibility workarounds no longer sully the core OS files. (Not all classes of compatibility workarounds can be offloaded to a compatibility DLL, but it's a big help.)

⮜

Why 16-bit DOS and Windows are still with us

MANY PEOPLE ARE calling for the abandonment of 16-bit DOS and 16-bit Windows compatibility subsystems. And trust me, when it comes time to pull the plug, I'll be fighting to be the one to throw the lever. (How's that for a mixed metaphor.)

But that time is not yet here.

You see, folks over in the Setup and Deployment group have gone and visited companies around the world, learned how they use Windows in their businesses, and one thing keeps showing up, as it relates to these compatibility subsystems: Companies still rely on them. Heavily.

Every company has its own collection of line-of-business (LOB) applications. These are programs that the company uses for its day-to-day business, programs the company simply cannot live without. For example, at Microsoft two of our critical LOB applications are our defect tracking system and our build system.

And like Microsoft's defect tracking system and build system, many of the LOB applications at major corporations are not commercially available software; they are internally developed software, tailored to the way that company works, and treated as trade secrets. At a financial services company, the trend analysis and prediction software is what makes the company different from all its competitors.

The LOB application is the deal-breaker. If a Windows upgrade breaks a LOB application, it's game over. No upgrade. No company is going to lose a program that *is critical to their business.*

And it happens that a lot of these LOB applications are 16-bit programs. Some are DOS. Some are 16-bit Windows programs written in some ancient version of Visual Basic.

"Well, tell them to port the programs to Win32."

Easier said than done.

- Why would a company go to all the effort of porting a program when the current version still works fine? If it ain't broke, don't fix it.

- The port would have to be debugged and field tested in parallel with the existing system. The existing system is probably ten years old. All its quirks are well understood. It survived that time in 1998 when there was a supply-chain breakdown and when production finally got back online, they had to run at triple capacity for a month to catch up. The new system hasn't been stress tested. Who knows whether it will handle these emergencies as well as the last system?

• Converting it from a DOS program to a Windows program would incur massive retraining costs for its employees. "I have always used F4 to submit a purchase order. Now I have this toolbar with a bunch of strange pictures, and I have to learn what they all mean." Imagine if somebody took away your current editor and gave you a new one with different key bindings. "But the new one is better."

• Often the companies don't have the source code to the programs any more, so they couldn't port it if they wanted to. It may use a third-party VB control from a company that has since gone out of business. It may use a custom piece of hardware for which they have the driver but no source code. And even if they did have the source code, the author of the program may no longer work at the company. In the case of a driver, there may be nobody at the company qualified to maintain the 32-bit Windows driver.

Perhaps with a big enough carrot, these companies could be convinced to undertake the effort (and risk!) of porting (or in the case of lost source code and/or expertise, rewriting from scratch) their LOB applications.

But it'll have to be a really big carrot.

Real example: Just this past weekend I was visiting a friend who lived in a very nice, professionally managed apartment complex. We had occasion to go to the office, and I caught a glimpse of their computer screen. The operating system was Windows XP. And the program they were running to do their apartment management? It was running in a DOS box.

🖜

What's the deal with those reserved filenames such as NUL and CON?

SET THE WAYBACK machine to DOS 1.0.

DOS 1.0 didn't support subdirectories, lowercase, or filenames longer than 8.3.

When you ran the assembler (or compiler if you were really fancy) the conversation went something like this:

```
A>asm foo          the ".asm" extension on "foo" is implied
Assembler version blah blah blah
Source file: FOO.ASM
Listing file [FOO.LST]:   just hit Enter to accept the default
Object file [FOO.OBJ]:    just hit Enter to accept the default
Assembler cranks away
```

You only had to type the base name of the file; the .LST and .OBJ extensions were appended automatically. In fact, I don't think you could disable the extensions; they were always added.

But what if you didn't want a listing file? The assembler demanded a filename, and if you didn't type any filename at all, it created one with the same basename as your source file.

That's where the magic filenames come in. Suppose you wanted the listing file to go straight to the printer. You didn't want to create a file on your floppy drive because there might not be enough space to hold it or because you didn't want to waste the time creating a file just to delete it anyway. So you typed PRN as the filename.

Now, the assembler doesn't know about these magic filenames. So the assembler will try to create the file PRN.LST and then start writing to it. Little does the assembler realize that the output is actually going to the printer.

If you wanted to discard the output entirely, you would type NUL, of course. And if you wanted it to go to the screen, you would type CON.

Now, if you followed closely, you can see that this story explains two things already:

• Why are the magic filenames magical even if I add an extension?

   Answer: If an extension removed the magic, then when the assembler added .LST to the filename, it would no longer be recognized as magical, thereby defeating the purpose of the magic.

• Why do these magic files exist in every directory?

   Answer: Because DOS 1.0 didn't have subdirectories. There was only one directory, which today we would call the root directory; but back then, there was no such thing as a subdirectory, so there was no need to talk about directories in the first place, much less give the only one you have a name. It was just called "the files on your disk." If magic files didn't work in subdirectories, then when you tried to, for example, chdir into a subdirectory and then run the assembler, you wouldn't be able to type NUL as the filename and get the magic.

But why do we carry these magic filenames forward even today?

Because everybody still relies on them. Just look at all the batch files that do things such as redirect to >NUL or test whether a directory exists by asking if exist directoryname\nul, or all the documentation that says to create a file with copy CON filename.

⌁

Why is a drive letter permitted in front of UNC paths (sometimes)?

A LITTLE-KNOWN quirk is that the file system accepts and ignores a drive letter in front of a UNC path. For example, if you have a directory called \\server\share\directory, you can say

```
dir P:\\server\share\directory
```

and the directory will be listed to the screen. The leading P: is ignored. Why is that?

Rewind to 1984 and the upcoming release of MS-DOS 3.1, which added networking support. Up to this point, all fully qualified file specifications consisted of three components: a drive letter, a path, and a filename. Many programs relied on this breakdown and did things like "helpfully" prepend a drive letter if it looks like you "forgot" one. For example, if you told it to save the results to \\server\share\file.txt, it would say, "Oh dear, that's not good, the user forgot the drive letter! I'll put the current drive in front to make things better," resulting in C:\\server\share\file.txt. Other programs would prompt you with "Please enter a drive letter," and you couldn't say, "No, there's no drive letter, just take the path and use it." They insisted on a drive letter, and you darn sure better give them one.

(Compare the UNIX programs that "helpfully" rewrite `//server/volume/file` as `/server/volume/file` because they "know" that consecutive slashes collapse, unaware of the special exception for two leading slashes.)

To retain compatibility with programs that provided this sort of "unwanted help," the designers of the networking support in MS-DOS decided to allow the strange syntax `C:\\server\share\directory` and treat it as if the drive letter simply weren't there. Some (but not all) of this quirk of path parsing persists today.

⤳

Do not underestimate the power of the game Deer Hunter

DURING THE RUN-UP to Windows XP Service Pack 2 Beta, there was a list of five bugs that the release management team decided were so critical that they were going to slip the beta until those bugs got fixed.

The third bug on the list: Deer Hunter 4 won't run.

Deer Hunter has the power to stop a beta.

⤳

Sometimes the bug isn't apparent until late in the game

I DIDN'T DEBUG it personally, but I know the people who did. During Windows XP development, a bug arrived on a computer game that crashed only after you got to one of the higher levels.

After many saved and restored games, the problem was finally identified.

The program does its video work in an offscreen buffer and transfers it to the screen when it's done. When it draws text with a shadow, it first draws the text in black, offset down one and right one pixel, and then draws it again in the foreground color.

So far so good.

Except that it didn't check whether moving down and right one pixel was going to go beyond the end of the screen buffer.

That's why it took until one of the higher levels before the bug manifested itself. Not until then did you accomplish a mission whose name contained a lowercase letter with a descender! Shifting the descender down one pixel caused the bottom row of pixels in the character to extend past the video buffer and start corrupting memory.

After the problem had been identified, fixing it was comparatively easy. The application compatibility team has a bag of tricks, and one of them is called "HeapPadAllocation." This particular compatibility fix adds padding to every heap allocation so that when a program overruns a heap buffer, all that gets corrupted is the padding. Enable that fix for the bad program (specifying the amount of padding necessary, in this case, one row's worth of pixels), and run through the game again. No crash this time.

What made this interesting to me was that you had to play the game for *hours* before the bug finally surfaced.

⌒

The long and sad story of the Shell Folders key

WHEN YOU ARE attempting to architect an operating system, backward compatibility is something you just have to accept. But when new programs *rely on* application hacks designed for old programs, that makes you want to scream.

Once upon a time, in what seems like a galaxy far, far away (a Windows 95 beta release known as M3), we documented a registry key called Shell Folders that programs could read to obtain the locations of various special folders like the Fonts folder or the My Documents folder.

The developers who received Windows 95 M3 Beta followed the documentation and used that key.

In the meantime, Windows 95 work continued, and we realized that a registry key was the wrong place to store this information. In part, because a lot of things (such as the Control Panel) aren't disk directories and so they wouldn't be expressible there. And in another part, because we had forgotten to take into account a feature of Windows NT called roaming user profiles, where your user profile can move around from place to place, so a hard-coded path in the registry is no good.

So we created the function SHGetSpecialFolderLocation, and updated the documentation to instruct developers to use this new function to obtain the locations of various special folders. The documentation on the old Shell Folders key was removed.

But to ease the transition from the M3 documentation to the final documentation, we left the old Shell Folders registry key around, "temporarily," but it was no longer the location where this information was kept. It was just a shadow of the "real" data stored elsewhere (User Shell Folders).

We shipped Windows 95 with this "temporary" key because there were still a small number of programs (let's say four) that hadn't finished converting to the new SHGetSpecialFolderLocation function. But the support for this registry key was severely scaled back, so it was just barely good enough for those four programs. After all, this was just a backward compatibility hack. All new programs should be using SHGetSpecialFolderLocation.

In other words, the Shell Folders key exists solely to permit four programs written in 1994 to continue running on the release version of Windows 95.

You can guess what happened next.

Windows 95 came out and everybody wanted to write programs for it. But reading documentation is a lot of work. So when there's some setting you want to retrieve, and you don't want to read documentation, what do you do? You search the registry! (Sound familiar? People still do this today.)

So now there were hundreds, thousands of programs which didn't call SHGetSpecialFolderLocation; they just went directly for the Shell Folders key. But they didn't realize that the support for Shell Folders was only barely enough to keep those four original programs working.

For example, did you know that if you never open your Fonts folder, and if no program ever calls SHGetSpecialFolderLocation(CSIDL_FONTS), there will not be a Fonts entry in the Shell Folders key? That's because those entries are created only if somebody asks for them. If nobody asks for them, they aren't created. No point setting up an application hack until it is needed.

Of course, when you're testing your program, you don't reformat your hard disk, install Windows 95 from scratch, and then run your program. You just put your program on a Windows 95 machine that has been running for months and see what happens. At some point during all those months, you opened your Font folder at least one time. As a result, the "Fonts" entry exists and you are happy.

And then back in our application compatibility labs, your program gets a "Fail" grade because our lab reformats the computer before installing each application to make sure there is nothing left over from the previous program before installing the next one.

And then the core development team gets called in to figure out why this program is getting a Fail grade, and we find out that in fact, this program, when faced with a freshly formatted machine, *never worked in the first place.*

Philosophical question: If a program never worked in the first place, is it still a bug that it doesn't work today?

Now there are those of you who are licking your lips and saying, "Wow, there's this User Shell Folders key that's even cooler than the Shell Folders key, let me go check it out." I implore you to exercise restraint and not rely on this new key. Just use the function `SHGetFolderPath`, which returns the path to whatever folder you want. Let the User Shell Folders key rest in peace. Because in Windows Vista, we're doing even more stuff with user profiles, and I would personally be very upset if we had to abandon the User Shell Folders key as "lost to backward compatibility" and set up shop in a new Real User Shell Folders key.

I strongly suspect that of those four original programs for which the Shell Folders key was originally created, not a single one is still in existence today.

The importance of error code backward compatibility

I REMEMBER A bug report that came in on an old MS-DOS program (from a company that is still in business, so don't ask me to identify them) that attempted to open the file "". That's the file with no name.

This returned error 2 (file not found). But the program didn't check the error code and thought that 2 was the file handle. It then began writing data to handle 2, which ended up going to the screen because handle 2 is the standard error handle, which by default goes to the screen.

It so happened that this program wanted to print the message to the screen anyway.

In other words, this program worked completely by accident.

Because of various changes to the installable file system in Windows 95, the error code for attempting to open the null file changed from 2 (file not found) to 3 (path not found) as a side effect.

Watch what happens.

The program tries to open the file "". Now it gets error 3 back. It mistakenly treats the 3 as a file handle and writes to it. What is handle 3? The standard MS-DOS file handles are as follows:

Handle	Name	Meaning
0	stdin	standard input
1	stdout	standard output
2	stderr	standard error
3	stdaux	standard auxiliary (serial port)
4	stdprn	standard printer

What happens when the program writes to handle 3? It tries to write to the serial port. Most computers don't have anything hooked up to the serial port. The write hangs. Result: dead program.

The file system folks had to tweak their parameter validation so that they returned error 2 in this case.

Sure, we do that

THE DIRECTX VIDEO driver interface for Windows 95 had a method that each driver exposed called something like DoesDriverSupport(REFGUID guidCapability) where we handed it a capability GUID and it said whether or not that feature was supported.

There were various capability GUIDs defined, things such as GUID_Can StretchAlpha to ask the driver whether it was capable of stretching a bitmap with an alpha channel.

There was one driver that returned TRUE when you called DoesDriver Support(GUID_XYZ), but when DirectDraw tried to use that capability, it failed, and in a pretty spectacular manner.

One of the DirectDraw developers called the vendor and asked them, "Does your card do XYZ?"

Their response: "What's XYZ?"

Turns out that their driver's implementation of DoesDriverSupport was something like this:

```
BOOL DoesDriverSupport(REFGUID guidCapability)
{
    return TRUE;
}
```

In other words, whenever DirectX asked, "Can you do this?" they answered, "Sure, we do that," without even checking what the question was.

(The driver must have been written by the sales department.)

So the DirectDraw folks changed the way they queried for driver capabilities. One of the developers went into his boss's office, took a network card, extracted the MAC address, and then smashed the card with a hammer.

You see, this last step was important: The GUID generation algorithm is based on a combination of time and space. When you ask the CoCreateGuid function to create a new GUID, it encodes the time of your request in the first part of the GUID and information that uniquely identifies your machine (the network card's MAC address, which is required to be unique by the standards that apply to network cards).

By smashing the network card with a hammer, he prevented that network card from ever being used to generate a GUID.

Next, he added code to DirectDraw so that when it starts up, it manufactures a random GUID based on that network card (which, by its having been destroyed, can never be validly created) and passes it to `DoesDriverSupport`. If the driver says, "Sure, we do that," DirectDraw says, "Aha! Caught you! I will not believe anything you say from now on."

⤐

When programs patch the operating system and mess up

HAVING YOUR PROGRAM patch portions of the operating system to hook into various functions is a bad idea, but that doesn't stop people from trying. And messing up.

As you saw earlier, the `ExtTextOut` function is a fast way of drawing a solid rectangle. But we discovered on Windows 95 that if you were running a particular piece of software, Explorer would start crashing in a location outside the normal operating system code, but inside a call to the `ExtTextOut`-based fast solid rectangle fill function, where it passed NULL as the string pointer and zero as the character count.

The reason for the crash is that the software product patched several operating system functions, including `ExtTextOut`, redirecting the call to code installed by that product. And the redirected version of the `ExtTextOut` function dereferenced the string parameter without checking whether the character count parameter was zero. I guess it never occurred to them that somebody would be crazy enough to call a text-drawing function without any text! As a result, when Explorer attempted to draw a solid rectangle, the system crashed inside the patched `ExtTextOut` function.

The shell team was forced to change their "draw solid rectangle" function to pass a pointer to a valid (but unused) string as the string pointer parameter. In other words, the function went something like this:

```
BOOL DrawSolidRect(HDC hdc, LPCRECT prc, COLORREF clr)
{
 BOOL fDrawn = FALSE;
 COLORREF clrPrev = SetBkColor(hdc, clr);
 if (clrPrev != CLR_INVALID) {
  fDrawn = ExtTextOut(hdc, 0, 0,ETO_OPAQUE, prc, TEXT(""), 0, NULL);
  SetBkColor(hdc, clrPrev);
 }
 return fDrawn;
}
```

Explorer continues to use this modified function even though the product that was responsible for it no longer exists. Once bitten, twice shy.

The compatibility constraints of even your internal bookkeeping

THE LISTVIEW CONTROL, when placed in report mode, has a child header control that it uses to display column header titles. This header control is the property of the listview, but the listview is kind enough to let you retrieve the handle to that header control.

And some programs abuse that kindness.

It so happens that the original listview control did not use the lParam of the header control item for anything. So some programs said, "Well, if you're not using it, then I will!" and stashed their own private data into it.

Then a later version of the listview decided, "Gosh, there's some data I need to keep track of for each header item. Fortunately, because this is my header control, I can stash my data in the lParam of the header item."

And then the application compatibility team takes those two ingredients (the program that stuffs data into the header control and the listview that does the same) to their laboratory, mixes them, and an explosion occurs.

After some forensic analysis, the listview development team figures out what happened and curses that they have to work around yet another program that grovels into internal data structures. The auxiliary data is now stored in some other less-convenient place so that those programs can continue to run without crashing.

The moral of the story: Even if you change something that nobody should be relying on, there's a decent chance that somebody is relying on it.

(I'm sure there will be the usual chorus of people who will say, "You should've just broken them." What if I told you that one of the programs that does this is a widely used system administration tool? Eh, that probably wouldn't change your mind.)

⌒

Why does Windows keep your BIOS clock on local time?

EVEN THOUGH WINDOWS NT uses UTC internally, the BIOS clock stays on local time. Why is that?

There are a few reasons. One is a chain of backward compatibility.

In the early days, people often dual-booted between Windows NT and MS-DOS/Windows 3.1. MS-DOS and Windows 3.1 operate on local time, so Windows NT followed suit so that you wouldn't have to keep changing your clock each time you changed operating systems.

As people upgraded from Windows NT to Windows 2000 to Windows XP, this choice of time zone had to be preserved so that people could dual-boot between their previous operating system and the new operating system.

Another reason for keeping the BIOS clock on local time is to avoid confusing people who set their time via the BIOS itself. If you hit the magic key during the power-on self-test, the BIOS will go into its configuration mode, and one of the things you can configure there is the time. Imagine how confusing it would be if you set the time to 3 p.m., and then when you start Windows, the clock reads 11 a.m.

"Stupid computer. Why did it even ask me to change the time if it's going to screw it up and make me change it a second time?"

And if you explain to them, "No, you see, that time was UTC, not local time," the response is likely to be "What kind of totally propeller-headed nonsense is that? You're telling me that when the computer asks me what time it is, I have to tell it what time it is in London? (Except during the summer in the northern hemisphere, when I have to tell it what time it is in Reykjavik!?) Why do I have to remember my time zone and manually subtract four hours? Or is it five during the summer? Or maybe I have to add. Why do I even have to think about this? Stupid Microsoft. My watch says three o'clock. I type three o'clock. End of story."

(What's more, some BIOSes have alarm clocks built in, where you can program them to have the computer turn itself on at a particular time. Do you want to have to convert all those times to UTC each time you want to set a wake-up call?)

⌒

Bad version number checks

VERSION NUMBERS. Very important. And so many people check them wrong.

This is why Windows 95's GetVersion function returned 3.95 rather than 4.0. A lot of code checked the version number like this:

```
UINT Ver = GetVersion();
UINT MajorVersion = LOBYTE(uVer);
UINT MinorVersion = HIBYTE(uVer);
if (MajorVersion < 3 || MinorVersion < 10) {
 Error("This program requires Windows 3.1");
}
```

Now consider what happens when the version number is reported as 4.0. The major version check passes, but the minor version check fails because 0 is less than 10.

This bug was so rife that we gave up adding a compatibility entry every application that had the problem and just decided, "Fine. If anybody asks, say that the Windows version is 3.95."

The ways people mess up IUnknown::QueryInterface

WHEN YOU'RE DEALING with application compatibility, you discover all sorts of things that worked only by accident. Consider some of the "creative" ways people mess up the IUnknown::QueryInterface method.

Now, you'd think, "This interface is so critical to COM, how could anybody possible mess it up?" Here's how:

+ Forgetting to respond to IUnknown

    Sometimes you get so excited about responding to all these great interfaces that you forget to respond to IUnknown itself. We have found objects where

```
IShellFolder *psf = some object;
IUnknown *punk;
psf->QueryInterface(IID_IUnknown, (void**)&punk);
```

    fails with E_NOINTERFACE!

+ Forgetting to respond to your own interface

    There are some methods that return an object with a specific interface. And if you query that object for its own interface, its sole reason for existing, it says, "Huh?"

```
IShellFolder *psf = some object;
IEnumIDList *peidl, *peidl2;
psf->EnumObjects(..., &peidl);
peidl->QueryInterface(IID_IEnumIDList, (void**)&peidl2);
```

There are some objects which return E_NOINTERFACE to the
QueryInterface call, even though you're asking the object for
itself! "Sorry, I don't exist," it seems they're trying to say.

+ Forgetting to respond to base interfaces

When you implement a derived interface, you implicitly implement
the base interfaces, so don't forget to respond to them, too.

```
IShellView *psv = some object;
IOleView *pow;
psv->QueryInterface(IID_IOleView, (void**)&pow);
```

Some objects forget and the QueryInterface fails with
E_NOINTERFACE.

+ Requiring a secret knock

In principle, the following two code fragments are equivalent:

```
IShellFolder *psf;
IUnknown *punk;
CoCreateInstance(CLSID_xyz, ..., IID_IShellFolder, (void**)&psf);
psf->QueryInterface(IID_IUnknown, (void**)&punk);
```

and

```
CoCreateInstance(CLSID_xyz, ..., IID_IUnknown, (void**)&punk);
punk->QueryInterface(IID_IShellFolder, (void**)&psf);
```

In reality, some implementations mess up and fail the second call to
CoCreateInstance. The only way to create the object successfully
is to create it with the IShellFolder interface.

+ Forgetting to say "no" properly

One of the rules for saying "no" is that you have to set the output
pointer to NULL before returning. Some people forget to do that.

```
IMumble *pmbl;
punk->QueryInterface(IID_IMumble, (void**)&pmbl);
```

If the `QueryInterface` succeeds, then `pmbl` must be non-NULL
on return. If it fails, `pmbl` must be NULL on return.

The shell has to be compatible with all these buggy objects because if it
weren't, customers would get upset and the press would have a field day. Some
of the offenders are big-name programs. If they broke, people would report,
"Don't upgrade to Windows XYZ, it's not compatible with ‹big-name program›." Conspiracy-minded folks would shout, "Microsoft intentionally broke
‹big-name program›! Proof of unfair business tactics!"

〜

When programs assume that the system will never change, Episode 1

AN EXAMPLE, ALL too frequent, of ways programs assume that the user interface will never change is reaching into system binaries and sucking out undocumented resources. In the shell, we have fallen into the reluctant position of
carrying "dead" icons around for the benefit of programs that assumed that
they would always be available. However, we often make these "orphaned"
icons blank so that these programs don't crash, but they don't necessarily look
all that wonderful either.

Recently, I learned of a new type of resource stealing: stealing animations.
For Windows Vista, there have been many changes to the way the system
internally organizes its resources to support the Multilingual User Interface
feature. One of the things we found was a handful of programs that reach
directly into Shell32.dll to obtain the file copy animation.

Remember, resources in system files should be treated as implementation
details, unless explicitly documented otherwise.

When programs assume that the system will never change, Episode 2

ONE OF THE stranger application compatibility puzzles was solved by a colleague of mine who was trying to figure out why a particular program couldn't open the Printers Control Panel. Upon closer inspection, the reason became clear. The program launched the Control Panel, used FindWindow to locate the window, and then accessed that window's "File" menu and extracted the strings from that menu looking for an item that contained the word *Printer*. It then posted a WM_COMMAND message to the Control Panel window with the menu identifier it found, thereby simulating the user clicking on the Printers menu option.

With Windows 95's Control Panel, this method fell apart pretty badly. There is no Printers option on the Control Panel's File menu. It never occurred to the authors of the program that this was a possibility. (Mind you, it was a possibility even in Windows 3.1; if you were running a non-English version of Windows, the name of the Printers option would be something like *Skrivare* or *Drucker*. Not that it mattered, because the File menu will be called something like *Arkiv* or *Datei!* The developers of this program simply assumed that everyone in the world speaks English.)

The code never checked for errors; it plowed ahead on the assumption that everything was going according to plan. The code eventually completed its rounds and sent a garbage WM_COMMAND message to the Control Panel window, which was, of course, ignored because it didn't match any of the valid commands on that window's menu.

The punch line is that the mechanism for opening the Printers Control Panel was rather clearly spelled out on the very first page of the "Control Panel" chapter of the Windows 3.1 SDK:

> *The following example shows how an application can start Control Panel and the Printers application from the command line by using the* WinExec *function:*
>
> ```
> WinExec("control printers", SW_SHOWNORMAL);
> ```

In other words, they didn't even read past the first page.

The solution: Create a "decoy" Control Panel window with the same class name as Windows 3.1, so that this program would find it. The purpose of these "decoys" is to draw the attention of the offending program, taking the brunt of the mistreatment and doing what they can to mimic the original behavior enough to keep that program happy. In this case, the decoy waited patiently for the garbage `WM_COMMAND` message to arrive and dutifully launched the Printers Control Panel.

Nowadays, this sort of problem would probably be solved with the use of a shim. But this was back in Windows 95, when application compatibility technology was still comparatively immature. All that was available at the time were application compatibility flags and hot-patching of binaries, wherein the values are modified as they are loaded into memory. Using hot-patching technology was reserved for only the most extreme compatibility cases, because getting permission from the vendor to patch their program was a comparatively lengthy legal process. Patching was considered a "last-resort" compatibility mechanism not only for the legal machinery necessary to permit it, but also because patching a program fixes only the versions of the program the patch was developed to address. If the vendor shipped ten versions of a program, ten different patches would have to be developed. And if the vendor shipped another version after Windows 95 was delivered to duplication, that version would be broken when Windows 95 hit the shelves.

It is important to understand the distinction between what is a documented and supported feature and what is an implementation detail. Documented and supported features are contracts between Windows and your program. Windows will uphold its end of the contract for as long as that feature exists. Implementation details, on the other hand, are ephemeral; they can change at any time, be it at the next major operating system release, at the next service pack, even with the next security hotfix. If your program relies on implementation details, you're contributing to the compatibility cruft that Windows carries around from release to release.

The decoy Display Control Panel

WHEN SUPPORT FOR multiple monitors was being developed, a major obstacle was that a large number of display drivers hacked the Display Control Panel directly instead of using the documented extension mechanism. For example, instead of adding a separate page to the Display Control Panel's property sheet for, say, virtual desktops, they would just hack into the Settings page and add their button there. Some drivers were so adventuresome as to do what seemed like a total rewrite of the Settings page. They would take all the controls, move them around, resize them, hide some, show others, add new buttons of their own, and, generally speaking, treat the page as a lump of clay waiting to be molded into their own image. (Here's a handy rule of thumb: If your technique works only if the user speaks English, you probably should consider the possibility that what you're doing is relying on an implementation detail rather than something that will be officially supported going forward.)

To support multiple monitors, the Settings page on the Display Control Panel underwent a major overhaul. But when you tried to open the Display Control Panel on a system that had one of these aggressive drivers installed, it would crash because the driver ran around rearranging things like it always did, even though the things it was manipulating weren't what the developers of the driver intended!

The solution was to create a "decoy" Settings page that looked exactly like the classic Windows 95 Settings page. The decoy page's purpose in life was to act as bait for these aggressive display drivers and allow itself to be abused mercilessly, letting the driver have its way. Meanwhile, the real Settings page (which is the one that was shown to the user), by virtue of having been overlooked, remained safe and unharmed.

There was no attempt to make this decoy Settings page do anything interesting at all. Its sole job was to soak up mistreatment without complaining. As a result, those drivers lost whatever nifty features their shenanigans were trying to accomplish, but at least the Display Control Panel stayed alive and allowed users to do what they were trying to do in the first place: adjust their display settings.

The decoy visual style

DURING THE DEVELOPMENT of Windows XP, the visual design team was very cloak-and-dagger about what the final visual look was going to be. They had done a lot of research and put a lot of work into their designs and wanted to make sure that they made a big splash at the Electronic Entertainment Expo (nicknamed E[3]) when the Windows XP design, code-named Luna, was unveiled. Nobody outside the visual styles team, not even me, knew what Luna was going to look like.

On the other hand, the programmers who were setting up the infrastructure for visual styles needed to have something to test their code against. And something had to go out in the betas.

The visual styles team came up with two styles. In secret, they worked on Luna. In public, they worked on a "decoy" visual style called Mallard. The ruse was so successful that people were busy copying the decoy and porting it to other operating systems.

CHAPTER FOURTEEN

ETYMOLOGY AND HISTORY

WE TAKE A break from explicit programming topics to look at historical topics, with some attention paid to how things got their names. Some of this discussion may lead to some insight into how Win32 evolved from 16-bit Windows, but most of it is just for fun.

What do the letters W and L stand for in WPARAM and LPARAM?

ONCE UPON A time, Windows was 16 bit. Each message could carry with it two pieces of data, called WPARAM and LPARAM. The first one was a 16-bit value (word), so it was called W. The second one was a 32-bit value (long), so it was called L. You used the W parameter to pass things like handles and integers. You used the L parameter to pass pointers.

When Windows was converted to 32 bit, the WPARAM parameter grew to a 32-bit value, too. So even though the W stands for word, it isn't a word any more. (And in 64-bit Windows, both parameters are 64-bit values!)

It is helpful to understand the origin of the terms. If you look at the design of window messages, you will see that if the message takes a pointer, the pointer is usually passed in the LPARAM; whereas if the message takes a handle or an integer, it is passed in the WPARAM. (And if a message takes both, the integer goes in the WPARAM and the pointer goes in the LPARAM.)

Once you learn this, it makes remembering the parameters for window messages a little easier. Conversely, if a message breaks this rule, it sort of makes your brain say, "No, that's not right."

Why was nine the maximum number of monitors in Windows 98?

WINDOWS 98 WAS the first version of Windows to support multiple monitors. And the limit was nine.

Why nine?

Because that allowed you to arrange your monitors in a three-by-three grid, just like in the television program *The Brady Bunch*. You have early 1970s television to thank.

Why is a registry file called a hive?

BECAUSE ONE OF the original developers of Windows NT hated bees. So the developer who was responsible for the registry snuck in as many bee references as he could, just to annoy his colleague. A registry file is called a hive, and registry data are stored in cells, which is what honeycombs are made of.

The management of memory for resources in 16-bit Windows

IN 16-BIT WINDOWS, resources were not loaded until explicitly requested:

- The FindResource function located the entry for the resource in the resource directory and returned it in the form of a HRSRC.

- The `LoadResource` function took that resource handle, allocated some movable memory (`HGLOBAL`), and loaded the referenced resources off the disk into that memory.

- The `LockResource` function took that global handle and locked it, returning a pointer to the resource bytes themselves.

- The `UnlockResource` function unlocked the global handle.

- The `FreeResource` function freed the memory that had been allocated to hold the resource.

Actually, it was more complicated than this. Additional bookkeeping ensured that if two people tried to load the same resource, the same memory block got used for both, and the `FreeResource` didn't actually free the memory until the reference count went back to zero.

Actually, it was even more complicated than this. If the resource was marked `DISCARDABLE`, the memory wasn't actually freed when the reference count dropped to zero. Instead, the global handle was marked as discardable (`GMEM_DISCARDABLE`), so the handle remained valid, but when the system came under memory pressure, the memory behind the handle would get freed, and the next time you did a `LoadResource`, it would get reloaded from disk.

So now you know what that `DISCARDABLE` keyword in resource files means. Or at least what it used to mean. Win32 doesn't do any of this; the `DISCARDABLE` flag is ignored but remains for compatibility.

What is the difference between HINSTANCE and HMODULE?

THEY MEAN THE same thing today, but at one time they were quite different. It all comes from 16-bit Windows.

In those days, a module represented a file on disk that had been loaded into memory, and the module handle was a handle to a data structure that described the parts of the file, where they come from, and where they had been loaded into memory (if at all). On the other hand, an instance represented a set of variables.

One analogy that might (or might not) make sense is that a module is like the code for a C++ class: It describes how to construct an object, it implements the methods, it describes how the objects of the class behave. On the other hand, an instance is like a C++ object that belongs to that class: It describes the state of a particular object that is a member of the class.

In C# terms, a module is like a type, and an instance is like an object. (Except that modules don't have things like static members, but it was a weak analogy anyway.)

Here's a diagram:

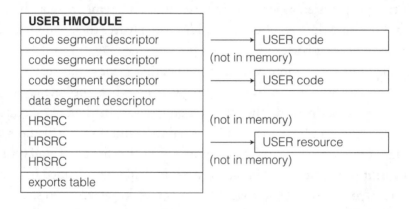

In 16-bit Windows, all programs ran in a single address space, and if a DLL was used by five programs, it was loaded only one time into memory. In particular, it got only one copy of its data segment. (In C++/C# terms, a DLL is like a singleton class.)

That's right, DLLs were system global rather than per process. The DLL did not get a separate copy of its data for each process that loaded it. If that was important to your DLL, you had to keep track of it yourself.

In geek terms, there was only one instance of a DLL in the system.

NOTEPAD HMODULE	
code segment descriptor	──────▶ NOTEPAD code
code segment descriptor	(not in memory)
data segment descriptor	
HRSRC	(not in memory)
HRSRC	──────▶ NOTEPAD resource

NOTEPAD HINSTANCE
NOTEPAD data

NOTEPAD HINSTANCE
NOTEPAD data

On the other hand, if you ran two copies of a program, say, Notepad, each one got its separate set of variables; there were two instances.

Both running copies of Notepad shared the NOTEPAD module (so the code and resources were shared), but each had its own copy of its variables (separate data segment). There were two instances of Notepad.

The instance handles in the above diagrams are the data segments.

Programs were identified by their instance handle. You can't use the module handle, because the two copies of Notepad have the same module handle (because the same code is running in each). The thing that makes them different is that each has its own set of global variables.

This is why the WinExec and ShellExecute functions return a HINSTANCE: They are holdovers from 16-bit Windows, where HINSTANCEs were the way to identify running programs.

When it came time to design Win32, the question then arose, "What do we do with HINSTANCE and HMODULE for Win32?" Because programs ran in separate address spaces, you didn't have instance handles visible across process boundaries. So the designers took the only thing they had: the base address of the module. This was analogous to the HMODULE, because the file header describes the contents of the file and its structure. And it was also analogous to the HINSTANCE, because the data was kept in the data segment, which was mapped into the process directly. In Win32, therefore, HINSTANCE and HMODULE are both just the base address of the module.

What was the purpose of the hPrevInstance parameter to WinMain?

AFTER YOUR AVERAGE Windows program picks itself up off the ground, control begins at your WinMain function. The second parameter, hPrevInstance, is always zero in Win32 programs. Certainly it had a meaning at some point?

Of course it did.

In 16-bit Windows, there was a function called GetInstanceData. This function took an HINSTANCE, a pointer, and a length, and copied memory from that instance into your current instance. (It's sort of the 16-bit equivalent to the ReadProcessMemory function, with the restriction that the second and third parameters had to be the same.)

> **NOTE:** Because 16-bit Windows had a common address space, the GetInstanceData function was really nothing more than an hmemcpy, and many programs relied on this and just used raw hmemcpy instead of using the documented method. The 16-bit version of Windows was actually designed with the possibility of imposing separate address spaces in a future version—observe flags such as GMEM_SHARED—but the prevalence of tricks such as hmemcpying your previous instance reduced this potential to an unrealized dream.

This was the reason for the hPrevInstance parameter to WinMain. If hPrevInstance was non-NULL, it was the instance handle of a copy of the program that is already running. You can use GetInstanceData to copy data from it, getting yourself up off the ground faster. For example, you might want to copy the main window handle out of the previous instance so you could communicate with it.

Whether hPrevInstance was NULL or not told you whether you were the first copy of the program. Under 16-bit Windows, only the first instance of a program registered its classes; second and subsequent instances continued to use the classes that were registered by the first instance. (Indeed, if they tried, the registration would fail because the class already existed.) Therefore, all 16-bit Windows programs skipped over class registration if hPrevInstance was non-NULL.

The people who designed Win32 found themselves in a bit of a fix when it came time to port WinMain: what to pass for hPrevInstance? The whole module/instance thing didn't exist in Win32, after all, and separate address spaces meant that programs that skipped over reinitialization in the second instance would no longer work. So Win32 always passes NULL, making all programs believe that they are the first one.

And amazingly, it actually worked.

⌒

Why is the GlobalWire function called GlobalWire?

FIRST, SOME BACKGROUND for those who never had to write 16-bit Windows programs: The GlobalWire function was similar to the 16-bit GlobalLock function, except that it had the bonus feature of relocating the memory to the lowest available linear address. You used this function as a courtesy if you intended to leave the memory locked for a long time. Moving it to the edge of the address space means that it is unlikely to become an obstacle in the middle of the address space that would otherwise prevent future large memory allocations from succeeding.

But why *wire*?

This employs a colloquial sense of the word *wire* as a verb that has lost its currency in the intervening years. To wire means to fasten securely in a very strong sense. It is probably related to the phrase *hard-wired*, which means "permanently attached in circuitry." Therefore, "wiring" memory into place ensures that it doesn't move around.

What was the difference between LocalAlloc and GlobalAlloc?

BACK IN THE days of 16-bit Windows, the difference was significant. In 16-bit Windows, memory was accessed through values called selectors, each of which could address up to 64KB. There was a default selector called the data selector; operations on so-called near pointers were performed relative to the data selector. For example, if you had a near pointer p whose value was 0x1234 and your data selector was 0x012F, when you wrote *p, you were accessing the memory at 012F:1234. (When you declared a pointer, it was near by default. You had to say FAR explicitly if you wanted a far pointer.)

Important: Near pointers are always *relative to* a selector, usually the data selector.

The GlobalAlloc function allocated a selector that could be used to access the amount of memory you requested. (If you asked for more than 64KB, something exciting happened, which is not important here.) You could access the memory in that selector with a far pointer. A far pointer is a selector combined with a near pointer. (Remember that a near pointer is relative to a selector; when you combine the near pointer with an appropriate selector, you get a far pointer.)

Every instance of a program and DLL got its own data selector, known as the HINSTANCE, which we learned about earlier. The default data selector for code in a program executable was the HINSTANCE of that instance of the program; the default data selector for code in a DLL was the HINSTANCE of that DLL. Therefore, if you had a near pointer p and accessed it via *p from a program executable, it accessed memory relative to the program instance's HINSTANCE. If you accessed it from a DLL, you got memory relative to your DLL's HINSTANCE.

The memory referenced by a selector could be turned into a local heap by calling the LocalInit function. Initializing the memory referenced by the HINSTANCE selector as a local heap was typically one of the first things a program or DLL did when it started up. (For DLLs, it was usually the *only* thing it did!) When you have a local heap, you can call `LocalAlloc` to allocate memory from it. The `LocalAlloc` function returned a near pointer relative to the default selector, so if you called it from a program executable, it allocated memory from the executable's `HINSTANCE`; if you called it from a DLL, it allocated memory from the DLL's `HINSTANCE`.

If you were clever, you realized that you could use `LocalAlloc` to allocate from memory other than `HINSTANCE`s. All you had to do was change your default selector to the selector for some memory you had allocated via `GlobalAlloc`, call the `LocalAlloc` function, and then restore the default selector. This gave you a near pointer relative to something *other than the default selector*, which was a very scary thing to have; but if you were smart and kept careful track, you could keep yourself out of trouble.

Observe, therefore, that in 16-bit Windows, the `LocalAlloc` and `Global Alloc` functions were completely different! `LocalAlloc` returned a near pointer, whereas `GlobalAlloc` returned a selector.

Pointers that you intended to pass between modules had to be in the form of far pointers because each module has a different default selector. If you wanted to transfer ownership of memory to another module, you had to use `GlobalAlloc` because that permitted the recipient to call `GlobalFree` to free it. (The recipient can't use `LocalFree` because `LocalFree` operates on the local heap, which would be the local heap of the recipient, not the same as your local heap.)

This historical difference between local and global memory still has vestiges in Win32. If you have a function that was inherited from 16-bit Windows and it transfers ownership of memory, it will take the form of an `HGLOBAL`. The clipboard functions are a classic example of this. If you put a block of memory onto the clipboard, it must have been allocated via `HGLOBAL` because you are transferring the memory to the clipboard, and the clipboard will call `GlobalFree` when it no longer needs the memory. Because OLE data objects are based on the clipboard, the `STGMEDIUM` structure used to represent clipboard data also uses an `HGLOBAL` to represent blocks of memory.

Even in Win32, you have to be careful not to confuse the local heap with the global heap. Memory allocated from one cannot be freed on the other. The functional differences have largely disappeared; the semantics are pretty much identical by this point. All the weirdness about near and far pointers disappeared with the transition to Win32. But the local heap functions and the global heap functions are nevertheless two distinct heap interfaces.

Because all the data-sharing functions use the global heap, the local heap functions in Win32 can be fractionally faster than the corresponding global heap functions. The global heap functions have to perform a small amount of additional bookkeeping to make data sharing possible, bookkeeping which the local heap functions (and the low-level heap functions like HeapAllocate) do not need to do.

Although the historical background of the LocalAlloc and GlobalAlloc functions is not essential information for writing programs in Win32, understanding how the functions evolved to their current state may help you understand why certain classes of functions prefer memory from one heap or another, such as we saw with the clipboard functions.

⟨

What was the point of the GMEM_SHARE flag?

THE GLOBALALLOC FUNCTION has a GMEM_SHARE flag. What is it for?

In 16-bit Windows, the GMEM_SHARE flag controlled whether the memory should outlive the process that allocated it. By default, all memory allocated by a process was automatically freed when that process exited.

Passing the GMEM_SHARE flag suppresses this automatic cleanup. That's why you have to use this flag when allocating memory to be placed on the clipboard or when you transfer it via OLE to another process. Because the clipboard exists after your program exits, any data you put on the clipboard needs to outlive the program. If you neglect to set this flag, then when your program exits, the memory that you put on the clipboard will be cleaned up, resulting in a crash the next time someone tries to read that data from the clipboard. (The GMEM_SHARE flag also controls whether the memory can be freed by a process other than the one that allocated it. This makes sense given the preceding semantics.)

Note that the cleanup rule applies to global memory allocated by DLLs on behalf of a process. Authors of DLLs had to be careful to keep track of whether any particular memory allocation was specific to a process (and should be freed when the process exited) or whether it was something the DLL was planning on sharing across processes for its own internal bookkeeping (in which case it shouldn't be freed). Failure to be mindful of this distinction would lead to puzzling crashes.

Thank goodness this is all gone in Win32.

Why do I sometimes see redundant casts before casting to LPARAM?

IF YOU READ through old code, you will often find casts that seem redundant:

```
SendMessage(hwndListBox, LB_ADDSTRING, 0, (LPARAM)(LPSTR)"str");
```

Why was `"str"` cast to `LPSTR`? It's already an `LPSTR`!

These are leftovers from 16-bit Windows. Recall that in 16-bit Windows, pointers were near by default. Consequently, `"str"` was a near pointer to a string. If the code had been written as

```
SendMessage(hwndListBox, LB_ADDSTRING, 0, (LPARAM)"str");
```

it would have taken the near pointer and cast it to a long. Because a near pointer is a 16-bit value, the pointer would have been zero-extended to the 32-bit size of a long.

However, all pointers in window messages must be far pointers because the window procedure for the window might very well be implemented in a different module from the sender. Recall that near pointers are interpreted relative to the default selector, and the default selector for each module is different. Sending a near pointer to another module will result in the pointer being interpreted relative to the *recipient's* default selector, which is not the same as the *sender's* default selector.

The intermediate cast to `LPSTR` converts the near pointer to a far pointer, LP being the Hungarian prefix for far pointers (also known as long pointers).

Casting a near pointer to a far pointer inserts the previously implied default selector, so that the cast to LPARAM captures the full 16:16 far pointer.

Aren't you glad you don't have to worry about this any more?

Why do the names of the registry functions randomly end in Ex?

SOME PEOPLE HAVE noticed that the names of the recommended registry functions sometimes end in Ex and sometimes don't:

RegCreateKeyEx	RegCloseKey
RegEnumKeyEx	RegDeleteKey
RegOpenKeyEx	RegDeleteValue
RegQueryValueEx	RegEnumValue
RegSetValueEx	RegQueryValue
	RegSetValue

The reason, as you might suspect, is historical. For this to make sense, you need to know about the original 16-bit registry.

A section of the 16-bit registry might look like this:

```
HKEY_CLASSES_ROOT
    .txt = "txtfile"
    txtfile = "Text Document"
       DefaultIcon = "notepad.exe,1"
```

There are three keys in this registry (aside from HKEY_CLASSES_ROOT), namely HKEY_CLASSES_ROOT\.txt, HKEY_CLASSES_ROOT\txtfile, and HKEY_CLASSES_ROOT\txtfile\DefaultIcon. Those three keys have the corresponding values txtfile, Text Document, and notepad.exe,1.

There are several things to notice about the 16-bit registry:

• Each key had a value, which was always a string.

- There was nothing that corresponds to what the 32-bit registry calls a named value. Each key contained only one piece of information, namely that string value (what in the 32-bit registry goes by the name *default* value).

The 16-bit registry had only seven functions:

- `RegOpenKey` opened an existing key given a name.
- `RegCreateKey` opened an existing key given a name or created it if it did not already exist.
- `RegCloseKey` closed the key handle returned by `RegOpenKey` or `RegCreateKey`.
- `RegDeleteKey` deleted a key by name.
- `RegEnumKey` enumerated the subkeys of a given key.
- `RegQueryValue` and `RegSetValue` read and wrote the string data associated with a registry key.

This is why the `RegQueryValue` and `RegSetValue` functions operate only on strings rather than accepting a registry data type: The original 16-bit registry supported only strings to begin with.

The people responsible for porting the registry to 32-bit Windows added security, which necessitated the Ex functions `RegOpenKeyEx` and `RegCreateKeyEx`, which accept a security access mask. Additional metadata such as the last-write time were exposed via the new Ex function `RegEnumKeyEx`.

They also added the concept of named values, name-associated data of arbitrary type that can be stored underneath a key. I think the choice of the word *value* to represent this concept was a poor one, because the word *value* was already being used for something else. Overloading the term just creates confusion. I would have used a word such as *item*.

At any rate, what's done is done, and functions needed to be created to access these "new values." Because they chose the same word *value* to represent these new objects, the functions that access them need to be named Ex to distinguish them from the old 16-bit versions (hence, `RegQueryValueEx` and `RegSetValueEx`).

Brand new functions for manipulating these new values didn't need the Ex because there was no old function to conflict with. Hence we have the non-Ex functions `RegDeleteValue` and `RegEnumValue` that operate on new values.

With the introduction of 64-bit Windows, a new `RegDeleteKeyEx` function was added that permits you to specify which registry (the 32-bit or 64-bit registry) you want to delete your key from. In Windows Vista, even more registry helper functions have been introduced, such as `RegCopyTree`: These do not have an Ex because there was no old function by the same name that it would have conflicted with.

In summary, then, the rule for whether a function is Ex or non-Ex is simple: If there is already a function by the same name, the new function must be called Ex. The historical background is knowing which functions existed at the point a new function was introduced.

⬅

What's the difference between SHGetMalloc, SHAlloc, CoGetMalloc, and CoTaskMemAlloc?

IF YOU'VE DONE programming with the Windows shell, you've no doubt seen (and possibly even used) the `SHGetMalloc` function, which returns a pointer to the shell task allocator, the memory allocator that is used by shell interfaces to allocate and free memory. On the other hand, there is also the `CoGetMalloc` function, which returns a pointer to the COM task allocator, which is the memory allocator used by COM interfaces to allocate and free memory. To confuse matters even more, there are the functions `SHAlloc` and `CoTaskMemAlloc`, which also allocate memory. Why are there so many functions that seem to do the same thing? How are they related?

Let's get the easy ones out of the way. First, CoTaskMemAlloc is exactly the same as allocating memory with the COM task allocator, and CoTaskMemFree is the same as freeing memory with the COM task allocator. In other words, calling CoTaskMemAlloc is the same as calling CoGetMalloc to obtain the COM task allocator, and then allocating memory from it. The CoTaskMemAlloc and CoTaskMemFree functions (and the less-used CoTaskMemRealloc) are just convenience functions that save you the trouble of having to mess with CoGetMalloc yourself. Consequently, you can safely allocate memory by using CoGetMalloc(), and then free it with CoTaskMemFree, and vice versa. It's all the same allocator.

Similarly, SHAlloc and SHFree are just wrappers around SHGetMalloc, which allocate/free the memory via the shell task allocator. Memory you allocated via SHGetMalloc can be freed with SHFree and vice versa.

So far, we have this diagram:

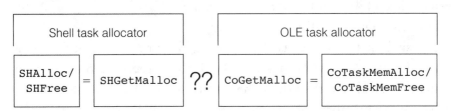

Now what about those question marks? If you read the comments in shlobj.h, you may get a bit of a hint:

```
//
// Task allocator API
//
//  All the shell extensions MUST use the task allocator (see OLE 2.0
// programming guild for its definition) when they allocate or free
// memory objects (mostly ITEMIDLIST) that are returned across any
// shell interfaces. There are two ways to access the task allocator
// from a shell extension depending on whether or not it is linked with
// OLE32.DLL or not (purely for efficiency).
//
// (1) A shell extension which calls any OLE API (i.e., linked with
//  OLE32.DLL) should call OLE's task allocator (by retrieving
//  the task allocator by calling CoGetMalloc API).
//
```

```
// (2) A shell extension which does not call any OLE API (i.e., not
//   linked with OLE32.DLL) should call the shell task allocator API
//   (defined below), so that the shell can quickly loads it when
//   OLE32.DLL is not loaded by any application at that point.
//
// Notes:
//   In next version of Windowso release, SHGetMalloc will be replaced
//   by the following macro.
//
// #define SHGetMalloc(ppmem)    CoGetMalloc(MEMCTX_TASK, ppmem)
//
```

(Yes, those typos like "guild" and "Windowso" have been there since 1995.)
This discussion strongly hints at what's going on.

When Windows 95 was being developed, computers typically had just 4MB of memory. (The cool people got 8MB.) But Explorer was also heavily reliant upon COM for its shell extension architecture, and loading OLE32.DLL into memory was a significant kick in the teeth. Under such tight memory conditions, even the loss of 4KB of memory was noticeable.

The solution: Play "OLE Chicken."

The shell, it turns out, used only a very limited subset of COM. As a result, the shell team wrote a "mini-COM" that supported only those operations and used it rather than the real thing. (It helped that one of the high-ranking members of the shell team was a COM super-expert.) The shell had its own miniature task allocator (SHGetMalloc), its own miniature binder (SHCoCreateInstance), its own miniature drag-drop loop (SHDoDragDrop), everything it needed *provided* you didn't run any other programs that used OLE32.

Once some other program that used OLE32 started running, you had a problem: There were now two separate versions of OLE in the system: the real thing and the fake version inside the shell. Unless something was done, you wouldn't be able to interoperate between real-COM and fake-shell COM. For example, you wouldn't be able to drag/drop data between Explorer (using fake-shell COM) and a window that was using real COM.

The solution: With the help of other parts of the system, the shell detected that "COM is now in the building" when anybody loaded OLE32.DLL, and it transferred all the information it had been managing on its own into the world of real COM. When it did this, all the shell pseudo-COM functions switched to real COM, too. For example, after OLE32.DLL got loaded, calls to the shell's fake task allocator just went to the real task allocator.

But what is OLE Chicken? This is another variation of the various "chicken"-type games, perhaps the most famous of which is Schedule Chicken. Schedule Chicken is a game of nerves played by groups in a dysfunctional project. Each group promises an unreasonably optimistic schedule, knowing full well that they cannot make it, but betting that some other group is lying about their schedule even more. The game is "won" when that other group becomes the one to miss a target date and force the schedule to slip, thereby buying your group more time. In extreme cases, the game can play out multiple times within a single release cycle. The name comes from a deadly test of nerves in the movie *Rebel Without a Cause* wherein two cars race toward a cliff, and the first driver to leap out of his car is declared the "chicken."

In OLE Chicken, each program would avoid loading OLE32.DLL as long as possible, so that it wouldn't be the one blamed for the long pause as OLE32.DLL got itself off the ground and ready for action. (Remember, we're talking 1995-era machines where allocating 32KB of memory would bring the wrath of the performance team down upon your head.)

Okay, so let's look at that comment block again.

The opening paragraph mentions the possibility that a shell extension does not itself link with OLE32.DLL. Option (1) discusses a shell extension that does use OLE32, in which case it should use the official OLE functions such as `CoGetMalloc`. But Option (2) discusses a shell extension that does not use OLE32. Those shell extensions are directed to use the shell's fake-COM functions such as `SHGetMalloc`, rather than the real-COM functions, so that no new dependency on OLE32 is created. Therefore, if OLE32 is not yet loaded, loading these shell extensions will also not cause OLE32 to be loaded, thereby saving the cost of loading and initializing OLE32.DLL.

The completion of our diagram for 1995-era programs would therefore be something like this:

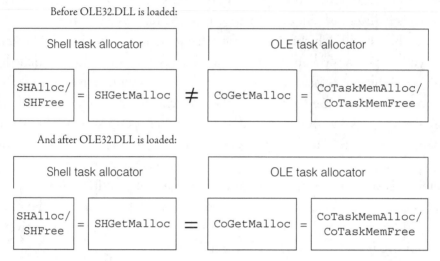

Before OLE32.DLL is loaded:

And after OLE32.DLL is loaded:

The final "Note" hints at the direction the shell intended to go. Eventually, loading OLE32.DLL would not be as painful as it was in Windows 95, and the shell can abandon its fake COM and just use the real thing. At this point, asking for the shell task allocator would become the same as asking for the COM task allocator.

That time actually arrived a long time ago. The days of 4MB machines are now the stuff of legend. The shell has ditched its fake COM and now just uses real COM everywhere.

Therefore, *the diagram today is the one with the equals sign.* All four functions are interchangeable in Windows XP and beyond.

What if you want to run on older systems? Well, it is always acceptable to use CoTaskMemAlloc/CoTaskMemFree. Why? You can puzzle this out logically. Because those functions are exported from OLE32.DLL, the fact that you are using them means that OLE32.DLL is loaded—*you* loaded it! At this point the "After" diagram above with the equals sign kicks in, and everything is all one big happy family.

The case where you need to be careful is if your DLL does *not* link to OLE32.DLL. In that case, you don't know whether you are in the "Before" or

"After" case, and you have to play it safe and use the shell task allocator for the things that are documented as using the shell task allocator.

I hope this discussion also provides the historical background of the function SHLoadOLE, which today doesn't do anything because OLE is already always loaded. But in the old days, this signaled to the shell, "Okay, now is the time to transfer all the information being maintained by your fake COM into the real COM." But because the shell no longer uses fake COM, there is no longer any information to transfer.

Why is Windows Error Reporting nicknamed Dr. Watson?

THE NICKNAME FOR the feature known as Windows Error Reporting is Dr. Watson. Where did that name come from?

As you have probably guessed, the name Dr. Watson was inspired by the character of Dr. Watson, the assistant to Sherlock Holmes in the stories by Arthur Conan Doyle.

It is my understanding that the doctor was originally developed as part of Windows 3.0 beta testing. His job was to record data about application crashes to a file so that the file could be uploaded and included with bug reports. The icon was (and continues to be) a friendly doctor using his stethoscope to investigate a problem.

The doctor has remained true to the "capture information about an error" aspect of his job. In the meantime, the word *Watson* has expanded its meaning to encompass anonymous end-user feedback mechanisms in general, such as Content Watson, which is a feedback tool the Office division uses to improve their documentation.

But if you hear "Watson" by itself, the speaker is almost certainly talking about error reporting.

What most people probably don't know is that Dr. Watson's name wasn't originally Dr. Watson. The original name of the diagnostic tool was Sherlock, whose icon was a lit drop-stem pipe. I remember chatting about the doctor with its original author, whose office was just a few doors down from mine. In 1991, he had to change the name from Sherlock to Dr. Watson because there was already a debugging tool called Sherlock that had come out a few years previously. The name had to change, and the doctor stepped in to fill Sherlock's shoes. The icon was originally a doctor's bag, but it changed to the stethoscope-wielding general practitioner a few months later. (I'm told that the Windows NT team was slow to learn of the doctor's new icon, and they used a medical bag, only to have to change the icon at the last minute because the red cross on the bag incorrectly suggested an affiliation with the international relief organization.)

⬿

What happened to DirectX 4?

IF YOU GO through the history of DirectX, you'll see that there is no DirectX 4. It went from DirectX 3 straight to DirectX 5. What's up with that?

After DirectX 3 was released, development on two successor products took place simultaneously: a shorter-term release called DirectX 4 and a more substantial longer-term release called DirectX 5.

But the feedback from the game development community said that they didn't really care about the small features in DirectX 4; what they were much more interested in were the features of DirectX 5. So it was decided to cancel DirectX 4 and roll all of its features into DirectX 5.

So why wasn't DirectX 5 renamed to DirectX 4?

Because there were already hundreds upon hundreds of documents that referred to the two projects as DirectX 4 and DirectX 5. Documents that said things such as "Feature XYZ will not appear until DirectX 5." Changing the name of the projects mid-cycle was going to create even more confusion. You would end up with headlines like "Microsoft removes DirectX 5 from the table; kiss good-bye to feature XYZ" and conversations reminiscent of the Abbott and Costello routine "Who's on First?"

"I have some email from you saying that feature ABC won't be ready until DirectX 5. When do you plan on releasing DirectX 5?"

"We haven't even started planning DirectX 5; we're completely focused on DirectX 4, which we hope to have ready by late spring."

"But I need feature XYZ and you said that won't be ready until DirectX 5."

"Oh, that email was written two weeks ago. Since then, DirectX 5 got renamed to DirectX 4, and DirectX 4 was cancelled."

"So when I have a letter from you talking about DirectX 5, I should pretend it says DirectX 4, and when it says DirectX 4, I should pretend it says 'a project that has since been cancelled'?"

"Right, but check the date at the top of the letter, because if it's newer than last week, then when it says DirectX 4, it really means the new DirectX 4."

"And what if it says DirectX 5?"

"Then somebody screwed up and didn't get the memo."

"Okay, thanks. Clear as mud."

Why are HANDLE return values so inconsistent?

IF YOU LOOK at the various functions that return HANDLEs, you'll see that some of them return NULL (like `CreateThread`) and some of them return INVALID_HANDLE_VALUE (like `CreateFile`). You have to check the documentation to see what each particular function returns on failure.

Why are the return values so inconsistent?

The reasons, as you may suspect, are historical.

The values were chosen to be compatible with 16-bit Windows. The 16-bit functions `OpenFile`, `_lopen` and `_lcreat` return –1 on failure, so the 32-bit `CreateFile` function returns INVALID_HANDLE_VALUE to facilitate porting code from Win16.

(Armed with this, you can now answer the following trivia question: Why do I call `CreateFile` when I'm not actually creating a file? Shouldn't it be called `OpenFile`? Answer: Yes, `OpenFile` would have been a better name, but that name was already taken.)

On the other hand, there are no Win16 equivalents for `CreateThread` or `CreateMutex`, so they return `NULL`.

Because the precedent had now been set for inconsistent return values, whenever a new function got added, it was a bit of a toss-up whether the new function returned `NULL` or `INVALID_HANDLE_VALUE`.

This inconsistency has multiple consequences.

First, of course, you have to be careful to check the return values properly.

Second, it means that if you write a generic handle-wrapping class, you have to be mindful of two possible "not a handle" values.

Third, if you want to pre-initialize a `HANDLE` variable, you have to initialize it in a manner compatible with the function you intend to use. For example, the following code is wrong:

```
HANDLE h = NULL;
if (UseLogFile()) {
    h = CreateFile(...);
}
DoOtherStuff();
if (h) {
    Log(h);
}
DoOtherStuff();
if (h) {
    CloseHandle(h);
}
```

This code has two bugs. First, the return value from `CreateFile` is checked incorrectly. The code above checks for `NULL` rather than `INVALID_HANDLE_VALUE`. Second, the code initializes the h variable incorrectly. Here's the corrected version:

```
HANDLE h = INVALID_HANDLE_VALUE;
if (UseLogFile()) {
    h = CreateFile(...);
}
DoOtherStuff();
if (h != INVALID_HANDLE_VALUE) {
    Log(h);
}
DoOtherStuff();
```

```
if (h != INVALID_HANDLE_VALUE) {
    CloseHandle(h);
}
```

Fourth, you have to be particularly careful with the INVALID_HANDLE_VALUE value: By coincidence, the value INVALID_HANDLE_VALUE happens to be numerically equal to the pseudo-handle returned by GetCurrentProcess(). Many kernel functions accept pseudo-handles; so if you mess up and accidentally call, say, WaitForSingleObject on a failed INVALID_HANDLE_VALUE handle, you will actually end up waiting on your own process. This wait will, of course, never complete, because a process is signaled when it exits, so you ended up waiting for yourself.

Why do text files end in Ctrl+Z?

ACTUALLY, TEXT FILES don't need to end in Ctrl+Z, but the convention persists in certain circles. (Though, fortunately, those circles are awfully small nowadays.)

This story requires us to go back to CP/M, the operating system that MS-DOS envisioned itself as a successor to. (Because the 8086 envisioned itself as the successor to the 8080, it was natural that the operating system for the 8086 would view itself as the successor to the primary operating system on the 8080.)

In CP/M, files were stored in sectors of 128 bytes each. If your file was 64 bytes long, it was stored in a full sector. The kicker was that the operating system tracked the size of the file as the number of sectors. If your file was not an exact multiple of 128 bytes in size, you needed some way to specify where the "real" end of file was.

That's where Ctrl+Z came in.

By convention, the unused bytes at the end of the last sector were padded with Ctrl+Z characters. According to this convention, if you had a program that read from a file, it should stop when it reads a Ctrl+Z, because that meant that it was now reading the padding.

To retain compatibility with CP/M, MS-DOS carried forward the Ctrl+Z convention. That way, when you transferred your files from your old CP/M machine to your new PC, they wouldn't have garbage at the end.

Ctrl+Z hasn't been needed for years; MS-DOS records file sizes in bytes rather than sectors. But the convention lingers in the COPY command, for example.

🙰

Why is the line terminator CR+LF?

THIS PROTOCOL DATES back to the days of teletypewriters. CR stands for "carriage return"; the CR control character returned the print head (carriage) to column 0 without advancing the paper. LF stands for "linefeed"; the LF control character advanced the paper one line without moving the print head. So if you wanted to return the print head to column zero (ready to print the next line) and advance the paper (so it prints on fresh paper), you needed both CR and LF.

If you go to the various Internet protocol documents, such as RFC 0821 (SMTP), RFC 1939 (POP), RFC 2060 (IMAP), or RFC 2616 (HTTP), you'll see that they all specify CR+LF as the line termination sequence. So the real question is not "Why do CP/M, MS-DOS, and Win32 use CR+LF as the line terminator?" but rather "Why did other people choose to differ from these standards documents and use some other line terminator?"

UNIX adopted plain LF as the line termination sequence. If you look at the stty options, you'll see that the onlcr option specifies whether a LF should be changed into CR+LF. If you get this setting wrong, you get stair-step text, where each
        line
             begins where the previous line left off. So even UNIX, when left in raw mode, requires CR+LF to terminate lines. The implicit CR before LF is a UNIX invention, probably as an economy, because it saves one byte per line.

The UNIX ancestry of the C language carried this convention into the C language standard, which requires only \n (which encodes LF) to terminate lines, putting the burden on the runtime libraries to convert raw file data into logical lines.

The C language also introduced the term *newline* to express the concept of "generic line terminator." I'm told that the ASCII committee changed the name of character 0x0A to newline around 1996, so the confusion level has been raised even higher.

⤳

TEXT vs. _TEXT vs. _T, and UNICODE vs. _UNICODE

So what's with all these different ways of saying the same thing?

There's actually a method behind the madness.

The plain versions without the underscore affect the character set the Windows header files treat as default. So if you define UNICODE, GetWindowText will map to GetWindowTextW rather than GetWindowTextA, for example. Similarly, the TEXT macro will map to L"..." rather than "...".

The versions with the underscore affect the character set the C runtime header files treat as default. So if you define _UNICODE, _tcslen will map to wcslen rather than strlen, for example. Similarly, the _TEXT macro will map to L"..." rather than "...".

What about _T? Okay, I don't know about that one. Probably it was just to save somebody some typing.

⤳

Why are dialog boxes initially created hidden?

You might not have noticed it until you looked closely, but dialog boxes are actually created hidden initially, even if you specify WS_VISIBLE in the template. The reason for this is historical.

Rewind back to the old days (we're talking Windows 1.0): Graphics cards are slow, and CPUs are slow and memory is slow. You can pick a menu option that displays a dialog and wait a second or two for the dialog to get loaded off the floppy disk. (Hard drives are for the rich kids.) And then you have to wait for the dialog box to paint.

To save valuable seconds, dialog boxes are created initially hidden and all typeahead is processed while the dialog stays hidden. Only after the type ahead is finished is the dialog box finally shown. And if you typed far ahead enough and press Enter, you might even have been able to finish the entire dialog box without it ever being shown! Now that's efficiency.

Of course, nowadays, programs are stored on hard drives and you can't (normally) out-type a hard drive, so this optimization is largely wasted, but the behavior remains for compatibility reasons.

Actually this behavior still serves a useful purpose: If the dialog were initially created visible, the user would be able to see all the controls being created into it, and watch as WM_INITDIALOG ran (changing default values, hiding and showing controls, moving controls around …) This is both ugly and distracting. ("How come the box comes up checked, then suddenly unchecks itself before I can click on it?")

⟞

When you change the insides, nobody notices

I FIND IT puzzling when people complain that Calc and Notepad haven't changed. In fact, both programs have undergone changes over the years. (Notepad gained some additional menu and status bar options. Calc got a severe workover.)

I wouldn't be surprised if these are the same people who complain, "Why does Microsoft spend all its effort on making Windows 'look cool'? They should spend all their efforts on making technical improvements and just stop making visual improvements."

And with Calc, that's exactly what happened: massive technical improvements. No visual improvement. And nobody noticed. In fact, the complaints just keep coming. "Look at Calc, same as it always was."

The innards of Calc—the arithmetic engine—were completely thrown away and rewritten from scratch. The standard IEEE floating-point library was replaced with an arbitrary-precision arithmetic library. This was done after people kept writing ha-ha articles about how Calc couldn't do decimal arithmetic correctly (that, for example, computing 10.21 – 10.2 resulted in 0.0100000000000016). These all came from people who didn't understand how computers handle floating point. Everybody should read the essay "What every computer scientist should know about floating point." Use your favorite search engine to find a copy.

Today, Calc's internal computations are done with infinite precision for basic operations (addition, subtraction, multiplication, division) and 32 digits of precision for advanced operations (square root, transcendental operators).

Try it: 1 / 3 * 10000000000 – 3333333333 =. The result is one-third exactly. Type 1/x – 3 = and you get zero back. (Of course, if you don't believe that, repeat the sequence * 10000000000 – 3333333333 = until you're bored and notice that the answer always comes back as 0.333333333333333333333333333333333. If it were fixed precision, the 3s would eventually stop coming.)

Thirty-two positions of precision for inexact results not good enough? The Power Calculator PowerToy uses the same arithmetic engine as Calc and lets you crank the precision to an unimaginable 512 digits.

Anyway, my point is that—whether you like it or not—if you don't change the UI, nobody notices. That's why so much effort is spent on new UI.

⌒

If FlushInstructionCache doesn't do anything, why do you have to call it?

IF YOU LOOK at the implementation of FlushInstructionCache on Windows 95, you'll see that it's just a return instruction. It doesn't actually do anything. So why do you have to call it?

Because the act of calling it is the whole point. The control transfers implicit in calling a function suffice to flush the instruction cache on a Pentium. The function doesn't have to do anything else; it is the fact that you called a function that is important.

If InitCommonControls doesn't do anything, why do you have to call it?

ONE OF THE problems beginners run into when they start using shell common controls is that they forget to call the InitCommonControls function. But if you were to disassemble the InitCommonControls function itself, you'll see that it, like the FlushInstructionCache function, doesn't actually do anything.

Then why do you need to call it?

As with FlushInstructionCache, what's important is not what it performs, but just the fact that you called it.

Recall that merely listing an import library in your dependencies doesn't actually cause your program to be bound to the corresponding dynamic link library (DLL). You have to call a function in that DLL in order for there to be an import entry for that DLL. And InitCommonControls is that function.

Without the InitCommonControls function, a program that wants to use the shell common controls library would otherwise have no reference to COMCTL32.DLL in its import table. This means that when the program loads, COMCTL32.DLL is not loaded and therefore is not initialized. Which means that it doesn't register its window classes. Which means that your call to the CreateWindow function fails because the window class has not been registered.

That's why you have to call a function that does nothing. It's for your own good.

The documentation for the InitCommonControls function recommends that you call the InitCommonControlsEx function instead. The reason is that the InitCommonControlsEx function lets you specify which controls you wish to initialize. The older InitCommonControls function remains for compatibility with Windows 95; if you call it, you initialize the controls that were available in the Windows 95 version of the common controls library (see the documentation of the ICC_WIN95_CLASSES flag for details). If you want access to any of the newer controls (such as the date and time picker), you need to use the InitCommonControlsEx function.

⟐

Why did InterlockedIncrement/ Decrement only return the sign of the result?

IF YOU READ the fine print of the InterlockedIncrement and Interlocked-Decrement functions, you'll see that on Windows NT 3.51 and earlier and on Windows 95, the return value only matches the sign of the result of the increment or decrement. Why is that?

The 80386 instruction set supports interlocked increment and decrement, but the result of the increment/decrement operation is not returned. Only the flags are updated by the operation. As a result, the only information you get back from the CPU about the result of the operation is whether it was zero, positive, or negative. (Okay, you also get some obscure information such as whether there were an even or odd number of 1 bits in the result, but that's hardly useful nowadays.)

Because those operating systems supported the 80386 processor, their implementations of the InterlockedIncrement and InterlockedDecrement functions were limited by the capabilities of the processor.

The 80486 introduced the XADD instruction, which returns the original value of the operand. With this additional information, it now becomes possible to return the result of the operation exactly.

Windows NT 4 dropped support for the 80386 processor, requiring a minimum of an 80486, so it could take advantage of this instruction. Windows 98 still had to support the 80386, so it couldn't.

So how did Windows 98 manage to implement an operation that was not supported by the CPU?

Windows 98 detected whether you had a CPU that supported the new XADD instruction. If not, it used an alternate mechanism that was mind-bogglingly slow: It called a driver whenever you wanted to increment or decrement a variable. The driver would then emulate the XADD instruction by disabling interrupts and performing the operation in locked memory. Because Windows 98 was a uniprocessor operating system, it didn't have to worry about a second processor changing the memory at the same time; all it needed to ensure was that the single processor didn't get interrupted while it was performing the "atomic" operation.

⤳

Why does the function WSASetLastError exist?

WHY DOES THE function WSASetLastError exist when there is already the perfectly good function SetLastError?

Actually, you know the answer, too, if you sit down and think about it.

Winsock was originally developed to run on both 16-bit Windows and 32-bit Windows. Notice how the classic Winsock functions are based on window messages for asynchronous notifications. In the 16-bit world, there was no SetLastError function. Therefore, Winsock had to provide its own version for the 16-bit implementation. And because source code compatibility is important, there was a 32-bit version, too. Of course, the 32-bit version looks kind of stupid in retrospect if you aren't aware of the 16-bit version.

⤳

Why are there broadcast-based mechanisms in Windows?

MANY WINDOWS INFORMATION mechanisms are based on message broadcasts, among them DDE, WM_FONTCHANGE, and changes in system settings. Why do these mechanisms use broadcasts, when we know that broadcasts can result in the system grinding to a halt because of windows that have stopped processing messages?

Because in 16-bit Windows, you didn't have this problem.

Recall that 16-bit Windows was cooperatively multitasking. When a program received control of the CPU, it could do anything it wanted, knowing that no other programs could run until it explicitly yielded control by calling a function such as GetMessage or PeekMessage. The downside of this, of course, was that a single hung program caused the entire system to hang, because it wasn't releasing the CPU.

The upside, however, was that if your program was running, you knew, *a priori*, that there were no hung programs in the system. How do you know that? Because if there were a hung program, *it would be running and not you.*

If there's only one thing, and you have it, you know that nobody else is hogging it.

Therefore, broadcasting messages was completely safe in 16-bit Windows. You didn't have to worry about nonresponsive programs because you had proof that there weren't any.

Of course, when the switch to preemptive multitasking occurred, this assumption no longer applied, but by then it was too late. The broadcast-based model was already in use, and consequently had to be preserved for compatibility reasons. (It would be bad if, for example, Lotus 1-2-3 stopped working on Windows NT because DDE broadcasts were no longer supported. If the Windows NT team had tried that gambit, nobody would have upgraded and Windows NT wouldn't have survived to make a second version.)

On the other hand, given the risks involved in DDE broadcasts, you probably would be better off designing *your* program to not use dynamic data exchange as a data communication mechanism, thereby avoiding the pitfall of message broadcasts. No point contributing to the problem.

Where did windows minimize to before the taskbar was invented?

Before Explorer was introduced in Windows 95, the Windows desktop was a very different place.

The icons on your desktop did not represent files; rather, when you minimized a program, it turned into an icon on the desktop. To open a minimized program, you had to hunt for its icon, possibly minimizing other programs to get them out of the way, and then double-click it. (You could also Alt+Tab to the program.)

Explorer changed the desktop model so that icons on your desktop represent objects (files, folders) rather than programs. The job of managing programs fell to the new taskbar.

But where did the windows go when you minimized them?

Under the old model, when a window was minimized, it displayed as an icon, the icon had a particular position on the screen, and the program drew the icon in response to paint messages. (Of course, most programs deferred to `DefWindowProc`, which just drew the icon.) In other words, the window never went away; it just changed its appearance.

But with the taskbar, the window really does go away when you minimize it. Its only presence is in the taskbar. The subject of how to handle windows when they were minimized went through several iterations, because it seemed that no matter what we did, some program somewhere didn't like it.

The first try was very simple: When a window was minimized, the Windows 95 window manager set it to hidden. That didn't play well with many applications, which cared about the distinction between minimized (and visible) and hidden (and not visible).

Next, the Windows 95 window manager minimized the window just like the old days, but put the minimized window at coordinates (−32000, −32000). This didn't work because some programs freaked out if they found their coordinates were negative.

So the Windows 95 window manager tried putting minimized windows at coordinates (32000, 32000). This still didn't work because some programs freaked out if they found their coordinates were positive and too large!

Finally, the Windows 95 window manager tried coordinates (3000, 3000). This seemed to keep everybody happy. Not negative, not too large, but large enough that it wouldn't show up on the screen (at least not at screen resolutions that were readily available in 1995).

If you have a triple-monitor Windows 98 machine lying around, you can try this: Set the resolution of each monitor to 1200x1024 and place them corner to corner. At the lower-right corner of the third monitor, you will see all your minimized windows parked out in the boonies.

(Windows NT stuck with the −32000 coordinates and didn't pick up the compatibility fixes for some reason. I guess they figured that by the time

Windows NT became popular, all those broken programs would have been fixed. In other words: Let Windows 95 do your dirty work!)

⤳

Why didn't the desktop window shrink to exclude the taskbar?

THE TASKBAR CREATED all sorts of interesting problems because the work area was not equal to the entire screen dimensions. (Multiple monitors created similar problems.) "Why didn't the functions that that returned the screen dimensions return the usable workspace instead?"

That would have made things even worse.

Lots of programs want to cover the entire screen. Games, for example, are very keen on covering the entire screen. Slideshow programs also want to cover the entire screen. (This includes both slideshows for digital pictures as well as business presentations.) Screen savers of course must cover the entire screen.

If the desktop window didn't include the taskbar, those programs would leave a taskbar visible while they did their thing. This is particularly dangerous for screen savers because a user could just click on the taskbar to switch to another program without going through the screen saver's password lock!

And if the taskbar were docked at the top or left edge of the screen, this would have resulted in the desktop window not beginning at coordinates (0, 0), which would no doubt have caused widespread havoc. (Alternatively, one could have changed the coordinate system so that (0, 0) was no longer the upper-left corner of the screen, but that would have broken so many programs it wouldn't have been funny.)

⤳

Why does the caret stop blinking when I tap the Alt key?

HERE'S A LITTLE quiz. Open the Run dialog. Observe the happily blinking caret in the edit control. Now tap the Alt key. The caret stops blinking. What happened?

Here are some clues:

- After tapping the Alt key, pressing any other key results in a beep. With two exceptions. Find those two exceptions and see if the result sheds any light.

- Perform this same exercise, but with Notepad rather than the Run dialog. Pay close attention to what changes on the screen. Press the right arrow key a few times. But observe what happens when you press the right arrow key when the highlight is on the Help menu.

- (Somewhat unfair.) If you have access to a computer running Windows 3.1, repeat the experiment there.

What happened is that tapping the Alt key once highlights the System menu button. The System menu is the menu you get when you click on the mini-icon in the upper-left corner of a window or right-click on the caption bar. Back in Windows 3.1, the System menu got its own button that looked like a horizontal bar. (I'm sure part of this was to provide a mnemonic for the keyboard accelerator that opens the System menu: Alt+Space.) If you tapped the Alt key, you put the window into "menu browsing mode." That's why you see the Notepad menu highlight after you tap the Alt key once, and why the arrow keys let you browse around the Notepad menu.

The System menu participates in menu browsing mode; indeed, if the window doesn't have a menu, then the System menu is the only menu available to be browsed! In Windows 3.1, when the System menu button was selected, it turned gray. But starting in Windows 95, there is no System menu button any more. You just have to use your imagination and pretend you see a highlighted System menu button.

Why does this oddity persist? For keyboard backward compatibility. Tapping the Alt key to enter menu browsing mode was a common scenario, and preserving it avoided having to retrain people's "muscle memory."

What is the deal with the ES_OEMCONVERT flag?

THE ES_OEMCONVERT EDIT control style is a holdover from 16-bit Windows. An ancient MSDN article from the Windows 3.1 SDK describes the flag thus:

> ES_OEMCONVERT *causes text entered into the edit control to be converted from* ANSI *to* OEM *and then back to* ANSI. *This ensures proper character conversion when the application calls the AnsiToOem function to convert a Windows string in the edit control to* OEM *characters.* ES_OEMCONVERT *is most useful for edit controls that contain filenames.*

Set the wayback machine to, well, January 31, 1992, the date of that article. At this time, the predominant Windows platform was Windows 3.0. Windows 3.1 was still a few months away from release, and Windows NT 3.1 was over a year away. The predominant file system was 16-bit FAT, and the relevant feature of FAT of this era for the purpose of this discussion is that filenames were stored on disk in the OEM character set. (We'll see more of the history behind the schism between the OEM and ANSI code pages in Chapter 16.)

Because GUI programs used the ANSI character set, but filenames were stored in the OEM character set, the only characters that could be used in filenames from GUI programs were those that exist in both character sets. If a character existed in the ANSI character set but not the OEM character set, there would be no way of using it as a filename; and if a character existed in the OEM character set but not the ANSI character set, the GUI program couldn't manipulate it.

The ES_OEMCONVERT flag on an edit control ensures that only characters that exist in both the ANSI and OEM character sets are used, hence the remark "ES_OEMCONVERT is most useful for edit controls that contain filenames."

Fast-forward to today.

All the popular Windows file systems support Unicode filenames and have for ten years. There is no longer a data loss converting from the ANSI character set to the character set used by the file system. Therefore, there is no need to filter out any characters to prevent the user typing a character that will be lost during the conversion to a filename. In other words, the ES_OEMCONVERT flag is pointless today. It's a leftover from the days before Unicode.

Indeed, if you use this flag, you make your program worse, not better, because it unnecessarily restricts the set of characters that the user will be allowed to use in filenames. A user running the U.S.-English version of Windows would not be allowed to enter Chinese characters as a filename, for example, even though the file system is perfectly capable of creating files whose names contain those characters.

∽

The story behind file system tunneling

ONE OF THE file system features you may find yourself surprised by is tunneling, wherein the creation timestamp and short/long names of a file are taken from a file that existed in the directory previously. In other words, if you delete some file "File with long name.txt" and then create a new file with the same name, that new file will have the same short name and the same creation time as the original file.

Why does tunneling exist at all?

When you use a program to edit an existing file, then save it, you naturally expect the creation timestamp on the updated file to be the same as the creation timestamp on the original. After all, you're editing a file, not creating a new one. But internally, many programs save a file by performing a combination of save, delete, and rename operations, and without tunneling, the creation time of the file would seem to change even though from the end user's point of view, no new file got created.

As another example of the importance of tunneling, consider that file "File with long name.txt," whose short name is, say, FILEWI~1.TXT. You load this file into a program that is not long-filename aware and save it. It deletes the old FILEWI~1.TXT and creates a new one with the same name. Without tunneling, the associated long name of the file would be lost. Instead of a friendly long name, the filename got corrupted into this thing with squiggly marks. Not good.

But where did the name *tunneling* come from? From quantum mechanics.

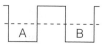

Consider the following analogy: You have two holes in the ground, and a particle is in the first hole (A) and doesn't have enough energy to get out. It only has enough energy to get as high as the dotted line.

You get distracted for a little while, maybe watch the Super Bowl halftime show, and when you come back, the particle somehow is now in hole B. This is impossible in classical mechanics, but thanks to the wacky world of quantum mechanics, it is not only possible, but *actually happens*. The phenomenon is known as tunneling because it's as if the particle "dug a tunnel" between the two holes, thereby allowing it to get from one hole to another without ever going above the dotted line.

In the case of file system tunneling, it is information that appears to violate the laws of classical mechanics. The information was destroyed (by deleting or renaming the file), yet somehow managed to reconstruct itself on the other side of a temporal barrier.

The developer who was responsible for implementing tunneling on Windows 95 got kind of carried away with the quantum mechanics analogy: The fragments of information about recently deleted or recently renamed files are kept in data structures called quarks.

Why do NTFS and Explorer disagree on filename sorting?

IF YOU'VE USED the FindFirstFile and FindNextFile functions to enumerate the contents of a directory on an NTFS drive, you may have noticed that the filenames are returned in sorted order, but sorted in a manner different from Explorer. Why is that?

For illustration purposes, I created files with the following names:

Name	Code Point	Description
a	U+0061	Latin small letter A
b	U+0062	Latin small letter B
×	U+00D7	Multiplication sign
å	U+00E5	Latin small letter A with ring above
ø	U+00F8	Latin small letter O with stroke

And here's the sort order for various scenarios, at least on my machine. (You'll later see why it's important whose machine you test on.)

+ Plain `dir` command

Name	Code Point	Description
a	U+0061	Latin small letter A
b	U+0062	Latin small letter B
å	U+00E5	Latin small letter A with ring above
×	U+00D7	Multiplication sign
ø	U+00F8	Latin small letter O with stroke

+ `dir /on`

Name	Code Point	Description
×	U+00D7	Multiplication sign
a	U+0061	Latin small letter A
å	U+00E5	Latin small letter A with ring above
b	U+0062	Latin small letter B
ø	U+00F8	Latin small letter O with stroke

+ Explorer sorted by name

Name	Code Point	Description
×	U+00D7	Multiplication sign
a	U+0061	Latin small letter A

å	U+00E5	Latin small letter A with ring above
b	U+0062	Latin small letter B
ø	U+00F8	Latin small letter O with stroke

First, notice that Explorer and `dir/on` agree on the alphabetic sort order. (When you throw digits into the mix, things diverge.) This is not a coincidence. Both are using the default locale's word sort algorithm.

Why does the raw NTFS sort order differ? Because NTFS's raw sort order has different goals.

The `dir /on` and Explorer output are sorting the items for humans. When sorting for humans, you need to respect their locale. If my computer were in Sweden, Explorer and `dir /on` would have sorted the items in a different order:

Name	Code Point	Description
×	U+00D7	Multiplication sign
a	U+0061	Latin small letter A
b	U+0062	Latin small letter B
å	U+00E5	Latin small letter A with ring above
ø	U+00F8	Latin small letter O with stroke

You can ask a Swede why this is the correct sort order if you're that curious. My point is that different locales have different sorting rules.

NTFS's raw sort order, on the other hand, is not for humans. As we saw above, sorting for humans can result in different results depending on which human you ask. But there is only one order for files on the disk, and NTFS needs to apply a consistent rule so that it can find a file when asked for it later.

To maintain this consistency, the NTFS raw sort order cannot be dependent upon such fickle properties as the current user's preferred sort order. It needs to lock in a sort algorithm and stick to it for the lifetime of the volume. And because NTFS is case preserving but not case sensitive (under normal circumstances), it needs to know the relationship between lowercase and uppercase letters. It does this by capturing the case mapping table at the time the drive is formatted and using that table to convert filenames from lowercase to uppercase, even if the operating system's case mapping tables change subsequently. After the filename has been converted to uppercase, it then needs to be sorted. Because this is not for humans, there's no need to implement the complex rules regarding secondary and tertiary weights, the interaction between alphanumerics and punctuation, and all the other things that make sorting hard. It just compares the code points as numbers.

In summary, therefore, Explorer sorts the items so you (a human) can find them. NTFS sorts the items so it (the computer) can find them.

⤔

The Date/Time Control Panel is not a calendar

ALTHOUGH MANY PEOPLE use the Date/Time Control Panel to flip through a calendar, that's not what it is for. In fact, if you use it that way, you can create all sorts of havoc!

In its original incarnation in Windows 95, the Date/Time Control Panel changed your date and time. If you clicked through the calendar to see next month, you *actually changed your system clock to next month*. If you changed your mind and clicked Cancel, the Date/Time Control Panel undid its changes and restored the date to the original date.

In other words, here's what happened, step by step:

- On April 1, you open the Date/Time Control Panel.

- You change the month to May. The Date/Time Control Panel changes your system date to May 1. If you are running an appointment calendar program, all appointments from the month of April will fire (for example, your April 15 alarm to remind you to file your income taxes). You are annoyed by all these alerts and you cancel them.

- You decide you didn't want to change the month to May after all and click Cancel.

- The Date/Time Control Panel changes the date back to April 1.

- On April 15, your income tax alarm *fails to fire* because you cancelled it, remember?

In other words, the Date/Time Control Panel was not designed for letting you flip through a calendar. It was designed for changing the system date and time.

Unaware of its design, people have been using the Date/Time Control Panel as if it were a calendar, not realizing that it was doing all sorts of scary things behind the scenes. It's like using a cash register as an adding machine. Sure, it does a great job of adding numbers together, but you're also messing up the accounting back at the main office!

For Windows 2000, in reluctant recognition of the way people had been misusing the Date/Time Control Panel, it was rewritten so that it doesn't change the system time until you hit the Apply button.

⤳

How did Windows 95 rebase DLLs?

When you produce a DLL, one of the things you specify is its preferred base address, the virtual address at which the DLL will be optimized to be loaded. When a DLL must be loaded at an address different from its preferred address (because the preferred address is unavailable), the kernel must rebase the DLL, which consists of updating (fixing up) all addresses in the DLL so that they refer to its new location in memory. A table of fix-ups describes all the places in the DLL that need to be adjusted in this way.

Windows 95 handled DLL rebasing very differently from Windows NT.

When Windows NT detects that a DLL needs to be loaded at an address different from its preferred load address, it maps the entire DLL into memory as copy-on-write, fixes it up (causing all pages that contain fix-ups to be copied into the page file), and then restores the original read-only/read-write state to the pages.

Windows 95, on the other hand, rebases the DLL incrementally, subscribing to the principle "Don't save anything you can recalculate." This is another concession to Windows 95's very tight memory requirements. Remember, it had to run on a 4MB machine. If it fixed up DLLs the way Windows NT did, then loading a 4MB DLL and fixing it up would consume all the memory on the machine, pushing out all the memory that was actually worth keeping!

When a DLL needed to be rebased, Windows 95 would merely make a note of the DLL's new base address but wouldn't do much else. The real work happened when the pages of the DLL ultimately got swapped in. The raw page was swapped off the disk, and then the fix-ups were applied on-the-fly to the raw page, thereby relocating it. The fixed-up page was then mapped into the process's address space and the program was allowed to continue.

This method has the advantage that the cost of fixing up a page is not paid until the page is actually needed, which can be a significant savings for large DLLs of mostly dead code. Furthermore, when a fixed-up page needed to be swapped out, it was merely discarded, because the fix-ups could just be applied to the raw page again.

And there you have it, demand-paging rebased DLLs instead of fixing up the entire DLL at load time. What could possibly go wrong?

Hint: It's a problem that is peculiar to the x86.

The problem is fix-ups that straddle page boundaries. This happens only on the x86 because the x86 architecture is the weirdo, with variable-length instructions that can start at any address. If a page contains a fix-up that extends partially off the start of the page, you cannot apply it accurately until you know whether or not the part of the fix-up you can't see generated a carry. If it did, then you have to add one to your partial fix-up.

To record this information, the memory manager associates a flag with each page of a relocated DLL that indicates whether the page contained a carry off the end. This flag can have one of three states:

- Yes, there is a carry off the end.
- No, there is no carry off the end.
- I don't know whether there is a carry off the end.

To fix up a page that contains a fix-up that extends partially off the start of the page, you check the flag for the previous page. If the flag says, "Yes," add one to your fix-up. If the flag says, "No," do not add one.

But what if the flag says, "I don't know?"

If you don't know, you have to go find out. Fault in the previous page and fix it up. As part of the computations for the fix-up, the flag will get to indicate whether there is a carry out the end. After the previous page has been fixed up, you can check the flag (which will no longer be a "Don't know" flag), and that will tell you whether to add one to the current page.

And there you have it, demand-paging rebased DLLs instead of fixing up the entire DLL at load time, even in the presence of fix-ups that straddle page boundaries. What could possibly go wrong?

Hint: What goes wrong with recursion?

The problem is that the previous page might itself have a fix-up that straddled a page boundary at its start, and the flag for the page two pages back might be in the "I don't know" state. Now you have to fault in and fix up a third page.

In theory, this recursion could continue for quite some time, but in practice it never went beyond three fix-ups.

(Of course, another way to stop the recursion is to do only a partial fix-up of the previous page, applying only the straddling fix-up to see whether there is a carry out and not attempting to fix up the rest. But Windows 95 went ahead and fixed up the rest of the page because it figured, hey, I paid for this page, I might as well use it.)

⟿

What are SYSTEM_FONT and DEFAULT_GUI_FONT?

AMONG THE THINGS you can get with the GetStockObject function are two fonts called SYSTEM_FONT and DEFAULT_GUI_FONT. What are they?

They are fonts nobody uses any more.

Back in the old days of Windows 2.0, the font used for dialog boxes was a bitmap font called System. This is the font that SYSTEM_FONT retrieves, and it is still the default dialog box font for compatibility reasons. Of course, nobody nowadays would ever use such an ugly font for the dialog boxes. (Among other things, it's a bitmap font and therefore does not look good at high resolutions, nor can it be anti-aliased.)

DEFAULT_GUI_FONT has an even less illustrious history. It was created during Windows 95 development in the hopes of becoming the new default GUI font, but by July 1994, Windows itself stopped using it in favor of the various fonts returned by the SystemParametersInfo function, but nobody remembered to remove it from the header file.

That these two stock fonts continue to exist is merely a remnant of history.

Why do up-down controls have the arrows backward?

WHEN YOU CREATE an up-down control (some people call it a "spinner" control) in its default configuration, the up-arrow decrements the value and the down-arrow increments it. Most people expect the up-arrow to increment and the down-arrow to decrement. Why is it backward?

The up-down control is a victim of Windows' reversed y-axis.

Mathematically, the (0, 0) coordinate should be at the lower-left corner of the screen (and in fact that's where OS/2 puts it), with y increasing as you move up the screen. Windows, on the other hand, puts the (0, 0) coordinate at the *upper*-left corner, with y increasing as you move *down* the screen.

What does that have to do with anything?

The up-down control can be positioned horizontally or vertically. Let's first look at the less problematic horizontal configuration. Windows and mathematics agree that the x coordinate increases to the right, and the right-arrow (the arrow with higher x coordinate) causes the value to increase. (Let's leave right-to-left languages out of the picture for the purpose of this discussion.)

After you have the horizontal version of the control working, converting it to a vertical control is a simple matter of interchanging the x- and y-axes.

That's why the up-arrow decreases the value. The up-arrow points toward smaller y coordinates and consequently decrements the value.

It's perfectly logical and simultaneously counterintuitive. (It's slightly more intuitive if you imagine the value attached to the up-down control as controlling the y coordinate of an imaginary object on the screen. In that case, clicking the up-arrow causes the y coordinate to decrease and the object moves up the screen.)

Fortunately, this wackiness doesn't last long, because the moment you change the range of the up-down control from the (not very useful) default of 0–100 to whatever you actually need, the arrows behave "normally" again.

Perhaps intuitiveness should have won out over logic. But what's done is done, and, as noted above, the problem goes away soon enough.

⌁

A ticket to the Windows 95 launch

A LIMITED NUMBER of seats at the Windows 95 launch were available to the product team, so there was a lottery to see who would get one of those tickets. The remainder of the team would be standing on bleachers hidden behind the stage, to be unveiled at the grand climax of the product launch festivities.

I happened to have been a winner in the ticket lottery, but the fact that there weren't enough seats for everybody created some degree of grousing among the have-nots. As a show of solidarity, I forewent the special VIP pass and ticket, instead taking my place in the crowd of red, blue, yellow, and green T-shirts waiting backstage and giving the pass and ticket to a colleague who really wanted to be in the tent.

While I waited in the staging room to be positioned for the grand finale, I was somewhat surprised to see my colleague in the room with me. She gave me back my unused VIP pass and ticket, saying, "It didn't feel right being out there in the tent. This is where I belong."

I probably have the only unused ticket to the Windows 95 launch.

While standing on the bleachers behind the screen, we could hear everything going on. When Jay Leno disappeared backstage to head off to his next scene, he emerged between the two sets of bleachers. We silently waved at him, but he was obviously focused on his job and didn't have time to schmooze with us.

It was very hard staying quiet for so long backstage. Our presence was supposed to be a surprise; any noise would give us away. There were moments where whispers got out of hand and people had to wave frantically (or—heavens—shush!) to restore quiet. I thought for certain one of our out-of-control moments had let the cat out of the bag, but from talking to people afterward who were in the tent, I learned that nobody noticed a thing.

Our only instructions from the director were "Wave, clap, and cheer!" (keeping up the energy until the last of the crowd had filed out). Everything beyond that was improvised. Somebody started up a cheer, with half of the bleachers shouting "Windows!" and the other half responding "95!" I'm sure there were other things we did to maintain the excitement, though I can't remember any of it now. I just remember that after a while I got tired of smiling and clapping but kept it up because I was on the aisle next to all the attendees, and that's show business!

My colleague Danny Glasser also won the lottery, but unlike me, he decided to watch the launch from within the tent. He admits, "While it was very exciting there, I knew from that day that I'd made the wrong decision."

Not everything related to the Windows 95 launch went well. As with many heavily anticipated products, many stores held a "midnight madness" sale, wherein the product would be available for purchase at the stroke of midnight. The *St. Louis Post-Dispatch* reported that a local CompUSA store found that their cash registers crashed at midnight, forcing eager customers to wait 90 minutes before the problem could be resolved. The cause: A bug in the cash register software that had lain undiscovered because the store had never stayed open past midnight before! In a sense, Windows 95 crashed a cash register.

⁓

CHAPTER FIFTEEN

How Window Messages Are Delivered and Retrieved

I N MY INTERACTIONS with Windows programmers, I often find that the understanding of how window messages are delivered and retrieved is not entirely complete. Nearly everyone gets the basic idea, but some details—often crucial details—end up garbled. (Unfortunately, the MSDN documentation is often a source of this garbling.) Because many people have already attempted to explain the basics and the intricacies of window message delivery, it was not clear to me at first how to go about this task, but then I realized the solution is not to add to the existing information, but merely to restate it in a different way.

Optional prerequisite reading for this section is the discussion in MSDN on queued and nonqueued messages and their interaction with the `GetMessage` and `PeekMessage` functions, which you can find in MSDN in the section titled "About Messages and Message Queues." If you've read that discussion or discussion from other authors, you may find the explanation below redundant; but if you find things still somewhat hazy in your mind, you may find that a fresh angle on the subject may help clarify.

Sent and posted messages

THE TERMINOLOGY I will use here is nonstandard, but I'm using it because I think it's a little clearer than the standard terminology. For the purpose of this discussion, I'm going to say that the messages associated with a thread fall into three buckets rather than the more standard two:

What I'll call them	Standard terminology
Incoming sent messages	Non-queued messages
Posted messages	Queued messages
Input messages	

In reality, the message breakdown is more complicated than this, but we'll stick to the above model for now, because it's "true enough."

Note also that under standard terminology, nonqueued messages are not considered to be in the thread's message queue. Only queued messages are *in the queue*.

One immediate consequence of the above breakdown of messages into three categories is that it gives the first indication why you cannot simulate input with the PostMessage function: Posted messages go into the posted message list, whereas input messages go into the input message list, and you'll see later in this chapter that the two are processed at different times.

The members of the SendMessage family of functions (which includes SendNotifyMessage, SendMessageCallback, and SendMessageTimeout) all behave the same with respect to the message bookkeeping: If the sender and receiver are on the same thread, then the window procedure of the receiver is called directly (bypassing the message pump). If the sender and receiver are on different threads, the message is added to the incoming sent messages of the receiver, and the receiver is "woken" to process the incoming message.

The PostMessage and PostThreadMessage functions add the message to the posted messages and wake the receiver.

User input (or synthesized user input, such as that produced by the SendInput function) is added to the input messages, and they also wake the receiver.

Because some people do better with pictures, here's a picture of a hypothetical thread showing how messages arrive in each of the three buckets:

incoming sent messages	posted messages	input messages
message S1	message P1	message I1
message S2	message P2	
	message P3	

↑   ↑   ↑

SendMessage   PostMessage   input

Waking the receiver means that if the receiver is blocked in a `GetMessage`, `WaitMessage`, `MsgWaitForMultipleObjects`, or similar function, the receiving thread is unblocked so that it can process the new messages, assuming that the receiving thread is waiting for the type of message that was added.

Now that you've seen how messages enter a thread, let's look at how they get back out.

On the message receiving side, there are three ways messages can be received, and each of them processes messages slightly differently, but they all follow the same basic principles:

- Incoming sent messages are delivered directly to the window procedure.

- Posted messages are retrieved (if `GetMessage` or `PeekMessage`).

- Input messages are retrieved (if `GetMessage` or `PeekMessage`).

Because the message receiving functions are all variations on the same basic idea, I'm going to write some pseudo-code helper functions so that the similarities are clearer. The first pseudo-function is one that delivers a message. Delivering a message is the climax of the entire message process; it consists of calling the window procedure with the message directly, and it goes roughly like this:

```
LRESULT DeliverMessage(HWND hwnd, UINT uMsg, WPARM wParam,
    LPARAM lParam)
```

```
{
 WNDPROC lpfnWndProc =
                   (WNDPROC)GetWindowLongPtr(hwnd, GWLP_WNDPROC);
 return CallWindowProc(lpfnWndProc, hwnd, uMsg, wParam, lParam);
}
```

All the complexity of message processing resides in how the system gets to the point where it can deliver the message and what it does with the answer.

As noted previously, one of the principles of message processing is the delivery of incoming sent messages. You'll see that this operation is performed at very specific points in the course of message processing:

```
void DeliverIncomingSentMessages()
{
 while (an incoming sent message exists) {
  MSG msg = that message;
  remove it from the incoming sent message list;
  if (it is a special pseudo-message) {
   handle the pseudo-message; // we'll learn about these later
  } else {
   DeliverMessage(msg.hwnd, msg.message, msg.wParam, msg.lParam);
   get return value back to sender somehow;
  }
 }
}
```

Armed with these helper functions, we can start looking at each of the message retrieval functions in turn and see how they follow the preceding guidelines.

First, there's `PeekMessage`. The pseudo-code for `PeekMessage` goes like this:

```
BOOL PeekMessage(LPMSG pmsg, HWND hwnd, UINT wMsgFilterMin,
                 UINT wMsgFilterMax, UINT flags)
{
 DeliverIncomingSentMessages();
 if (a posted message exists that satisfies the filter) {
  *pmsg = that message;
  if (flags & PM_REMOVE) remove it from the posted message list;
  return TRUE;
 }
 if (an input message exists that satisfies the filter) {
  *pmsg = that message;
  if (flags & PM_REMOVE) remove it from the input message list;
```

```
  return TRUE;
}
  return FALSE;
}
```

In other words, the `PeekMessage` function first delivers all incoming sent messages that are waiting to be processed (if any). After that's done, it looks for a candidate message in the posted message list, and, failing that, in the input message list. If one such is found, the message is removed from the corresponding message list (if the `PM_REMOVE` flag was passed), and that message is *retrieved* (not delivered). If there are no such messages, `PeekMessage` returns `FALSE`.

Note that incoming sent messages are handled very differently from posted and input messages. You cannot filter out incoming sent messages; they are always processed. Filtering applies only to posted and input messages. Also, incoming sent messages are dispatched internally by `PeekMessage`, whereas posted and input messages are merely returned to the caller via the `pmsg` parameter, and it is the caller's responsibility to decide what to do with the message. (Usually, the decision is, "Dispatch it," but you'll see below that that is not always the case.)

The `GetMessage` function is just like `PeekMessage`, except that it doesn't return until it gets a posted or input message. If there is no message to be retrieved, it just keeps waiting until one finally arrives:

```
BOOL GetMessage(LPMSG pmsg, HWND hwnd, UINT wMsgFilterMin,
                UINT wMsgFilterMax)
{
  while (!PeekMessage(pmsg, hwnd,
                      wMsgFilterMin, wMsgFilterMax, PM_REMOVE)) {
    WaitMessage(); // wait for a new message to arrive
  }
  return pmsg->message != WM_QUIT;
}
```

The final case in which incoming sent messages are dispatched is when the thread is waiting for an inter-thread `SendMessage` to complete. All the `SendMessage`-like functions are basically the same, just with slightly different frills, so I discuss them all together. For expository purposes, I am ignoring error checking and assuming that the sender and receiver are on different threads, because messages sent within a thread are converted into direct calls to the window procedure, as already noted.

```
SendToAnotherThread(...)
{
 add the message to the incoming sent message list
 of the receiver;

 // these two functions wait for the receiver to respond
 if (Function == SendMessage || Function == SendMessageTimeout) {
  while (!message reply received && !timed out) {
   DeliverIncomingSentMessages();
   wait for a new message or (if SendMessageTimeout)
   timeout elapses;
  }
 }
}
```

The message is added to the incoming sent message list of the thread that the target window belongs to; and in the case of SendMessage and SendMessageTimeout, the sending thread dispatches incoming sent messages until the target window returns an answer (or the message times out). There are additional details concerning how SendMessageCallback performs the callback and how SendMessageTimeout cleans up if the message times out, but those details aren't relevant to the discussion here, so I defer them for now.

One point to bear in mind is that these three scenarios (PeekMessage, GetMessage, and inter-thread SendMessage) are the only ones that will dispatch incoming sent messages. If you're debugging a problem with a thread that isn't receiving incoming sent messages, make sure it's actually doing one of these three things.

That's it for the basics of sent and posted messages. It's really not that complicated. Just keep those three ground rules in mind, and you've got it in a nutshell.

The life of a sent message

So FAR, WE'VE been looking at messages from the thread's point of view, how a thread delivers and receives messages. Let's change our point of view to that of the message itself, starting by following a sent message through the system.

The easy case is when a thread sends a message to a window that belongs to that same thread. In that case, the window procedure of the receiving window is called directly:

```
LRESULT SendMessage_SameThread(HWND hwnd, UINT uMsg,
                               WPARAM wParam, LPARAM lParam)
{
  return DeliverMessage(hwnd, uMsg, wParam, lParam);
}
```

Notice that an intra-thread sent message bypasses everything. It doesn't go onto the posted message list or even the incoming sent message list. Consequently, it doesn't go through the message pump either. It goes straight to the destination window procedure.

The more interesting case for a sent message is the inter-thread case. As noted previously, the message is added to the incoming sent message list of the destination window. There it waits until the thread responsible for the destination window does one of the three things listed above that processes incoming sent messages: `PeekMessage`, `GetMessage`, or an inter-thread `SendMessage`. When the thread that receives the message returns from the window procedure, the message result is transferred back to the sending thread, at which point the sending thread can continue on its merry way.

There is a variation on this message life cycle that involves the `ReplyMessage` function. If the receiving thread calls `ReplyMessage` during the processing of an incoming sent message, the value passed to the `ReplyMessage` function is returned to the sending thread as if the receiving thread had returned from its window procedure. As a result, both the sending thread and the receiving thread are executing simultaneously. The sending thread is executing because it is no longer waiting for the message result, while the receiving thread is executing because it hasn't yet returned from its window procedure. (When the window procedure finally returns a value, that value is ignored, of course, because the sender was already given a result and you can't go back in time and change a value that was already returned!)

The life of a posted message

THE LIFE OF a posted message is a bit more complicated than that of a sent message. As noted previously, a posted message is appended to the posted message list of the thread that owns the destination window. There it waits until the receiving thread calls the GetMessage or PeekMessage function, at which point the message is copied to the MSG structure provided by the application. What happens next depends on who retrieved the message.

In principle, a program can do anything it wants with that message. It could throw it away or it could modify it or it could even (horrors!) dispatch the message. Because anything could happen, a comprehensive list of possibilities is impossible, but let's look at some of the more likely scenarios.

Most likely the message was retrieved by the thread's primary message pump, which goes something like this:

```
while (GetMessage(&msg, NULL, 0, 0)) {
  if (!TranslateAccelerator(hwndMain, hacc, &msg)) {
   TranslateMessage(&msg);
   DispatchMessage(&msg);
  }
}
```

If that's the case, the retrieved message will be checked against the accelerator table and, if a match is found, a WM_COMMAND (or WM_SYSCOMMAND) message will be posted to the window specified by hwndMain. In that case, message processing ends, and the message *is never delivered to the window procedure* (something to bear in mind if you're debugging a problem where a posted message appears never to reach its destination window).

If the message does not match an accelerator, it is typically delivered to the window procedure by the DispatchMessage function, but exceptions apply:

- If the message is a thread message, there is no window to deliver the message to. Consequently, thread messages are not dispatched.

- If the message is a WM_TIMER message and the lParam is nonzero, the lParam is treated as a TIMERPROC, and the callback function is called directly.

The next most common scenario is the dialog loop. As you already know, the basic dialog loop looks like this:

```
while (<dialog still active> &&
       GetMessage(&msg, NULL, 0, 0, 0)) {
 if (!IsDialogMessage(hdlg, &msg)) {
  TranslateMessage(&msg);
  DispatchMessage(&msg);
 }
}
```

This looks like a normal message pump but for the introduction of IsDialogMessage. Thus, the new twist is that an additional class of messages will never reach their destination window: dialog box navigation messages. (We discussed the details of IsDialogMessage in Chapter 10, "The Inner Workings of the Dialog Manager.")

A small fraction of modal loops do not fall into the two categories above, but they tend to share the same basic characteristics. The posted message is retrieved, preprocessed, and (assuming it survives preprocessing) is delivered to the destination window. And because the message is posted, the return value of the message is discarded since there is nowhere to return it to.

Generated posted messages

WHEN I INTRODUCED the three types of messages, I admitted that reality is more complicated. Some "special" types of messages don't fall neatly into one of those three buckets.

One of those special messages is the WM_MOUSEMOVE message. As you saw earlier, the message is not added as an input message when the mouse moves; instead, a "the mouse moved" flag is set. When the window manager goes looking for an input message and the "the mouse moved" flag is set, it clears the flag and generates a WM_MOUSEMOVE message on the fly, adding it to the list of input messages (or coalescing it with an existing WM_MOUSEMOVE message).

Other special messages that fall into this "generated on the fly" category are the WM_PAINT, WM_TIMER and WM_QUIT messages. The first two messages are generated even later in the message search process, only after no applicable input message list was found, and only if the message filter indicates that that type of message is being requested. (The WM_QUIT message is even shier than the paint and timer messages, because it emerges only after the posted message list is empty. On the other hand, the WM_QUIT message is also bolder, in that it ignores the message filter.)

Given these adjustments, the PeekMessage function takes the following more complex form:

```
BOOL PeekMessage(LPMSG pmsg, HWND hwnd, UINT wMsgFilterMin,
               UINT wMsgFilterMax, UINT flags)
{
 DeliverIncomingSentMessages();

 if (a posted message exists that satisfies the filter) {
  *pmsg = that message;
  if (flags & PM_REMOVE) remove it from the posted message list;
  return TRUE;
 }

 // note that WM_QUIT ignores the filter
 if (a WM_QUIT message is pending and
     there are no posted messages) {
  clear the "WM_QUIT is pending" flag;
  *pmsg = a WM_QUIT message;
  return TRUE;
 }

 if (the mouse has moved and input messages satisfy the filter) {
  clear the "mouse has moved" flag;
  append a WM_MOUSEMOVE message into the input message list;
```

```
    }

    if (an input message exists that satisfies the filter) {
     *pmsg = that message;
     if (flags & PM_REMOVE) remove it from the input message list;
     return TRUE;
    }

    if (a window needs to be painted and
        the WM_PAINT message satisfies the filter) {
     *pmsg = a WM_PAINT message;
     return TRUE;
    }

    if (a timer has elapsed and
        the WM_TIMER message satisfies the filter) {
     append a WM_TIMER message to the posted message list;
     *pmsg = that message;
     if (flags & PM_REMOVE) remove it from the posted message list;
     return TRUE;
    }

    return FALSE;
}
```

Here's a puzzle: I noted earlier that the generated WM_MOUSEMOVE message might be coalesced with an existing message. How can that be if the message isn't generated until the application requests it?

The WM_MOUSEMOVE and WM_TIMER messages are particularly strange: When it is time for them to be generated, they become real messages in the queue! This has subtle consequences for programs that call PeekMessage with the PM_NOREMOVE flag. If you peek and don't remove a WM_MOUSEMOVE or WM_TIMER message, the message stays in the queue. If you are sufficiently devious, you can inadvertently fill your queue with multiple copies of these messages by assiduously refusing to remove them.

This quirk of the WM_MOUSEMOVE and WM_TIMER messages also answers our puzzle: If the mouse message was generated but left in the queue because the caller passed PM_NOREMOVE, the message remains in the input message list, at which point a subsequent mouse move message will be coalesced with it.

≋

When does SendMessageCallback call you back?

WHEN YOU CALL the SendMessageCallback function, you pass a function pointer that the system will call when the sent message is processed by the recipient. How does that callback happen?

Basically, it arrives "as if" the recipient sent a message back to you.

In other words, when the recipient finishes processing the message, it performs the moral equivalent of a SendMessage to the thread that sent the message: A pseudo-message is added to the incoming sent message list, and the window manager "dispatches" the pseudo-message by calling the callback function you provided. These are the pseudo-messages we mentioned briefly when we sketched out the DeliverIncomingSentMessages function.

The window manager uses these pseudo-messages as a way to transfer execution between threads in a controlled manner. Because the pseudo-message is retrieved as part of normal message processing, the window manager knows that when the pseudo-message is processed, the application is in a stable state. This is a general principle of thread interruptions: You cannot interrupt a thread unpredictably because you will have no idea what the thread was in the middle of doing.

For example, if you interrupt a thread while it owns a critical section, the code in your interrupt will find itself running while that critical section is owned, something the code was probably not designed to handle, which can in turn result in deadlocks. Worse, you might attempt to enter that same critical section (which will succeed, because the thread that owns a critical section is allowed to enter it again), and you are now under the mistaken belief that you are the only code that is modifying the data structure that the critical section protects, when in fact the code you interrupted is also modifying it.

More generally, if you interrupt the thread while some data structures are unstable (say, for example, while it was in the middle of updating a linked list), the code in your interrupt had better not attempt to access those data structures. Effectively, your interrupt *can't reliably do much of anything*, which makes it a not-very-useful sort of interrupt.

That's why the window manager uses pseudo-messages to transfer control between threads: When the code runs on the target thread, the thread is in a known stable state. (This is entirely analogous to how overlapped I/O and asynchronous procedure calls in general run only at specific points, again, because running them as interrupts would make it effectively impossible to use them in any meaningful way.)

What happens in SendMessageTimeout when a message times out?

When the SendMessageTimeout function times out, what happens to the message you were trying to send?

The message is cancelled, subject to the laws of physics as we currently understand them.

If the timeout period elapses without the receiving thread having replied to the message, the SendMessageTimeout cancels the message. If the message has yet to be delivered, the cancellation is complete: The destination window never receives the message. However, if the message has been delivered, but the recipient has not replied, the cancellation is only partial. The window manager ignores any attempt by the recipient to return a result, but it can't go back in time and prevent the recipient from receiving the message in the first place.

The bad news for the programmer is that there is no indication from the SendMessageTimeout function which of the two scenarios has occurred.

Applying what you've learned to some message processing myths

ARMED WITH ALL this new knowledge about how messages are delivered and retrieved, we can bust the following myths, each of which came from an actual Win32 developer:

- **Myth**. SendNotifyMessage behaves just like PostMessage if the window is on another thread.

  The SendNotifyMessage belongs to the SendMessage family of functions and as such shares much more with SendMessage than it does with PostMessage. The message sent with SendNotifyMessage is added to the incoming sent message list, not to the posted message list; this distinction is important because it alters the order in which the message is processed relative to other messages. Sending with SendNotifyMessage puts the message ahead of all existing posted messages (since incoming sent messages are processed before posted messages), whereas PostMessage puts the message after any existing posted messages. Also, messages sent with SendNotifyMessage are delivered as part of the DeliverIncomingSentMessages step we discussed above, which means that they not only bypass the message pump, but they can also be delivered while waiting for a response from an outbound SendMessage; neither of these statements apply to posted messages.

- **Myth**. Posting a message is just an asynchronous send.

  Actually, the SendNotifyMessage function produces an asynchronous send. The differences between PostMessage and the asynchronous send produced by SendNotifyMessage were discussed above.

- **Myth**. If you send a message to a window that belongs to another thread, the message is posted into the destination thread's message queue at a higher priority than posted messages.

Sent messages go into the incoming sent messages list, not the posted messages list. Because the sent messages list is processed before the posted messages list, it may look like a high-priority posted message, but as noted previously, sent and posted messages are processed very differently by the window manager.

How can you tell who sent or posted you a message?

You can't, because not even the window manager knows. The window manager doesn't keep track of this information for posted messages or messages sent via SendNotifyMessage. The window manager does keep track of the sender if the sender needs to be informed of the result of the message (for example, if the message was sent via SendMessage), but this information is not exposed by the window manager.

If you need this information, you must provide it yourself. For example, the WM_NOTIFY message specifies that the sender of the message must set the hwndFrom member of the NMHDR structure to the handle of the window to which the message applies. Similarly, the rules for the Dynamic Data Exchange (DDE) messages require the sender to pass an appropriate window handle as the messages' wParam.

But these are all conventions. They aren't enforced by the system. If people really want to confuse you, they can send you a WM_NOTIFY message with incorrect information in the NMHDR structure. But of course, they then deserve what they get!

You can't simulate keyboard input with PostMessage

Some people attempt to simulate keyboard input to an application by posting keyboard input messages, but this is not reliable for many reasons.

First of all, keyboard input is a more complicated matter than those who imprinted on the English keyboard realize. Languages with accent marks have dead keys, Far East languages have a variety of Input Method Editors, and I have no idea how complex script languages handle input. There's more to typing a character than just pressing a key.

Second, even if you manage to post the input messages into the target window's queue, that doesn't update the other state associated with input. For example, when the code behind the window calls the GetKeyState function or the GetAsyncKeyState function, it's going to see the "real" keyboard state and not the fake state that your posted messages have generated. Similarly, GetQueueState will report a posted message (QS_POSTMESSAGE) rather than input (QS_INPUT), which in turn has consequences for programs that are dependent on the queue state, for example, those that use the MsgWait ForMultipleObjects function.

The SendInput function was designed for injecting input into Windows. If you use that function, at least the states of the shift and other modifier keys will be reported correctly. You still have other problems ahead of you, however. For example, many keyboard layouts (such as those for East Asian languages) have complicated input states that go beyond simply converting character codes to scan codes.

What should you do, then? If your program exposes an automation interface, your tests can use that. Alternatively, you can use your program's accessibility interfaces. Indeed, using the accessibility interfaces in your tests is an excellent way of validating that your program is in fact accessible to people with physical disabilities. We will get our feet wet with accessibility in Chapter 20, "Taxes."

CHAPTER SIXTEEN

INTERNATIONAL PROGRAMMING

THE WORLD IS an international place, and although few people intentionally exclude portions of the world from using their software, you may end up inadvertently creating problems as the result of design and implementation decisions taken during software development. Here are some musings on the topic of international programming. I also wholeheartedly recommend the Web site of my colleague Michael Kaplan. *Sorting It All Out*, http://blogs.msdn.com/michkap/, goes into even greater depth on the subject of international programming, Unicode, and (as you might surmise from the site's title) collation.

Case mapping on Unicode is hard

OCCASIONALLY, I'M ASKED, "I have to identify strings that are identical, case-insensitively. How do I do it?"

The answer is, "Well, it depends. Whose case-mapping rules do you want to use?"

Sometimes the reply is, "I want this to be language-independent."

Now you have a real problem.

Every locale has its own case-mapping rules. Many of them are in conflict with the rules for other locales. For example, which of the following pairs of words compare case-insensitive equal? (In the mind of a native speaker, not necessarily how Windows treats them.)

1. Gif   GIF

2. Maße   MASSE

3. Maße   Masse

4. Même   MEME

The answers may surprise you:

1. No in Turkey, yes in the United States.

2. No in the United States, yes in Germany.

3. No in the United States, no in Germany, yes in Switzerland!
   (Though you would probably never see it written as "Maße" in Switzerland.)

4. Yes in France, no in Québec!

(And I've heard that the capitalization rules for German are context-sensitive. Maybe that changed with the most recent spelling reform.) Unicode Technical Report 21 has more examples.

Just because you're using Unicode doesn't mean that all your language problems are solved. Indeed, being able to represent characters in nearly all the world's languages means that you have more things to worry about, not fewer.

⪾

An anecdote about improper case mapping

INTERNET EXPLORER HAD a case-mapping bug that transformed somebody's name into a dead body.

This bug occurred because Internet Explorer tried to convert the characters in the name "Yamada" to lowercase but was not mindful of the character-combining rules of the double-byte 932 character set used for Japanese. In this character set, a single glyph can be represented either by one or two bytes. The Roman character "A" is represented by the single byte 0x41. On the other hand, the character "の" is represented by the two bytes: 0x82 0xCC.

When you parse a Japanese string in this character set, you need to maintain state. If you see a byte that is marked as a "DBCS lead byte," then it and the byte following must be treated as a single unit. There is no relationship between the character represented by 0x8E 0x52 (山) and 0x8E 0x72 (屍) even though the second bytes happen to be related when taken on their own (0x52 = "R" and 0x72 = "r").

Internet Explorer forgot this rule and merely inspected and converted each byte to lowercase independently. So when it came time to convert the characters making up the name "Yamada," the second bytes in the pairs were erroneously treated as if they were Roman characters and were "converted to lowercase" accordingly.

Characters	Encoding	Meaning
山田	0x8E 0x52 0x93 0x63	Yamada
屍田	0x8E 0x72 0x93 0x63	corpse + rice field

The result was that the name "Yamada" turned into the characters meaning "corpse" and "rice field." You can imagine how Mr. Yamada felt about this.

Converting the string to Unicode would have helped a little, since the Unicode capitalization rules would certainly not have connected two unrelated characters in that way. But there are still risks in character-by-character capitalization: In some languages, capitalization is itself context-sensitive. For example, in Hungarian, "sZ" and "SZ" are not the same thing when compared case-insensitively.

⤳

Why you can't rotate text

WHEN PEOPLE READ the explanation about why the word "Start" disappears when you dock the taskbar vertically, some suggest, "Why not draw the text vertically?"

Ah, now you get to learn about the exciting world of vertical text.

We originally intended to run text vertically in the new XP Start menu. In original designs for the menu, your name ran vertically up the left side of the menu instead of running across the top.

Rotating text is problematic in languages that traditionally run vertically, such as Chinese. Consider my name, 陳瑞孟. In traditional vertical text, it would be written as shown in Example 1. In contexts where a person who doesn't read Chinese may encounter the name, the Western name can be appended to the Chinese name, as I have done here. Notice that the English text is rotated *clockwise*. This convention preserves the top-to-bottom reading order.

陳瑞孟 (Raymond Chen)

Example 1

As a concession to Western influences, it is permissible to render Chinese characters left-to-right, in which case my name would be written as "陳瑞孟 (Raymond Chen)".

Compare this to the traditional Western way of rotating text. Text that would normally be rendered as "Raymond Chen" is rotated *counterclockwise* (Example 2).

Raymond Chen

Example 2

Now consider what happens if you take a Chinese name rendered the Western way—"陳瑞孟 (Raymond Chen)"—and rotate it the Western way. The result is shown in Example 3. Notice that from a Chinese point of view, everything is upside-down! The character that is supposed to be at the top (陳) is now at the bottom.

陳瑞孟 (Raymond Chen)

Example 3

For many years now, Windows has been multilingual. This means that the same underlying code runs, regardless of language. Changing a language merely changes the strings being displayed. Consequently, there can be no language-specific user interface. In this case, it means that we can't have separate rotation rules for Chinese as opposed to English or German.

NOTE: Even if we were allowed to have separate rotation rules, we would have to be able to tell whether the name was in the form we've been working with so far, or was in the form Raymond Chen (陳瑞孟). In the "English first" form, we should rotate it as in Example 2, since this is an English string with Chinese characters embedded, as opposed to Example 1, where we had a Chinese string with English characters embedded. Those of you who have seen Arabic and English mixed together have seen punctuation marks bandied about with similar degrees of confusion.

Multilingual support also explains why you see things like "1 folder(s)" instead of "1 folder" and "2 folders." Why not have two format strings, one for when the number of items is exactly one, and another for when the number of items is two or more?

Well, for one reason, that would significantly increase the number of strings we would have to carry around. (If you say "just add *s* to make the plural," then you really need to get out more!)

For another reason, some languages (such as Slovene) have a "dual" number in addition to singular and plural. The Lahir language has singular (one), dual (two), trial (three), paucal (a few), and plural (many). So now you need perhaps five versions of every string that contains a replaceable number.

This also explains why you see a lot of strings of the form "Property: Value" (for example, "Last modified: Monday, September 29, 2003") instead of a phrase ("Last modified on Monday, September 29, 2003"). This is necessary to avoid problems caused by grammar. If you attempt to compose a phrase, you have to worry about subject-verb agreement, gender and number agreement, declensions, and all sorts of other things that computers aren't good at. The only safe solution is to avoid grammar entirely and use the "Property: Value" notation instead. (And even this isn't good enough for many languages. Swedish, for example, requires that adjectives be declined even when they are used absolutely.)

We did get one special exception to the grammar-independence rule: Personalized folders. When you view somebody else's My Documents folder, it says "Chris's Documents." We made this request to the translators, and they worked hard to make sure that the templates for possessive forms were accurate in all the languages we support. (Fortunately, we didn't have to deal with languages whose form of the template depended on us knowing whether Chris is a man or a woman.)

What are these directories called 0409 and 1033?

MICROSOFT PRODUCTS OFTEN have subdirectories called 0409 and 1033. Or at least they do if you're in the United States, because 1033 is the locale identifier for "English (United States)," whose hexadecimal value is 0x0409. You may also find directories called 0409. Some programs use hex codes and some use decimal. Go figure.

The value of a locale identifier is given by the formula

```
primary language + 1024 * sub-language
```

For example, Swiss German is `LANG_GERMAN + 1024 * SUBLANG_GERMAN_SWISS = 7 + 1024 * 2 = 2055`.

Why would a program create a directory named after a language code in the first place?

Many Microsoft products support a multilingual user interface. This means that the same program can be used to display its user interface in multiple languages. Office and Windows are the two biggest examples. Language-specific resources need to be broken out into their own directories so that they won't conflict with resources corresponding to some other language.

Keep your eye on the code page

REMEMBER THAT THERE are typically two 8-bit code pages active, the so-called ANSI code page and the so-called OEM code page. GUI programs usually use the ANSI code page for 8-bit files (though UTF-8 is becoming more popular lately), whereas console programs usually use the OEM code page. (We'll learn more about the names ANSI and OEM later.)

This means, for example, that when you open an 8-bit text file in Notepad, it assumes the ANSI code page. But if you use the TYPE command from the command prompt, it will use the OEM code page.

This has interesting consequences if you frequently switch between the GUI and the command line.

The two code pages typically agree on the first 128 characters, but nearly always disagree on the characters from 128 to 255 (the so-called extended characters). For example, on a U.S.-English machine, character 0x80 in the OEM code page is Ç, whereas in the ANSI code page it is €.

Consider a directory that contains a file named ç. If you type dir at a command prompt, you see a happy ç on the screen. On the other hand, if you do dir >files.txt and open files.txt in a GUI editor like Notepad, you will find that the Ç has changed to a €, because the 0x80 in the file is being interpreted in the ANSI character set instead of the OEM character set.

Stranger yet, if you mark/select the filename from the console window and paste it into Notepad, you get a Ç. That's because the console window's mark/select code saves text on the clipboard as Unicode; the character saved into the clipboard is not 0x80 but rather U+00C7, the Unicode code point for "Latin Capital Letter C With Cedilla." When this is pasted into Notepad, the character is converted from Unicode to the ANSI code page, which on a U.S.-English system encodes the Ç character as 0xC7.

But wait, there's more. The command processor has an option (/U) to generate all piped and redirected output in Unicode rather than the OEM code page.

If you run the command

```
cmd /U /C dir >files.txt
```

then the output will be in Unicode and therefore will record the Ç character as U+00C7, which Notepad will then be able to read back.

This has serious consequences for batch files.

Batch files are 8-bit files and are interpreted according to the OEM character set. This means that if you write a batch file with Notepad or some other program that uses the ANSI character set for 8-bit files, and your batch file contains extended characters, the results will not match what you see in your editor.

Following through on this topic, let's take a look at the consequences of code page selection on source code. Here's a trick question. Predict the output of the following program:

```
#include <stdio.h>

int __cdecl main(int argc, char **argv)
{
 printf("Ç"); // capital C cedilla
 return 0;
}
```

Why is this a trick question?

I didn't tell you what code page the source code is in. In fact, depending on what text editor you used, you will get different results. Note: For the purpose of this discussion, I'll take a U.S.-centric view of the various system code pages. The ANSI code page will be assumed to be 1252 (Western European), and the OEM code page 437. The principles involved apply generally, but I chose these two code pages for concreteness.

Perhaps you created the file from an editor that uses the OEM code page. This is typical of text-mode editors like edit.com. It's also what you get if you use the `copy con` command to create a file directly from the command prompt:

```
> copy con test.cpp
#include <stdio.h>

int __cdecl main(int argc, char **argv)
{
 printf("Ç"); // capital C cedilla
 return 0;
}
^Z
        1 file(s) copied.
```

If you went the OEM code page route, the character in the source file is `0x80`, because that is the value for Ç in the OEM code page (437).

On the other hand, perhaps you used an editor that employs the ANSI code page, which is typical of graphical editors like Notepad. In that case, the character in the source file is 0xC7, which is the value for ç in the ANSI code page (1252).

Because I didn't specify what code page the source file was in, the problem was underspecified. (Besides, the question was itself an illegal question; the ç character is not part of the required standard source character set. But we're going to soldier on, anyway, because people often find themselves in this situation and don't understand why they're getting what they're getting.)

Now that we understand the consequences of using non-ASCII characters on your text editor, let's next look at the consequences on the compiler.

In this case, the compiler doesn't have to do any work. It just takes the bytes between the quotation marks and emits them into the object file.

In our example in which the source file used the OEM code page, the string generated into the object file is 0x80 0x00, because the source file contains the byte 0x80 between the quotation marks. Similarly, in the second example with the ANSI code page, the string generated into the object file is 0xC7 0x00, because in that case, the source file contains the byte 0xC7 between the quotation marks.

Okay, now that we know how the string being passed to the printf function is interpreted at compile time, we can next look at how the string behaves at run time.

Because printf sends its output to the console, the characters will be displayed in the OEM code page. In the first case, then, the string 0x80 0x00 is interpreted as ç, which is what you see on the screen. On the other hand, if your text editor uses the ANSI code page, then you get the string 0xC7 0x00, which is interpreted as the line-drawing character ╟.

As you can see, the factor that controls what actually gets printed to the screen isn't the compiler or the runtime; it's your text editor!

And the weirdness doesn't stop there. Let's change the printf to

```
MessageBox(NULL, "Ç", "Test", MB_OK);
```

If you understood what happened with printf, then predicting what this will do should be a piece of cake.

If your text editor uses the OEM character set, then, as we noted, the string generated into the object file is 0x80 0x00. Because the MessageBox function is a GUI function, it treats 8-bit character strings in the ANSI character set, which means that 0x80 x00 becomes €.

If your text editor uses the ANSI character set, then the string generated into the object file is 0xC7 0x00, which when interpreted in the ANSI character set results in ç.

You might decide that the lesson here is that if you are writing a console program, you should use a console-based text editor, whereas if you're writing a GUI program, you should use a GUI text editor. But what if you have a program that does both? Consider the program that uses both printf (for debugging) and MessageBox.

```
printf("Ç");
MessageBox(NULL,  "Ç",  "Test",  MB_OK);
```

In this case, no matter which editor you use, somebody will lose. But in fact it's even worse than that.

Instead of using an 8-bit string, let's create a Unicode string in our little program by changing the printf and MessageBox calls to

```
wprintf(L"Ç");
MessageBoxW(NULL,  L"Ç",  L"Test",  MB_OK);
```

Again, there are two cases, depending on whether your text editor uses the OEM or ANSI code page. As before, let's look at the OEM case first.

When the compiler sees an L"..." string, it takes the bytes between the quotation marks and converts them to Unicode according to an implementation-defined mapping between the so-called source character set and the so-called execution character set. The Microsoft Visual Studio compiler by default uses the CP_ACP code page to perform this conversion, although you can change this with the #pragma setlocale() directive. (Just what we need, yet another variable that influences the interpretation of bytes as characters.)

Taking all this into consideration, we see that the string L"Ç", if stored in the OEM character set, comes out as 0x80 0x00. When interpreted according to the CP_ACP code page, the 0x80 is treated as the € character. Consequently, the resulting Unicode string is U+20AC U+0000.

The wprintf function takes its Unicode input and converts it to 8-bit output according to the current locale as set by the setlocale function in C or the std::locale object in C++. Since we did not modify the locale in our test program, the runtime library uses the default locale, which is the "C" locale. The "C" locale is a bare-bones locale that assumes that the 8-bit values 0 to 255 map to the same values 0 to 255 as a wchar_t. Conversely, the mapping from a wchar_t to an 8-bit value is to convert wchar_t values 0 to 255 to 8-bit values 0 to 255. Wide characters whose values are 256 or greater are considered inconvertible.

Therefore, when the preceding code fragment is run, the wprintf function attempts to convert the Unicode string to an 8-bit string, but cannot because the character U+20AC has a numerical value greater than 255. As a result, you get no output at all from the wprintf, because the conversion from Unicode failed. (If you step through with the debugger, you'll see that wprintf returns –1, which indicates that an error occurred, and errno is EILSEQ, which indicates an encoding error.)

The call to MessageBoxW is much easier to predict. It prints the € character, because there is no conversion involved; MessageBoxW can display Unicode strings directly.

Now let's consider the result if the source code were written in the ANSI code page. The analysis is similar: The string L"Ç", if stored in the ANSI code page, comes out as 0xC7 0x00. Converting this to Unicode according to the CP_ACP code page results in the rather unsurprising U+00C7 U+0000. When this string is passed to the wprintf function, the conversion from a Unicode string to an 8-bit string is successful because all the code points have numerical values less than or equal to 255. The result is the string 0xC7 0x00, which appears on the console as the line-drawing character ╟ because the console uses the OEM character set. When that same string is passed to the MessageBoxW function, it displays as Ç, again because MessageBoxW does not perform any conversion, rendering the Unicode string directly.

Well, that exercise was influenced by the runtime library's choice of "C" as the default locale. What if we bypass the runtime library and generate our output directly to the console?

```
DWORD cchWritten;
WriteConsoleW(GetStdHandle(STD_OUTPUT_HANDLE), L"Ç", 1,
              &cchWritten, NULL);
```

As we've already seen, the string that is passed to WriteConsoleW will be either U+20AC U+0000 or U+00C7 U+0000, depending on whether the source code is in the OEM or ANSI character set. As we saw with the wprintf function, the U+20AC character cannot be converted to the OEM character set, but instead of failing, the WriteConsoleW function succeeds and prints a question mark. Working backward, you can infer that the conversion from Unicode to the OEM character set is performed with the WideCharToMultiByte function, which by default uses a question mark to represent characters that could not be converted. On the other hand, if the source code is in the ANSI character set, the string U+00C7 U+0000 converts to 0x80 0x00 in the OEM character set, which displays on the screen as a capital C with cedilla.

As I noted earlier, the #pragma setlocale() directive adds another wrinkle to this exercise by changing the rules that govern how the compiler converts bytes to characters. As a result, even if you can somehow control which editor various people are using to edit source code, you still don't know how 8-bit character strings are going to be converted to Unicode. An include file somewhere may have decided to use that #pragma to change the ambient code page behind your back.

Believe it or not, it gets even worse than this. We've so far been looking at the mass mayhem that occurs if you embed characters outside the 7-bit ASCII character set in your source code. Let's move on to integer promotions.

Consider the following program:

```
#include <stdio.h>

int __cdecl main(int argc, char **argv)
{
 int i1 = 'Ç';
 int i2 = L'Ç';
 printf("%d %d\n", i1, i2);

 wchar_t wch1 = 'Ç';
 wchar_t wch2 = L'Ç';
```

```
printf("%d %d\n", wch1, wch2);

return 0;
}
```

Again, we need to look at the two possible source code character sets. If saved in the OEM character set, the output will be

```
-128 8364
65408 8364
```

Do you understand why?

The value of i1 is set from an integer character constant. In the OEM character set, 'Ç' has the value 0x80, which as a signed character has the decimal value –128. On the other hand, L'Ç' follows the rules for 8-bit-to-Unicode conversion that we saw earlier. The result is the character U+20AC, which has the decimal value 8364. That explains the first line.

On the second line, the values are stored into variables of type wchar_t, which in Win32 is a 16-bit unsigned type. Consequently, the value –128 is sign-extended to 0xFF80, which then has the unsigned value 65408. The second value 8364 is determined by the same logic that we used to obtain the value on the first line.

If the file were saved in the ANSI code page, the output would be

```
-57 199
65479 199
```

The character 'Ç' has the numeric value 0xC7, which as a signed character has the decimal value –57. When sign-extended to a 16-bit unsigned value, it becomes 65479. The value 199 is the Unicode code point value for L'Ç' = U+00C7.

Observe the importance of distinguishing your 8-bit character literals from your wide character literals. Adding or removing an L can result in wild changes in the values you ultimately obtain from the compiler. And if you don't understand where these results come from, then you may have difficulty tracking down these issues to the presence or absence of that crucial L.

What's the moral of the story? In my opinion, the moral is never to put characters that do not fit in the 7-bit ASCII range in source code. As we saw, the interpretation of such characters depends heavily on what type of editor you use and what language is preferred by the person compiling your program. The interpretation can also be influenced by what #pragma directives are buried in your header files. Even worse, the simple error of omitting the L prefix on character constants can generate the wrong constants.

Given all the variables (many of which may be beyond your control), it is simply not reasonable to expect that everybody who uses your source code is going to edit and compile it with the same environmental conditions that you used. If you need to encode character or string constants that do not fit in the 7-bit ASCII range, specify their code points explicitly. If we change our previous sample program to the following:

```
#include <stdio.h>

int __cdecl main(int argc, char **argv)
{
  int i1 = '\xC7';
  int i2 = L'\x00C7';
  printf("%d %d\n", i1, i2);

  int wch1 = '\xC7';
  int wch2 = L'\x00C7';
  printf("%d %d\n", wch1, wch2);

  return 0;
}
```

expressing the character code point explicitly via the \x escape, then the program no longer depends on the text editor or the ambient code page. If you find yourself doing this a lot, you may wish to set up some macros:

```
#define CH_CAPCCEDILLA_850    '\xC7'    // correct value for code
                                        // page 850
#define WCH_CAPCCEDILLA       L'\x00C7'
#define STR_CAPCCEDILLA_850   "\xC7"    // correct value for code
                                        // page 850
#define WSTR_CAPCCEDILLA      L"\x00C7"

wprintf(WSTR_CAPCCEDILLA "a va?");
```

I admit that this technique is extremely unwieldy, but in practice there should be little need to embed language-specific strings into source code, since all language-specific strings should have been placed into resources to begin with.

⤲

Why is the default 8-bit code page called "ANSI"?

THIS APPARENT INCONSISTENCY is explained by Kathy Wissink, program manager at Microsoft:

> *The term "ANSI" as used to signify Windows code pages is a historical reference, but is nowadays a misnomer that continues to persist in the Windows community. The source of this comes from the fact that the Windows code page 1252 was originally based on an ANSI draft, which became ISO Standard 8859-1. However, in adding code points to the range reserved for control codes in the ISO standard, the Windows code page 1252 and subsequent Windows code pages originally based on the ISO 8859-x series deviated from ISO. To this day, it is not uncommon to have the development community, both within and outside … Microsoft, confuse the 8859-1 code page with Windows 1252, as well as see "ANSI" or "A" used to signify Windows code page support.*[1]

⤲

Why is the default console code page called "OEM"?

NOT ONLY IS the ANSI code page not actually ANSI, but the OEM code page isn't actually OEM, either.

Back in the days of MS-DOS, there was only one code page, namely, the code page that was provided by the original equipment manufacturer in the form of glyphs embedded in the character generator on the video card. When Windows came along, the so-called ANSI code page was introduced and the name *OEM* was used to refer to the MS-DOS code page.

---

1. Kathy Wissink, "Unicode and Windows XP," 21st International Unicode Conference, Dublin, May 2002, available at http://download.microsoft.com/download/5/6/8/56803da0-e4a0-4796-a62c-ca920b73bb17/21-Unicode_WinXP.pdf.

Why the discrepancy between GUI programs and console programs over how 8-bit characters should be interpreted?

The reason is, of course, historical.

In the long-ago days when MS-DOS reigned, the code page was what today is called the OEM code page. For U.S.-English systems, this is the code page with the box-drawing characters and the fragments of the integral signs. It contained accented letters, but not a very big set of them, just enough to cover the German, French, Spanish, and Italian languages. And Swedish. (Why Swedish, yet not Danish and Norwegian, I don't know.) The characters in the OEM code page were controlled by the video card provided by the original equipment manufacturer. (At the time, the original manufacturer was effectively synonymous with IBM, there being no other significant manufacturer of PCs.)

When Windows came along, it decided that those box-drawing characters were wasting valuable space that could be used for adding still more accented characters, so out went the box-drawing characters and in went characters for Danish, Norwegian, Icelandic, and Canadian French. (As we saw earlier, Canadian French uses characters that European French does not.)

Thus began the schism between console programs (MS-DOS) and GUI programs (Windows) over how 8-bit character data should be interpreted.

Over the years, Windows has relied less and less on the character generator embedded in the video card, to the point that the term *OEM character set* no longer has anything to do with the original equipment manufacturer. It is just a convenient term meaning "the character set used by MS-DOS and console programs." Indeed, if you take a machine running U.S.-English Windows (OEM code page 437) and install, say, Japanese Windows, then when you boot into Japanese Windows, you'll find that you now have an OEM code page of 932.

⬱

Why is the OEM code page often called ANSI?

IT HAS BEEN pointed out that the documentation for the cmd.exe program says

```
/A Causes the output of internal commands to a pipe or file
   to be ANSI
```

even though the output is actually in the OEM code page. Why do errors such as this persist?

Because ANSI sometimes means OEM.

The "A" versions of the console functions accept characters in the OEM code page despite the "A" suffix that would suggest ANSI. What's more, if you call the SetFileAPIsToOEM function, then "A" functions that accept filenames will also interpret the filenames in the OEM code page rather than the ANSI code page.

I've heard it said that there are two types of people in the world: those who believe that the world can be divided into two types of people, and those who do not.

And there are those who mentally divide the world of characters into two groups: Unicode and 8-bit. And as you can see, many of these people were involved in the original design of Win32. There are "W" functions (Unicode) and "A" functions (ANSI). There are no "O" functions (OEM). Instead, the OEM folks got lumped in with the ANSI folks.

There are also those (like me) who realize the distinction, but out of laziness or convenience often use ANSI as an abbreviation for "an appropriate 8-bit character set, determined from context." In the context of console programming, the appropriate 8-bit character set is the OEM character set.

Let's take another look at the online help for cmd.exe:

```
/A Causes the output of internal commands to a pipe or file to be
   ANSI
/U Causes the output of internal commands to a pipe or file to be
   Unicode
```

The person who wrote this clearly meant ANSI to mean "that thing that isn't Unicode." I'll leave you to decide whether this author belongs to the "Everything is either Unicode or ANSI" camp or the "just being casual" camp.

Logical but perhaps surprising consequences of converting between Unicode and ANSI

CONSIDER THE FOLLOWING code fragment:

```
...
WIN32_FIND_DATA wfd;
HANDLE hff = FindFirstFile("*.xyz", &wfd);
if (hff != INVALID_HANDLE_VALUE) {
 FindClose(hff);
 HANDLE h = CreateFile(wfd.cFileName, ...);
 ...
}
```

If you compile this code as ANSI, you can find yourself in a difficult situation: The FindFirstFile function might return a filename that isn't legal.

The mapping between Unicode and ANSI is not one-to-one. Many Unicode characters have no equivalent ANSI representation. If you have one of those characters in a filename, calling the ANSI version of the FindFirstFile function will return a cFileName with question marks for the characters that could not be converted. Too bad the question mark is not a legal filename character. This problem is unavoidable due to the inability of expressing all Unicode characters in the ANSI character set. When faced with one of these inexpressible characters, you have to punt.

You might try using the short filename as a fallback, but that won't get you anywhere if the file system doesn't support short filenames (say, if it's HPFS, or it's NTFS with short names disabled).

But wait, it's worse.

Even if the string can be converted, remember that there is no requirement that the length of the Unicode string in WCHARs be the same as the length of the ANSI equivalent in CHARs. For example, consider the situation in which the ANSI code page is DBCS and you have a filename consisting of 200 copies of a Unicode character that requires two bytes to represent. This is a perfectly valid filename, well under the MAX_PATH limit. But if a program compiled in ANSI tries to find it, the program can't, because the equivalent ANSI string is 400 CHARs long, which exceeds the MAX_PATH limit.

The solution to all this nonsense is just to use the Unicode versions of the functions. That way, there is no conversion and no loss of data.

CHAPTER SEVENTEEN

SECURITY

IF I HAD a nickel each time somebody asked for a feature that was a security hole …

I'd have a lot of nickels.

We begin this chapter by looking at features that are actually security holes and then move on to other security-related matters.

World-writable files

"I WANT A file that all users can write to. My program will use it as a common database of goodies."

This is a security hole. For a start, there's an obvious denial-of-service attack by having a user open the file in exclusive mode and never letting go. There's also a data-tampering attack, where the user opens the file and writes zeros all over it or merely alters the data in subtle ways. Your music index suddenly lost all its Britney Spears songs. (Then again, maybe that's a good thing. Sneakier would be to edit the index so that when somebody tries to play a Britney Spears song, they get Madonna instead.)

A colleague from the security team pointed out another problem with this design: disk quotas. Whoever created the file is charged for the disk space consumed by that file, even if most of the entries in the file belong to someone else. If you create the file in your Setup program, it will most likely be owned by an administrator. Administrators are exempt from quotas, which means that everybody can party data into the file for free! (Particularly devious users might hide the data inside what's known as an *NTFS alternate data stream* so that it won't affect normal users of the file.) And if the file is on the system partition (which it probably is), users can try to fill up all the available disk space and crash the system.

If you have a shared resource that you want to let people mess with, one way to do this is with a service. Users do not access the resource directly but rather go through the service. The service decides what the user is allowed to do with the resource. Maybe some users are permitted only to increment the "number of times played" counter, whereas others are allowed to edit the song titles. If a user is hogging the resource, the server might refuse connections from that user for a while.

A file doesn't give you this degree of control over what people can do with it. If you grant write permission to a user, that user can write to *any* part of the file. The user can open the file in exclusive mode and prevent anybody else from accessing it. The user can put fake data in the file in an attempt to confuse the other users on the machine.

In other words, the user can make a change to the system that impacts how other users can use the system. This sort of "impact other users" behavior is something that is reserved for administrators. Unprivileged users should be allowed only to mess up their own lives; they shouldn't be allowed to mess up other users' lives.

⁓

Hiding files from Explorer

BY DEFAULT, EXPLORER does not show files that have the FILE_ATTRIBUTE_ HIDDEN flag, because somebody deliberately wanted to hide those files from view.

You can, of course, ask that such files be shown anyway by going to Folder Options and selecting Show hidden files and folders. This shows files and folders even if they are marked as FILE_ATTRIBUTE_HIDDEN.

On the other hand, files that are marked as both FILE_ATTRIBUTE_HIDDEN and FILE_ATTRIBUTE_SYSTEM remain hidden from view. These are typically files that are involved in the plumbing of the operating system; messing with these can cause various types of "excitement." They are files like the page file, folder configuration files, and the System Volume Information folder.

If you want to see those files, too, you can uncheck Hide protected operating system files.

Let's look at how far this game of hide/show Ping-Pong has gone:

Show	Hide
1. Normal file	
2.	Hidden file
3. "Show hidden files"	
4.	Hidden + System
5. "Show protected operating system files"	

You'd think this would be the end of the hide/show arms race, but this doesn't stop people from wanting to add a sixth level and make something invisible to Explorer, overriding the five existing levels.

At some point this back and forth has to stop, and for now, it has stopped at level five. Adding just a sixth level without a seventh would create a security hole, because it would allow a file to hide from the user. As a matter of security, a sufficiently privileged user must always have a way of seeing what is there or at least know that there is something there that can't be seen. Nothing can be undetectably invisible.

If you add a sixth level that lets a file hide from level five, there must be a level seven that reveals it.

⤙⤙

Stealing passwords

SOMETIMES PEOPLE ASK for features that are such blatant security holes I don't know what they were thinking.

"Is there a way to get the current user's password? I have a program that does some stuff, then reboots the system, and I want to have the current user's password so I can log that user back in when I'm done, then my program can resume its operation."

This is if you're lucky and they explain why they need the user's password. Often they just come right out and ask for it without any background.

Imagine the fantastic security hole if this were possible. Anybody could write a program that steals your password *without even having to trick you into typing it*. The person would just call the imaginary `GetPasswordOf-CurrentUser` function, and bingo! there is your password.

Even if you didn't want the password itself but merely some sort of "cookie" that could be used to log users on later, you still have a security hole. Let's call this imaginary function `GetPasswordCookieOfCurrentUser`; it returns a "cookie" that can be used to log users on instead of using their password.

This is just a thinly disguised `GetPasswordOfCurrentUser` because that "cookie" is *equivalent to a password*. Log on with the cookie and you are now that person.

⤜⤏

Silent install of uncertified drivers

PROBABLY THE SINGLE greatest source of blue-screen crashes in Windows XP is buggy device drivers. Because drivers run in kernel mode, no higher authority is checking what they're doing. If some user-mode code runs amok and corrupts memory, it's just corrupting its own memory. The process eventually crashes, but the system stays up. On the other hand, if a driver runs amok and corrupts memory, it's corrupting your system and eventually your machine dies.

In acknowledgment of the importance of having high-quality drivers, Windows XP warns you when an uncertified driver is being installed. Which leads to a question from a device driver author.

"When I try to install any driver, I get a User Consent Dialog box that tells the user that this is an unsigned driver. Is it possible to author a driver installation package that bypasses this user consent dialog box?"

The whole purpose of that dialog is to prevent the situation you desire from happening! If you don't want the warning dialog, submit your driver for certification. (For testing purposes, you can sign your drivers with the test root certificate and install the test root certificate before running your setup program. Of course, installing the test root certificate also causes the desktop to read "For test purposes only" as a reminder that your machine is now allowing test-signed drivers to be installed.)

Driver writers, of course, find the certification process cumbersome and will do whatever they can to avoid it. Because, naturally, if they submit their driver for certification, it might fail! As we saw in "Defrauding the WHQL driver certification process" (Chapter 9), this has led to varying degrees of shenanigans to trick the WHQL team into certifying a driver different from the one they intend to use.

My favorite stunt was related to me by a colleague who was installing a video card driver whose setup program displayed a dialog that read, roughly, "After clicking OK, do not touch your keyboard or mouse while we prepare your system." After you click OK, the setup program proceeds to move the mouse programmatically all over the screen, opening the Display Control Panel, clicking on the Advanced button, clicking through various other configuration dialogs, a flurry of activity for what seems like a half a minute. When faced with a setup program that does this, your natural reaction is to scream, "Aaaiiiigh!"

Your debugging code can be a security hole

WHEN YOU'RE DEVELOPING your debugging code, don't forget that just because it's only for debugging doesn't mean that you can forget about security.

I remember one vendor who asked, "We have a service and for testing purposes we want to be able to connect to this service and extract the private data that the service is managing, the data that normally nobody should be allowed to see. That way, we can compare it against what we think the data should be. This is just for testing purposes and will not be called during normal operation. How do you recommend we do this?"

Remember that hackers don't care whether the code you wrote was for normal use or for diagnostic purposes. If it's there, they will attack it.

The vendor went to a lot of effort to protect this internal data, making sure that none of the service operations disclose it directly, but then in a haze of "this would make debugging easier," they lost their heads and added a debugging backdoor that gives direct access to this data that they had worked so hard to protect.

It doesn't matter how much you protect the front door if you leave the service entrance wide open.

I have a printer driver that insists on creating a log file in the root of the drive. This log file, which is world-readable, contains among other things, the URLs of every single Web page I have printed. If I log on as an administrator and delete the log file, it just comes back the next time I print a document.

I assume the printer vendor created this log file for diagnostic purposes, but it also creates a security hole. Everybody on the system can see the URL of any Web page that was printed by anybody else.

⟡

Why shared sections are a security hole

MANY PEOPLE RECOMMEND using shared data sections as a way to share data between multiple instances of an application. This sounds like a great idea, but in fact it's a security hole.

Proper shared memory objects created by the CreateFileMapping function can be secured. They have security descriptors that let you specify which users are allowed to have what level of access. By contrast, anybody who loads your EXE or DLL gets access to your shared memory section.

Consider the following program:

```
#include <stdio.h>
#include <windows.h>
```

```
// These directives place the g_iShared variable inside a shared
// memory section.
#pragma comment(linker, "/SECTION:.shared,RWS")
#pragma data_seg(".shared")
int g_iShared = 0;
#pragma data_seg()

void printit()
{
  char sz[5];
  sprintf(sz, "%d", g_iShared);
  puts(sz);
}

int __cdecl main(int argc, char **argv)
{
 while (true) {
  printit();
  // ignore the race condition; that's not the point here
  int iNew = g_iShared + 1;
  if (iNew == 10) iNew = 0;
  g_iShared = iNew;
  Sleep(1000);
  }
}
```

Go ahead and run this program. It counts from 0 to 9 over and over again. Because we never let g_iShared go above 9, the sprintf is safe from buffer overflow.

Or is it?

Run this program. Then use the runas utility to run a second copy of this program under a different user. For extra fun, make one of the users an administrator and another a nonadministrator.

Notice that the counter counts up at double speed. That's to be expected because the counter is shared.

Okay, now close one of the copies and relaunch it under a debugger. (It's more fun if you let the administrator's copy run free and run the nonadministrator's copy run under a debugger.) Let both programs run, and then break into the debugger and change the value of the variable g_iShared to something really big, say, 1000000.

Now, depending on how intrusive your debugger is, you might or might not see the crash. Some debuggers try to be "helpful" and "unshare" shared memory sections when you change their values from the debugger. Helpful for debugging (maybe), bad for my demonstration (definitely).

Here's how I did it with the ntsd debugger that comes preinstalled with Windows XP. (You are not expected to understand all these steps; I provide it only to "show my work.") I opened a command prompt, which runs as myself (and I am not an administrator). I then used the runas utility to run the scratch program as administrator. It is the administrator's copy of the scratch program that I'm going to cause to crash even though I am just a boring normal nonadministrative user.

From the normal command prompt, I typed ntsd sample to run the scratch program under the debugger. From the debugger prompt, I typed u main to disassemble the main function, looking for

```
01001143 a300300001      mov      [g_iShared (01003000)],eax
```

(Note: your numbers may differ.) I then typed g 1001143 to instruct the debugger to execute normally until that instruction is reached. When the debugger reached that one-time breakpoint, I typed r eax=0n1000000;t to change the value of the eax register to the decimal value 1000000 and then trace one instruction. That one-instruction trace wrote the out-of-range value into shared memory, and one second later, the administrator version of the program crashed with a buffer overflow.

What happened?

Because the memory is shared, all running copies of the scratch program have access to it. All I did was use the debugger to run a copy of the scratch program and change the value of the shared memory variable. Because the variable is shared, the value also changes in the administrator's copy of the program, which then causes the sprintf buffer to overflow, thereby crashing the administrator's copy of the program.

You might argue, "Well, obviously the bug is that the program used the unsafe sprintf function," but you're missing the forest for the trees. Suppose there is a pointer in the shared memory block. (In practice, because the address of a shared memory block is not guaranteed to be the same between processes, the programmer would have used a so-called *based* pointer; that is, a pointer relative to another location. This detail does not affect the underlying attack, however, so we will ignore it.) An attacker can corrupt that shared pointer, causing the copy of the program running under the administrator account to access any memory you choose. You can set the pointer to a garbage value and get the other copy of the program to crash, or you can set it to a value that causes the program to read or modify memory that you find particularly valuable. If there is a string in the shared memory block, you can remove the null terminator and cause it to become "impossibly" long, resulting in a potential buffer overflow if somebody copies it without checking the length. Or you can just modify the string: Perhaps it's a filename, and you've thereby tricked the administrator's copy of the program to operate on a file of your choosing.

And if there is a C++ object with a vtable, you have just hit the mother lode! (The program of course couldn't share the C++ object because the function pointers wouldn't necessarily be meaningful in other processes, but perhaps the administrator's copy of the program placed the object in shared memory even though only no other process actually uses it.) If you find yourself in this situation, you can redirect the vtable to a bogus vtable (which you construct in the shared memory section), and put a function pointer entry in that vtable that points into some code that you generated (also into the shared memory section) that takes over the machine. (If Data Execution Prevention is enabled, the scope of the attack is reduced, but there is still an attack.)

Even the most paranoid program that carefully validates everything in shared memory before using it is still vulnerable because an attacker can just modify the shared variables (by filling the page with random numbers, say) to the point where the program can't make any sense of them any more. The program may not crash, but you've at least accomplished a denial of service because whatever those shared variables were supposed to be doing, they sure aren't doing it now!

Moral of the story: Avoid shared memory sections. Because you cannot attach an access control list (ACL) to the section, any process which can load your EXE or DLL can modify your variables and cause havoc in another instance of the program that is running at a higher security level.

⁓

Internet Explorer's Enhanced Security Configuration doesn't trust the intranet

WINDOWS SERVER 2003 comes with a feature called Internet Explorer Enhanced Security Configuration that cranks the security settings for Explorer and Internet Explorer through the roof. Think of it as "Internet Explorer with a tinfoil hat." It's special to the Server edition of Windows because companies who shell out thousands of dollars for a server-class machine typically don't want their employees reading online comics on the company's central payroll database server! The payroll database server should be browsing only to Web sites that have to do with managing the payroll database server.

One of the more significant changes is that *the intranet is considered just as unsafe as the Internet*. Why is that?

Because the intranet is also a scary place.

Any random employee on your intranet can plug in and start hosting Web pages that are not trustworthy. Server administrators are paranoid and don't even normally allow scripts to execute.

If there is an intranet site that you do trust, you can add it to your trusted sites list.

The term *intranet* is not as well defined as one would like. If you're in a college dorm, is everybody in your building your "intranet"? Why should you trust a student two floors downstairs more than you trust a computer in a country you've never heard of? Many (most?) cable modem providers are set up so that everybody in your neighborhood is on the same local-area network (LAN) (gives a whole new meaning to *network neighborhood*). Why should you trust that creepy neighbor down the street just because that person lives in your neighborhood?

⁓

CHAPTER EIGHTEEN

WINDOWS 2000 AND WINDOWS XP

WINDOWS 2000 AND Windows XP continued the evolution of the Windows user interface introduced in Windows 95. They faced the dual challenge of changing the user interface while still maintaining backward compatibility as well as coping with an increasingly hostile software environment. Gone are the days when you could assume that software vendors wouldn't actively abuse their customers.

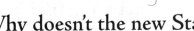

Why doesn't the new Start menu use Intellimenus in the All Programs list?

COMMON REQUEST: "I want to be able to turn on personalized menus (Intellimenus) when in XP Start Menu mode."

Imagine if Intellimenus were enabled with the XP Start menu.

You use five programs; the rest are not used much. (Studies show that five is the typical number of unique applications users run on a regular basis. All the rest are rare.)

Those five programs are on the "most frequently used (MFU) programs" list on the Start menu.

You decide today you want to run some other program, one of those other programs that you run rarely.

You click All Programs.

You can't find the program because it was hidden by Intellimenus because it's a rarely run program. If it were a popular program, it would be on the MFU already!

If you are a naive user, you say, "Hey, who uninstalled all my programs? It's missing from All Programs!" It's kind of a misnomer to call it "All Programs" when in fact it doesn't show all your programs.

If you are an experienced user, you say, "Sigh, why do I have to keep clicking this chevron? The whole reason I'm going to 'All Programs' is that I want to run a program I haven't run in a long time, *duh*. The chevrons should be pre-expanded, save me a click!"

In other words, if we had Intellimenus enabled on All Programs, it would just show you your MFU again, because the MFU and Intellimenus are both showing the same information, just in different ways. That's clearly pointless.

Think of All Programs as a *really big* chevron. The MFU is the collapsed version. All Programs is the expanded version.

Why is there no programmatic access to the Start menu pin list?

WE LEARNED OUR lesson the hard way.

In the earlier, simpler days, Windows was designed in a more open manner. Internal file formats were documented. Programs could manipulate the system in a wide variety of ways. The assumption was that software developers would exercise this power responsibly and for the benefit of the user. After all, if a program abused its customers, it wouldn't have customers for very long. Programs therefore had an incentive to treat the user with respect. That was then.

In Windows 95, we gave programmatic access to the Start menu "Fast items" list, the list of items that appear at the top of the classic Start menu above the Programs list. This area was meant for users to customize with their favorite links, but programs quickly saw an opportunity and added themselves to it every chance they got.

In Internet Explorer, we gave programmatic access to the Favorites menu, and once again, programs took it upon themselves to add an entry to it.

In Windows XP, we intentionally did not give programmatic access to the bold list of items at the top of the Start menu (the "pin list"). The pin list is for users to list their favorite icons. It is not the place for a program to decide unilaterally, "I am so cool. I am your favorite icon. I just know it. So I'll put myself there because, well, I'm so cool."

From our experience with the Fast Items list and the Favorites menu, we knew that the moment we let programs mess with the pin list, they would install themselves into it, and the pin list would become meaningless (and annoying).

What's particularly galling are the programs that, as part of their install, decide that they are so cool they want to be *everywhere* to make sure you don't *miss out* on the *coolest most amazing program ever written in the history of mankind*, so they go into the Start menu, into the Fast items, and onto the desktop. They go into the Quick Launch, onto your Favorites, and take over as your default autoplay handler. They even hang out as an icon next to the clock on the taskbar just in case you somehow missed all those other places. And each time you run them, they go and re-create those icons and settings in case you "accidentally lost them."

I hate those programs.

There are plenty of other examples of things for which there exist no programmatic control out of fear that the power would be used for evil. There is no interface for manipulating the taskbar notification icons of another program, nor is there one for adding or removing a band in the taskbar. Imagine the havoc if programs were allowed to manipulate these highly sensitive components of the user interface.

System policies suffer as a consequence of all these decisions. Each system policy that controls these highly attractive features becomes an attractive target for these unscrupulous programs. Your typical home user does not have a domain. Under this configuration, there is no domain policy to override local machine policy, and therefore a malicious program can abuse the user by setting a local machine policy that promotes their program.

We're sorry it turned out this way, but at least I hope you'll understand what brought us to this state.

⌒

Why does Windows XP Service Pack 2 sometimes forget my CD autoplay settings?

IT DIDN'T FORGET them; it's just double-checking with you.

There were two problems with the way the original version of Windows XP handled CD autoplay.

First, when you installed a new program that included CD autoplay capability, many users didn't know how to select that new program as their default CD autoplay program. If they had previously selected a program and ticked "Always perform this action," there was no easily discoverable way to undo the "always" flag to make the dialog reappear and allow the user to select the new program instead.

Second, many programs, upon installation, secretly hacked the undocumented CD autoplay settings to set themselves as the default CD autoplay handler, gleefully overriding the user's previously stated preference (because these programs egotistically believed themselves to be the coolest most amazing program ever written in the history of mankind).

In other words, the two problems were, "I just installed this program and I want it to be the CD autoplay program," and its converse, "I just installed this program and I *don't* want it to be the CD autoplay program."

Windows XP Service Pack 2 (SP2) introduced new behavior related to CD autoplay in an attempt to address these problems: When it sees that a new CD autoplay handler is available, it shows you the CD autoplay dialog one more time. This gives you a chance to (a) pick that new program you just installed, or (b) unpick that program you just installed (if it was presumptuously rude enough to set itself as your default).

The first time you insert a CD into your computer after upgrading to Windows XP SP2, you will also get the CD autoplay dialog. This is a "better late than never" dialog to cover for any handlers that were installed before you upgraded to Windows XP SP2.

What's the moral of the story? Whereas in the old days you only had to worry about helping other programmers interface with your feature, in the new software landscape you also have to worry about *stopping* programmers who are trying to abuse your interface.

The unsafe device removal dialog

WHAT WAS THE deal with the unsafe device removal dialog in Windows 2000, and why is it gone in Windows XP?

When Windows 2000 showed the unsafe device removal dialog, the device was indeed removed unsafely. If it was a USB storage device, for example, there may have been dirty I/O buffers. If it were a printer, there may have been an active print job. The USB subsystem doesn't know for sure. (Those are concepts at a higher layer that the USB subsystem doesn't know about.) All it knows is that it had an active channel with the device and now the device is gone, so it gets upset and yells at you.

In Windows XP, it still gets upset, but it now keeps its mouth shut. You're now on your honor not to rip out your USB drive while a program still has a file open on the drive, to wait two seconds for all I/O to flush before removing the drive, not to unplug your printer while a job is printing, etc. If you do, your drive gets corrupted or a print job is lost and you're on your own.

The "Safely Remove Hardware" icon is still there, and it still works. All that changed is that Windows XP no longer scolds you when you remove a device unexpectedly. Personally, I recommend using the "Safely Remove Hardware" icon anyway. More than once that icon saved me when I thought I had exited all programs that were using my USB drive, only to have the "Safely Remove Hardware" icon remind me that I had forgotten one of them.

Two brief reminiscences on the Windows XP Comments? button

IN BETA VERSIONS of Windows XP, there was special code in the window manager to give every window a link in the upper-right corner called *Comments?* which if clicked displayed a dialog that allowed you to submit feedback to Microsoft about that window.

Because this was a beta release, there was no anonymity when you submitted feedback. (You signed away your anonymity when you agreed to the special beta license agreement and typed in your beta ID number.) Yet we got more than one feedback submission that began, "Hi, I pirated this copy of Windows XP, and here's some feedback."

In its initial incarnation, the word in the title bar was *Lame*, but people with a weaker sense of humor changed it to the less-confrontational *Comments?* The name *Lame* was a tribute to a recurring sketch on a local comedy show *Almost Live!* called "The Lame List, or What's Weak This Week (brought to you with the help of Seattle's Heavy Metal community)." In this sketch, members of the Seattle band Soundgarden would respond to proposed topics by shouting "Lame!" It was a simple but oddly effectively sketch.

Why does Explorer eject the CD after you finish burning it?

PARTLY AS A convenience, but partly to work around buggy hardware.

Most CD drives cache information about the disc in their internal memory to improve performance. However, some drives have a bug where they fail to update the cache after the CD has been written to. As a result, you can write some data to a CD, then ask the CD drive for the data you just wrote, and it won't be there! The drive is returning the old cached data rather than the new data. For most drives, ejecting and reinserting the CD is enough to force the drive to update its internal cache.

"But wait, it gets worse!" I'm told.

Some drives are "smart" and realize you've reinserted the same media, and then don't update. These drives require that you put in another type of media (or pressed CD-ROM media) to force them to update. These drives were manufactured around 2002, and new drives don't have it *this* bad, but some still have the above problem requiring an eject/insert cycle.

So there's your tip for the day. If you are burning data to a CD and you find the data isn't there, try ejecting the disc and reinserting it. If your drive is particularly buggy, you'll have to eject the disc, insert a *different* disc, and then eject that second disc and reinsert the first one.

Why does Windows setup lay down a new boot sector?

BECAUSE THE ALTERNATIVE is worse.

You would expect that after installing an operating system, the operating system should boot. If your boot sector is damaged—perhaps because this is a brand new hard drive with no boot sector, or because it was infected with a boot sector virus—you expect the operating system's setup program to replace the boot sector with a good one. If it didn't, you'd have an operating system that didn't boot.

Not the greatest introduction to a new operating system.

I know some people are going to suggest, "Why doesn't the setup program ask before overwriting the boot sector?" But think about it. It's Christmas Day, you're installing Windows XP on your computer, you go through the setup process, and it asks you a question you can't answer. "Gosh, the computer says that I have a custom boot sector. It says that this could be for legitimate reasons, or it could be due to a virus. How the heck am I supposed to know the difference?" That's assuming they even read the dialog. A much more realistic scenario is, "Eek! The computer is asking me a scary question! How do I cancel out of this? I hate computers. They're so hard to use."

Yes, this means that if you are an ultradweeb with a custom boot sector, you will lose it when you install Windows. But Windows isn't picking on you. It even destroys itself. If you take a Windows XP machine and install Windows 2000 onto it, the Windows 2000 setup program will lay down a new boot sector that knows how to boot Windows 2000 but doesn't know about Windows XP. You'll have to restore the Windows XP boot files to restore that functionality.

Things are a little better starting with Windows XP SP2 and Windows Server 2003 SP1, though. Those and future versions of Windows setup check the version of the Windows NT boot loader file and will leave a newer version of the boot loader intact rather than overwriting it with an older version.

⌇

Psychic debugging: Why your expensive four-processor machine is ignoring three of its processors

ON ONE OF our internal mailing lists, someone was wondering why his expensive four-processor computer appeared to be using only one of its processors. From Task Manager's Performance tab, the chart showed that the first processor was doing all the work and the other three processors were sitting idle. Using Task Manager to set each process's processor affinity to use all four processors made the computer run much faster, of course. What happened that messed up all the processor affinities?

At this point, I invoked my psychic powers. Perhaps you can, too.

First hint: My psychic powers successfully predicted that Explorer also had its processor affinity set to use only the first processor.

Second hint: Processor affinity is inherited by child processes.

Here was my psychic prediction:

"My psychic powers tell me that

+ Explorer has had its thread affinity set to one processor ...

+ because you previewed an MPG file ...

+ whose decoder calls `SetProcessAffinityMask` in its
  `DLL_PROCESS_ATTACH` ...

+ because the authors of the decoder couldn't fix their multiprocessor
  bugs ...

+ and therefore locked the process's thread affinity to a single processor
  in order to 'fix' the bugs."

Although my first psychic prediction was correct, the others were wide of the mark, although they were on the right track and successfully guided further investigation to uncover the culprit.

The real problem was that there was a third-party shell extension whose authors presumably weren't able to fix their multiprocessor bugs, so they decided to mask them by calling the `SetProcessAffinityMask` function to lock the current process (Explorer) to a single processor. Woo-hoo, we fixed all our multiprocessor bugs at one fell swoop! Let's all go out and celebrate!

Because processor affinity is inherited, every program launched by Explorer winds up using only one of the four available processors. One bad shell extension can ruin your whole day.

(Yes, the vendor of the offending shell extension has been contacted, and they claim that the problem has been fixed in more recent versions of the software.)

Psychic debugging: Why your CPU usage is hovering at 50%

SOMETIMES PSYCHIC DEBUGGING consists merely of seeing the bigger picture.

On one of our internal bug-reporting mailing lists, someone asked, "How come when I do XYZ, my CPU usage goes to 50%?"

My psychic answer: "Because you have two processors."

The response was genuine surprise and amazement. How did I know they had two processors? Simple: If they had only one processor, the CPU usage would be 100%. This seems unhelpful on its face, but it actually does help diagnose the problem, because now they can search the bug database for bugs in the XYZ feature tagged "100% CPU" to see whether any of those apply to their situation. (And in this case, it turns out that one did.)

⁓

What's the deal with the DS_SHELLFONT flag?

IT INDICATES THAT you want the Windows 2000 default shell font. But that doesn't mean that you're going to get it.

To indicate that you would like the "Windows 2000" look for your dialog, you have to do three things and hope for a fourth:

- Use a DIALOGEX template rather than a DIALOG template.
- Set the DS_SHELLFONT flag in your dialog styles.
- Set the dialog font to MS Shell Dlg.
- Hope that you're running on Windows 2000 or later on a system that has the new Windows 2000 dialog font enabled.

If all four conditions are satisfied, your dialog gets the Windows 2000 look.

If any condition fails, you get the "classic" dialog font. Note that the fourth condition is not within your program's control. Consequently, you have to make sure your dialog looks good in *both* the classic dialog font and the new one.

For property sheet pages, things are more complicated.

It would be visually jarring for there to be a mix of fonts on a property sheet. You wouldn't want the Advanced button to be in MS Sans Serif but the Apply button in Tahoma. To avoid this problem, the property sheet manager looks at all the pages in the property sheet. If they are all using the Windows 2000 look, the property sheet uses the Windows 2000 look, too. But if there is even a single page that does not use the Windows 2000 look, the property sheet reverts to the classic look *and converts all the Windows 2000-look pages to classic look.*

In this way, all the pages in the property sheet have the classic look instead of having a mishmash of some pages with the classic look and some with the Windows 2000 look.

That's why you will occasionally find that a shell property sheet has reverted to the classic look. Some shell extension infected the property sheet with a page that does not have the Windows 2000 look, and for the sake of visual consistency, the property sheet manager set all the pages on the property sheet to classic look.

This is another reason it is important that you test your property sheet pages both with the Windows 2000 look and the classic look. If your property sheet page ends up sharing a property sheet with a non-Windows 2000-look page, your page is going to be reverted to classic look.

🌊

Why does DS_SHELLFONT = DS_FIXEDSYS | DS_SETFONT?

You MIGHT HAVE noticed that the numeric value of the DS_SHELLFONT flag is equal to DS_FIXEDSYS | DS_SETFONT.

```
#define DS_SETFONT      0x40L
#define DS_FIXEDSYS     0x0008L
#define DS_SHELLFONT    (DS_SETFONT | DS_FIXEDSYS)
```

Surely that isn't a coincidence.

The value of the DS_SHELLFONT flag was chosen so that older operating systems (Windows 95, Windows 98, Windows NT 4) would accept the flag while nevertheless ignoring it. This allowed people to write a single program that got the Windows 2000 look when running on Windows 2000 and got the classic look when running on older systems. (If you make people have to write two versions of their program, one that runs on all systems and one that runs only on the newer system and looks slightly cooler, they will usually not bother writing the second one.)

The DS_FIXEDSYS flag met these conditions. Older systems accepted the flag because it was indeed a valid flag, but they also ignored it because the DS_SETFONT flag takes precedence.

This is one of those backward compatibility exercises: How do you design something so that it is possible to write one program that gets the new features on new systems while at the same time degrading gracefully on old systems?

What other effects does DS_SHELLFONT have on property sheet pages?

When you invent a new flag, you can start using it to fix errors of the past without breaking backward compatibility.

One of the errors of the past was that property sheet page dimensions were taken relative to the MS Sans Serif font, even if the page used some other font.

```
DLG_SAMPLE DIALOGEX 32, 32, 212, 188
CAPTION "Caption"
FONT "Lucida Sans Unicode"
...
```

This sample dialog template says that it is 212 dialog units (DLUs) wide and 188 DLUs tall. If the dialog template were used for a standalone dialog, those DLU values would be calculated relative to the font on the dialog, namely Lucida Sans Unicode.

However, if the dialog template were used for a property sheet page, earlier versions of Windows would interpret the values 212 and 188 relative to the font of the *property sheet frame* (usually MS Sans Serif), not relative to the font associated with the page itself. Many people worked around this problem by giving their pages pre-adjusted sizes, so that when Windows measured the dialog against MS Sans Serif, the adjustments cancelled out.

In other words, suppose that Lucida Sans Unicode is 25% wider than MS Sans Serif. (I'm just making up numbers.) Then to get a 212-DLU-wide dialog relative to Lucida Sans Unicode, the dialog template would specify a width of 212 DLU + 25% = 265 DLU.

Because people were now relying on this behavior, it couldn't be changed. If you went in and "fixed" it, all those pre-adjusted dialogs would now come out at the wrong size.

Ah, but now there is a new flag, DS_SHELLFONT. Starting in Windows 2000, if you specify the DS_SHELLFONT dialog style for your DIALOGEX dialog template, the dialog dimensions are taken relative to the font you specified in your template (which is probably what you wanted) rather than relative to the property sheet frame font. If you leave off the flag (as older programs will), the property sheet measurement code remains bug-for-bug compatible with previous versions.

〜

CHAPTER NINETEEN

WIN32 DESIGN ISSUES

By now you've probably gotten a feel for some of the types of decisions that went into the design of Win32. Making it easier to port a program from 16-bit Windows to 32-bit Windows, for example, was a major motivator in the early days. Here, we dig a little deeper into the philosophy of Win32, starting with how Win32 was shaped by lessons learned from 16-bit Windows.

Why does Win32 fail a module load if an import could not be resolved?

BECAUSE WE TRIED it the other way and it was much worse.

In 16-bit Windows, a module that didn't satisfy all its imports would still load. So long as you didn't call a missing import, you were fine. If you did try to call a missing import, you crashed pretty spectacularly with the dreaded Unrecoverable Application Error dialog.

The Win32 folks decided that this was a bad design, because often people would take Fred Application, designed for Windows 3.1, and run it on Windows 3.0, and it would run great for about an hour, at which point Fred Application would call a function that was available only in Windows 3.1 (such as, say, `GetSaveFileName`) and crash as a result.

The Win32 folks decided that if an import could not be resolved, the program should fail loading. If the makers of Fred Application wanted to run on Windows 3.0 after all, they could indicate this by using `GetProcAddress` explicitly. Because if you have to call `GetProcAddress` explicitly, it'll probably occur to you to check the return value.

This issue comes up occasionally when people wish out loud, "Gosh, there should be a way I could mark an import as 'optional.' If an optional import can't be resolved, the load should not fail. It would be the program's responsibility to verify that the bind succeeded before calling it." These people are unwittingly asking for history to repeat itself.

Note that Microsoft's Visual C linker does provide functionality called "delay-load" that allows you to return to something similar to the 16-bit Windows behavior regarding missing imports. References to functions in a dynamic-link library that has been marked for delay-loading are not resolved until the first time each function is called. If the function does not exist, an exception is raised (although you can override this behavior).

🙠

Why are structure sizes checked strictly?

YOU MIGHT HAVE noticed that Windows as a general rule checks structure sizes strictly. For example, consider the MENUITEMINFO structure:

```
typedef struct tagMENUITEMINFO {
    UINT     cbSize;
    UINT     fMask;
    UINT     fType;
    UINT     fState;
    UINT     wID;
    HMENU    hSubMenu;
    HBITMAP  hbmpChecked;
    HBITMAP  hbmpUnchecked;
    ULONG_PTR dwItemData;
    LPTSTR   dwTypeData;
```

```
    UINT    cch;
#if(WINVER > = 0x0500)
    HBITMAP hbmpItem; // available only on Windows 2000 and higher
#endif
} MENUITEMINFO, *LPMENUITEMINFO;
```

Notice that the size of this structure changes depending on whether WINVER >= 0x0500 (that is, whether you are targeting Windows 2000 or later). If you take the Windows 2000 version of this structure and pass it to Windows NT 4, the call will fail because the sizes don't match.

"But the old version of the operating system should accept any size that is greater than or equal to the size it expects. A larger value means that the structure came from a newer version of the program, and it should just ignore the parts it doesn't understand."

We tried that. It didn't work.

Consider the following imaginary-sized structure and a function that consumes it. This will be used as the guinea pig for the discussion to follow:

```
typedef struct tagIMAGINARY {
  UINT cbSize;
  BOOL fDance;
  BOOL fSing;
#if IMAGINARY_VERSION > = 2
  // v2 added new features
  IServiceProvider *psp; // where to get more info
#endif
} IMAGINARY;

// perform the actions you specify
STDAPI DoImaginaryThing(const IMAGINARY *pimg);

// query what things are currently happening
STDAPI GetImaginaryThing(IMAGINARY *pimg);
```

First, we found lots of programs that simply forgot to initialize the cbSize member altogether:

```
IMAGINARY img;
img.fDance = TRUE;
img.fSing = FALSE;
DoImaginaryThing(&img);
```

They got stack garbage as their size. The stack garbage happened to be a large number, so it passed the "greater than or equal to the expected cbSize" test and the code worked. Then the next version of the header file expanded the structure, using the cbSize to detect whether the caller is using the old or new style. Now, the stack garbage is still greater than or equal to the new cbSize, so version 2 of DoImaginaryThing says, "Oh cool, this is somebody who wants to provide additional information via the IServiceProvider field." Except of course that there is no psp member in the structure that the program allocated. Version 2 of DoImaginaryThing ends up reading from whatever memory happens to follow the version 1 IMAGINARY structure, which is highly unlikely to be a pointer to an IServiceProvider interface. The most likely result is a crash when version 2 tries to call the IServiceProvider::QueryService method on an invalid pointer.

Now consider this related scenario:

```
IMAGINARY img;
GetImaginaryThing(&img);
```

The next version of the header file expanded the structure, and the stack garbage happened to be a large number, so it passed the "greater than or equal to the expected cbSize" test, so it returned not just the fDance and fSing flags, but also returned a psp. Oops, but the caller was compiled with version 1, so its structure doesn't have a psp member. The psp gets written past the end of the structure, corrupting whatever came after it in memory. Ah, so now we have one of those dreaded buffer overflow bugs.

Even if you were lucky and the memory that came afterward was safe to corrupt, you still have a bug: By the rules of COM reference counts, when a function returns an interface pointer, it is the caller's responsibility to release the pointer when no longer needed. But the caller that was compiled with version 1 of the header file doesn't know about this psp member, so it certainly doesn't know that it needs to be Release()d. So now, in addition to memory corruption (as if that wasn't bad enough), you also have a memory leak.

Wait, I'm not done yet. Now let's see what happens when a program written in the future runs on an older system.

Suppose somebody is writing a program intending it to be run on version 2. The program sets the cbSize to the larger version 2 structure size and sets the psp member to a service provider that performs security checks before allowing any singing or dancing to take place (for example, makes sure everybody paid the entrance fee). Now somebody takes this program and runs it on version 1. The new version 2 structure size passes the "greater than or equal to the version 1 structure size" test, so version 1 will accept the structure and Do the Imaginary Thing. Except that version 1 didn't support the psp field, so your service provider never gets called and your security module is bypassed. Now everybody is coming into your club without paying.

Now, you might say, "Well those are just buggy programs. They deserve to lose." You might be able to argue this for the first case of a caller who failed to initialize the cbSize member, but what of the caller who is expecting version 2 but gets version 1 instead? If you stand by that argument, prepare to take the heat when you read magazine articles like "Microsoft intentionally designed ‹Product X› to be incompatible with ‹software from a major competitor›. Where is the Justice Department when you need them?"

Why do I have to return this goofy value for WM_DEVICECHANGE?

To DENY a device removal query, you must return the special value BROADCAST_QUERY_DENY, which has the curious value 0x424D5144. What's the story behind that?

Well, we first tried following the pattern set by WM_QUERYENDSESSION, where returning TRUE allows the operation to proceed and returning FALSE causes the operation to fail. But when we did this, we found that lots of programs were denying all Plug and Play removal requests—programs that were written for Windows 3.1 which didn't have Plug and Play! How could this be?

These programs decided, "Well, I have the Windows 3.1 documentation right here in front of me and I looked at all the messages. The ones I care about, I handled, and for all the others, I will just return zero instead of calling `DefWindowProc`." And they managed to get this to work in Windows 3.1 because they read the SDK carefully and found the five or six messages that require a nonzero return value and made sure to return that nonzero value. The rest got zero.

And then when we added a new message that required a nonzero return value (which `DefWindowProc` provided), these programs continued to return zero and caused all device removal queries to fail.

So we had to change the "cancel" return value to something that wasn't zero. To play it extra safe, we also made the "cancel" return value something other than 1, because we suspected that there would be lots of programs who were just returning TRUE to all messages and we didn't want to have to rewrite the specification another time.

That's why the special return value is `0x424D5144`: It's a value that nobody is likely to be returning by mistake. (And if you know your ASCII character codes, you recognize it as the letters BMQD, which stand for "broadcast message query deny.")

The arms race between programs and users

THERE IS A constant struggle between people who write programs and the people who actually use them. For example, you often see questions such as, "How do I make my program so the user can't kill it?"

Now, imagine if there were a way to do this. Ask yourself, "What would the world be like if this were possible?"

Well, then there would be some program, say, xyz.exe, that is unkillable. Now suppose you're the user. There's this program xyz.exe that has gone haywire, so you want to exit it. But it won't let you exit. So you try to kill it, but you can't kill it, either.

This is just one of several arms races that you can imagine.

"I don't want anybody to kill my process" versus "How do I kill this runaway process?"

- "I want to shove this critical dialog in the user's face" versus "How do I stop programs from stealing focus?"
- "I don't want anybody to delete this file" versus "How do I delete this file that refuses to be deleted?"
- "How do I prevent this program from showing up in Task Manager?" versus "How can I see all the programs that are running on my computer?"

Eventually you have to decide which side wins, and Windows has decided to keep users in control of their own programs and data, keep administrators in control of their own computer, and keep network administrators in control of all computers on the network. Thus, users can kill any process they want (given sufficient privileges), they can stop any program from stealing focus, and they can delete any file they want (again, given sufficient privileges).

Programs can try to make themselves more difficult to kill (deny PROCESS_TERMINATE access, deny PROCESS_CREATE_THREAD access so that people can't CreateRemoteThread(EndProcess), deny PROCESS_VM_WRITE so that people can't scribble into your stack and make you double fault, deny PROCESS_SUSPEND_RESUME so that they can't suspend you), but eventually you just can't stop them from, say, elevating to Debug privilege, debugging your process, and jumping to ExitProcess.

Notice that you can kill CSRSS.EXE and WINLOGON.EXE if you like. Your computer will get very angry at you, but you can do it. (Save your work first!)

Another useful question to ask yourself: "What's to prevent a virus from doing the same thing?" If there were a way to do these things, then a virus could take advantage of them and make itself invisible to Task Manager, undeletable, and unkillable. Clearly you don't want that, do you?

⁓

Why can't you trap TerminateProcess?

IF A USER fires up Task Manager and clicks the End Task button on the Applications tab, Windows first tries to shut down your program nicely, by sending WM_CLOSE messages to GUI programs and CTRL_CLOSE_EVENT events to console programs. But you don't get a chance to intercept TerminateProcess. Why not?

TerminateProcess is the low-level process-killing function. It bypasses DLL_PROCESS_DETACH and anything else in the process. When you kill with TerminateProcess, no more user-mode code will run in that process. It's gone. Do not pass go. Do not collect $200.

If you could intercept TerminateProcess, you would be escalating the arms race between programs and users. Suppose you could intercept it. Well, then if you wanted to make your program unkillable, you would just hand in your TerminateProcess handler! And then people would ask for "a way to kill a process that is refusing to be killed with TerminateProcess," and we'd be back to where we started.

⁓

Why do some processes stay in Task Manager after they've been killed?

WHEN A PROCESS ends (either of natural causes or because of something harsher like TerminateProcess), the user-mode part of the process is thrown away. But the kernel-mode part can't go away until all drivers are finished with the thread, too.

For example, if a thread was in the middle of an I/O operation, the kernel signals to the driver responsible for the I/O that the operation should be cancelled. If the driver is well-behaved, it cleans up the bookkeeping for the incomplete I/O and releases the thread.

If the driver is not as well behaved (or if the hardware that the driver is managing is behaving strangely), it may take a long time for the driver to clean up the incomplete I/O. During that time, the driver holds that thread (and therefore the process that the thread belongs to) hostage. This is a simplification of what actually goes on, but it's close enough for the purpose of this discussion.

Note to kernel-mode debugging nerds: If you think your problem is a wedged driver, you can drop into the kernel debugger, find the process that is stuck, and look at its threads to see why they aren't exiting. You can use the !irp debugger command to view any pending IRPs (I/O request packets) to see what device is not completing.

After all the drivers have acknowledged the death of the process, the meat of the process finally goes away. All that remains is the process object, which lingers until all handles to the process and all the threads in the process have been closed. (You did remember to CloseHandle the handles returned in the PROCESS_INFORMATION structure that you passed to the CreateProcess function, didn't you?)

In other words, if a process hangs around after you've terminated it, it's really dead, but its corpse will remain in the system until all drivers have cleaned up their process bookkeeping, and all open handles to the process have been closed.

Understanding the consequences of WAIT_ABANDONED

ONE OF THE important distinctions between mutexes and the other synchronization objects is that mutexes have owners. If the thread that owns a mutex exits without releasing the mutex, the mutex is automatically released on the thread's behalf.

But if this happens, you're in big trouble.

One thing many people gloss over is the WAIT_ABANDONED return value from the synchronization functions such as WaitForSingleObject. They typically treat this as a successful wait, because it does mean that the object was obtained, but it also tells you that the previous owner left the mutex abandoned and that the system had to release it on the owner's behalf.

Why are you in big trouble when this happens?

Presumably, you created that mutex to protect multiple threads from accessing a shared object while it is an unstable state. Code enters the mutex, then starts manipulating the object, temporarily making it unstable, but eventually restabilizes it, and then releases the mutex so that other threads can access the object.

For example, you might have code that manages an anchored doubly linked list in shared memory that goes like this:

```
void MyClass::ReverseList()
{
 WaitForSingleObject(hMutex, INFINITE);
 int i = 0; // anchor
 do {
  int next = m_items[i].m_next;
  m_items[i].m_next = m_items[i].m_prev;
  m_items[i].m_prev = next;
  i = next;
 } while (i != 0);
 ReleaseMutex(hMutex);
}
```

There is nothing particularly exciting going on. Basic stuff, right?

But what if the program crashes while holding the mutex? (If you believe that your programs are bug-free, consider the possibility that the program is running over the network and the network goes down, leading to an in-page exception. Or simply that the user went to Task Manager and terminated your program while this function is running.)

In that case, the mutex is automatically released by the operating system, leaving the linked list in a corrupted state. The next program to claim the mutex will receive WAIT_ABANDONED as the status code. If you ignore that status code, you end up operating on a corrupted linked list. Depending on how that linked list is used, it might result in a resource leak or the system creating an unintended second copy of something, or perhaps even a crash. The unfortunate demise of one program causes other programs to start behaving strangely.

Then again, the question remains, "What do you do, then, if you get WAIT_ABANDONED?" The answer is, "Good question."

You might try to repair the corruption, if you keep enough auxiliary information around to recover a consistent state. You might even design your data structures to be transactional, so that the death of a thread manipulating the data structures does not leave them in a corrupted state. Or you might just decide that because things are corrupted, you should throw away everything and start over, losing the state of work in progress, but at least allowing new work to proceed unhindered. (Although in this case, you probably should let the user know that there was loss of data.)

Or you might just choose to ignore the error and continue onward with a corrupt data structure, hoping that whatever went wrong won't result in cascade failures down the line. This is what most people do, although usually without even being aware that they're doing it. And it's really hard to debug the crashes that result from this approach.

Exercise: Why did we use subscripts instead of pointers in our linked list data structure?

Answer: Because the data structure resides in shared memory, it can have a different virtual address in different processes; therefore, simple pointers cannot be used because the address of a particular element varies depending on which process is looking at it. Therefore, some sort of relative addressing is necessary, and subscripts are one way of implementing said relative addressing.

⋑

Why can't I put hyperlinks in notification icon balloon tips?

THE SHORT ANSWER: because there is no NIF_PARSELINKS flag.

The long answer:

When balloon tips were first developed, there was no support for links. Consequently, programs were free to put insecure text in balloon tips, because there was no risk that they would become "live." So, for example, a virus scanner might say, "The document 'XYZ' has been scanned and found to be free of viruses."

Now suppose hyperlinks were supported in balloon tips. Look at how this can be exploited: I can write a Web page that goes

```
<TITLE>&lt;A HREF="file:C:\Windows\system32\format.com?C:"&gt;
Party plans&lt;/A&gt;</TITLE>
```

I then rename the file to `Party plans.html`, attach it to some email, and send it to you.

You download the message and because you are a cautious person, you ask your virus scanner to check it out. The balloon appears:

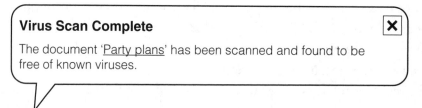

"Oh, how convenient," you say to yourself. "The virus scanner even included a hyperlink to the document so I can read it."

And then you click on it and your hard drive gets reformatted.

"So why don't you add an `NIF_PARSELINKS` flag, so people who want to enable hyperlinks in their balloon tips can do so, and still remain compatible with people who wrote to the old API?" (I've heard of one person trying to pass a `TTF_PARSELINKS` flag in the `NOTIFYICONDATA.uFlags` member. I hope it's obvious to everybody why this had no chance of working.)

Because that would just be passing the buck. Anybody who used this proposed flag would then have to be extra careful not to put untrusted links in the balloon tips. Most people would just say, "Wow! A new flag! That's awesome!" and start using it without considering the serious security implications. Then somebody can trick the program into putting untrusted text into a balloon tip and thereby exploit the security hole.

"Aw, come on, who would be so stupid as to write code without considering all the security implications?"

I hope that was a joke question.

The best way to make sure things are secure is to make it impossible to be insecure.

⤢

Why can't I use the same tree item multiple times?

IT'S THE CONTINUING balance between ease of use and generality.

At a literal level, you can't use the same tree items in multiple places in the tree, because then various properties would become ambiguous, properties like TVGN_PARENT or TVIS_EXPANDED. (If a tree item could be in two places, it would have two parents, for example.)

Of course, this problem could have been solved by separating the item content from the item presence. So instead of just having an HTREEITEM, there would be, say, HTREENODE and HTREENODECONTENTS. The node would represent a physical location in the tree, and the item contents would represent the contents of that node: its name, icon, and so on.

Sure, that could have been done, but remember the balance. You're making the common case hard in order to benefit the rare case. Now everybody who is manipulating tree views has to worry about twice as many objects. (What used to be one item is now a node plus contents.) This is generally not the balance you want to strike when designing an interface.

When you design an interface, you want to make the common case easier than the rare case.

A program that wants this separation can, of course, do the separation manually. Put all the contents in a separate sharable structure and have your HTREEITEMs refer to that shared structure in their lParams. This is more work for the program, but now the cost is being shouldered by the one who wants the extra functionality.

⤢

The kooky STRRET structure

IF YOU'VE DEALT with the shell namespace, you've no doubt run across the kooky STRRET structure, which is used by the IShellFolder::GetDisplayNameOf method to return names of shell items. If you read its documentation, you'll see that a STRRET is sometimes an ANSI string buffer, sometimes a pointer to a Unicode string, sometimes (and this is the kookiest bit) an offset into a shell data structure called an item ID list. What is going on here?

The STRRET structure burst onto the scene during the Windows 95 era. Computers during this time were still comparatively slow and memory constrained. (Windows 95's minimum hardware requirements were for 4MB of memory and a 386DX processor, which ran at a whopping 25MHz.) It was much faster to allocate memory off the stack (a simple sub instruction) than to allocate it from the heap (which might take *thousands* of instructions!), so the STRRET structure was designed so the common (for Windows 95) scenarios could be satisfied without needing a heap allocation.

The STRRET_OFFSET flag took this to an even greater extreme. Often, you kept the name inside the pidl, and copying it into the STRRET structure would take, gosh, 200 clocks! To avoid this wasteful memory copying, STRRET_OFFSET allowed you to return just an offset into the pidl, which the caller could then copy out of directly.

Woo-hoo, you saved a string copy.

Of course, as time passed and computers got faster and memory became more readily available, these micro-optimizations have turned into annoyances. Saving 200 clock cycles on a string copy operation is hardly worth it any more. On a 1GHz processor, a single soft page fault costs you more than a million cycles; a hard page fault costs you tens of millions.

You can copy a lot of strings in twenty million cycles.

What's more, the scenarios that were common in Windows 95 aren't quite so common any more, so the original scenario that the optimization was tailored for hardly occurs any more. It's an optimization that has outlived its usefulness.

Fortunately, you don't have to think about the STRRET structure any more. Several helper functions such as StrRetToBSTR and StrRetToStr take the STRRET structure and turn it into something much easier to manipulate.

The kookiness of the STRRET structure has now been encapsulated away. Thank goodness.

Why can't you set UTF-8 as your ANSI code page?

AFTER ALL, IF you could set your ANSI code page to UTF-8, the program could call the A versions of all the Win32 functions and avoid all the UTF-8 to UTF-16 conversions that would have to be done to call the W version. All the benefit of Unicode without the hassle of having to rewrite.

There are a few reasons why this is not practical, pointed out to me by my colleague Michael Grier.

First, some programs expect to get locale information from code pages. You might roll your eyes at the thought of it, but it's something people do. "Oh, your default code page is 949? You must be in Korea." Or even stranger, "What is the name of the second month of the year in code page 950?" But UTF-8 doesn't carry any locale information, because it's not associated with any culture or part of the world.

The second point, however, is much worse. There's a boatload of code out there that assumes that the maximum length of a character encoding is two bytes. In other words, they support SBCS (single byte character sets), DBCS (double byte character sets), but not a generalized MBCS (multi-byte character set). If the GetCPInfo function ever returned a CPINFO.MaxCharSize greater than two, the programs would keel over. For UTF-8, CPINFO.MaxCharSize is a whopping four.

Sometimes this dependency on a maximum of two bytes per character is subtle. For example, suppose you're writing your own Read-type function that reads characters from stdin and converts them to Unicode. The basic algorithm is to read bytes from stdin and produce Unicode characters as they are complete. At the end of the buffer, there may be some bytes that do not fully encode a character; you just push those bytes back into the input stream via ungetch so that they can be processed later. Eventually, the trail bytes for that partial character show up, and you successfully read the bytes for that (now complete) character out of stdin, convert that character to Unicode, and continue on your way.

But this algorithm fails on UTF-8, because a single UTF-8 character can be as large as four bytes, requiring up to 4 – 1 = 3 bytes of pushback. Too bad ungetch provides only one pushback character.

What's more, when you have a three- or four-byte character, the first character is obviously a lead byte, and the last character isn't, but what about the middle characters? Very few programs are prepared for the existence of these "middle bytes." Consider, for example, the trick of identifying character boundaries by looking for runs of lead bytes and placing boundaries depending on whether the run length is even or odd. That would fall apart when faced with a three-byte UTF-8 character.

Which is all too bad because making the ANSI code page UTF-8 would certainly have made many things simpler. But you can't always get what you want.

⮑

When should you use a sunken client area?

THE WS_EX_CLIENTEDGE EXTENDED window style allows you to create a window whose client area is "sunken." When should you use this style?

The section "Design of Visual Elements," in *Guidelines for User Interface Developers and Designers* (http://msdn.microsoft.com/library/default.asp?url=/library/en-us/dnwue/html/ch14c.asp), says that the sunken border should be used "to define the work area within a window."

Specifically, what this means is that a sunken client area indicates that the window is a "container." So, for example, the Explorer contents pane gets a sunken client area because a folder "contains" its elements. Users expect to be able to manipulate the items inside a container. By contrast, a dialog box is not a container, so it doesn't get a sunken client area.

Why is there no all-encompassing superset version of Windows?

WHY IS THERE no single version of Windows that contains everything? Instead, as you move up the ladder, say, from Windows XP Professional to Windows Server 2003, you gain server features and lose workstation features. Why lose features when you add others?

Because it turns out no actual customers want to keep the workstation features on their servers. Only developers want to have this "all-encompassing" version of Windows, and making it available to them would result in developers testing their programs on a version of Windows no actual customer owns.

I think one of my colleagues who works in security support explained it best: "When customers ask why their server has Internet Explorer, NetMeeting, Media Player, Games, Instant Messenger, and so forth installed by default, it's hard for the support folks to come up with a good answer. Many customers view each additional installed component as additional risk, and want their servers to have the least possible amount of stuff installed."

If you're the CIO of a bank, the thought that your servers are ready to play Quake must give you the heebie-jeebies.

Why is it even possible to disable the desktop, anyway?

THIS IS SIMPLY an artifact of the history of the philosophy of the Windows operating system design.

Back in the old days, memory was tight, hard drives were luxuries, the most popular CPU for the IBM PC didn't have memory protection, and software development was reserved for the rarefied elite who could afford to drop a few thousand dollars on the Windows Software Development Kit. This had several consequences:

- Tight memory means that anything optional had to be left behind.
- Software developers were trusted not to be stupid.
- Software developers were trusted not to be malicious.
- Software developers were trusted to do the right thing.

Certainly there could have been a check in all the places where windows can be disabled to reject attempts to disable the desktop window, but that would have made one window "more special" than others, undermining the "simplicity" of the window manager. Anything optional had to be left behind.

Software developers were trusted not to make the sort of stupid mistakes that led to the desktop being disabled. If such a serious mistake were to creep in, certainly their testing department would have caught it before the program was released. Software development was hard because *nobody said this was going to be easy.*

Software developers were trusted to treat their customers with respect. Because, after all, software developers who abuse their customers won't have customers for very long. If a program put itself in the Startup group, it was doing so not for selfish reasons but rather because the customer actually wanted it.

The window manager was left fairly exposed, granting software developers the power to do things such as install hooks, subclass windows that were owned by other processes, and manipulate the contents of the Startup group, with the assumption that software developers would use the power for good, not for evil. Don't bother stopping a program from disabling the desktop window, because maybe that program is doing it for a good reason that we hadn't thought of. Similarly, don't stop a program from disabling the focus window or even setting focus to NULL, because we're trusting that the program is doing this for a good reason we hadn't anticipated.

The world of software has changed much since those simpler days.

What are the window and menu nesting limits?

IN THE OLD days, Windows didn't bother enforcing a nesting limit because, well, if you wanted to nest windows 200 deep, that was your decision. (In the same way that if you wanted to disable the desktop, well, that was your decision, too.) Many window operations are recursive, but because everything happened on the application's stack, it was your own responsibility to make your stack big enough so that it didn't overflow.

But Windows NT moved the window manager off the application stack (first into a separate process, then into kernel mode). So now the window manager needs to watch out for stack overflow attacks from people creating too many nested windows.

The window nesting limit was set to 100 for the early days of Windows NT. For Windows XP, it dropped to 50 because increased stack usage in some internal functions caused the stack to overflow at around 75. Dropping to 50 created some breathing room.

The menu nesting limit is 25 on Windows XP. This limit, like the window nesting limit, is subject to change at any time. (As with window nesting, Windows 95 let you go ahead and nest menus all you wanted. In fact, you could go really evil and create an infinite loop of menus. You crashed pretty quickly thereafter, of course.)

What's the difference between HWND_TOP and HWND_TOPMOST?

THE SPECIAL VALUES HWND_TOP and HWND_TOPMOST have similar names but do completely different things when passed as the hWndInsertAfter parameter to the DeferWindowPos function (or its moral equivalents such as SetWindowPos).

As a backgrounder, you should start off by reading the MSDN Documentation for the `DeferWindowPos` function, which is perfectly accurate as far as it goes. Here, I discuss the issue from a historical perspective in the hopes that looking at it from a different direction might improve understanding.

Sibling windows are maintained in an order called the Z-order. (For the purpose of this discussion, top-level windows are also treated as siblings. In fact, it is the Z-order of top-level windows that most people think of when they say "Z-order.")

The Z-order should be visualized as a vertical stack, with windows "above" or "below" siblings.

Before Windows 3.0, the behavior was simple: `HWND_TOP` brings the window to the top of the Z-order.

Windows 3.0 added the concept of "topmost" windows. These are top-level windows that always remain "above" non-topmost windows. To make a window topmost, call `DeferWindowPos` (or one of its moral equivalents) with `HWND_TOPMOST` as the `hWndInsertAfter`. To make a window non-topmost, use `HWND_NOTOPMOST`.

As a result of the introduction of "topmost" windows, `HWND_TOP` now brings the window "as high in the Z-order as possible without violating the rule that topmost windows always appear above non-topmost windows." What does this mean in practice?

- If a window is topmost, `HWND_TOP` puts it at the very top of the Z-order.

- If a window is not topmost, `HWND_TOP` puts it at the top of all non-topmost windows (that is, just below the lowest topmost window, if any).

Owner and owned windows add a layer of complication to the discussion, but the underlying principle is still valid: Topmost windows always appear over non-topmost windows, and `HWND_TOP` puts you as high as you can go in the Z-order without violating that principle.

CHAPTER TWENTY

TAXES

A T THE 2005 Professional Developer Conference, the Tablet PC team had a tough task ahead of them: They had to get people to care about power management.

The reason why this is tough is that power management is rarely a deal-maker. If a user is evaluating, say, personal finance software, how much weight are they going to place on which program consumes less battery power? That's probably a third- or fourth-level tiebreaker. No amount of power management is going to overcome the fact that your program's interface is harder to use than your competitor's. Nobody ever said, "Oh, yeah, I switched my word processor from X to Y because X was chewing too much battery power." When a battery doesn't last very long, users tend to blame the battery, not the software that is draining it.

Power management falls into a category some development teams call "taxes." It's something you do, not because it actually benefits you specifically, but because it benefits the software landscape as a whole. We'll spend this chapter looking at a variety of software taxes and how you should go about paying them.

Of course, not all development teams in the world are so diligent as to pay all their taxes. I suspect most cheat on their taxes, and some of them just don't pay any at all. Are you a tax cheat?

⁓

Hierarchical Storage Management

THE SHORT DESCRIPTION of Hierarchical Storage Management is that it is a way of archiving data transparently. When a file is due for archival, it is transferred to a slower (but less expensive) storage medium, such as magnetic tape, leaving a stub behind. The stub retains some of the file's original metadata, such as last-modified time and file size, but none of the original file's contents are recorded by the stub. If a program tries to read from or write to the stub, the original file is "recalled" from tape backup, a process that can take minutes.

Programmatically, you can detect that you stumbled across one of these stubs by checking for the FILE_ATTRIBUTE_OFFLINE file attribute. (Note that this is not the same as Offline Files.) We already saw that Explorer indicates such files with a black clock. The command prompt indicates such files by putting the file size in parentheses. If your program encounters a file with this attribute, it should not read from or write to the file unless the user explicitly asked it to do so. Examples of operations that should be suppressed for an offline file in the absence of explicit user action include the following:

* Auto-preview
* Content indexing
* Searching
* Scanning for viruses
* Extracting data from file content

For example, a context menu handler should not read from an offline file just to see which context menu options to offer. Right-clicking a file is not a strong enough reason to recall it from tape. Note that merely opening the file doesn't recall the file. The recall happens when you access data that has been archived to tape; for example, by reading the file contents or accessing alternate data streams. (There is also the strange flag FILE_FLAG_OPEN_NO_RECALL, which indicates that the file should not be recalled, even if you access offline data. When you access the offline data, the file data are retrieved from tape but the stub remains a stub and the data remain on tape.)

Failing to respect the FILE_ATTRIBUTE_OFFLINE file attribute when performing a search would result in all files accessed during the search being recalled from tape. If left unchecked, this will eventually recall every single file on the system, completely negating the act of archiving the files to tape in the first place!

Geopolitics

WE'VE ALREADY SEEN that the Windows time zone and regional settings dialogs created international unrest. When Internet-based maps burst onto the scene in 2005, companies rediscovered the minefield known as international mapmaking. Those new to the business failed to recognize extremely sensitive issues such as the name of the body of water that lies between Korea and Japan or how to label the island of Taiwan. Like many issues regarding naming, these subjects are tied up in history with strong feelings on both sides. As we saw in the time zone example, deferring to United Nations-approved boundaries or terminology is not always sufficient to calm the parties involved in a dispute.

This is why you tend to see the word *region* used in Microsoft products rather than *country*. There are still many parts of the world where sovereignty is a highly contentious issue. If you call something a country, you have effectively taken sides in a dispute you probably would be better off staying out of.

Geopolitics wasn't so much of an issue in the past, when you could control where in the world your program was running by virtue of controlling where your distributors were. But with the Internet, everything you post instantly becomes available to an international audience.

Unfortunately, I don't have any good advice on this particular tax. My personal rule is this: Stay far, far away from maps.

Remote Desktop Connection and Painting

AN INCREASINGLY IMPORTANT developer tax is supporting Remote Desktop Connection properly. When the user is connected via a Remote Desktop Connection, video operations are transferred over the network connection to the client for display. Because networks have high latency and nowhere near the bandwidth of a local video card, you need to adapt to the changing cost of drawing to the screen.

If you draw a line on the screen, the "draw line" command is sent over the network to the client. If you draw text, a "draw text" command is sent (along with the text to draw). So far so good. But if you copy a bitmap to the screen, the entire bitmap needs to be transferred over the network.

Let's write a sample program that illustrates this point. Start with our scratch program and make the following changes:

```
// new function
void Draw(HWND hwnd, HDC hdc, PAINTSTRUCT *pps)
{
 FillRect(hdc, &pps->rcPaint, (HBRUSH)(COLOR_WINDOW + 1));
 RECT rc;
 GetClientRect(hwnd, &rc);
 for (int i = -10; i < 10; i++) {
  TextOut(hdc, 0, i * 15 + rc.bottom / 2, TEXT("Blah blah"), 9);
 }
}

void PaintContent(HWND hwnd, PAINTSTRUCT *pps)
{
 Draw(hwnd, pps->hdc, pps);
}

// Add to WndProc
case WM_ERASEBKGND: return 1;

BOOL
InitApp(void)
{
```

```
    WNDCLASS wc;

    wc.style = CS_VREDRAW | CS_HREDRAW; // change
    ... as before ...
}
```

There is an odd division of labor here; the `PaintContent` function doesn't actually do anything aside from handing the work off to the `Draw` function to do the actual drawing. (You'll see why soon.) Make sure the Show window contents while dragging option is enabled and run this program and resize it vertically. Ugh, what ugly flicker. We fix this by the traditional technique of double-buffering:

```
void PaintContent(HWND hwnd, PAINTSTRUCT *pps)
{
 if (!IsRectEmpty(&pps->rcPaint)) {
  HDC hdc = CreateCompatibleDC(pps->hdc);
  if (hdc) {
   int x = pps->rcPaint.left;
   int y = pps->rcPaint.top;
   int cx = pps->rcPaint.right - pps->rcPaint.left;
   int cy = pps->rcPaint.bottom - pps->rcPaint.top;
   HBITMAP hbm = CreateCompatibleBitmap(pps->hdc, cx, cy);
   if (hbm) {
    HBITMAP hbmPrev = SelectBitmap(hdc, hbm);
    SetWindowOrgEx(hdc, x, y, NULL);

    Draw(hwnd, hdc, pps);

    BitBlt(pps->hdc, x, y, cx, cy, hdc, x, y, SRCCOPY);

    SelectObject(hdc, hbmPrev);
    DeleteObject(hbm);
   }
   DeleteDC(hdc);
  }
 }
}
```

Our new `PaintContent` function creates an offscreen bitmap and asks the `Draw` function to draw into it. After that's done, the results are copied to the screen at one go, thereby avoiding flicker. If you run this program, you'll see that its resizing behavior is nice and smooth.

Now connect to the computer via a Remote Desktop Connection and run it again. Because Remote Desktop Connection disables the Show window contents while dragging option, you can't use resizing to trigger redraws. Instead, maximize the program and restore it a few times. Notice the long delay before the window is resized when you maximize it. That's because we are pumping a huge bitmap across the Remote Desktop Connection as part of that BitBlt call.

Go back to the old version of the PaintContent method, the one that just calls Draw, and run it over Remote Desktop Connection. Ah, this one is fast. That's because the simpler version doesn't transfer a huge bitmap over the Remote Desktop Connection; it just sends 20 TextOut calls on a pretty short string of text. These take up much less bandwidth than a 1024×768 bitmap.

We have one method that is faster over a Remote Desktop Connection, and another method that is faster when run locally. Which should we use?

We use both, choosing our drawing method based on whether the program is running over a Remote Desktop Connection:

```
void PaintContent(HWND hwnd, PAINTSTRUCT *pps)
{
 if (GetSystemMetrics(SM_REMOTESESSION)) {
  Draw(hwnd, pps->hdc, pps);
 } else if (!IsRectEmpty(&pps->rcPaint)) {
  ... as before ...
 }
}
```

Now we get the best of both worlds. When run locally, we use the double-buffered drawing, which draws without flickering; but when run over a Remote Desktop Connection, we use the simple Draw method, which draws directly to the screen rather than to an offscreen bitmap.

This is a rather simple example of adapting to Remote Desktop Connection. In a more complex world, you might have more complicated data structures associated with the two styles of drawing, or you might have background activities related to drawing that you may want to turn on and off based on whether the program is running over a Remote Desktop Connection. Because the user can dynamically connect and disconnect, you can't just assume that the state of the Remote Desktop Connection when your program starts will be the state for the lifetime of the program. You'll see next how we can adapt to a changing world.

Fast User Switching and Terminal Services

WHEN THE WORKSTATION is locked or disconnected, you should turn off nonessential timers, minimize background activities, and generally send your program into a quiet state. If you already used the technique of painting only when your window is visible on the screen, you get all of this for free, because a locked workstation and a disconnected session do not generate paint messages.

If you have other activities that you want to scale back or shut down when the user has locked the workstation or disconnected, you can register to be notified when the state changes. Knowing about these state changes is also important so that you can tell when your display is local or remote. As we saw last time, drawing on Remote Desktop Connection is much slower than on a local display, because all the bitmaps need to be transferred over the network to the Remote Desktop client.

Because locking a workstation and disconnecting a session prevent us from using visual feedback to indicate our program's state, we'll use the speaker. Start with our scratch program and make the following changes:

```
#include <wtsapi32.h>

BOOL OnCreate(HWND hwnd, LPCREATESTRUCT lpcs)
{
 WTSRegisterSessionNotification(hwnd, NOTIFY_FOR_THIS_SESSION);
 return TRUE;
}

void OnWTSSessionChange(WPARAM wParam)
{
 switch (wParam) {
 case WTS_CONSOLE_DISCONNECT:
 case WTS_REMOTE_DISCONNECT:
```

```
case WTS_SESSION_LOCK:
case WTS_SESSION_LOGOFF:
  Beep(440, 250); break;
case WTS_CONSOLE_CONNECT:
case WTS_REMOTE_CONNECT:
case WTS_SESSION_UNLOCK:
case WTS_SESSION_LOGON:
  Beep(880, 250); break;
  }
}

// add to WndProc
    case WM_WTSSESSION_CHANGE:
        OnWTSSessionChange(wParam);
        return 0;
```

In this program, we register for a session notification when we create our main window, and listen for the session change message in our window procedure. If we see one of the "going away" messages, we make a low beep; if we see one of the "coming back" messages, we make a high beep.

Run this program and then lock the workstation or use Fast User Switching to switch away. You should be greeted by a low beep, although you might have to listen carefully if you have a sound associated with the action you performed, because the low beep will be mixed in with it. When you switch back, you should hear a high beep.

Of course, a real program would respond to the notifications by starting or stopping its background tasks. The purpose of this program was merely to show how to get the notifications in the first place.

◌

Multiple users

REMEMBER THAT THE Windows directory and the HKEY_LOCAL_MACHINE portion of the registry are system-wide, whereas the user's profile and the HKEY_CURRENT_USER portion of the registry are per user. Many programs make the unfortunate assumption that the computer has only one user and consequently do not maintain the separation between global and per-user state.

User preferences, such as window positions, most recently used files, and auto-complete history, must be stored in per-user locations. The obvious reason is that if there are two users, both of whom use your program, each one may have different customizations and history. It would not only be annoying for one user to see another user's auto-complete history, but it would also most likely be an information-disclosure security vulnerability. Furthermore, the users running your program might not have administrator privileges on the local computer, which means your program can't modify global state even if it wanted to.

The existence of multiple users also means that programs should be wary of requesting exclusive access to shared files. If you open a global configuration file with exclusive access, for example, only one user can run your program at a time; the second copy of the program will get a sharing violation when it tries to open the global configuration file.

Another consequence of multiple users is that a program cannot use the computer name or computer's IP address as a unique identifier when communicating with a server. The consequences of this type of mistake will vary depending on how this allegedly unique identifier is used. For example, when a second copy of the program is run by another user, the first copy may lose its connection to the server (because the server assumes that the first copy crashed when the second copy connects), or even worse, the data from the two copies of the program may get mixed together.

Fortunately, these type of multiple-user problems have become rarer now that Windows XP and Fast User Switching have become prevalent. When simultaneous multiple users required an expensive Terminal Server, these types of errors often went unnoticed.

Roaming user profiles

ONE OF THE less-known features of Windows is the roaming user profile. I know that this is not well known because I often see suggestions that fail to take the roaming user profile scenario into account. Indeed, if your program behaves badly enough, you can cause data loss. (More on this later.) Let's start with the obvious question: What is a roaming user profile?

Well, your user profile is the collection of things that reside under your `%USERPROFILE%` directory. (This is not quite true, but it's a good enough approximation for the purpose of this discussion. We look at an important exception later.) Your per-user registry is kept in `%USERPROFILE%\ntuser.dat`, so your per-user registry is part of your user profile.

In highly managed environments (corporations), system administrators can set up user profiles on a centralized server, so that users log on to any machine and have available their files and settings. This is accomplished by copying the user profile from the server when the user logs on and copying it back to the server when the user logs off. (Of course, there is also caching involved to save time if the user logs back on to the same machine.)

What does this mean for you, the programmer?

For one thing, it means that the path to the user's profile can change from one logon session to the next. If the user runs your program from Computer A, the user profile directory might be `C:\Documents and Settings\Fred`, but when the user logs off from Computer A and logs on to Computer B, the directory to the user profile might change to `C:\WINNT\Profiles\Fred`. In particular, that file that used to be at `C:\Documents and Settings\Fred\My Documents\Proposal.txt` has moved to `C:\WINNT\Profiles\Fred\My Documents\Proposal.txt`. If your program has a feature where it offers a list of recently used files (or auto-opens the most recently used file), you might find that the file no longer exists at its old location. The solution is to use profile-relative paths, or even better, shell virtual folder-relative paths (for example, recording the path relative to `CSIDL_MYDOCUMENTS`), so that when the profile roams to a machine with a different user profile path, your program can still find its files.

For another thing, you cannot just cruise through the `HKEY_LOCAL_MACHINE\SOFTWARE\Microsoft\Windows NT\CurrentVersion\ProfileList` registry key expecting to find all the user profiles and possibly even modify them, because the copy of the user profile on the local computer might not be the authoritative one. If the profile is a cached roaming profile, any changes you make will either (1) be lost when the user roams back to the computer after using another computer, or (2) cause the local profile to be considered newer than the master copy on the server, causing the changes the user made to the copy on the server to be lost! (Which of the two bad scenarios you find yourself in depends on the time you change the cached profile and the time the target user logs off that other computer.)

Another consequence of roaming user profiles is that your program can effectively see itself changing versions constantly. If Computer A has version 1.0 of your program and Computer B has version 2.0, as the profile roams between the two computers, both versions 1.0 and 2.0 will be operating on the user profile in turn. If versions 1.0 and 2.0 use the same registry keys to record their settings, your registry formats had better be both upward and downward compatible. This is a particularly painful requirement for operating system components, which consequently need to maintain bidirectional registry format compatibility with systems as old as Windows NT 4. (Windows NT 3.51 had a different model for roaming user profiles.)

Yet another consequence of roaming user profiles applies to services. Prior to Windows XP, if a service holds a registry key open after the user logged off, the registry hive cannot be unloaded and consequently (1) consumes memory for that profile even though the user is no longer logged on, and (2) prevents the user's local registry changes from being copied back to the server. This "hive leakage" problem was so rampant that in Windows XP, the profile unload code takes a more aggressive stance against services that hold keys open too long: If 60 seconds after a user logs off there are still open keys, the profile manager copies the user's registry to the server anyway. The profile still takes up memory until the last key is closed, but at least the user's registry is updated on the server.

Redirected folders

A POPULAR FEATURE used in conjunction with (or as an alternative to) roaming user profiles is redirected folders, which is a way for a domain administrator to specify that selected folders in the user profile (for example, the Desktop, the Start menu, the My Documents directory) are not stored in the user profile but rather on a separate server, which for the purpose of discussion I call the "folder server," although that is hardly standard terminology. Note that this feature can be turned on independently of roaming user profiles. Roaming user profiles copies the user profile around; redirected folders let you pull folders out of the user profile. There are four combinations of these two settings, and each of them has its merits. If you've been following along so far, you already see how they interact, but I'll spell it out in pictures this time. I will abbreviate the "roaming" and "nonroaming" portions of the user profile as simply *R profile* and *NR profile*. For illustration purposes, I show only two redirectable folders, although in reality there are plenty more.

Local computer

| NR profile |
| R profile |
| Start menu |
| My Documents |

The first case is the common case: The profile neither roams nor contains redirected folders. Because there is nothing roamed or redirected, the fact that everything is kept on the local computer is hardly surprising. This is the most common configuration on consumer machines, where there is no IT department running the show.

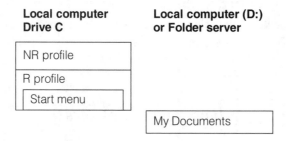

Local computer
Drive C

| NR profile |
| R profile |
| Start menu |

Local computer (D:)
or Folder server

| My Documents |

In this second configuration, the profile is still local, but we've redirected the My Documents folder to another location. (Although just to prove a point, I left the Start menu unredirected.) Some people redirect their My Documents to another, presumably much larger, drive on the same machine. Another common configuration in this same model (local profile + redirected folder) consists of redirecting My Documents to a folder server. This alternate configuration might be seen in a corporate network, so that each user's documents are kept on a file server that is regularly backed up and has shadow copies enabled so that the files can be recovered easily. You might even see it in a home network if you have accounts on multiple machines but want to keep all your documents in a central location. The downside of this arrangement is that if your My Documents server becomes unavailable, you lose access to all your documents.

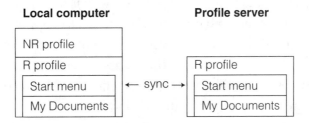

Next is the configuration with a roaming user profile but no redirected folders. As we learned earlier, the master copy of the user profile resides on the profile server. When you log on, the server copy of the profile is pulled down to update the local profile, and when you log off, changes to the local profile are pushed back to the server. This is the classic roaming profile configuration where all user data lives in the profile. Because the document folders are not redirected, the profile server can go offline and you can still do your work because your documents are cached locally.

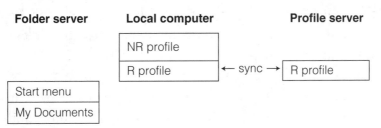

In our final configuration, we have enabled both roaming profiles and redirected folders. This is another common corporate configuration because it reduces the amount of copying that happens at logon and logoff but still keeps the user's profile and documents on managed servers so that they can be backed up and otherwise centrally administered.

A common gotcha for keeping the files entirely on a folder server is that if the folder server becomes unavailable, you lose access to your documents. This is particularly painful in laptop scenarios where the computer spends a lot of its time not connected to the network that houses the folder server. You can use offline files, however, to make these scenarios much more tolerable.

What is the lesson here?

First, as previously noted when we discussed roaming profiles, one reason why you can't manipulate the profile of a user who is not logged on is that the profile you may happen to find might not be the master copy, and what's worse, modifying the local copy can result in it becoming the master, ultimately resulting in data loss when the two versions are reconciled.

Second, even if you somehow manage to get the user to log on so that the local copy is the master, and even if you are running as local administrator, the user's files may have been redirected to another server where the local computer's administrator account does not have access.

The upshot is that you simply cannot manipulate another user's profile without actually running in the context of that user. You need to be aware of these other scenarios where the user's data is simply not accessible to you.

☙

My Documents vs. Application Data

THE MOST IMPORTANT difference between My Documents and Application Data is that My Documents is where users store their files, whereas Application Data is where programs store their files.

In other words, if you put something in CSIDL_MYDOCUMENTS (My Documents), you should expect the user to be renaming it, moving it, deleting it, emailing it to their friends, all the sorts of things users do with their files. Therefore, files that go there should be things that users will recognize as "their stuff": documents they've created, music they've downloaded, that sort of thing.

On the other hand, if you put something in CSIDL_APPDATA (Application Data), the user is less likely to be messing with it. This is where you put your program's supporting data that isn't really something you want the user messing with, but which should still be associated with the user: high score tables, program settings, customizations, spell check exceptions, and so on.

There is another directory called CSIDL_LOCAL_APPDATA that acts like CSIDL_APPDATA, except that it does not get copied if the user profile roams. (The Local Settings branch is not copied as part of the roaming user profile.) Think of it as a per-user, per-machine storage location. Caches and similar nonessential data should be kept here, especially if they are large. Other examples of nonroaming per-user data are your %TEMP% and Temporary Internet Files directories.

⁓

Large address spaces

ALTHOUGH THE TRADITIONAL split in the 4GB address space of 32-bit Windows gives user mode 2GB and kernel mode 2GB, Windows can be put into a mode where the user/kernel mode address space split gives 3GB to user mode and squeezes kernel mode into 1GB. This is typically done on machines dedicated to heavy data processing such as computer-aided design or databases.

Programs have to opt into the expanded address space (by setting the /LARGEADDRESSAWARE flag in their header), but dynamic link libraries (DLLs) have no choice in the matter. If your DLL is used only by applications under your control, then you yourself decide whether the program will mark itself as large-address-space compatible, and presumably you won't set the /LARGEADDRESSAWARE flag until you've made sure that the program and all its DLLs are indeed ready for large address spaces.

On the other hand, there's a good chance that you do not control all the applications that can load your DLL. If your DLL is a COM in-process server, it can be loaded by any process that creates an object from your DLL. And, of course, if your DLL is a plug-in for another application, you are at the mercy of the address space established by your host application. Indeed, you might fall into this category without even realizing it: If you use the regsvr32 program to install your DLL, you are letting the regsvr32 program determine the address space, and it so happens that regsvr32 is marked as large-address-space aware.

In those cases where you do not have complete control over the applications that will load your DLL, you must code your DLL with the possibility in mind that your host will have a large address space.

What does it mean to be ready for large address spaces? It means that your program or DLL does not assume that all valid pointers lie below the 2GB boundary. There are many ways code can make this sort of assumption, sometimes explicit, but often inadvertent.

The most common explicit way code can make this sort of assumption is by using the high bit of the address as a tag bit. For example, you might decide to encode integers inside pointers by setting the high bit:

```c
// Do not use these macros or functions – see text
#define ENCODINGMASK 0x80000000
#define ENCODEINTEGERASLPWSTR(i)  (LPWSTR)(ENCODINGMASK | (i))
#define ISENCODEDINTEGER(p)       ((int)(p) & ENCODINGMASK)
#define DECODELPWSTRTOINTEGER(p)  ((int)(p) & ~ENCODINGMASK)

void DoSomething(LPWSTR pszNameOrInt)
{
 CommonBehavior();
 if (ISENCODEDINTEGER(pszNameOrInt)) {
  DoSomethingWithInteger(DECODELPWSTRTOINTEGER(pszNameOrInt));
 } else {
  DoSomethingWithString(pszNameOrInt);
 }
}

// Call it either with an integer (smuggled inside a pointer)
DoSomething(ENCODEINTEGERASLPWSTR(3));

// or call it with a proper string
DoSomething(L"hello");
```

These sorts of tricks are often pulled when you have an operation that can be performed either with an integer or a pointer, and you don't want to write two functions, so instead you write one function that takes a pointer or a "smuggled integer" and alters its behavior slightly depending on whether the actual parameter is a string or a smuggled integer. Using the high bit of the address as a tag bit means that when your DLL runs inside a large address space, it will mistake genuine pointers in the 2GB-to-3GB range for smuggled integers. For example, in that second call above, where we pass L"hello", it's possible that the string is stored at a high address, say, 0x90102030. In that case, the DoSomething function will treat it not as a string but rather as if it were an encoding of the integer 0x10102030. The result of this case of mistaken identity will almost certainly be undesirable.

Another place I've seen people explicitly use the high bit of an address as a tag bit is where they want to encode an error inside a pointer:

```
// Do not use these functions -- see text
LPWSTR GetNameOfThing(Thing *pThing)
{
  HRESULT hr = ...;
  if (FAILED(hr)) return (LPWSTR)hr;
  ...
  return pName;
}

// sample usage — do not use — see text
LPWSTR pszName = GetNameOfThing(pThing);
if (FAILED((HRESULT)pszName)) ...
```

The poorly designed GetNameOfThing function tries to be clever and returns either the thing's name or an HRESULT cast to a pointer. Callers cast the pointer back to an HRESULT to see whether the function succeeded. This trickery falls apart in a large address space, because the value 0x80070006 could either be a pointer that happens to point slightly above the 2GB boundary, or it could be the error E_HANDLE.

If you've been pulling stunts like this, how do you fix them? In the first example, where integers were being smuggled inside pointers, you can use the MAKEINTRESOURCE macro to do your integer smuggling. The encoding method used by MAKEINTRESOURCE takes advantage of the fact that the bottom 64KB of the address space are roped off as invalid; therefore, pointers in the range

0x00000000 through 0x0000FFFF must be smuggled integers. (Note that you can, in principle, remove the rope and allocate genuine memory at those very low addresses, but doing such is not recommended.) This technique does limit the range of integers you can encode in this manner to 16-bit values, however. If you need to encode a larger range, you should just pass two parameters, one a pointer and one an integer.

In the second case, where the encoding is happening in the return value, the MAKEINTRESOURCE trick won't work because HRESULTs are not 16-bit values. You should rewrite the function to return an HRESULT (either an error code or S_OK on success) and return the pszName through an additional output parameter:

```
HRESULT GetNameOfThing(Thing *pThink, OUT LPWSTR *ppwszOut);
```

A pleasant side effect of both of these solutions (the MAKEINTRESOURCE approach or merely using two values, one a pointer and one an integer) is that they also make your program Win64 compatible, because the code no longer assumes that pointers are 32-bit values.

An example of inadvertently assuming that the address space is only 2GB can be found in the following function:

```
// Do not use this function - see text
#define BUFFER_SIZE 32768
BOOL IsPointerInsideBuffer(const BYTE *p, const BYTE *buffer)
{
    return p >= buffer && p - buffer < BUFFER_SIZE;
}
```

If the address space is greater than 2GB, the pointer p may be more than 2GB away from the buffer. Consider, hypothetically, that buffer=0x20000000 and p=0x90000000. This pointer clearly does not point inside the buffer (which goes from 0x20000000 to 0x20007FFF), but look at how the function is evaluated.

First, we evaluate p >= buffer. This computes 0x90000000>= 0x20000000, which is true. Next, we evaluate p - buffer <BUFFER_SIZE. This computes 0x20000000-0x90000000<32768. The result of the subtraction is 0x90000000, but this is treated as a negative number because the

difference of two pointers is a signed integer. Consequently, the comparison also succeeds, because a negative number is less than the positive number 32768. Result: You think that p points into the buffer even though it doesn't.

There are many ways of fixing this function. My personal favorite is this:

```
BOOL IsPointerInsideBuffer(const BYTE *p, const BYTE *buffer)
{
    return (ULONG_PTR)(p - buffer) < BUFFER_SIZE;
}
```

One way of looking at this approach is to observe that negative numbers, when cast to unsigned, turn into extremely large positive numbers. (Win32 requires two's complement arithmetic.) A more clever way of seeing it is to observe that you're "rotating the address space" so that the buffer appears to begin at address zero, at which point a single range check suffices.

One particularly subtle case I've seen of code that inadvertently assumed a 2GB address space was a function that did a binary search through a byte array. It attempted to compute the midpoint between the low and high pointers by calculating `((UINT)low + (UINT)high) / 2`. In a large address space, the sum of the two pointers may overflow, resulting in inadvertent truncation and an access violation when the resulting midpoint pointer is dereferenced.

Power management
and detecting battery power

POWER MANAGEMENT WAS the topic that inspired the entire discussion of taxes. The simplest form of power management is just scaling back or cancelling background operations when the computer is running on battery power. Let's start our scratch program and make the following changes:

```
// If we cannot determine the power status,
// assume we're not on battery
BOOL IsOnBatteryPower()
{
    SYSTEM_POWER_STATUS sps;
    return GetSystemPowerStatus(&sps) && sps.ACLineStatus == 0;
```

```
}

BOOL g_fTimerRunning = FALSE;
char g_chBackground = '0';

void CALLBACK OnBackgroundTimer(HWND hwnd, UINT uMsg,
                                UINT_PTR idTimer, DWORD tm)
{
 g_chBackground++;
 if (g_chBackground == '9' + 1) g_chBackground = '0';
 InvalidateRect(hwnd, NULL, TRUE);
}

void OnPowerChange(HWND hwnd)
{
 BOOL fWantTimerRunning = !!IsOnBatteryPower();
 if (g_fTimerRunning != fWantTimerRunning) {
  g_fTimerRunning = fWantTimerRunning;
  if (fWantTimerRunning) {
   SetTimer(hwnd, IDT_BACKGROUND, 250, OnBackgroundTimer);
  } else {
   KillTimer(hwnd, IDT_BACKGROUND);
  }
 }
}

BOOL
OnCreate(HWND hwnd, LPCREATESTRUCT lpcs)
{
    OnPowerChange(hwnd);
    return TRUE;
}

LRESULT OnPowerBroadcast(HWND hwnd, WPARAM wParam, LPARAM lParam)
{
 switch (wParam) {
 case PBT_APMPOWERSTATUSCHANGE:
   OnPowerChange(hwnd);
   break;
 }
 return TRUE;
}
void
PaintContent(HWND hwnd, PAINTSTRUCT *pps)
{
 TextOut(pps->hdc, 0, 0, &g_chBackground, 1);
}
```

```
// Add to WndProc
   case WM_POWERBROADCAST:
     return OnPowerBroadcast(hwnd, wParam, lParam);
```

This simple program sets up a "background task" that simply counts from zero to nine over and over again. (Of course, in real life, your "background task" would probably be something much more complicated and presumably more useful.) There are two key functions here. The first is `IsOnBatteryPower`, which determines whether the computer is running on battery power. We use this function in `OnPowerChange` to decide whether we want the background task running or not and either starting or stopping it, accordingly.

The second key function is `OnPowerBroadcast`, which handles the `WM_POWERBROADCAST` message. When we are told that the power status has changed, we ask `OnPowerChange` to start or stop our background task. The `PBT_APMPOWERSTATUSCHANGE` notification can be raised for things other than going on and off battery power, such as the battery charge level crossing certain thresholds. See MSDN for additional information.

This is the most basic type of battery-sensitive power management. If you are feeling particularly generous, you can listen for other types of power notifications. For example, the `PBT_APMBATTERYLOW` notification tells you that the user's battery has reached a low-power state, at which point you might decide to become even more conservative with your background activities.

＞

Intermittent network connectivity

IN RECENT YEARS, it has become more common for network connectivity to be an intermittent resource. When your laptop computer is in the office, it is connected to the corporate network; when you go to the coffee shop, you're on an unsecured wireless network; and when you come home, you're on your home wireless network. Adapting to changes in network connectivity will become increasingly important for many classes of applications.

There is one simple function that you can use to be notified of changes in network connectivity, at least if your program uses TCP/IP for its networking. NotifyAddrChange will notify you when the IP address on any network interface has changed. Although the function has both blocking and nonblocking forms, you almost certainly want to use the nonblocking variant instead of consuming an entire thread merely to wait for something that happens only occasionally.

As always, start with our scratch program and make the following changes:

```
#include <iphlpapi.h>

OVERLAPPED g_o;
HANDLE g_hRegister;

void RegisterForAddrChange()
{
 HANDLE h;
 NotifyAddrChange(&h, &g_o);
}

void CALLBACK OnAddrChanged(void *p, BOOLEAN fTimedOut)
{
 MessageBeep(0);
 RegisterForAddrChange();
}

void Cleanup()
{
 if (g_hRegister) {
  UnregisterWaitEx(g_hRegister, INVALID_HANDLE_VALUE);
  g_hRegister = NULL;
 }
 if (g_o.hEvent) {
  CloseHandle(g_o.hEvent);
  g_o.hEvent = NULL;
 }
}

BOOL
OnCreate(HWND hwnd, LPCREATESTRUCT lpcs)
{
 g_o.hEvent = CreateEvent(NULL, FALSE, FALSE, NULL);
 if (g_o.hEvent &&
```

```
RegisterWaitForSingleObject(&g_hRegister, g_o.hEvent,
                            OnAddrChanged, NULL, INFINITE,
                            0)) {
  RegisterForAddrChange();
  return TRUE;
 }
 Cleanup();
 return FALSE;
}

void
OnDestroy(HWND hwnd)
{
 Cleanup();
 PostQuitMessage(0);
}
```

The key here is the `RegisterForAddrChange` function, which requests that the handle in the `OVERLAPPED` structure be signaled when an IP address changes. (If we had passed `NULL` as both parameters, the call would have blocked until an address change occurred.) We register the event handle with the thread pool so that the `OnAddrChanged` function is called when the event is signaled. All we do here is beep the speaker; although in a real program, you would probably inspect the condition of the network interfaces and perhaps attempt to initiate a connection after discarding any cached information you had about the previous network connection. For example, if the IP address changes, you might want to restart your network discovery process to figure out how the new network differs from the old one.

⁓

Anti-aliased fonts and ClearType

WINDOWS PROVIDES A variety of technologies for rendering monochrome text on color displays, taking advantage of display characteristics to provide smoother results. These include grayscale anti-aliasing as well as the more advanced ClearType technique. Both of these methods read from the background pixels to decide what pixels to draw in the foreground. This means that rendering text requires extra attention.

If you draw text with an opaque background, there is no problem because you are explicitly drawing the background pixels as part of the text-drawing call, so the results are consistent regardless of what the previous background pixels were. If you draw text with a transparent background, however, you must make sure the background pixels that you draw against are the ones you really want.

The most common way people mess this up is by drawing text multiple times. I've seen programs that draw text darker and darker the longer you use them. We'll see here how this can happen and what you need to do to avoid it. Start with the scratch program and make these changes:

```
HFONT g_hfAntialias;
HFONT g_hfClearType;

BOOL
OnCreate(HWND hwnd, LPCREATESTRUCT lpcs)
{
  g_hfAntialias = CreateFont(-20, 0, 0, 0, FW_NORMAL, 0, 0, 0,
     DEFAULT_CHARSET, OUT_DEFAULT_PRECIS, CLIP_DEFAULT_PRECIS,
     ANTIALIASED_QUALITY, DEFAULT_PITCH, TEXT("Tahoma"));
  g_hfClearType = CreateFont(-20, 0, 0, 0, FW_NORMAL, 0, 0, 0,
     DEFAULT_CHARSET, OUT_DEFAULT_PRECIS, CLIP_DEFAULT_PRECIS,
     CLEARTYPE_QUALITY, DEFAULT_PITCH, TEXT("Tahoma"));
  return g_hfAntiAlias && g_hfClearType;
}

void
OnDestroy(HWND hwnd)
{
  if (g_hfAntialias) DeleteObject(g_hfAntialias);
  if (g_hfClearType) DeleteObject(g_hfClearType);
  PostQuitMessage(0);
}


void MultiPaint(HDC hdc, int x, int y, int n)
{
  LPCTSTR psz =
            TEXT("The quick brown fox jumps over the lazy dog.");
  int cch = lstrlen(psz);
  for (int i = 0; i < n; i++) {
    TextOut(hdc, x, y, psz, cch);
  }
```

```
}

void
PaintContent(HWND hwnd, PAINTSTRUCT *pps)
{
  int iModePrev = SetBkMode(pps->hdc, TRANSPARENT);
  HFONT hfPrev = SelectFont(pps->hdc, g_hfAntialias);
  MultiPaint(pps->hdc, 10,  0, 1);
  MultiPaint(pps->hdc, 10, 20, 2);
  MultiPaint(pps->hdc, 10, 40, 3);
  SelectFont(pps->hdc, g_hfClearType);
  MultiPaint(pps->hdc, 10, 80, 1);
  MultiPaint(pps->hdc, 10,100, 2);
  MultiPaint(pps->hdc, 10,120, 3);
  SelectFont(pps->hdc, hfPrev);
  SetBkMode(pps->hdc, iModePrev);
}
```

Run this program and take a close look at the results. Observe that in each set of three rows of text, the more times we overprint, the darker the text. In particular, notice that overprinting the anti-aliased font makes the result significantly uglier and uglier! What went wrong?

The first time we drew the text, the background was a solid fill of the window background color. But when the text is drawn over itself, the background it sees is the previous text output. When the algorithm decides that "This pixel should be drawn by making the existing pixel 50% darker," it actually comes out 75% darker because the pixel is darkened twice. And if you draw it three times, the pixel comes out 88% darker.

When you draw text, draw it exactly one time, and draw it over the background you ultimately want. This allows the anti-aliasing and ClearType engines to perform their work with accurate information.

The programs that darken the text are falling afoul of the overprinting problem. When the programs decide that some text needs to be redrawn (for example, if the focus rectangle needs to be drawn or removed), they "save time" by refraining from erasing the background and merely drawing the text again (but with/without the focus rectangle). Unfortunately, if you don't erase the background, the text ends up drawn over a previous copy of itself, resulting in darkening. The solution here is to draw text over the correct background.

If you don't know what background is on the screen right now, you need to erase it to set it to a known state. Otherwise, you will be blending text against an unknown quantity, which leads to inconsistent (and ugly) results.

Another case where you run into the overprinting problem is if you don't pay close attention to the flags passed in the DRAWITEMSTRUCT that is passed to the WM_DRAWITEM message. For example, some people simply draw the entire item in response to the WM_DRAWITEM message, even though the window manager passed the ODA_FOCUS flag, indicating that you should only draw or erase the focus rectangle. This is not a problem if drawing the entire item includes erasing the background; but if you assume that the WM_ERASEBKGND message had erased the background, you will end up overprinting your text in the case where you were asked only to draw the focus rectangle. In that case, the control is not erased; all you have to do is draw the focus rectangle. If you also draw the text, you are doing what the MultiPaint function did: drawing text over text; and the result is text that gets darker each time it repaints.

⌒

High DPI displays

Video displays with high pixel density (measured in dots per inch or DPI) are becoming increasingly common. Whereas on an older display, 72 pixels made up one inch on the screen, newer displays can have 96 or over 200 pixels per inch. Windows allows users to specify the relationship between screen pixels and physical dimensions to accommodate these displays.

What does this mean for your program? First, because the mapping between point and pixels changes, all point-based computations are affected by changes to the DPI, and the most visible place this can be seen is with fonts. For example, on a 72DPI display, a font that is specified as 10 point will be 10 pixels high, but on a 96DPI display, the font will be closer to 13 pixels high. Because dialog units (DLUs) are relative to the font size, this means that a change in DPI will also change the size of your dialog boxes.

Fonts do not scale perfectly linearly. Increasing the height of a font by 50%, say, will not necessarily increase its width by the same amount. As a result, a dialog box layout that looked good at 96DPI may end up with truncated or overlapping elements when rendered at 120DPI. Unfortunately, these consequences are hard to predict; you will have to run your program at a variety of DPI settings to ensure that the dialog boxes look acceptable at each of them. (For Windows Vista, the recommended DPI settings are 96, 120, 144, and 192; so you should make sure your program looks acceptable at each of these settings at a minimum.)

Although the system automatically scales fonts with DPI, you're on your own with pixel-based computations. For example, if you blindly draw a one-pixel-wide separator line, you will find that at high DPI settings, the line becomes nearly invisible. Any hard-coded pixel size should be treated as suspect. Instead, you should operate with points (or some other physical unit) and convert it to pixels based on the current DPI setting.

Perhaps the easiest way to do this is to make your physical unit the 96DPI pixel. This allows you to operate internally in pixels as before, but perform a final DPI adjustment before drawing to the screen:

```
int g_xDPI, g_yDPI;

BOOL InitializeDPI()
{
 HDC hdc = GetDC(NULL); // get screen DC
 if (!hdc) return FALSE;
 g_xDPI = GetDeviceCaps(hdc, LOGPIXELSX);
 g_yDPI = GetDeviceCaps(hdc, LOGPIXELSY);
 ReleaseDC(NULL, hdc);
}

int AdjustXDPI(int cx)
{
 return MulDiv(cx, g_xDPI, 96);
}

int AdjustYDPI(int cy)
{
 return MulDiv(cy, g_yDPI, 96);
}

// Compute the size of some screen element in "96 DPI pixels"
x = GetWidth();
```

```
y = GetHeight();
// Convert it to real pixels based on DPI
x = AdjustXDPI(x);
y = AdjustXDPI(y);
```

The program should call the `InitializeDPI` function as part of its startup; the function retrieves the screen DPI in both the horizontal and vertical directions and saves them for future reference. Subsequently, after you've computed the size of a screen element in pixels (or at least, in "what would have been pixels if the screen were at 96DPI"), you can pass the dimensions to the `AdjustXDPI` and `AdjustYDPI` functions to do the final DPI scaling to adjust for the user's actual screen DPI.

Another place where you may be relying on pixel dimensions is bitmaps, in particular, bitmaps set into static controls on dialog boxes. As noted earlier, dialog boxes scale with DPI, which means that a static control which was perfectly sized for your 160×200 bitmap on a 96DPI screen ends up being too small when the dialog box is displayed on a 120DPI screen. The result of this mismatch depends on what styles you gave to the static control.

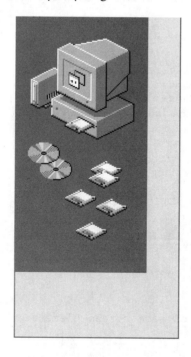

If you specify no special styles for the static bitmap control (aside from SS_BITMAP, of course), the bitmap will be aligned against the upper-left corner of the static control. If the static control is larger than the bitmap, there will be gaps where the bitmap failed to cover the entire control.

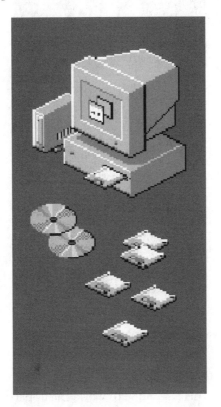

If you specify the SS_REALSIZECONTROL style, the bitmap will be stretched to the size of the static bitmap control. Depending on the type of image, this might be acceptable. Line drawings do not stretch well, but photographs tend to do better. Note, however, that the stretching is done by a simple StretchBlt; so even in the photograph case, you probably want to pre-stretch your bitmap using a higher-quality stretching algorithm so that the result is visually acceptable. If the image is a line drawing, you might simply have to have a series of bitmaps, each designed for one of the common DPI values, and select the closest match at runtime, stretching as necessary to reach the exact size desired.

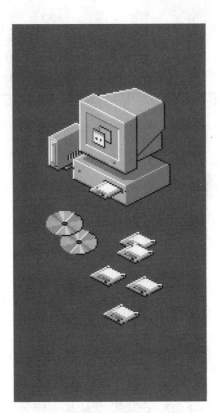

On the other hand, you can specify the SS_CENTERIMAGE style for the static bitmap control. In this case, the bitmap will be centered within the control and the gaps surrounding the bitmap will be filled with the color of the upper-left pixel of the bitmap. For this technique to work, the upper-left pixel of the bitmap must be a suitable fill color, but for line drawings this is typically not a problem.

Indeed, for line drawings, a combination of the second and third techniques may result in the best results: Author a series of images, one at each of the common DPI values, and choose the one that comes the closest to the target bitmap dimensions without going over, and then center it.

Finally, the window manager in Windows Vista has recognized that high DPI is so badly botched by most applications that it has taken the same approach as the power management team: If people can't get it right, take the decision out of their hands. In Windows Vista, the Desktop Window

Manager (DWM) emulates a 96DPI display, regardless of what the user specified. Programs that inquire after the screen DPI will merely get a value of 96 back. When the program draws its content, the DWM will scale the output to the actual screen DPI.

This virtualization has its advantages and disadvantages. The advantage is that the user will no longer see strange gaps, overlapping, or truncation when the DPI is set to a value other than 96. The disadvantage is that while those awful scenarios are avoided, the result is still not ideal because of the stretching. Programs are strongly encouraged to opt out of DPI virtualization. This can be done either programmatically by calling the SetProcessDPIAware function or, preferably, declaratively by specifying in your application manifest that your program is DPI aware and does not require virtualization:

```
<asmv3:application
 xmlns:asmv3="urn:schemas-microsoft-com:asm.v3">
 <asmv3:windowsSettings
  xmlns="http://schemas.microsoft.com/SMI/2005/WindowsSettings">
    <dpiAware>true</dpiAware>
 </asmv3:windowsSettings>
</asmv3:application>
```

If you do either of these things, your program gets to see the true screen DPI, but the responsibility is now yours to scale your user interface appropriately.

Multiple monitors

ALTHOUGH MULTIPLE MONITORS have been supported by Windows since 1998, it disappoints and frustrates me that so many applications fail to handle them properly. Eventually, you may want to investigate taking greater advantage of multiple monitors; but for now, here is the minimum you need to know so that your program at least doesn't fall apart on a multiple-monitor system.

First, only the primary monitor will have its upper-left corner at the coordinates (0, 0). Secondary monitors will have other positions; in particular, a secondary monitor can have *negative coordinates* relative to the primary. For example, consider the dual-monitor arrangement depicted here.

```
(-800,0)        (0,0)
Secondary
                Primary
      (0,600)
                    (1024,768)
```

In this monitor configuration, the secondary monitor has its upper-left corner at (−800, 0) and its lower-right corner at (0, 600). Observe also that the two monitors are different sizes. In fact, they could even be different color depths. (For example, the one on the left might be set to use 16 bits per pixel, whereas the one on the right could be using 24 bits per pixel.)

Make sure you don't assume that negative coordinates are invalid. In the above configuration, the coordinate (− 800, 0) is a perfectly acceptable position for a window to be. It corresponds to the upper-left corner of the secondary monitor. Some programs "helpfully" reposition items so that they have positive coordinates, thereby keeping them "on the screen"; these programs become very frustrating to use on a multiple-monitor system setup like we have here because they keep shoving their objects onto the primary monitor. For example, one program I use displays all its menus on the primary monitor, even if the program's main window is on the secondary.

Another thing to note is that the values of GetSystemMetrics (SM_CXSCREEN) and GetSystemMetrics(SM_CYSCREEN) refer only to the primary monitor. These system metrics remain behind in order to provide compatibility with applications written before the advent of multiple monitors, but new applications should avoid them because they do not take into account secondary monitors. If you want to know the size of the screen, you first have to decide which screen you're talking about!

You identify a display monitor to the window manager with an HMONITOR. There are two ways of obtaining monitor handles, either by the advanced technique of enumerating them explicitly (via a function such as EnumDisplayMonitors) or by the more basic technique of using one of the MonitorFromXxx functions.

If you want to do the least amount of work to support multiple monitors, you can just restrict yourself to the monitor the user has put your window on by calling the MonitorFromWindow function. (If the window straddles multiple monitors, the monitor that has the largest area of intersection with the window will be chosen.) You can then pass that monitor handle to `GetMonitorInfo` to get the coordinates of that monitor:

```
void GetMonitorRectFromWindow(HWND hwnd, OUT RECT *prc)
{
 MONITORINFO mi = { sizeof(mi) };
 HMONITOR hmon = MonitorFromWindow(hwnd,
                                    MONITOR_DEFAULTTONEAREST);
 if (hmon && GetMonitorInfo(hmon, &mi)) {
  *prc = mi.rcMonitor;
 } else {
  // Can't get monitor from window - use the primary monitor
  prc->left = prc->top = 0;
  prc->right = GetSystemMetrics(SM_CXSCREEN);
  prc->bottom = GetSystemMetrics(SM_CYSCREEN);
 }
}
```

This function takes the window and obtains the nearest monitor. The `MonitorFromXxx` functions let you specify which monitor you want if the window is not on any monitor; here, we ask for the window manager to give us the closest monitor. If we still cannot get a monitor from the window (perhaps the window handle was invalid), we return values appropriate for the primary monitor.

Your program should use this function (or a function like it) where it would have previously asked for the dimensions of the screen. Note that because a rectangle is returned, you need to position your objects within a rectangle rather than assuming that the rectangle's origin is (0, 0). For example, if you want to compute the center of a window's monitor, you would use something like this:

```
RECT rcMonitor;
GetMonitorRectFromWindow(hwnd, &rcMonitor);
int x = rcMonitor.left + (rcMonitor.right - rcMonitor.left) / 2;
int y = rcMonitor.top + (rcMonitor.bottom - rcMonitor.top) / 2;
```

Performing your computations on the correct monitor is essential if your program has a full-screen mode. Many laptop computers are capable of going into a multiple-monitor configuration with the laptop's built-in LCD as the primary and the external monitor as secondary. It would not be unreasonable for users to want to run your program full screen on the external monitor (which is, say, connected to a projector for a presentation) while keeping their notes visible on the LCD panel in another window. For this to work, your program needs to go full screen onto the correct monitor.

I know another program that tries to go full screen but misses. Although it does go onto the correct monitor, it uses the dimensions of the primary monitor! Because my primary and secondary monitors are not the same size, this results in a rather distorted full-screen window on the secondary monitor.

But wait, there's more to coordinate management than merely being monitor aware. We take up those additional topics next.

The work area

As you saw in "Why does the taskbar default to the bottom of the screen?" (Chapter 4), many programs fail to distinguish between screen coordinates and work area coordinates. Along the edges of each monitor, space can be reserved by the taskbar or application toolbars, leaving a rectangular region in the center for normal application windows. (Note that the taskbar can appear on a secondary monitor.) This region is known as the work area, and you can obtain its dimensions by calling GetMonitorInfo and looking at the rcWork member of the MONITORINFO structure:

```
void GetWorkAreaFromWindow(HWND hwnd, OUT RECT *prc)
{
 MONITORINFO mi = { sizeof(mi) };
 HMONITOR hmon = MonitorFromWindow(hwnd,
                                    MONITOR_DEFAULTTONEAREST);
 if (hmon && GetMonitorInfo(hmon, &mi)) {
  *prc = mi.rcWork;
 } else {
  // Can't get monitor from window - use the primary monitor
  SystemParametersInfo(SPI_GETWORKAREA, 0, prc, 0);
 }
}
```

This is basically the same as the GetMonitorRectFromWindow function except that we return the rcWork member to get the work area of the monitor the window resides on. If we cannot obtain the monitor for the window, we use the work area of the primary monitor.

To be honest, few programs run afoul of the work area when they do their coordinate computations because most programs just let the user do the window positioning. The place where they run into trouble is when they try to mix GetWindowPlacement with SetWindowPos. The restored window rectangle in the WINDOWPLACEMENT structure (used by the GetWindowPlacement and SetWindowPlacement functions) is given in work area coordinates, not screen coordinates. When programs "slide up under the taskbar" they are using a WINDOWPLACEMENT as screen coordinates, causing the window to slide up and to the left by the amount of space taken up by application bars at the top and left of the screen.

The simple solution to this problem is not to mix the two coordinates. If you retrieve the window position via GetWindowPlacement, use the SetWindowPlacement function to restore it.

The SetWindowPlacement function is the preferred way to restore window positions because it takes into account changes in screen resolution, multiple monitors, and changes in the work area. The function checks that the window coordinates passed in, when converted from workspace coordinates to screen coordinates, will result in a window that is visible on at least one monitor. If the result is a window that would be completely off the screen, the SetWindowPlacement function moves the window back onscreen.

⬯

Displaying your pop-up windows in the right place

WHEN YOU DECIDE to display a centered window, make sure you center it against the correct thing. If you are displaying a pop-up message, you should position it based on the location of the object that generated the pop-up. For example, if a particular window wants to display a pop-up, the pop-up should be positioned relative to that window (centered, corner-aligned, whatever). Many times I see programs that blindly center the window onto the primary monitor, which is wrong for multiple reasons.

First, of course, is that the window might be on the wrong monitor entirely. If the program is running on a secondary monitor, its pop-ups should display on that same monitor.

Second, you may have noticed that monitors have been getting bigger over the years. If you center your pop-up on the monitor rather than on the owner window, you might end up putting your pop-up far away from its owner, causing users to overlook it and be baffled as to why your program appears to have disabled itself. To get your program reenabled, the users have to deal with a pop-up window that is so far away from the main window that it appears unrelated.

The problem of poorly chosen centering is a special case of the more general problem of using absolute positioning rather than relative positioning. Absolute positioning is appropriate only if you have control of the entire screen (for example, if your program has gone into full-screen presentation mode). If your program is sharing the screen with other programs, you should present your interface elements in locations relative to other interface elements. Failing to adhere to this principle results in your interface elements appearing in inappropriate (and possibly confusing) locations.

Accessibility

PERHAPS THE MOST-NEGLECTED software tax is accessibility. Indeed, accessibility is a tax that I myself have been glossing over throughout this book in the interest of not cluttering the presentation. (The discussion here is brief, too, because my goal is merely to raise awareness of the issue rather than explore it in depth.)

Let's go back to our program that illustrated painting only when the window is visible on the screen and make it accessible. This particular program is both complicated and simple from an accessibility point of view.

It's complicated because the program paints its own text rather than relying on a system-provided control such as a static text control or a list box. If you use a system-provided control, you can take advantage of the accessibility functionality of those controls. For example, if a program uses a dialog box that consists entirely of system-provided controls and doesn't use owner-draw, it doesn't need to take any special actions to make the dialog box accessible because all the system-provided controls take care of the accessibility for you. Unfortunately, our sample draws text directly and therefore must also shoulder the accessibility burden of exposing that text to assistive technology programs.

On the other hand, our sample is a simple case of a custom accessible window because it consists of just one element (the text) with no subelements.

Before we start tweaking our program, let's set some groundwork:

```cpp
#include <oleacc.h>

class BaseAccessible : public IAccessible
{
public:
 // *** IUnknown ***
 STDMETHODIMP QueryInterface(REFIID riid, void **ppv)
 {
  IUnknown *punk = NULL;
  if (riid == IID_IUnknown)  {
   punk = static_cast<IUnknown*>(this);
  } else if (riid == IID_IDispatch)  {
   punk = static_cast<IDispatch*>(this);
  } else if (riid == IID_IAccessible)  {
   punk = static_cast<IAccessible*>(this);
  }
  *ppv = punk;
  if (punk) {
   punk->AddRef();
   return S_OK;
  } else {
   return E_NOINTERFACE;
  }
 }
 STDMETHODIMP_(ULONG) AddRef()
    { return InterlockedIncrement(&m_cRef); }
 STDMETHODIMP_(ULONG) Release()
 {
   ULONG cRef = InterlockedDecrement(&m_cRef);
```

```
    if (cRef == 0) delete this;
    return cRef;
}

// *** IDispatch ***
STDMETHODIMP GetTypeInfoCount(UINT *pctinfo)
{
  return m_paccStd->GetTypeInfoCount(pctinfo);
}
STDMETHODIMP GetTypeInfo(UINT iTInfo, LCID lcid,
                         ITypeInfo **ppTInfo)
{
  return m_paccStd->GetTypeInfo(iTInfo, lcid, ppTInfo);
}
STDMETHODIMP GetIDsOfNames(REFIID riid, LPOLESTR *rgszNames,
                           UINT cNames, LCID lcid, DISPID
                           *rgDispId)
{
  return m_paccStd->GetIDsOfNames(riid, rgszNames, cNames,
                                  lcid, rgDispId);
}
STDMETHODIMP Invoke(DISPID dispIdMember, REFIID riid, LCID lcid,
                    WORD wFlags, DISPPARAMS *pDispParams,
                    VARIANT *pVarResult, EXCEPINFO *pExcepInfo,
                    UINT *puArgErr)
{
  return m_paccStd->Invoke(dispIdMember, riid, lcid,wFlags,
            pDispParams, pVarResult, pExcepInfo, puArgErr);
}

// *** IAccessible ***
STDMETHODIMP get_accParent(IDispatch **ppdispParent)
{
  return m_paccStd->get_accParent(ppdispParent);
}
STDMETHODIMP get_accChildCount(long *pcountChildren)
{
  return m_paccStd->get_accChildCount(pcountChildren);
}
STDMETHODIMP get_accChild(VARIANT varChild,
                          IDispatch **ppdispChild)
{
  return m_paccStd->get_accChild(varChild, ppdispChild);
}
STDMETHODIMP get_accName(VARIANT varChild, BSTR *pbsName)
{
```

```
  return m_paccStd->get_accName(varChild, pbsName);
}
STDMETHODIMP get_accValue(VARIANT varChild, BSTR *pbsValue)
{
  return m_paccStd->get_accValue(varChild, pbsValue);
}
STDMETHODIMP get_accDescription(VARIANT varChild, BSTR *pbsDesc)
{
  return m_paccStd->get_accDescription(varChild, pbsDesc);
}
STDMETHODIMP get_accRole(VARIANT varChild, VARIANT *pvarRole)
{
  return m_paccStd->get_accRole(varChild, pvarRole);
}
STDMETHODIMP get_accState(VARIANT varChild, VARIANT *pvarState)
{
  return m_paccStd->get_accState(varChild, pvarState);
}
STDMETHODIMP get_accHelp(VARIANT varChild, BSTR *pbsHelp)
{
  return m_paccStd->get_accHelp(varChild, pbsHelp);
}
STDMETHODIMP get_accHelpTopic(BSTR *pbsHelpFile,VARIANT varChild,
                              long *pidTopic)
{
  return m_paccStd->get_accHelpTopic(pbsHelpFile, varChild,
                                     pidTopic);
}
STDMETHODIMP get_accKeyboardShortcut(VARIANT varChild,BSTR
                                     *pbsKey)
{
  return m_paccStd->get_accKeyboardShortcut(varChild, pbsKey);
}
STDMETHODIMP get_accFocus(VARIANT *pvarChild)
{
  return m_paccStd->get_accFocus(pvarChild);
}
STDMETHODIMP get_accSelection(VARIANT *pvarChildren)
{
  return m_paccStd->get_accSelection(pvarChildren);
}
STDMETHODIMP get_accDefaultAction(VARIANT varChild,BSTR
                                  *pbsDefAction)
{
  return m_paccStd->get_accDefaultAction(varChild, pbsDefAction);
}
```

```
STDMETHODIMP accSelect(long flagsSelect, VARIANT varChild)
{
    return m_paccStd->accSelect(flagsSelect, varChild);
}
STDMETHODIMP accLocation(long *pxLeft, long *pyTop,
                         long *pcxWidth, long *pcyHeight,
                         VARIANT varChild)
{
  return m_paccStd->accLocation(pxLeft, pyTop, pcxWidth,pcyHeight,
                            varChild);
}
STDMETHODIMP accNavigate(long navDir, VARIANT varStart,VARIANT
                         *pvarEndUpAt)
{
  return m_paccStd->accNavigate(navDir, varStart, pvarEndUpAt);
}
STDMETHODIMP accHitTest(long xLeft, long yTop,VARIANT *pvarChild)
{
  return m_paccStd->accHitTest(xLeft, yTop, pvarChild);
}
STDMETHODIMP accDoDefaultAction(VARIANT varChild)
{
  return m_paccStd->accDoDefaultAction(varChild);
}
STDMETHODIMP put_accName(VARIANT varChild, BSTR bsName)
{
  return m_paccStd->put_accName(varChild, bsName);
}
STDMETHODIMP put_accValue(VARIANT varChild, BSTR bsValue)
{
  return m_paccStd->put_accValue(varChild, bsValue);
}

protected:
 BaseAccessible(IAccessible *paccStd)
  : m_cRef(1), m_paccStd(paccStd)
 {
  m_paccStd->AddRef();
 }
 ~BaseAccessible() { m_paccStd->Release(); }

private:
 LONG m_cRef;
protected:
 IAccessible *m_paccStd;
};
```

As you can see, this class is not particularly interesting. It just wraps an existing `IAccessible` object inside another one. The value of this class is to allow you to modify the behavior of the wrapped `IAccessible` interface by overriding selected methods. In our case, we will override the `get_accName` and `get_accValue` methods to return our custom data:

```
class ScratchAccessible : public BaseAccessible
{
public:
 static HRESULT Create(HWND hwnd, LONG idObject,REFIID riid,
                       void **ppv)
 {
  *ppv = NULL;
  IAccessible *paccStd;
  HRESULT hr = CreateStdAccessibleObject(hwnd, idObject,
                                         IID_IAccessible,
                                         (void **)&paccStd);
  if (SUCCEEDED(hr)) {
   // note: uses non-throwing "new"
   ScratchAccessible *psa = new ScratchAccessible(paccStd);
   if (psa) {
    hr = psa->QueryInterface(riid, ppv);
    psa->Release();
   } else {
    hr = E_OUTOFMEMORY;
   }
   paccStd->Release();
  }
  return hr;
 }

 // Selective overriding of IAccessible
 STDMETHODIMP get_accName(VARIANT varChild, BSTR *pbsName)
 {
  if (varChild.vt == VT_I4 && varChild.lVal == CHILDID_SELF) {
   *pbsName = SysAllocString(L"Current time");
   return *pbsName ? S_OK : E_OUTOFMEMORY;
  }
  return m_paccStd->get_accName(varChild, pbsName);
 }
 STDMETHODIMP get_accValue(VARIANT varChild, BSTR *pbsValue)
 {
  if (varChild.vt == VT_I4 && varChild.lVal == CHILDID_SELF) {
   WCHAR szTime[100];
   if (GetTimeFormatW(LOCALE_USER_DEFAULT, 0, NULL, NULL,
```

```
                     szTime, 100)) {
    *pbsValue = SysAllocString(szTime);
    return *pbsValue ? S_OK : E_OUTOFMEMORY;
   }
  }
  return m_paccStd->get_accValue(varChild, pbsValue);
 }
private:
 ScratchAccessible(IAccessible *paccStd)
   : BaseAccessible(paccStd) { }
};
```

Our static `Create` method uses the `CreateStdAccessibleObject` function to get the `IAccessible` that would have been used if we didn't provide our own implementation. We wrap that interface inside our `ScratchAccessible` object, which overrides the `get_accName` method by returning "Current time" as the accessible name for the object and the current time as its value.

Now we can hook this up to our sample program:

```
void
PaintContent(HWND hwnd, PAINTSTRUCT *pps)
{
    TCHAR szTime[100];
    if (GetTimeFormat(LOCALE_USER_DEFAULT, 0, NULL, NULL,
                      szTime, 100)) {
        // SetWindowText(hwnd, szTime); // delete
        TextOut(pps->hdc, 0, 0, szTime, lstrlen(szTime));
    }
}

void CALLBACK
InvalidateAndKillTimer(HWND hwnd, UINT uMsg,
                       UINT_PTR idTimer, DWORD dwTime)
{
    KillTimer(hwnd, idTimer);
    InvalidateRect(hwnd, NULL, TRUE);
    NotifyWinEvent(EVENT_OBJECT_VALUECHANGE, hwnd,
            OBJID_CLIENT, CHILDID_SELF);
}

// new function
LRESULT OnGetObject(HWND hwnd, WPARAM wParam, LPARAM lParam)
{
 if (lParam == OBJID_CLIENT) {
```

```
    IAccessible *pacc;
    HRESULT hr = ScratchAccessible::Create(hwnd,(LONG)lParam,
                                        IID_IAccessible,
                                        (void**)&pacc);
    if (FAILED(hr)) return hr;
    LRESULT lr = LresultFromObject(IID_IAccessible, wParam, pacc);
    pacc->Release();
    return lr;
  }
  return DefWindowProc(hwnd, WM_GETOBJECT, wParam, lParam);
}

// Add to WndProc
    case WM_GETOBJECT: return OnGetObject(hwnd, wParam, lParam);
```

The change to the PaintContent function merely removes the caption change from our timer. We do this just to reduce the number of things changing in the system so that it's easier to watch the effect of the accessibility changes without being distracted by other changes.

The change to the InvalidateAndKillTimer function is one that is often overlooked by people who implement the IAccessible interface: firing accessible events when the state of an object changes. You need to fire accessible events for your custom IAccessible implementation so that accessibility tools will know that the onscreen content has changed. They can then fetch the new accessible properties and take action such as reading the new value to the user.

The ball is set into motion by the WM_GETOBJECT handler. If we are being asked for the accessible object for the window client area, we create our wrapper object and return it. Note the careful way this object is returned: The LresultFromObject function takes the accessible object and encodes it into an LRESULT, which we return. The encoding process (assuming it is successful) takes its own reference on the interface; we are still on the hook for releasing our reference.

With these changes, you can run the program in conjunction with accessibility tools such as Narrator (which comes with Windows XP) or Inspect (which is part of the Active Accessibility SDK) to see that your custom-painted window now exposes its name and value via Active Accessibility, thereby allowing accessible technology programs such as screen readers to retrieve information about your program's display and present it to users with disabilities.

Now, this seems like an awful lot of work, and it is. As noted before, this work was necessary because we are custom painting our content rather than using a system-provided window class such as a static control. If we had used a static control to display the time, the accessibility support already built in to the static control would have done this work for us.

Our job was also complicated by the fact that the value constantly changes. If the value were static, we could have used Direct Annotation to set the value when the window was created and allow the default `IAccessible` implementation to do all the work. You can learn more about Direct Annotation and the rest of Active Accessibility from the Active Accessibility documentation in MSDN.

Remember also that accessibility is not just for users with disabilities. Because the accessibility interfaces are programmable, any program can use them to extract text and other information from your application. For example, a dictionary program can use the accessible interfaces to retrieve the text beneath the mouse cursor and display a translation or definition in a helper window. If your program doesn't support accessibility, those helper programs will be unable to retrieve text from your program, leaving the user stymied.

CHAPTER TWENTY-ONE

Silliness

LIFE IS NOT all seriousness, of course. Here are some sillier things that happened.

The much-misunderstood "nop" action

THE PRINTERS WERE reconfigured in our building, and we got an announcement that went like this:

> **Subject:** *Printer/Copier Reconfiguration*
>
> **Action Required**
>
> *blah blah blah printers are being reconfigured blah blah blah*
>
> **Action(s) to be taken:** *No action is required, as the print path information will remain the same.*

Sometimes you have to do nothing, and that counts as doing something.

Don't let Marketing mess with your slides

I FORGET WHICH conference it was, maybe GCDC 1996. We were all busy preparing our presentations and submitted them to the Microsoft conference representatives so that they could apply the standard template, clean them up, print out copies to go into the handouts, all that stuff.

What about that "clean them up" step?

We didn't realize what clean them up meant until we showed up at the conference and looked at the handouts.

Part of cleaning up was inserting ® and ™ symbols as necessary, which meant that they also took every occurrence of the abbreviation VB and changed it to Microsoft Visual Basic®. They even did this to the presentation on vertex buffers. The abbreviation for vertex buffers is also VB.

You can imagine what the effect was.

Whimsical bug reports

WHIMSICAL BUG REPORTS, although not a common occurrence, aren't exactly unheard of either. They are a popular way to vent a shared frustration and lighten the mood.

The company changed milk suppliers for our cafeterias. Well, more accurately, the previous milk supplier was bought by another milk company. The problem is that the single-serving milk cartons from the new company are hard to open.

So, of course, what you do is file a bug.

Bug: *New milk cartons are hard to open.*

To Reproduce: *Go to cafeteria, get milk carton, attempt to open it, get napkins, and clean up mess.*

(The reason is that the milk company bought a brand new machine that seals the cartons with too much glue. The fix was to adjust the seal.)

A few workarounds were suggested, including bringing your own cow and a three-step process of freezing the milk, tearing the carton open, then allowing the milk to thaw. Others explained that the fix is held up in testing: "Currently only three testers are handling this component and they can only drink eight cartons a day. The team could conduct more carton-opening tests but carton-tasting, milk-flow testing, and carton pressure tests are still remaining." Plus, of course, a security review needs to be made of the consequences of a weaker seal.

This is a particularly software-oriented joke, because it highlights how hard it is to make bug fixes in software—by applying the software testing regimen to something that isn't software. You can't assume that a simple, local change such as adjusting the amount of glue applied to the carton will result in a simple, local change in the final product (a more acceptable seal strength). Software is nonlinear. A simple change can have effects (some catastrophic, some subtle) far, far away from the point of change.

⤸

Watch out for those sample URLs

WHEN WRITING DOCUMENTATION, you might have to come up with a sample URL to illustrate some point or other. When you do, make sure the sample URL is under your control. I remember a Windows beta that used the sample URL http://www.xxxxx.com/ in a dialog box. You can imagine where that actually goes.

(Raymond's strange dream story: One night I dreamed that I found a Web site devoted to the cartoon *Dilbert*, and for some reason the name of the site was "Wally World." In the morning, I checked out the site and was in for a big surprise: It's a gay porn site.)

So play it safe. When you need a sample URL, don't just make something up. If you do, odds are good that somebody is going to rush in and register it. Make your sample URLs point back to your company's home page, or use http://www.example.com, which has been reserved for use in sample URLs.

(The promise is only that the domain example.com will always be safe to use in documentation; there is no promise that visiting the site will actually reveal anything interesting.) If that's too unsatisfying, you can always go out and register the domain you want to use as your sample, so that nobody else can sneak in and steal it. (And with the price competition for domain names nowadays, it won't cost you much at all.) If you choose to register your own domain, make sure to renew it when its registration expires. The scripting team used the Web site scripthappens.com as a sample URL, but they were slow to renew the domain when it came up for expiration, and it's been a porn site ever since. Plenty of other companies have fallen into the same trap. Learn from their mistakes.

⮞

No code is an island

As an example of the nonlocal effects of a simple change, consider that on Windows 2003 Server the Display Adapter Troubleshooting slider still lists "full acceleration" as the recommended setting even though the default for Server is "full minus one."

This is one of those "Oh, that's an easy change" bugs. The discussion probably went like this:

> **Some guy whose idea this was:** "For stability reasons, we want to lower the default video acceleration for Server a notch. Dear Video Setup team, can you do that for us?"
>
> **Video Setup team:** "Sure thing, that's no problem. The default setting is all done by us; it should not have any impact on anybody else. We'll just do it and be done with it."
>
> **Guy:** "Sweet. Thanks."

And bingo, the default video acceleration dropped to one notch below full on Server, and everyone was happy.

Except that there's this text tucked away in the Display Control Panel that has the word (*recommended*) next to "full acceleration." That didn't get updated.

Oops. (I wouldn't be surprised if there is also some help text that didn't get updated for this change.)

No code is an island.

So when you complain, "Aw come on, it's a one-line change. What's taking so long?" think about the little video acceleration slider.

But I have Visual Basic Professional

BACK IN 1995, I was participating in a chat room on MSN on the subject of Windows 95 kernel-mode device drivers (known as VxDs). One of the people in the chat room asked, "Can I write a VxD in Visual Basic?"

I replied, "VxDs are typically written in low-level languages such as C or even assembly language."

Undaunted, the person clarified: "But I have Visual Basic *Professional*."

It's all about the translucent plastic

A FRIEND OF mine used to work on the development of the USB specification and subsequent implementation. One of the things that happens at these meetings is that hardware companies would show off the great USB hardware they were working on. It also gave them a chance to try out their hardware with various USB host manufacturers and operating systems to make sure everything worked properly together.

One of the earlier demonstrations was a company that was making USB floppy drives. The company representative talked about how well the drives were doing and mentioned that they make two versions, one for PCs and one for Macs.

"That's strange," the committee members thought to themselves. "Why are there separate PC and Mac versions? The specification is very careful to make sure that the same floppy drive works on both systems. You shouldn't need to make two versions."

One of the members asked the obvious question. "Why do you have two versions? What's the difference? If there's a flaw in our specification, let us know and we can fix it."

The company representative answered, "Oh, the two floppy drives are completely the same electronically. The only difference is that the Mac version comes in translucent blue plastic and costs more."

This company was, of course, hardly the first to capitalize on the iMac-inspired translucent plastic craze. My favorite is the iMac-styled George Foreman Grill. (I'm told the graphite ones cook faster.)

⁓

My first death threat

ACTUAL FEEDBACK SUBMITTED to the microsoft.com Web site many years ago:

id: *13726*

Date: *1996-07-29 17:27:41.997*

Name: **********

Email: ************

Area: *Windows 95*

Comments:

PLEASE read this entire email as it is quite serious. I just discovered today that in the Windows 95 operating system, there are no switches, command line options, or any way whatsoever to have the XCOPY command include hidden/system files in its operations. It is clear that at some point in the development of the Windows 95 product, that somebody made a conscious decision to implement the xcopy command in this manner. It is also clear from looking at the Windows NT XCOPY command that it can be implemented in the manner I describe. Therefore, let me give fair warning. This may not be easy, and I will expect no help from Microsoft in finding out who this person (or persons) was that made this decision, but ... eventually I will find out who made this decision, and I will kill them. This is not an idle threat — I will pursue this matter until it is resolved ... whoever is responsible for this incredibly ridiculous implementation of what would be an otherwise useful tool will die at my hands, hopefully in a bloody, painful fashion. You will not get away. —J*hn ******

J*hn, if you're still out there ... the switch for copying hidden files on Windows 95 is /H. Same as Windows NT.

Please don't kill me.

⮑

You can't escape those AOL CDs

ONE OF MY colleagues was unpacking one of those $30,000 quad-processor more-memory-than-you-know-what-to-do-with super-server computers. The kind that require their own electrical substation.

And it came with an AOL CD.

It's like buying a giant plasma television set and finding an advertisement for an aerial antenna in the box.

Apparently, one of the questions AOL tech support asks when people call in complaining that they can't get their AOL CD to work is, "Do you have a computer?"[1] because so many people who don't have computers stick the CD into their stereo or DVD player and can't get it to work.

⮑

Giving fair warning before plugging in your computer

THAT COLLEAGUE WHO gave me the AOL CD that came with his big-iron server later received a prototype Itanium computer for testing purposes. The early Itaniums were behemoths. They weighed a ton, sounded like a weed whacker, and put out enough heat to keep you comfortably warm through the winter. (If you opened them up, you would probably see several carefully shaped Styrofoam blocks with the label "Do not remove! Engineering Styrofoam!" I never though I would ever see the phrase *engineering Styrofoam* used seriously.)

Never one to read all the safety labels before playing with a new toy, my colleague took the heavy-duty double-capacity power cables and ran them to the normal wall socket. Then he threw the power switch.

And the power went out in the entire building wing.

---

1. *Wait, Wait, Don't Tell Me*, National Public Radio, November 13, 2004. Opening Panel Round, second question, available at http://www.npr.org/programs/waitwait/archrndwn/2004/nov/041113.waitwait.html.

The power surge from the Itanium overloaded the poor wall socket and tripped the wing's circuit breaker. Everybody went through the standard power-outage drill, while speculating with one another what the cause for this one might be.

It didn't take long for word to get out. "X plugged in his Itanium."

After the electricians came by to check that everything was okay, they reset the circuit breaker and everybody got back to work.

My colleague re-cabled the machine to be more friendly to the building's power circuitry. Then he sent out email to the entire team.

"I'm turning it on!"

We all saved our work and waited.

The power stayed up.

Then we all smiled to ourselves and resumed our typing.

Spider Solitaire unseats the reigning champion

SOME TIME AGO, the usability research team summarized some statistics they had been collecting on the subject of what people spend most of their time doing on the computer at home. Not surprisingly, surfing the Internet was number one. Number two was playing games, and in particular, I found it notable that the number one game is no longer Klondike Solitaire (known to most Windows users as just plain Solitaire).

That title now belongs to Spider Solitaire. The top three games (Spider Solitaire, Klondike Solitaire, and FreeCell) together account for more than half of all game-playing time.

Personally, I'm a FreeCell player.

Exercise: Why aren't games such as Unreal Tournament or The Sims in the top three?

⪾

There's something about Rat Poker

WHEN PERFORMING USABILITY tests, one of the standard tasks we give people is to install a game, and the game we usually use is The Puzzle Collection. (Yes, it's an old game, but changing the game makes it less valid to compare results from one year to the next.)

One of the things that the game's setup does that always confuses people is that it asks you where you want to install it and suggests a directory. If you accept the default, a warning box appears that reads, "The directory C:\Program Files\Microsoft Puzzle Collection does not exist. Do you wish to create it?"

People see this dialog box and panic.

Why?

Because it's an unexpected dialog, and unexpected dialogs create confusion and frustration. From a programming perspective, this is a stupid dialog because it's hardly a surprise that the directory doesn't exist. You're installing a new program! From a usability point of view, this is a stupid dialog because it makes users second-guess themselves. "Gosh, did I do something wrong? The computer is asking me if I'm sure. It only does that when I'm about to do something really stupid." They then click No (it's always safest to say No), which returns them to the dialog asking them to specify an installation directory, and they'll poke around trying to find a directory that won't generate an "error message." I've seen users install the Puzzle Collection into their Windows directory because that was the first directory they could think of that didn't generate the error message.

Anyway, after the program is installed (one way or another), we tell them to relax and play a game. We say it as if we're giving them a reward for a job well done, but it's actually still part of the test. We want to see how easily users can find whatever it is they just installed.

One thing you can count on is that when faced with the collection of games available, for some reason, they always pick Rat Poker.

Always.

Each of us has our own pet theory why people always pick Rat Poker. Personally, I think it's that the Rat Poker icon is the most friendly looking of the bunch. Many of them are abstract, or they depict scary creatures, but awww, look at that cute rat with the big nose. He looks so cheerful!

Click. Another vote for Rat Poker.

Be careful what you name your product group

THEY THOUGHT THEY were so clever when they named the Desktop Applications Division. "And the abbreviation is DAD, isn't that cute? It complements the Microsoft Office Manager toolbar (MOM)."

And then the troubles started.

Shortly after the new product group was formed, everybody in the product group started getting email talking about strange nonbusiness things. How's the garden doing? Did you get my letter? When will the twins be coming home from college?

The reason is that the email address for sending mail to the entire division was, naturally, DAD. But it so happens that many people have a nickname for their father in their address book, named, of course, dad. People thought they were sending email to their dad, when in fact it was going to DAD.

The email address for sending mail to the entire division was quickly changed to something like deskapps or dappdiv.

The psychology of naming your internal distribution lists

ONE PROBLEM THAT I'm sure everybody has run into is what I'm going to call the comp.unix.wizards problem. People who have a problem with UNIX are looking for someone who can help them, and given the choice between a general questions group and a wizard group, they're obviously going to choose the wizards because that's where the smart people are! Of course, this annoys the wizards who created the group so they could focus on advanced UNIX topics.

Here's a trick. Give your nontechnical discussion group the name XYZ Technical Discussion. Meanwhile, name your technical discussion group something less attractive like XYZ Infrastructure Committee. Your "technical discussion" distribution list will get the support questions, and people will feel like they're getting a "more direct line" to the technical staff. In reality, of course, the technical staff read both the XYZ Technical Discussion and the XYZ Infrastructure Committee groups.

(Now, by revealing this trick, I risk ruining it.)

⁀

Differences between managers and programmers

IF YOU FIND yourself in a meeting with a mix of managers and programmers, here's one way to tell the difference between them: Look at what they brought to the meeting.

Did they bring a laptop computer? Score bonus points if the laptop computer is actually *turned on* during the meeting or if the laptop is special in some way. (Back when I developed this rule, having a wireless card or a Tablet PC was special enough.) If so, that person is probably a manager.

Did they come to the meeting empty-handed or with a spiral-bound notebook? If so, that person is probably a programmer.

It's not an infallible test, but it works with surprisingly high accuracy.

Here's another trick: If you are attending a talk, you can tell whether the person at the lectern is a manager or a programmer by looking at their PowerPoint presentation.

If it's black-and-white, all-text, multimedia free, and rarely has more than ten bullet points on a page, the presenter is probably a programmer.

If it's colorful, with graphics, animation, and pages crammed with information bordering on illegibility, the presenter is probably a manager.

It's fun watching a manager try to rewind their presentation to a particular page. As you step over pages, you still have to sit through the animations, which means that instead of "hit space five times" to go forward five pages, you have to "hit space fifteen times, waiting three seconds between each press of the spacebar" because each page has three animations that you must sit through and experience again.

Using floppy disks as semaphore tokens

IN THE VERY early days of Windows 95, the distribution servers were not particularly powerful. The load of having the entire team installing the most recent build when it came out put undue strain on the server. The solution (until better hardware could be obtained) was to have a stack of floppy disks in the office of the "build shepherd." (The job of build shepherd was to perform the initial diagnosis of problems with the build itself or with verification testing and make sure the right developer is called in to address the problem.)

If you wanted to install the latest build, you had to go to the build shepherd's office and take one of the specially marked floppy disks. When you finished installing, you returned the disk.

In other words, the floppy disk acted as a real-world semaphore token.

When a token changes
its meaning midstream

THE PROJECT LEADER for the Microsoft Virtual Machine for Java was well known for wearing Hawaiian shirts. I'm told that the team managers decided to take one of those shirts and use it as an award to the team member who fixed the most bugs or some similar thing. What the team managers failed to take into account was that nobody actually liked being given a Hawaiian shirt ("Does this mean I have to wear it?"), especially not one that had been worn by somebody else. If you happened to be the person who fixed the most bugs, you sort of reluctantly accepted the shirt even though you really didn't want it.

And then a wonderful thing happened. The meaning of the shirt flipped.

The details are lost to the mists of time, but it happened while the project leader was out on vacation. During this time, the holder of the "shirt award" chose to "reward" the person responsible for a build break by giving him the shirt. This proved to be the turning point: The shirt became a symbol of disapproval. I believe the unofficial rule was that to get rid of the shirt, you had to find somebody who messed up at least as bad as whatever you did to earn the shirt in the first place.

When the project leader returned from vacation, he was rather surprised to see what had happened to his "award."

My colleague Jeff Davis explains that a similar thing happened in the MSN Explorer team. The development manager bought a singin'-dancin' James Brown as a reward. It was cool but incredibly annoying to have people stop in, press the button, and have to listen to "I Feel Good." After about the twentieth listen, the trophy instantly metamorphosed into something you got when you broke the build or otherwise made a horrific mistake.

The team was reorganized, and James Brown continued its duties on the shell team. Eventually Jeff ended up with it when the guy across the hall from him moved offices and left it in his office rather than pack it, the sneaky devil. Jeff retired the James Brown doll and found it a nice home away from the office where it can do no more harm.

〜

Whimsical embarrassment as a gentle form of reprimand

DURING THE DEVELOPMENT of Windows Vista project, I messed up a cross-component check-in and broke the build. I'm not proud of it. (In my excitement over finally having passed a few weeks' worth of testing requirements, I absently submitted only one of the components for check-in! My change was 99% within one component, and I forgot about the other 1%.) My submission cleared the "single-component check-in" queue at around 4:30 a.m., and before I got a chance to fix the problem at 8 a.m., a complex job was submitted into the "multi-component check-in" queue. That job failed, of course, because I neglected to update the second component.

A few hours later, I was greeted with a large inflatable bunny rabbit in my office. His name is "Bug Bunny," and it is my lot to be Bug's keeper until somebody else breaks the build. (But hey, at least I fixed it before 5 p.m. At 5 p.m., my team's lab kicks off its nightly builds; and if you break those builds, the next morning's "official team build" doesn't get released, and testers don't have anything to install.)

Many groups have an object with a similar purpose, namely to be "bestowed upon" the person who most recently messed up. And as we saw earlier, the "object of shame" may not even have started out its life with that purpose.

∽

Using a physical object as a reminder

ON OUR TEAM, we have a mailing list where people can report problems. Those people could be testers from our team or they could be people from elsewhere in the company. All members of the team are expected to keep an eye on the messages and debug problems in their areas. The job of monitoring the mailing list to ensure that every issue is addressed rotates according to a predetermined schedule; and in addition to receiving a piece of reminder mail at 4 p.m. the business day before it's your turn, you will also find a Mickey Mouse ears hat on your desk when you arrive in the morning.

I bought this hat in Disneyland a few years ago and somehow managed to convince the person operating the sewing machine to stitch the name Dev O'Day on the back. It's an Irish name, I explained, but it also stands for Developer of the Day, which is the title we use for the person who monitors the mailing list.

One of our team members went on vacation to Disneyland the following year and brought back a backup hat, which sits in my office. The backup hat is occasionally brought into service when the primary Dev O'Day hat goes missing, at which point a Search and Rescue mission is undertaken to locate the hat and restore it to circulation. (It's usually just sitting in the office of someone who was Developer of the Day recently and merely forgot to hand the hat off at the end of the day.)

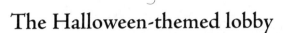

The office disco party

ONE OF THE long-standing traditions at Microsoft is to play a prank on someone's office while that person is away on vacation. You can imagine what most of these pranks are like, filling someone's office with packing peanuts or other materials, or relocating the office to an unlikely part of the building (the bathroom, the cafeteria), or something more subtle like mirror-reversing all the furniture in the office. Redecorating an office is a common theme, such as turning a co-worker's office into a French bistro or a golf course (with real grass).

One particularly memorable office redecoration was from 1996 or so. One of the managers, let's call him Bob, had a bit of a reputation for being cool in a nightclubby sort of way. While Bob was away on vacation, his team set to work. They emptied his office completely, painted the walls black, removed the ceiling tiles to give it that "industrial" look, and installed a disco dance floor, disco lights, and a stereo with turntable.

It was Disco Bob's Party Palace.

When Bob returned, there was quite a happenin' disco party waiting for him.

The Halloween-themed lobby

DURING THE WINDOWS 95 project, the window manager team stayed late one night and redecorated the lobby. They suspended a variety of Halloween-themed objects from fishing lines: spiders, ghosts, witches, jack-o'-lanterns, that sort of thing. The fishing line went up and over pulleys, rigged so that the objects spookily rose and fell seemingly of their own volition. It was quite an impressive display.

The fishing lines were anchored to various doors in the building. Because the doors they chose were highly trafficked, this ensured a random pattern of motion for the objects suspended from the fishing line. Of course, no spooky Halloween display would be complete without a spider rigged to the front door, rapidly descending upon the poor victim coming in for a meeting.

Index

THIS BOOK IS SAFARI ENABLED

INCLUDES FREE 45-DAY ACCESS TO THE ONLINE EDITION

The Safari® Enabled icon on the cover of your favorite technology book means the book is available through Safari Bookshelf. When you buy this book, you get free access to the online edition for 45 days.

Safari Bookshelf is an electronic reference library that lets you easily search thousands of technical books, find code samples, download chapters, and access technical information whenever and wherever you need it.

TO GAIN 45-DAY SAFARI ENABLED ACCESS TO THIS BOOK:

- Go to **http://www.awprofessional.com/safarienabled**

- Complete the brief registration form

- Enter the coupon code found in the front of this book on the "Copyright" page

Addison
Wesley

If you have difficulty registering on Safari Bookshelf or accessing the online edition, please e-mail customer-service@safaribooksonline.com.